VATICAN II

VATICAN II

FORTY YEARS LATER

William Madges
Editor

THE ANNUAL PUBLICATION
OF THE COLLEGE THEOLOGY SOCIETY
2005
VOLUME 51

Maryknoll, New York 10545

Founded in 1970, Orbis Books endeavors to publish works that enlighten the mind, nourish the spirit, and challenge the conscience. The publishing arm of the Maryknoll Fathers and Brothers, Orbis seeks to explore the global dimensions of the Christian faith and mission, to invite dialogue with diverse cultures and religious traditions, and to serve the cause of reconciliation and peace. The books published reflect the views of their authors and do not represent the official position of the Maryknoll Society. To learn more about Maryknoll and Orbis Books, please visit our website at www.maryknoll.org.

Copyright © 2006 by the College Theology Society.

Published by Orbis Books, Maryknoll, New York 10545-0308.
Manufactured in the United States of America.

All rights reserved. No part of this publication may be reproduced or transmitted in any form or by any means, electronic or mechanical, including photocopying, recording or any information storage or retrieval system, without prior permission in writing from the publisher.

Queries regarding rights and permissions should be addressed to: Orbis Books, P.O. Box 308, Maryknoll, New York 10545-0308.

Library of Congress Cataloging-in-Publication Data

Vatican II : forty years later / William Madges, editor.
p. cm. — (College Theology Society annual volume ; 51)
Includes bibliographical references (p.).
ISBN-13: 978-1-57075-633-7 (pbk.)
1. Vatican Council (2nd : 1962-1965) I. Title: Vatican 2. II. Title: Vatican Two. III. Madges, William, 1952- IV. Annual publication of the College Theology Society ; v. 51.
BX8301962 .V333 2006
262'.52—dc22

2005037783

Contents

PART II
THE CATHOLIC CHURCH ENGAGES THE MODERN WORLD

PART III
THE ENCOUNTER WITH OTHER CHRISTIANS AND OTHER RELIGIONS

Acknowledgments

Many individuals have labored hard to make this volume possible and I wish to acknowledge my great debt to them. First, I wish to express my gratitude to the authors of the essays included here. They help us to understand the achievements of Vatican II and to imagine the future of the church. I am especially appreciative of their responsiveness to my editorial requests. Second, I am deeply grateful to my colleagues who evaluated the submitted essays, helped to determine which should be published, and suggested ways in which the essays could be improved: Gillian Ahlgren, Michael Barnes, Peter Bernardi, Regina Boisclair, Joseph Bracken, James Buchanan, Christopher Key Chapple, John Connolly, Charles Curran, Carol Dempsey, Joseph Devlin, Dennis Doyle, William French, Richard Gaillardetz, Marie Giblin, Chester Gillis, George Gilmore, Elizabeth Groppe, Edward Hahnenberg, Mary Ann Hinsdale, Bradford Hinze, Sally Kenel, Paul Knitter, William Loewe, Patrick Lynch, Robert Masson, Judith Merkle, Ronald Modras, Theresa Moser, Kenneth Overberg, Patricia Plovanich, William Portier, Bernard Prusak, Thomas Rausch, Susan Ross, William Shea, Shannon Schrein, Daniel Sheridan, John Sniegocki, Springs Steele, Jonathan Tan, Terrence Tilley, and James Zeitz.

I also wish to thank my research assistant, Sara Knutson, for her organizational and research assistance, and my departmental assistant and secretary, Darleen Frickman, for assistance in formatting the essays. Finally, I would like to acknowledge Susan Perry, our wonderful editor at Orbis Books, with whom it has been a delight to work.

Introduction

William Madges

Forty years ago, on December 8, 1965, Archbishop Pericle Felici, General Secretary of the Council, read a letter from Pope Paul VI that declared the Second Vatican Council closed. In that letter, the Pope stated that the Council, which was the largest, the most momentous, and the most opportune of councils, "numbered without doubt among the greatest events of the Church."[1] Although many would still agree with that judgment, at least some today would deny that the promise of the Council has been extensively fulfilled. What was the promise of Vatican II? It was the promise of a church internally renewed and externally engaged with the world. It was the promise of a church in which the laity would share equal responsibility with the clergy for advancing God's reign. It was the promise of a church in which Catholics would feel compelled to join other Christians and members of other religious traditions or no religion in effectively addressing the joys, hopes, and anxieties of the world's peoples, especially the poor and the marginalized. In short, it was the promise of a church that would be not only a sign, but also an effective instrument of union with God and unity among all people.[2]

Certainly, the Catholic Church today is significantly different from the church of January 25, 1959, the day on which Pope John XXIII, having been pope for only ninety days, announced his decision to convoke a new council. Certainly the Council caused fresh air to blow into and through the house of the church as it set about the updating that John XXIII requested.[3] But, just as certainly, people today are divided about how to properly interpret the legacy of Vatican II and how to implement it. The years immediately following the close of the Council were filled with excitement. The excitement sprang initially from the pastoral orientation and dialogical attitude of the church's leaders. This attitude, first articulated by Pope John XXIII and then echoed by large numbers of Catholic bishops, is expressed well in the Pope's opening address to the Council on October 11, 1962. Vatican II, unlike other councils, was not convened to condemn specific heresies or to oppose dangerous social movements. Although he acknowledged the presence of fallacious teaching and dangerous concepts in the modern world, Pope John directed the church to "make use of the medicine of mercy rather than that of severity." He declared that the church would meet the needs of the present day "by demonstrating the validity of her teaching rather than by condemnations." In short, he wanted the church to be seen as "the loving mother of all, benign, patient, full of mercy and goodness toward the brethren who are separated from her."[4] By teaching the full dignity of every human being and by promoting social justice and world peace, Pope John believed that the church could be a positive, transformative power in the world. His words were welcomed by many in the 1960s and 1970s, a time awash in various social and political liberation movements (such as the civil rights, feminist, and peace movements; political independence movements against colonial powers; and so on) and expectant of change.

The years immediately following the close of the Council were also filled with some confusion. Former strict rules governing Catholic practice (such as abstinence from meat on Fridays) were relaxed; many nuns abandoned their habits, and priests, their Roman collars; and catechesis was transformed from the memorization of stock answers to an exploration of biblical stories with regard to their application to life. The Council's acknowledgment of the common priesthood of believers and the affirmation of the principles of collegiality and subsidiarity appeared to make the church less hierarchical and more "democratic." The Council's recognition of the many elements of church existing outside of the visible boundaries of the Catholic Church (*Unitatis Redintegratio*, 3) and its affirmation of true and holy elements in other religions (*Nostra Aetate*, 2) made clear that salvation was possible outside of the Roman communion. The closer the bonds between the Catholic Church and other churches or religions became, the more some Catholics wanted to know: Had the Catholic Church simply abandoned its past traditions? What remained truly distinctive and essential to Catholic identity?

Such questions have continued to be posed throughout the past forty years, and the answers have been quite different. In more recent times, those who judge that the new emphases and directions introduced by Vatican II have been taken to inappropriate conclusions appeal to the Council documents themselves to stem the tide of change. On the other hand, those who judge that the new emphases and directions introduced by Vatican II have been blocked or misrouted by the hierarchy appeal to the same documents. Arguments rage concerning the "letter" versus the "spirit" of the Council. Who is right? Both sides can claim the Council as theirs because the conciliar documents juxtapose the old and the new. Vatican II brought change, but it just as certainly maintained continuity with the past.[5]

The conciliar documents bear the impress of two different orientations that have been yoked together, if not always smoothly blended.[6] On the one hand, there is an open, pastoral, and ecumenical stance oriented toward the future, exemplified by Pope John XXIII. On the other, there is a closed, doctrinal, and apologetic stance oriented toward the past, exemplified by Cardinal Alfredo Ottaviani, secretary of the Sacred Congregation of the Holy Office and head of the Theological Commission that prepared the initial schemas to be considered by the Council.[7] After the death of John XXIII in 1963, Pope Paul VI sought to harmonize these different orientations. Thirty years after the Council, Pope John Paul II acknowledged the reality of old and new, of both continuity and change, in the achievements of the Council. In his 1994 Apostolic Letter, "Tertio Millennio Adveniente," he stated:

> The Second Vatican Council is often considered as the beginning of a new era in the life of the Church. This is true, but at the same time it is difficult to overlook the fact that the Council drew much from the experiences and reflections of the immediate past, especially from the intellectual legacy left by Pius XII. In the history of the Church, the "old" and the "new" are always closely interwoven. The "new" grows out of the "old," and the "old" finds a fuller expression in the

> "new." Thus it was for the Second Vatican Council and for the activity of the Popes connected with the Council, starting with John XXIII, continuing with Paul VI and John Paul I, up to the present Pope.

The fortieth anniversary of the conclusion of Vatican II provides us with the following opportunities: 1) to recall what the Council did or attempted to do; 2) to explain how the teachings of the Council have been received and interpreted by describing the current state of the church; and finally 3) to imagine what the future of the church might look like based upon the different ways in which the legacy of the Council is interpreted. That is the task of this volume. Obviously the expanse of topics treated at Vatican II, and the subsequent four decades of often competing interpretations of the Council preclude the possibility of an extensive treatment of all or even most of the important developments promulgated by Vatican II. The essays included in this volume were chosen largely because they describe and analyze some of the most important themes and topics of the Council or because they assess significant recent developments in the church in light of the legacy of the Council. The volume is divided into three parts that explore 1) aspects of the renewed understanding of church that emerged from Vatican II, 2) the church's engagement with the modern world, and 3) the encounter with other believers and the transformation of the church's relation to other religious traditions.

In Part One, the authors describe and evaluate the implications of Vatican II's understanding of the church and the role of scripture and tradition in the church's life. A renewed understanding of the church is articulated primarily in the "Dogmatic Constitution on the Church" (*Lumen Gentium*), which many regard as "the most momentous achievement of the Council, both because of its important contents and because of its central place among the Council documents."[8] The initial draft (schema) of *Lumen Gentium,* which was prepared by the Theological Commission headed by Cardinal Ottaviani, articulated an understanding of church that was consistent with the then standard emphasis upon the hierarchical and juridical aspects of the church. When first presented to the Council fathers toward the end of the first session of the Council (December 1962), the draft was roundly criticized by many for triumphalism, clericalism, and juridicism, yet it was defended by others.[9] When the second session of the Council began in September 1963, the Council fathers had an entirely new document on the church to consider.[10] This draft was revised in light of the debates at the second (1963) and the third session (1964) of the Council. The final version of the Constitution, overwhelmingly approved by 2,151 bishops on November 21, 1964, supplemented the initial draft's juridical and hierarchical emphasis with the inclusion of more pastoral and communitarian elements.[11]

The idea of "community," whether expressed as the "mystical body of Christ" or as the "people of God," is a significant aspect of Vatican II's ecclesiology. Although the word itself did not occupy a central place in the Council, *communio*, especially since the time of the 1985 Extraordinary Synod, has come to be regarded as an appropriate synthesis of the essential elements of Vatican II's understanding of church.[12] In its fundamental meaning, *communio* suggests that the church is an instrumental sign of union with God, made possible through Christ and in the Holy Spirit. Because of this union with God through communion with Christ, the baptized are also able to experience communion with one another. Whereas some theologians since the time of the Council have emphasized the horizontal dimension of this union, Pope John Paul II and Pope Benedict XVI have stressed the priority of its vertical dimension.[13] In "The Communion Ecclesiology of Joseph Ratzinger" Philip A. Franco explores Pope Benedict XVI's (formerly Cardinal Joseph Ratzinger's) interpretation of communion and its implications for the life of the church in the years following Vatican II.

In the composition of its voting members, Vatican II reflected the broad and diverse geographical communion of the modern Catholic Church. Not only was Vatican II the largest of the twenty-one ecumenical councils, it also was the most culturally diverse. Approximately 42 percent of the prelates came from Latin America, Asia, and Africa. As Karl Rahner observed in his essay "Basic Theological Interpretation of the Second Vatican Council," Vatican II represented a "qualitative leap" forward toward becoming a world church. Despite the large non-European representation, however, European theological perspectives retained ascendancy during much of the Council. Nonetheless, the windows had been opened to new voices and new concerns. Even though the consequences of this fact for the post-conciliar life of the church were still limited, Rahner conceded, that did not alter "the essential fact that the Council made manifest and brought into activity a Church which was no longer the European church with its American areas of dissemination and its exports to Asia and Africa."[14] In short, the church was beginning to live and work in a new way. In his essay " 'Reception' or 'Subversion' of Vatican II by the Asian Churches?" Peter Phan explores how the culture and the context of Asian Catholics have promoted this new way of being church. He first describes the contributions of the Asian churches at the Second Vatican Council and then details the various areas of contemporary church life in Asia in which Vatican II has been positively received. Finally, he discusses the challenges as well as the contributions of the Asian churches to the church universal by focusing on the Asian Synod.

The next two essays in Part One examine other important facets of Vatican II ecclesiology. Christopher D. Denny describes how John Courtney Murray's understanding of Catholic Action helped to prepare the way for greater participation of the laity in the mission of the church. Although Murray's later writings on the relationship between church and state, and especially his contribution to Vatican II's "Declaration on Religious Freedom," have received the lion's share of scholarly attention, Denny argues that Murray's early lectures reveal that this later interest in church-state relations and religious freedom arose from his concern about the ability of the Catholic Church to present a traditional yet timely message to the modern world.

In "Vatican II and the Role of Women," Harriet A. Luckman scrutinizes developments since Vatican II in understanding the role of the laity, especially women, in the life of the church. The "Dogmatic Constitution on the Church" (*Lumen Gentium*) declared that by virtue of their baptism and incorporation into Christ, the laity share in the threefold offices of Christ and therefore share with the clergy responsibility for the mission of the church. Luckman measures the degree to which the implementation of this declaration has been successful.

The "Dogmatic Constitution on Divine Revelation" (*Dei Verbum*) constituted a second important pillar of Vatican II. As R. A. F. Mackenzie remarked forty years ago, other conciliar documents might have more obvious effects upon members of the church, but few could be more fundamental than *Dei Verbum* because it speaks of the divine revelation that gives the church its direction and nourishes its life.[15] This Constitution, like *Lumen Gentium*, had a difficult gestation period. The discussion of the first draft of the document in 1962 centered upon the notion of two sources of revelation. Although the Council of Trent (1545-63) had applied the term "source" to the gospel, the first draft of this Constitution applied the term to scripture and tradition, which were regarded as the two "fountains" of revelation. This way of thinking about "two sources" had emerged in the context of Catholic apologetics vis-à-vis Protestantism. By regarding scripture and tradition as two separate, virtually independent sources of divine revelation, Catholic apologists could justify as authentically Christian those Catholic beliefs and practices that Protestants claimed had little or no basis in scripture.

However, the wave of renewal that was coursing through some channels of theology in the first half of the twentieth century challenged this idea of two sources. Instead of regarding scripture and tradition as two independent sources, this new theological movement spoke of them as a cohesive whole that transmits God's Word to successive generations in different ways. Scripture communicates in written form; tradition, in unwritten form. But neither is independent of or contrary to the other. Whereas the earlier, apologetic perspective presented a Catholic position clearly differentiated from, if not also antithetical to, the Protestant position, the later perspective offered a Catholic position that displayed considerable common ground with the Protestant insistence upon the authority and sufficiency of scripture. These two perspectives clashed at Vatican II.

After several days of sometimes heated debate, it appeared that the Council had reached a stalemate. Although most bishops were unhappy with the draft on revelation, they lacked the two-thirds majority required to reject the document. Only an intervention by Pope John XXIII made it possible for the draft to be rejected and a new beginning to be made.[16] The text underwent successive revisions and was finally approved during the fourth and last session of the Council in 1965.

Building upon Pope Pius XII's *Divino Afflante Spiritu* (1943), *Dei Verbum* insists that proper interpretation of scripture depends upon discerning the intention of the biblical authors through analysis of the literary forms the authors used and the socio-historical context in which they wrote.[17] In the decades leading up to the Council, the historical-critical method had become an important tool in gaining accurate knowledge about the socio-historical contexts in which the biblical books were produced. With Vatican II's approval of the modern tools of biblical analysis, Catholic biblical scholars felt further encouraged to use historical-critical and other interpretative tools in deciphering the meaning of scripture. In her essay, "Scripture after Vatican II," Alice L. Laffey critically assesses the historical-critical method and argues that the literary-critical method has been more successful in nurturing faith. She calls for reclaiming scripture studies as a theological discipline in the service of faith.

Dei Verbum identified not only scripture, but also tradition as an instrument for transmitting divine revelation. According to the Constitution, scripture is "the utterance of God as it is set down in writing under the guidance of God's Spirit," and "tradition preserves the word of God as it was entrusted to the apostles by Christ our lord and the holy Spirit." *Dei Verbum* insists that both scripture and tradition are to be accepted and honored with the same sense of devotion because "[t]radition and scripture together form a single sacred deposit of the word of God, entrusted to the church."[18] In "*Dei Verbum*: Its Historic Break from 'Curial Theology,' " Francis Holland identifies the ways in which this Constitution broke new ground in understanding the interrelationships of revelation, scripture, and tradition and in describing the role of the faithful and the magisterium in the interpretation of God's word. He argues that more recent church documents represent something of a retreat from the positions articulated in *Dei Verbum*.

The final essay in Part One deals with the most significant crisis to confront the Catholic Church since the close of Vatican II: the clergy sex abuse scandal. Since the beginning of the year 2002, when the *Boston Globe* broke the story about Cardinal Bernard Law's handling of cases of sex abuse by former priest John Geoghan and others, there has been an almost continuous series of revelations of the sexual abuse of children or young people by Catholic priests. Although it began in Boston, the disturbing story has been repeated in dioceses across the country, from Florida to California, from Louisiana to Wisconsin. Hundreds of priests have been removed from ministry or resigned in the wake of the revelations; in addition, a handful of bishops, including Bishop Anthony J. O'Connell of Palm Beach and Bishop J. Kendrick Williams of Lexington have resigned from their roles of pastoral leadership.

The shock of many Americans at the magnitude of the abuse crisis has been matched, if not surpassed, by anger at the way some bishops have dealt with cases of abuse in their dioceses. Some bishops have moved priests who were guilty of abuse to new parish assignments without informing parishioners. Some have used tough legal negotiations and out-of-court financial settlements to keep victims of abuse from creating "scandal" by bringing their allegations into public light. Some bishops have given the impression that they are more concerned about protecting the institutional church's reputation than with protecting children and young people from abuse. Survivors of sexual abuse have fought back, legally and financially. Some estimate that perhaps as much as one billion dollars have already been or are about to be paid in settlements.

Jason King, in "Vatican II's Ecclesiology and the Sexual Abuse Scandal," examines three recent books dealing with the clergy sexual abuse scandal and probes their underlying understanding of Vatican II ecclesiology. He suggests that they provide inadequate resources for developing an appropriate theology of reconciliation and insufficient measures for preventing future cases of abuse. He explores the Vatican II image of the church as pilgrim as a fruitful alternative. He suggest that this understanding of church provides better resources for dealing with the current crisis and for identifying a way forward.

Part Two of this volume, consisting of four essays, examines how Vatican II brought the Catholic Church into constructive engagement with the modern world. The first two essays examine the "Pastoral Constitution on the Church in the Modern World" (*Gaudium et Spes*), the longest of Vatican II's sixteen documents and the most substantive of its statements concerning the dignity of the human person and the social obligation to work for the common good in the context of the specific social, economic, and political problems facing contemporary society. The existence of the Constitution, which was not part of the initial plan for the Council, owes much to the intervention of Cardinal Joseph Suenens of Malines (Belgium) and the influence of bishops representing "the church of the poor."[19] Like other Vatican II documents, *Gaudium et Spes* was subjected to resistance from some quarters. Like those other documents, it also moved from a more abstract and conceptual perspective toward a more biblical and conciliar outlook.[20] It was formally approved at the very end of the Council in December 1965.

In "Straining Toward Solidarity in a Suffering World," Christine Firer Hinze analyzes the message, the reception, and the future of the "Pastoral Constitution." Her thesis is that the Constitution introduced a particular way of framing social ethics and enacting social mission, which is one of its most important and still undeveloped legacies. She argues that the Constitution presents "incarnational solidarity" as an essential key for authentically Christian and human living in today's world. While acknowledging the call of *Gaudium et Spes* for solidarity as an important ethical resource, William French insists that its understanding of solidarity must be broadened to include consideration of the nonhuman world. In "Greening *Gaudium et Spes*," French argues that a responsible solidarity today requires a reinterpretation of the theological anthropology operative in *Gaudium et Spes* and a recasting of solidarity within a broader creation-centered, ecologically informed frame of understanding.

The final two essays in Part Two explore post-Vatican II Catholic teaching concerning political aspects of our contemporary situation. In "Changing Views on the Relation of Christ and the State," Victor Lee Austin compares the position of Pope John Paul II on this matter vis-à-vis the position of Vatican II, as articulated in *Gaudium et Spes* and *Dignitatis Humanae* ("Declaration on Religious Freedom"). Austin describes how John Paul II selected and developed further one aspect of the Council's teaching—its modern affirmations of subjective rights—while silently editing out the elements of the Council's teaching that maintained traditional politico-theological claims about the role of the state. In "Catholic Teaching on War, Peace, and Nonviolence since Vatican II," John Sniegocki describes the significant transformation of magisterial thought on war and peace that has occurred in the wake of Vatican II. In particular, he highlights a renewed appreciation for pacifism, increased emphasis on establishing the conditions necessary for peace, and an emphasis upon nonviolence as a method to combat injustice. Sniegocki concludes his essay with a series of challenging questions concerning military service, the payment of taxes, reinterpretation of natural law, and a spirituality of nonviolence and reconciliation.

The essays in Part Three of this volume concern Catholicism's relationship to other churches and other religions. The first essay describes the historical ecumenical context in which Vatican II occurred. The next two essays deal with the broad issues of the interreligious trajectory created by the Council and the kind of practical dialogical skills needed today to advance interreligious understanding. The final two essays explore recent developments in two specific relationships: the Catholic-Jewish relationship and the Catholic-evangelical relationship.

Vatican II produced two different documents that describe relationships with those who are not Catholic: the "Decree on Ecumenism" (*Unitatis Redintegratio*) and the "Declaration on the Relationship of the Church to Non-Christian Religions" (*Nostra Aetate*). The former document lays out Catholic principles of ecumenism and discusses how concern for restoring unity among Christians is to be put into practice. The latter document, which was originally a chapter in the "Decree on Ecumenism," addresses relations with non-Christians, with special emphasis placed upon the relationship with Jews.

Pope John XXIII declared that one of the principal purposes of Vatican II was to contribute to the unity of the separated Christian churches. Prior to the Council, he established the Secretariat for Christian Unity (1960) and he named five official observers to attend the Third Assembly of the World Council of Churches in New Delhi, India (1961). In "Vatican II and the Twentieth Century's 'Conciliar Renaissance,'" Elaine Catherine MacMillan situates the Council within the historical context of the intense conciliar activity that was taking place in all the mainline churches. By "conciliar" MacMillan means to refer to representative assemblies, whether at the local, regional, or international level, that gather in order to answer the questions that the contemporary church faces. MacMillan examines whether the Roman Catholic Church, in the forty years since Vatican II, has successfully realized the Council's promise by recovering the conciliar dimension of ecclesial life.

As was noted above, the "Declaration on the Relationship of the Church to Non-Christian Religions" (*Nostra Aetate*) began as

Chapter Four of the "Decree on Ecumenism" and was focused exclusively on the Jewish people. The impetus behind the document was the desire to address the anti-Semitism that was rampant and so graphically embodied in the wide-scale murder of Jews during World War II. The declaration, however, was eventually enlarged to include reference to other religious adherents and to include consideration of the possibility of salvation for those outside the Catholic Church.[21]

After reading section 2 of *Nostra Aetate* together with section 16 of *Lumen Gentium*, some are left with the impression that Vatican II is proclaiming new doctrine about the possibility of salvation outside the Catholic Church.[22] In fact, the bishops at Vatican II, building upon several centuries of developing theological insight, articulated an understanding of the church that enabled them to affirm the possibility of salvation of those who were not explicitly members of the Catholic Church without repudiating the teaching of Lateran Council IV (that there "is one universal church of the faithful, outside of which no one is saved"). The "Dogmatic Constitution on the Church" (*Lumen Gentium*) declared that all people are called to be "church," understood fundamentally as the assembly or people of God. To the church all are called, "and they belong to it or are ordered to it in various ways, whether they be catholic faithful or others who believe in Christ or finally all people everywhere who by the grace of God are called to salvation."[23] Jews and Muslims are explicitly identified as included in the plan of salvation. The essence of the Constitution's teaching on the possibility of salvation outside of Christianity is summed up in section 16:

> There are others who search for the unknown God in shadows and images; God is not far from people of this kind since he gives to all life and breath and everything (see Acts 17: 25-28), and the Saviour wishes all to be saved (see 1 Tim 2:4). There are those who without any fault do not know anything about Christ or his church, yet who search for God with a sincere heart and, under the influence of grace, try to put into effect the will of God as known to them through the dictate of conscience: these too can obtain eternal salvation. Nor does divine Providence deny the helps that are necessary for salvation to those who, through no fault of their own,

> have not yet attained to the express recognition of God yet who strive, not without divine grace to lead an upright life.[24]

Acknowledging these significant statements from the Council, Paul F. Knitter in "Bridge or Boundary? Vatican II and Other Religions," asks whether Vatican II is a limit beyond which Christians cannot step without losing their own identity. Specifically, Knitter explores whether Vatican II provides the Catholic/Christian community with a bridge beyond "inclusivism" toward a mutualist theology of religions. Reid B. Locklin, in "Interreligious *Prudentia*," attempts to show how Peter Lombard's twelfth-century project for promoting prudence as *practical* intelligence can offer a fresh perspective on interreligious dialogue in the contemporary era, one that shifts our focus from the problematic, conflicting claims of different religious traditions, as such, to the persons Christians may become by engaging such claims with seriousness, creativity, and piety.

Elena Procario-Foley, in "Heir or Orphan?" sketches the history of the genesis of *Nostra Aetate*, describes the progress and regress in Christian-Jewish relations since *Nostra Aetate* and considers ways of moving the discussion into the next forty years. In the final essay of the volume, "Catholic Evangelicals and Ancient Christianity," Phillip Luke Sinitiere demonstrates that a "catholic evangelical" trend is present within evangelicalism. Noting that the pontificate of Pope John Paul II resulted in a "dramatic warming" of relations between evangelicals and Catholics, Sinitiere situates this trend within the wider stream of evangelical thought and constructively engages the future of evangelicalism in an ecumenical context.

Notes

[1]The opening paragraph of the letter states: "The Second Vatican Ecumenical Council, assembled in the Holy Spirit and under protection of the Blessed Virgin Mary, whom we have declared Mother of the Church, and of St. Joseph, her glorious spouse, and of the Apostles Sts. Peter and Paul, must be numbered without doubt among the greatest events of the Church. In fact it was the largest in the number of Fathers who came to the seat of Peter from every part of the world, even from those places where the hierarchy has been very recently established. It was the richest because of the questions which for four sessions have been discussed carefully and profoundly. And last of all it

was the most opportune, because, bearing in mind the necessities of the present day, above all it sought to meet the pastoral needs and, nourishing the flame of charity, it has made a great effort to reach not only the Christians still separated from communion with the Holy See, but also the whole human family" (Brief of Pope Paul VI, in *The Documents of Vatican II*, ed. Walter M. Abbott [New York: The America Press, 1966], 738).

[2]See "The Dogmatic Constitution on the Church" (*Lumen Gentium*), 1.

[3]Pope John XXIII identified *aggiornamento* (bringing up to date) as the general pastoral purpose of Vatican II. According to one famous anecdote, when the Pope sensed that he was having little success in explaining to a group of bishops what updating meant, he went to the nearest window, opened it and said, "The church needs to let in some fresh air."

[4]Pope John XXIII, Opening Speech to the Council, in *The Documents of Vatican II*, 716. Concerning this speech, see Giuseppe Alberigo and Joseph A. Komonchak, eds., *History of Vatican II*, 5 vols. (Maryknoll: Orbis Books, 1995-2006), 2:14-18.

[5]For additional insight, consult the reflections and comments by those intimately connected with or affected by Vatican II in William Madges and Michael J. Daleys, eds., *Vatican II: Forty Personal Stories* (Mystic, Conn.: Twenty-Third Publications, 2003).

[6]Avery Dulles has observed that it has been especially difficult to avoid conflict and to interpret the conciliar documents properly because the "council fathers, under the direction of Pope Paul VI, made every effort to achieve unanimity and express the consensus of the whole episcopate, not the ideas of one particular school. For this reason, they sought to harmonize differing views, without excluding any significant minority. In some cases they adopted deliberate ambiguities." See his essay, "Vatican II: The Myth and the Reality," in *America* 188/6 (February 24, 2003), 7-8.

[7]It is perhaps not surprising that the motto on Ottaviani's episcopal coat of arms was *Semper Idem*—"Always the same." See John Deedy, *A Book of Catholic Anecdotes* (Allen, Texas: Thomas More, 1997), 195.

[8]Avery Dulles, "Introduction to the Dogmatic Constitution on the Church," in *The Documents of Vatican II*, 10. Cardinal Léger of Montreal regarded the document on the church as the hinge of the entire Council. See Xavier Rynne (pseud.), *Letters from Vatican City. Vatican Council II (First Session): Background and Debates* (New York: Farrar, Straus & Co., 1963), 222. And Pope Paul VI believed that it would be the crowning achievement that "distinguishes this solemn and historic synod in the memory of future ages." See his "Opening Address for the Third Session (September 14, 1964)," in Rynne, *The Third Session: The Debates and Decrees of Vatican Council II, September 14 to November 21, 1964* (New York: Farrar, Straus & Giroux, 1965), 290.

[9]See Rynne, *Letters from Vatican City*, 215-19, 222-31; Alberigo and Komonchak, *History of Vatican II*, 2:330-40; Gérard Philips, "History of the

Constitution," in *Commentary on the Documents of Vatican II*, ed. Herbert Vorgrimler, 5 vols. (New York: Crossroad, 1989), 1:109.

[10]See Alberigo and Komonchak, *History of Vatican II*, 3:491-98.

[11]The reorientation is well illustrated in three areas: the relationship of clergy and laity within the church; the relationship between the Catholic Church and other Christian churches and communities; and the relationship of the bishops to the pope.

[12]See the lecture given by Cardinal Joseph Ratzinger at the Pastoral Congress of the Diocese of Aversa (Italy) on September 15, 2001; translation in *L'Osservatore Romano*, Eng. ed. (23 January 2002), 5.

[13]See John Paul II's 1988 Apostolic Exhortation, "Christifideles Laici," 19.

[14]Karl Rahner, *Theological Investigations XX* (New York: Crossroad, 1981), 20:80.

[15]"Important as the Constitution on the Church is generally agreed to be, it is equaled in stature by the Constitution on Divine Revelation; the two are the most fundamental documents produced by the Second Vatican Council. To the casual reader, the latter may not appear to be either novel or dramatic, but to the theologian it is of basic importance. Other constitutions and decrees will have more obvious practical effects for people within the Church (e.g., the Constitution on the Liturgy), or for those still separated from her (e.g., the Decree on Ecumenism), but all the documents depend on the faith in God's word to men, which the Council has spelled out in this Constitution" (MacKenzie's Introduction to *Dei Verbum*, in *The Documents of Vatican II*, 107).

[16]See Alberigo and Komonchak, *History of Vatican II*, 2:262-66. Pope John gave the task of creating a shorter, more ecumenical, and pastoral draft to a mixed commission, consisting of "liberals" (Cardinals Frings, Liénart, and Meyer), "traditionalists" (Cardinals Browne and Ruffini), and a centrist (Cardinal Lefebvre), with Cardinals Ottaviani and Bea serving as joint presidents.

[17]"In order to get at what the biblical writers intended, attention should be paid (among other things) to *literary genres*. This is because truth is presented and expressed differently in historical, prophetic or poetic texts, or in other styles of speech. The interpreter has to look for that meaning which a biblical writer intended and expressed in his particular circumstances, and in his historical and cultural context, by means of such literary genres as were in use at this time" (*Dei Verbum*, 12, in *Decrees of the Ecumenical Councils*, 2 vols., ed. Norman P. Tanner [Washington, D.C.: Georgetown University Press, 1990], 2:976).

[18]"Dogmatic Constitution on Divine Revelation" (*Dei Verbum*), 9 and 10, in *Decrees of the Ecumenical Councils*, 975.

[19]See Leon-Joseph Suenens, "A Plan for the Whole Council," in *Vatican II Revisited by Those Who Were There Then*, ed. Alberic Stacpoole (Minne-

apolis: Winston Press, 1986), 88-105; Charles Moeller, "History of the Constitution," in *Commentary on the Documents of Vatican II* Vorgrimler, 5:10-11; and Alberigo and Komonchak, *History of Vatican II*, 2:200-203.

[20]See Vorgrimler, *Commentary on the Documents of Vatican II*, 5:3; and Alberigo and Komonchak, *History of Vatican II*, 2:412.

[21]The Declaration goes far beyond a statement concerning Catholic relations with Jews. It affirms the unity of the human community (1). And it acknowledges that, although the fullness of religious life is to be found in Christ, there are elements of truth and goodness in other religions (2). Although expected to continue to witness to their own faith, Christians are therefore exhorted to acknowledge and encourage the spiritual and moral truths found among non-Christians. The statements dealing with Hinduism and Buddhism are very brief and descriptive, rather than evaluative. The statements dealing with Islam and Judaism are much fuller and appreciative. High regard for Muslims is expressed (3) while gratitude for the "nourishment" Christianity draws from Judaism is acknowledged (4). The Declaration concludes with an appeal to all Christians to be at peace with all people (5).

[22]For an excellent history of the development of Catholic thinking on the issue of salvation outside the church, see Francis A. Sullivan, *Salvation Outside the Church? Tracing the History of the Catholic Response* (New York: Paulist Press, 1992).

[23]*Lumen Gentium*, 13, in *Decrees of the Ecumenical Councils*, 2:860.

[24]*Lumen Gentium*, 16, in *Decrees of the Ecumenical Councils*, 2:861.

Part I

THE IMPLICATIONS OF VATICAN II'S UNDERSTANDING OF CHURCH

The Communion Ecclesiology of Joseph Ratzinger

Implications for the Church of the Future

Philip A. Franco

Inspired by the documents and spirit of the Second Vatican Council, few ecclesiological models have been more prominent in recent decades than that of the church as communion.[1] Since this decisive moment in the history of Catholicism, many Roman Catholics have been liberated from the view of the church as a completely immutable and hierarchical institution. Such a statement must be balanced by the recognition that the Council neither created the concept of the church as communion, nor have all Catholics embraced this concept. Even those who have adopted this understanding of church are not in full agreement as to what precisely it means.

In broad terms, communion ecclesiology presents the church as "a 'communion' or fellowship among human beings and God."[2] This approach to the church is ancient, with roots in scripture and the Fathers. Paul reminds us, "The Cup of blessing which we bless, is it not a participation in the blood of Christ? The Bread which we break, is it not a participation in the body of Christ? Because there is one bread, we who are many are one body" (1 Cor 10:16-17). Tillard notes that for the early tradition, "The nature of the Church . . . is, therefore, summed up in *communion, koinonia*. . . . This existence as *communion* constitutes its essence."[3] Ecclesiologist Dennis Doyle identifies six contemporary models of communion ecclesiology, noting important similarities and distinctions between them.[4]

Prominent among those who have contributed to this discussion on the church as communion is Joseph Ratzinger, former prefect of the Congregation for the Doctrine of the Faith, now known as Pope Benedict XVI. Ratzinger has written and spoken extensively on the topic of the church as communion. In fact, from his doctoral dissertation on Augustine's ecclesiology to his most recent pronouncements, ecclesiology permeates all of Ratzinger's ideas and decisions. His concept of communion is at the core of his theology and worldview. This has been the case since the beginning of his career. When asked to describe what was specific about his theology, Ratzinger replied, "I began with the theme of the Church, and it is present in everything."[5]

In *The Ratzinger Report: An Exclusive Interview on the State of the Church*, a well-known interview published in 1985, the then cardinal-prefect suggested that ecclesiology is among the most essential questions in contemporary theology. In Ratzinger's view, a widespread misunderstanding of the true nature of the church has been at the very root of contemporary controversies and disagreements within Catholicism.[6] Both before and after the interview, Ratzinger has repeatedly criticized those thinkers who have adopted a notion of church that grossly misinterprets the Council's true intentions and, worse yet, lacks continuity with the historical understanding of the church's origin, nature, and purpose. In the interview, Ratzinger lamented, "My impression is that the authentically Catholic meaning of the reality 'Church' is tacitly disappearing, without being expressly rejected. Many no longer believe that what is at issue is a reality willed by the Lord himself."[7]

Holding such a powerful position within the Roman Curia, Ratzinger's opinions and work surely found their way into official church pronouncements. Although he insists that his work as a private theologian was distinct from his work as prefect, one can effortlessly discover his theological fingerprints on numerous documents promulgated by the Vatican, whether from his congregation or others. Furthermore, his recent election as bishop of Rome obviously makes Ratzinger and his theology all the more pertinent to contemporary theological discourse as we wonder what course he will chart for the Catholic Church and for ecumenical dialogue with other Christian communities.

This essay will seek to examine this prominent theologian's

understanding of communion ecclesiology. It will then provide a brief overview of his critiques of alternate ecclesiologies and an examination of some implications of his ecclesiology for the future of the church. In pursuing these goals, Ratzinger's own works, particularly those that clearly present his current developed views, will be foundational. Secondary sources offering critical and alternative perspectives will also be used, including John Allen, Jr.'s biography of Ratzinger, *Cardinal Ratzinger: The Vatican's Enforcer of the Faith*, which will provide vital facts and background. This biography, reissued upon Ratzinger's election as pope, has been the subject of recent discussion since Allen has publicly acknowledged some shortcomings of the work as well as his own misgivings about the manner in which Ratzinger is depicted therein. Allen wrote quite candidly, "If I were to write the book again today, I'm sure it would be more balanced, better informed, and less prone to veer off into judgment ahead of sober analysis."[8] Despite its shortcomings, Allen's biography provides important facts about Ratzinger's life and tenure as prefect. Along with Ratzinger's personal memoir, *Milestones: Memoirs 1927-1977*, Allen's work provides some essential insights into Ratzinger's worldview and motivations.

Ratzinger—Some Background

From the time of his priestly ordination in 1951, Ratzinger enjoyed the reputation of a promising scholar. He completed his first dissertation on "The People and the House of God in Augustine's Doctrine of the Church,"[9] which has had a great influence on his subsequent theology. His second dissertation, the *Habilitation* for official university appointment, was on Bonaventure and revelation.[10] Ratzinger was a respected professor at various universities, including Tübingen. He also served as a *peritus* at the Second Vatican Council, a time he describes as very special in his life. [11] Created a cardinal in 1977, he was appointed Prefect of the Congregation for the Doctrine of the Faith in 1981.[12] Various authors note that this appointment was originally greeted with some level of enthusiasm by theologians, as they assumed that Ratzinger, a fellow theologian, would be more understanding of and sympathetic to the work of academic theologians than a traditional curial bureaucrat. Some have since revised this opinion. As we know, having uttered the word "*Accepto*" on April 19, 2005, after a brief conclave, he became Pope Benedict XVI.

A Brief Overview of Early Ratzinger

Before delving into the pope's ecclesiology, it is necessary to make mention of one more important biographical fact. There are many who contend that when studying the theology of this man there are two distinct, perhaps quite different, bodies of work. Some contend there is "early Ratzinger" and there is "late Ratzinger." Early Ratzinger is seen as one who contributed considerably to the progressive trends before and during the Council. Late Ratzinger, disheartened during the years after the Council, is seen as one who became increasingly conservative, culminating in his complete turn to the right when he became prefect. These terms, of course, require some clarification. As understood in this essay, "progressive" refers to those who were in favor of greater openness to and dialogue with the modern world, in line with John XXIII's attempt to open the proverbial windows of the church, including a wider role for the laity, a renewal of the liturgy, and a greater degree of collegiality in the administration of the church. "Conservatives," on the other hand, were those who sought less change resulting from the Council and favored, for the most part, the preservation of the Tridentine status quo. Here we will very briefly examine this issue in regard to Ratzinger and the progression of his thought.

One of the key *periti* at the Second Vatican Council, Ratzinger has been described as one who worked "energetically for a renewed vision of the church."[13] Allen points out that Ratzinger was one of the conciliar champions of bishops' conferences and even spoke negatively of the Holy Office and Roman theologians.[14] In 1964, Ratzinger was among those who founded the journal *Concilium*, certainly a progressive periodical that lauded many of the reforms achieved by the Second Vatican Council.[15] His earlier works do, for the most part, reflect this more progressive perspective. A few illustrative examples include his *Introduction to Christianity*, originally published in 1968. In this work, Ratzinger briefly treats the issue of the church in the context of his examination of the Apostles' Creed. He focuses on themes such as the sinfulness of the members of the church, stating,

> We are tempted to say, if we are honest with ourselves, that the Church is neither holy nor Catholic: the Second Vatican Council itself ventured to the point of speaking no longer merely of the holy Church but of the sinful Church, and the only reproach it incurred was that of still being far too timorous; so deeply aware are we all of the sinfulness of the Church.[16]

Ratzinger nuanced this approach in his later work, placing emphasis on the distinction between the individual who is sinful and the church, which is sinless. "Ratzinger stresses that it is only the Church considered insofar as it embraces sinners in its bosom that travels the path of penance and renewal, not the Church considered in its inner essence."[17] Ratzinger notes that there are certainly sinners in the Church, but he asserts that "this in no way means that the Church as such was also a sinner."[18]

Shortly after the Council, Ratzinger spoke of the church being present, "not where organizing, reforming and governing are going on but in those who simply believe. . . ."[19] Additionally, he wrote, "[T]he individual Church is a self-contained unity fully embodying the entire essence of the Church of God. . . ."[20] Such statements are significant because they seem to be in contrast with Ratzinger's more recent downplaying of the local church and his oft-repeated contention that the church must never be viewed as merely the sum of particular churches. Rather, there is one universal church in existence from the beginning, ontologically prior to particular churches.[21]

Some have suggested that these progressive themes, such as the sinfulness of the church and the importance of the local church, are muted in Ratzinger's later work and that this fact gives clear evidence of Ratzinger's move to the theological right in his late career. Ratzinger, however, rejects this interpretation. While he acknowledges growth in his thought, Ratzinger contends that it was not so much he who moved to the proverbial right, but members of the theological community who moved to the left. The community left him, for the most part, where he always was.[22] Ratzinger says quite directly, "The Professor and the Prefect are the same person, but the two terms refer to two offices that correspond to different tasks. In that sense, then, there is a difference but no contradiction."[23]

Despite Ratzinger's contention, various significant theologians continue to hold that Ratzinger has changed, with some even accusing him of betraying the Council. Among the most prominent of Ratzinger's critics has been Hans Küng, who accuses the current pope of being among those who betrayed the "true council," an accusation Ratzinger usually hurls at more progressive theologians.[24] Lamenting what he believes to be a selective use of conciliar documents and themes, Küng writes,

> [T]he emphasis is on what Joseph Ratzinger calls the "true council" as opposed to all the "council mischief"; this true council does not denote a new beginning but simply stands in continuity with the past. . . . Many people rightly speak of a betrayal of the council. . . . Instead of the words of the conciliar program there are again the slogans of a magisterium which once more is conservative and authoritarian.[25]

As we will see, Küng's statement is in direct contrast to Ratzinger's perennial contention that the Council must be viewed in continuity with the past.

Perhaps, as he claims, Ratzinger was never a thoroughly liberal, freethinking theologian who inexplicably changed his views and suddenly turned to the right, but it is also very clear that evolution did take place, making Ratzinger's contemporary, developed views distinct from the views he expressed during and shortly after the Council.

In subsequent sections of this essay, I will focus on the "late Ratzinger," that is, his more recent and decidedly conservative thought, expressed since he became prefect. Although a more detailed look at his earlier, progressive writings would be a very worthy endeavor indeed, the purpose here is to examine what the pontiff considers his current, developed ecclesiological vision and the manner in which this vision will shape the future of the church.

Setting the Stage—Ecclesiology since the Second Vatican Council

With the promulgation of *Lumen Gentium*, as well as the overall themes of the Second Vatican Council, there emerged a new emphasis within Roman Catholicism on the idea of the church as communion. The bishops of the Council referred to the church as having "the nature of sacrament—a sign and instrument, that is, of communion with God and unity among all men . . . a people brought into unity from the unity of the Father, the Son and the Holy Spirit" (*Lumen Gentium* 1).[26] As Doyle reminds us, "Catholic theologians cannot interpret either Vatican II or communion ecclesiology apart from one another."[27] In the time since the Council, however, theologians have emphasized different understandings of communion. Dennis Doyle argues that the various versions of communion ecclesiology can find support in the conciliar texts. Those documents present a multi-dimensional approach to the concept of communion, and justice cannot be done to the Council unless theologians are faithful to "the breadth and depth of this vision of the Church."[28]

Immediately after the Council, the description of the church as the "people of God," widely viewed as the most accurate expression of the Council's ecclesiology, became widespread within the Roman Catholic Church. Ratzinger notes that he initially embraced this trend, but soon became concerned that the term was not being used properly and therefore not expressing the profound reality that is the church.[29] In Ratzinger's view, this term was not being utilized in the manner intended by the Council Fathers and was not balanced by an adequate understanding of communion. As a result, the real meaning and profundity of "people of God" was lost. What evolved instead was a primarily sociological, horizontal understanding of the term that bore little resemblance to the ecclesiological intentions of the Council and little, if any, continuity with scripture and Christian history.[30]

Seeking to remedy this problem, Ratzinger proposed "communion" as a term preferable to "people of God" in speaking of Vatican II's renewed understanding of the church. Although there is certainly a connection between the two terms, both of which trace their contemporary popularity and usage to the Second Vatican Council, the term communion, Ratzinger argues, is a more accurate and profound way of expressing what "people of God" now fails to express because the latter has become a widely misunderstood and trivialized slogan.[31] Even many theologians, Ratzinger suggests, have torn the term "people of God" from its proper biblical roots, causing it to become a popular slogan used to promote democratization and dissent in the church.[32] The church is the "people of God," Ratzinger argues, only if we are fully united in communion with Christ and one another, not simply because we say we are the people of God.

After the term communion gained currency, it, too, according to Ratzinger, became trivialized. Despite this fact, he maintains that communion remains a profound manner of describing the church and one that clearly articulates the ecclesiology of Vatican II. On June 2, 2002, delivering a talk on this topic, Ratzinger gave an overview of his move toward communion ecclesiology and noted, "I decided that the word . . . which conveyed the very essence of the Church herself, was koinonia—communion."[33]

Ratzinger's Communion Ecclesiology

Having established that the term communion, according to Ratzinger, is the key to understanding the nature of the church, we must now ask: What precisely does communion mean? For Ratzinger, the essence of communion is understood as the intimate unity that exists between the believer and the Lord.[34] Flowing from this unity with the Triune God, the believer is united to all other believers, thus becoming one body, the body of Christ. Ratzinger explains:

> Communion means that the seemingly uncrossable frontier of my "I" is left wide open and can be so because Jesus has first allowed himself to be opened completely, has taken us all into himself and has put himself totally into our hands. Hence, Communion means the fusion of existences; just as in the taking of nourishment the body assimilates foreign matter to itself, and is thereby enabled to live, in the same way my "I" is "assimilated" to that of Jesus, it is made similar to him in an exchange that increasingly breaks through the lines of division. The same event takes place in the case of all who communicate; they are assimilated to this "bread" and thus are made one among themselves—*one* body.[35]

This communion is realized in the Eucharist, making the Eucharist the very center of the faith and the source of the church.[36] Ratzinger says, "The formula 'the Church is the Body of Christ' thus states that the Eucharist, in which the Lord gives us his body and makes us one body, forever remains the place where the Church is generated. . . ."[37] Communion is not primarily a social reality but exists first and foremost with Christ, without whom communion between believers would not be possible. For Ratzinger, therefore, a legitimate ecclesiology of communion cannot be centered solely on the word or the people, but must be thoroughly centered on Christ in the Eucharist. To reduce communion to a reality that is solely or primarily sociological, Ratzinger contends, is to misconstrue the historical understanding of the term.

In order to adequately define this notion of communion and root it firmly in Christian tradition, Ratzinger accentuates several passages from scripture. He cites 1 Corinthians 10:16-17, previously quoted, which helps us to understand that "the concept of communion is above all anchored in the most holy Sacrament of the Eucharist."[38] Ratzinger also turns to John, "If we walk in the light, as he is in the light, we are in communion with one another" (1 John 1:6), noting that this text "shows the same logic of *communio* that we already found in Paul: communion with Jesus becomes communion with God himself, communion with the light and with love. . . ."[39] In order to delve deeper into Ratzinger's definition of communion, let us first examine three terms that are essential to his approach to the topic. Ratzinger describes authentic communion as vertical, horizontal, and diachronic.

Communion as Vertical and Horizontal

Ratzinger frequently stresses the importance of understanding the term communion in this sense of intimate unity between the believer and the Lord, not simply as human community. He maintains that while variant definitions of the term communion exist, it can only be legitimately used in ecclesiological discussions when both the vertical and horizontal dimensions of communion are acknowledged and understood. In the "Letter to the Bishops of the Catholic Church on Some Aspects of the Church Understood as Communion," he stated, "If the concept of *communion*, which is not a univocal concept, is to serve as a key to ecclesiology, it has to be understood within the teaching of the Bible and the patristic tradition, in which *communion* always involves a double dimension: the *vertical* (communion with God) and the *horizontal* (communion among men)."[40]

As we shall see later, Ratzinger has frequently expressed frustration with theologies that do not adequately emphasize this vertical dimension of communion, but focus instead upon the horizontal dimension.

Communion as Diachronic

Since this communion is not to be understood in purely sociological terms, Ratzinger emphasizes that the horizontal dimension of communion must be understood as "diachronic." In other words, the horizontal dimension of communion does not extend simply to those believers who currently live in community with one another. Communion is not limited to the here and now, but, like no solely human institution can claim, ecclesial communion extends beyond the borders of this life and includes the countless members of the church who have gone before us and still live in Christ. The document goes on to state, "This communion exists not only among the members of the pilgrim Church on earth, but also between these and all who, having passed from this world in the grace of the Lord, belong to the heavenly Church or will be incorporated into it after having been fully purified."[41]

Therefore, one cannot speak of the *sensus fidei* in the church by referring solely to the opinions of contemporary believers, who make up but a small fraction of church membership. The church throughout time must be included in any articulation of the church's faith. Ratzinger says, "[The] Church lives not only synchronically but diachronically as well. This means that it is always all—even the dead—who live and are the whole Church."[42]

Communion and the Hierarchy

Some versions of communion ecclesiology de-emphasize the hierarchical view of the church and stress instead the unity and equality of all believers.[43] For Ratzinger, it is precisely the fact that the church is a communion that necessitates the hierarchy and underscores its importance. To suggest that the church be structured otherwise causes us to lose the essential notion of communion and reduces the church to a club or modern democracy. Ratzinger asserts that "the Church of Christ is not a party, not an association, not a club. Her deep and permanent structure is not *democratic* but *sacramental*, consequently *hierarchical*."[44] His works on this aspect of ecclesiology are many, but brevity requires a quick overview of Ratzinger's approach to the hierarchy within the communion of the church.

Ratzinger argues that the monarchical episcopate is essential to the nature of the church because an authentic church *communio* requires the unity of a community centered on the Eucharist. There is, therefore, one bishop who leads and whose role it is to preserve unity within his particular church and with the successor of Peter. The bishop ensures that the vertical and horizontal dimensions of communion are not divided.[45] There is also the ministerial priesthood, intimately connected to the episcopacy and the Eucharist, without which the Eucharist could not be confected. Therefore, Ratzinger provides us with the simple axiom, "A Church understood eucharistically is a Church constituted episcopally."[46]

The papacy, although it has been a stumbling block to unity in the course of church history, exists not for the exercise of temporal power but for the sake of unity and the preservation of the communion of the universal church, with which every particular church and bishop must necessarily be in communion.[47] This necessary communion, Ratzinger claims, is not a means of bolstering the authority of the church of Rome, but is simply an ecclesiological necessity because the papacy, as a unifying factor in the church, ensures that the church is not wounded by becoming a group of independent national churches that cannot speak with one voice.[48]

Ratzinger frequently points out that the exact manner in which papal primacy is exercised has differed over the years and may continue to evolve and change based on temporal necessities. However, such change in the exercise of the papacy could never involve any scenario in which final authority is vested in any place other than the Holy See. Petrine authority remains essential as long as the church is understood not as a federation of distinct communities, but as *communio*. Ratzinger rejects the notion that the papacy is a superfluous invention. Rather, it comes directly from Christ. Ratzinger states, "The Roman Primacy is not an invention of the popes, but an essential element of ecclesial unity that goes back to the Lord and was developed faithfully in the nascent Church."[49]

Ratzinger's Critique of Alternative Communion Ecclesiologies

Although very rarely identifying specific theologians and their works, Ratzinger has frequently and meticulously critiqued alternative ecclesiologies "misusing" terms such as "people of God" and "communion." The aforementioned 1992 document on communion signed by Ratzinger states: "Some approaches to ecclesiology suffer from a clearly inadequate awareness of the Church as a *mystery of communion*, especially insofar as they have not sufficiently integrated the concept of *communion* with the concepts of *People of God* and of the *Body of Christ*, and have not given due importance to the relationship between the Church as *communion* and the Church as *sacrament*."[50]

Since a detailed analysis of his critiques would be neither necessary nor practical given the scope of this essay, a brief overview covering the major theme of his critiques, namely the overemphasis of the horizontal dimension of communion, will suffice.

Generally, Ratzinger views many other notions of communion as purely or primarily horizontal, lacking the necessary balance between the horizontal and the vertical dimensions of communion. In a 2002 address he stated,

> Those who speak today of an "ecclesiology of communion" generally tend to mean two things: (1) They support a "pluralist" ecclesiology. Almost a "federalist" sense of union, opposing what they see as a centralist conception of the Church; (2) they want to stress, in the exchanges of giving and receiving among local Churches, their culturally pluralistic forms of worship in liturgy, in discipline and in doctrine.[51]

Such ecclesiologies, he says, focus on the human dimensions of communion. They reduce *koinonia* to simple human community and fail to understand the term in all its profundity. They neglect or downplay Christ, truly present in the Eucharist, as the very center and source of the church. Instead, they turn their gaze toward humanity as its center. In this view, the church is not generated and sustained by the Eucharist, but by the gathering of persons in Christ's name who become church simply by virtue of their gathering. The church is thereby reduced to a purely human society, a group of independent communities with varying practices and doctrines. What emerges is a church that is built from the people upwards, rather than a church that is a gift received from the Lord. In such a scenario, Ratzinger says, it is we who transform the church into what we wish it to be, rather than the church that forms us into what Christ wishes us to be. "[W]e 'make' the Church ourselves and do so in constantly new ways."[52]

For Ratzinger, such an approach to ecclesiology characterizes the fundamental mistake made by those individuals and groups who refer to the church as the "people of God" or claim, "We are church." These persons and groups are not technically incorrect, but they are misunderstanding or intentionally changing such terms by defining them in this purely horizontal, ahistorical manner. He sees great danger in such "misguided" approaches to communion ecclesiology. Envisioned in this way, the church can easily disappear as it divides along ideological lines of liberal or conservative. It can be viewed by its members as a superfluous association that can be discarded should it no longer represent one's personal ideology or preferences. He refers to these approaches as "North American Free Church"[53] ecclesiological models, reminiscent of the churches founded in the "new world," tailored to the wishes of members, in direct opposition to institutional and state churches.

Critiques of Ratzinger's Work

While Ratzinger has been critical of other approaches to communion ecclesiology, disapproving of their emphasis on the horizontal to the detriment of the vertical, it seems fair to suggest that the most obvious criticism of Ratzinger's work is his overemphasis of the vertical aspect of communion to the detriment of the horizontal. Ratzinger's ecclesiology puts precious little emphasis on the horizontal bonds of human community and therefore has little to say in terms of social justice and other issues of human solidarity. Indeed, in his work on communion, "Ratzinger scarcely refers to human solidarity and makes no ecclesial claims about it."[54] Furthermore, he generally "makes no mention of gross economic inequalities or of an option for the poor, and he argues against views that would analyze all social problems as structural."[55] This aspect of his ecclesiology is in direct contrast to the communion ecclesiology of various other theologians, particularly liberation theologians.

Other theologians have lamented Ratzinger's rigidity, suggesting that the communion of which he speaks is not sufficiently inclusive and egalitarian. Liberation theologian Juan Luis Segundo suggested that Ratzinger's insistence that the church not be a church "of the people," as he puts it, lies in Ratzinger's concern for the preservation of hierarchical authority.[56] Miroslav Volf, a Protestant theologian, rejecting Ratzinger's insistence on communion with Rome as essential to the legitimacy of every particular church, calls this aspect of Ratzinger's ecclesiology ecumenically offensive.[57]

Implications of Ratzinger's Ecclesiology for the Future of the Church

It is not difficult to speculate as to the practical implications of Ratzinger's ecclesiology because, in many instances, we have already seen the influence of his views within church decrees and decisions. The ways in which his ecclesiology will shape the church and its activity in the world are many and varied. Let us here examine just a few of its implications.

First, in general terms, as we can easily glean from what has already been stated, Ratzinger would take issue with the very phrase "church of the future." In his estimation, such a phrase must be understood in a very specific manner, lest it suggest a lack of continuity within the church and connote some sort of break between the church founded by Christ, living and growing throughout history, and the church as it exists today. Such a break is simply illogical in Ratzinger's theology. Ratzinger maintains that such a phrase, while not totally unacceptable, must be properly qualified, or it becomes an example of the incorrect interpretation of the ecclesiology and intentions of the Second Vatican Council. In *The Ratzinger Report*, he stated forcefully,

> This schematism of a *before* and *after* in the history of the Church, wholly unjustified by the documents of Vatican II, which do nothing but reaffirm the continuity of Catholicism, must be decidedly opposed. There is no "pre-" or "post-" conciliar Church: there is but one, unique Church that walks the path toward the Lord, ever deepening and ever better understanding the treasure of faith that he himself has entrusted to her. There are no leaps in this history, there are no

> fractures and there is no break in continuity. In no way did the Council intend to introduce a temporal dichotomy in the Church.[58]

Were the eminent theologian addressing us today concerning the theme of this volume, he would most likely contend that, as we look back on the Council and envision the future, we should know that there is not, properly understood, a *church of the future*. Rather, we look toward the *future of the church*, the *one* church as it continues journeying toward the Lord. His work contends that the teachings and effects of the Second Vatican Council must be viewed from this overarching perspective of the church throughout history, in continuity with the whole experience of Catholic Christianity. Therefore, flowing from his ecclesiology, the Council could not be viewed as a major change of the church, but as one significant, Spirit-guided development in the church's life. The Council was not, strictly speaking, an innovation or a substantial change, but one step on our walk toward the Lord. For Ratzinger, it is only when the Council is understood in this manner that its teachings will be fully grasped and the authentic reform it sought will be fully realized.

That is not to say that we should not discuss the future; quite the contrary, as much of Ratzinger's work has touched upon this issue. He has observed that the church in the future might be smaller in many ways, yet must never fail to be a communion open to all.[59] Noting what he deems a lack of Christian culture to support the church and the Faith, he envisions the church of the future as "having to find new ways of pilgrim fellowship."[60] In other words, the smaller church in the future will need to find ways to live in communion without relying on worldly power or great size.

In addition to these more general ways of envisioning the future, we may also opine as to some specific and perhaps more immediate implications of Ratzinger's view of the church. His ecclesiology offers numerous implications for the manner in which the church might function as we continue on this pilgrimage. Here I will focus on a select few. These will include the question of authority in the Catholic Church, the celebration of the liturgy, and the ecumenical movement. Of course, we must keep in mind that these implications are based on Ratzinger's most recent theological views, expressed primarily during his time as prefect. In light of the aforementioned shift in Ratzinger's thought over the years, perhaps we cannot completely rule out the possibility that his new office will afford us the opportunity to witness the emergence of a "third Ratzinger." Until such time, we look toward the future based on the evidence available.

Authority in Ratzinger's Communion Ecclesiology

One of the most significant aspects of a church shaped by Ratzinger's vision would be a very specific, centralized understanding of authority in the church and the manner in which this authority is exercised in regard to church members. Although Ratzinger frequently stresses that papal authority has its limitations and that it has been and can be exercised in numerous ways, it is nonetheless absolutely essential in Roman Catholicism. He rejects those notions of collegiality or "democratization" that would, in any way, remove complete authority within the church from the bishop of Rome. This safeguards the communion, as the pope is the "guarantor of obedience, so the church cannot simply do as she likes."[61] Thus, particular churches are only completely legitimate insofar as they are in union with Peter's successor. In such a scenario, it seems the centralization of authority is an absolute necessity.

Based on this, Ratzinger has taken a very cautious approach to bishops' conferences and their doctrinal decisions and status. Few would deny that it is his understanding of authority, based on his communion ecclesiology, that has been the source of limitations in the manner in which bishops' conferences function. Never could the particular church under one bishop, or a national church under a conference of bishops, be seen in any sense to be independent of or superior to the universal church. Ratzinger, in his years as prefect, frequently cautioned that while bishops' conferences do, of course, teach, there is not a separate level of magisterial authority granted to national bishops' conferences that stifles the teaching authority of each bishop in his own diocese.[62] This notion was manifested in John Paul II's *Apostolos Suos,* which states that episcopal conferences must have their doctrinal statements approved by the Vatican directly and must be unanimously agreed upon within the conference.[63]

Furthermore, Ratzinger's insistence that communion ecclesiology does not entail democratic structures greatly influences the manner in which dissent is handled and reform is achieved. He does not deny that ecclesial reform and change can be necessary.[64] However, the sole criterion for judging the legitimacy of such movements toward reform, he says, can never be popular trends or personal preferences of individual theologians or bishops, but must be fidelity to the teaching and intention of Christ as revealed in scripture and tradition. True reform seeks not so much what the people desire, but what Christ desires. Ratzinger explains that true reform involves not making the church as we want it, but simply removing that which is not part of its essential nature as founded by the Lord. To illustrate this point, he mentions Michelangelo, who said the sculptor does not, strictly speaking, *make* a work of art, but simply uncovers what is already present in the stone. In reforming the church, we must uncover what Christ desires, without modeling the church on our own preferences.[65] Properly understood, we *are* church, but we do not *make* the church, only Christ does, and he gives it to his people as gift. Therefore, final authority on what constitutes authentic reform must be the magisterium, understood as the teaching authority Christ gives his church in the person of the pope and the bishops in communion with him.

In light of this, it is important to note a statement Pope Benedict XVI made during his inaugural homily as bishop of Rome on April 24, 2005. He said, "My real programme of governance is not to do my own will, not to pursue my own ideas, but to listen, together with the whole Church, to the word and the will of the Lord, to be guided by Him, so that He himself will lead the Church at this hour of our history."[66] Although only time will demonstrate Benedict's success in fulfilling this promise, it is a promise firmly rooted in his communion ecclesiology.

Liturgy in Ratzinger's Communion Ecclesiology

In terms of the liturgy, Ratzinger has contended that the purely horizontal notions of communion have been manifested in the manner in which liturgy is celebrated in the church today. While he supports the reformed liturgy, he has also spoken of a "reform of the reforms"[67] by which certain perceived exaggerations would be corrected. Ratzinger's writings on liturgy give us a clear idea of what he believes these liturgical exaggerations to be.

Liturgy, he argues, has become focused on the people, the multiplication of their roles, and the creativity of the local community. His ecclesiology would remedy this and return the celebration of liturgy to its proper focus on the people's relationship with God. Active participation would be understood primarily as the laity consciously participating in the prayer of the church, and not primarily as requiring the performance of a variety of different functions. On this issue Ratzinger states, "The almost theatrical entrance of different players into the liturgy, which is so common today . . . quite simply misses the point. If the various external actions . . . become the essential in the liturgy, if the liturgy degenerates into general activity, then we have radically misunderstood the 'theo-drama' of the liturgy and lapsed almost into parody."[68] Essentially, Ratzinger argues that legitimate active participation, as intended by the Council, is not the multiplication of activity and roles for the laity, but prayerful participation in the sacrificial offering of the priest.[69]

Additionally, since Ratzinger's ecclesiology would demand that the liturgical celebration focus on the vertical dimensions of communion rather than the horizontal and sociological, he has demonstrated a propensity for a return to the custom of having the priest offer mass with his back to the congregation. More precisely, the priest should face the same direction as the people, focusing on the Lord. This, he claims, is the ancient and preferred practice, finding its roots in Judaism.[70] According to Ratzinger, the post-conciliar turn toward the people represents something the Council did not directly intend, as well as a misunderstanding of the origins of this practice. As contemporary ecclesiology focuses on the horizontal with insufficient reference to God, the idea of the priest facing the people is a reflection of this ecclesiology. Ratzinger argues,

> Less and less is God in the picture. . . . The turning of the priest toward the community has turned the community into a self-enclosed circle. . . . The common turning toward the East was not a "celebration toward the wall"; it did not mean "the priest had his back to the people" . . . it was much more a question of the priest and people facing in the same direction, knowing that together they were in procession toward the Lord. They did not close themselves into a circle; they did not gaze at one another, but as the pilgrim People of

> God they set off for the *Oriens*, for the Christ who comes to meet us.[71]

Another dimension of this proper emphasis on communion and God would involve a partial return to mandatory Latin, particularly in the liturgy of the Eucharist. In conformity with the documents of the Council, which did not completely reject Latin, Ratzinger would return to the use of Latin in selected areas in order to emphasize the universality of the liturgy and strengthen the bonds of communion. He believes this would be an antidote to the contemporary problem of localized and horizontal liturgies.[72]

Christian Unity in Ratzinger's Communion Ecclesiology

Finally, Ratzinger's ecclesiology has serious implications for the manner in which the ecumenical movement continues. John Allen, Jr., states quite bluntly, "On a practical level, Ratzinger the prefect has done very little to advance ecumenism and a fair bit to retard it."[73] Since his election, the new pope has spoken of his desire to continue on the path toward Christian unity. His ecclesiology is one key in determining how that path will be traveled. While perhaps similar to the trail blazed by John Paul II, it seems unlikely that Benedict will be as enthusiastic about common worship and other historic overtures made by his predecessor.

With the church as the body of Christ, a communion that finds its source and life in the Eucharist and is guided by the bishops in communion with Peter's successor, ecumenism must essentially be viewed, according to Ratzinger's ecclesiology, as the movement to bring these separated Christians into this communion. No other scenario, save that of Christian denominations entering into full communion with the bishop of Rome, would constitute true and complete unity.[74] In a church shaped by this vision, what must be emphasized in ecumenical dialogue is not compromise or even commonalities, but truth. Only then will Orthodox and Protestant Christians be completely within the communion of the church. This vision is evident in the document on the church as communion, in which the former prefect stated,

> Since, however, communion with the universal Church, represented by Peter's Successor, is not an external complement to the particular Church, but one of its internal constituents,

> the situation of those venerable Christian communities also means that their existence as particular Churches is *wounded*. The wound is even deeper in those ecclesial communities which have not retained the apostolic succession and a valid Eucharist. This in turn also injures the Catholic Church, called by the Lord to become for all "*one flock*" with "*one shepherd*" (77), in that it hinders the complete fulfillment of its universality in history.[75]

Any ecumenical movement that seeks to downplay doctrinal differences by simply gathering Christians for common worship would therefore be a false understanding of ecumenism.

Conclusion

For some, Joseph Ratzinger's church of the future bears a striking resemblance to the church of the past. For Ratzinger, the very manner in which that statement was phrased reveals a misunderstanding of what it means to speak of the church and its future. Some have accused him of tenuously adopting the decrees of the Council and using them to formulate an ecclesiology that is not essentially different from the authoritative, hierarchical model; others see him as a voice in the wilderness, authentically interpreting the Council and helping to save the church from inauthentic change. Whether one views Ratzinger as theological friend or foe, one thing cannot be denied: his voluminous, respected, and insightful writings have contributed significantly to the church of the present and will remain a force in the future. His election as pope guarantees that fact. As we look back on Vatican II and envision the future, I will end with these words from the pope, which are both representative of his ecclesiological work and quite fitting for this volume. He says,

> . . . to defend the true tradition of the Church today means to defend the Council. [We must not] view Vatican II as a "break" and an abandonment of the tradition. There is, instead, a continuity that allows neither a return to the past nor a flight forward, neither anachronistic longings nor unjustified impatience. We must remain faithful to the *today* of the Church, not the *yesterday* or *tomorrow*. And this today

of the Church is the documents of Vatican II, without *reservations* that amputate them and without *arbitrariness* that distorts them.[76]

As Pope Benedict XVI now stands prominently within this *today* of the Catholic Church, only time will tell how he will lead the people of God toward the church's *tomorrow.*

Notes

[1]Avery Dulles, *Models of the Church,* expanded edition (New York: Image Books, 2002), 22-23. At several points in this ecclesiological work, Dulles alludes to the widespread use of this model since Vatican II.

[2]Dennis Doyle, *Communion Ecclesiology: Vision and Versions* (Maryknoll, N.Y.: Orbis Books, 2000), 18.

[3]J. M. R. Tillard, *Church of Churches: The Ecclesiology of Communion* (Collegeville, Minn.: Liturgical Press 1992), 29.

[4]Doyle, *Communion Ecclesiology,* 19.

[5]Joseph Ratzinger, *Salt of the Earth, Christianity and the Catholic Church at the End of the Millennium. An Interview with Peter Seewald* (San Francisco: Ignatius Press, 1997), 65.

[6]Joseph Ratzinger with Vittorio Messori, *The Ratzinger Report: An Exclusive Interview on the State of the Church* (San Francisco: Ignatius Press, 1985), 45.

[7]Ibid.

[8]John Allen, Jr., *National Catholic Reporter* online, April 26, 2005 (4:29), available from http://www.nationalcatholicreporter.org/word/word042605.htm; Internet; accessed 25 July 2005.

[9]Joseph Ratzinger, *Milestones*: *Memoirs 1927-1977* (San Francisco: Ignatius Press, 1997), 97.

[10]Ibid., 108.

[11]See ibid., 121.

[12]Ratzinger with Messori, *The Ratzinger Report,* 17.

[13]John Allen, Jr., *Cardinal Ratzinger: The Vatican's Enforcer of the Faith* (New York: Continuum, 2000), 55.

[14]See ibid., 61-66.

[15]Ratzinger with Messori, *The Ratzinger Report*, 18.

[16]Joseph Ratzinger, *Introduction to Christianity* (San Francisco: Ignatius Press, 1990), 262.

[17]Doyle, *Communion Ecclesiology*, 54.

[18]Ratzinger with Messori, *The Ratzinger Report*, 52.

[19]Ratzinger, *Introduction to Christianity*, 266.

[20]Joseph Ratzinger, *Theological Highlights of Vatican II* (New York: Paulist Press, 1966), 121-22.

[21]See Stephan Otto Horn and Vizenz Pfnur, eds., *Pilgrim Fellowship of Faith: The Church as Communion* (San Francisco: Ignatius Press, 2005), 259.

[22]Ratzinger with Messori, *The Ratzinger Report*, 18.

[23]Joseph Ratzinger, "Letter to His Eminence Metropolitan Damaskinos of Switzerland," in Horn and Pfnur, eds., *Pilgrim Fellowship of Faith*, 230.

[24]See, for example, Ratzinger with Messori, *The Ratzinger Report*, 30.

[25]Hans Küng, *The Catholic Church: A Short History* (New York: Modern Library, 2003), 192.

[26]In Austin P. Flannery, ed., *Vatican Council II: The Conciliar and Post-Conciliar Documents* (Northport, New York: Costello Publishing, 1987), *Lumen Gentium* 1.

[27]Doyle, *Communion Ecclesiology*, 2.

[28]Ibid., 78.

[29]Joseph Ratzinger, "Eucharist, Communion and Solidarity," *Inside the Vatican*, August-September 2002, 13.

[30]Ibid.

[31]Ibid.

[32]See Ratzinger, *Salt of the Earth*, 188.

[33]Ratzinger, "Eucharist, Communion and Solidarity," 13.

[34]See the Congregation for the Doctrine of the Faith, "Letter to the Bishops of the Catholic Church on Some Aspects of the Church Understood as Communion," Origins 22 (25 June 1992), sect. 3, 108.

[35]Joseph Ratzinger, *Called to Communion: Understanding the Church Today* (San Francisco: Ignatius Press, 1996), 37.

[36]Ratzinger, "Eucharist, Communion and Solidarity," 14.

[37]Ratzinger, *Called to Communion*, 37.

[38]Ratzinger, "Eucharist, Communion and Solidarity," 14.

[39]Ibid., 15.

[40]Congregation for the Doctrine of the Faith, "Letter to the Bishops of the Catholic Church on Some Aspects of the Church Understood as Communion," sect. 3, 108.

[41]Ibid., 6.

[42]Ratzinger, *Salt of the Earth*, 188-89.

[43]See, for example, Doyle, *Communion Ecclesiology*, 34, and Dulles, *Models of the Church*, 40.

[44]Ratzinger with Messori, *The Ratzinger Report*, 49.

[45]Ratzinger, *Called to Communion*, 86.

[46]Ibid., 79.

[47]Ibid., 72.

[48]Ibid., 235.

[49]Ratzinger, *Called to Communion*, 72.

[50]Congregation for the Doctrine of the Faith, "Letter to the Bishops of the Catholic Church on Some Aspects of the Church Understood as Communion," 108.

[51]Ratzinger, "Eucharist, Communion and Solidarity," 14.

[52]Ratzinger, *Called to Communion*, 137.

[53]Ratzinger with Messori, *The Ratzinger Report*, 46.

[54]Doyle, *Communion Ecclesiology*, 113.

[55]Ibid., 114.

[56]Juan Luis Segundo, *Theology and the Church: A Response to Cardinal Ratzinger and a Warning to the Whole Church*, trans. John W. Diercksmeier (Minneapolis: Winston Press, 1985), 148.

[57]See Doyle, *Communion Ecclesiology*, 163.

[58]Ratzinger with Messori, *The Ratzinger Report*, 35.

[59]Joseph Ratzinger, *God and the World: Believing and Living in Our Time. A Conversation with Peter Seewald* (San Francisco: Ignatius Press, 2002), 443.

[60]Ratzinger, *Salt of the Earth*, 264.

[61]Ratzinger, *God and the World*, 377.

[62]Allen, *Cardinal Ratzinger*, 63.

[63]John Paul II, *Apostolos Suos. On the Theological and Juridical Nature of Episcopal Conferences*, 22-23.

[64]Ratzinger, *Called to Communion*, 140-41.

[65]Ibid.

[66]Benedict XVI, Inaugural Homily of April 24, 2005, available from http://www.vatican.va/holy_father/benedict_xvi/homilies/2005/documents/hf_benxvi_hom_20050424_inizio-pontificato_en.html: Internet; accessed 9 May 2005.

[67]Allen, *Cardinal Ratzinger*, 72.

[68]Joseph Ratzinger, *The Spirit of the Liturgy* (San Francisco: Ignatius Press, 2000), 175.

[69]Ibid., 173.

[70]Ibid., 80-81.

[71]Ibid., 80.

[72]See Ratzinger, *God and the World*, 417.

[73]Allen, *Cardinal Ratzinger*, 5.

[74]See, for example, Congregation for the Doctrine of the Faith, *Dominus Iesus*, 17.

[75]Congregation for the Doctrine of the Faith, "Letter to the Bishops of the Catholic Church on Some Aspects of the Church Understood as Communion," sect. 17, 111.

[76]Ratzinger with Messori, *The Ratzinger Report*, 31.

"Reception" or "Subversion" of Vatican II by the Asian Churches?

A New Way of Being Church in Asia

Peter C. Phan

Forty years, which is a long time in a person's life, may be sufficient to offer a perspective on its significance, but it is nothing more than a minuscule speck in the two-millennia history of the Catholic Church. Four decades would not even afford enough distance to assess the impact of an ecumenical council, especially one of such magnitude and complexity as Vatican II, which has been rightly described as the most important event of the twentieth century, both in secular and ecclesiastical history. Any current assessment of Vatican II, therefore, can be no more than fragmentary and provisional, pending the Archimedean viewpoint available perhaps at the *eschaton*.

The difficulty in presenting the impact of Vatican II on the Asian churches is compounded not only by the vastness of the field of inquiry and the scarcity of theological data but also by the fact that in many countries, particularly those under communist regimes (such as China, North Korea, and Vietnam), accurate information on the churches' activities is practically impossible to obtain. Even in other Asian countries, detailed empirical studies of the churches are almost non-existent, so that available data should be viewed with circumspection.

Furthermore, the two realities under investigation—Asian churches and Vatican II—are themselves hard to circumscribe, and unless it is clear what is meant by them, our discussion will be unfocused. "Asian churches" as used here refers to the members of the Federation of Asian Bishops' Conferences (FABC), a transnational organization comprising fourteen full members (Bangladesh, India, Indonesia, Japan, Korea, Laos-Cambodia, Malaysia-Singapore-Brunei, Myanmar [Burma], Pakistan, Philippines, Sri Lanka, Taiwan, Thailand, and Vietnam) and ten associate members (Hong Kong, Kazakhstan, Kyrgyzstan, Macau [Aomen], Mongolia, Nepal, Siberia, Tadjikistan, Turkmenistan, and Uzbekistan).[1] By "Vatican II" is meant not only the general council (1962-65) convoked by Pope John XXIII and concluded under Pope Paul VI, with its sixteen documents, but also the official postconciliar commissions and documents (such as the Council [*consilium*] for the Implementation of the Constitution on the Sacred Liturgy, numerous new liturgical books, the 1983 Code of Canon Law, the *Catechism of the Catholic Church*, and so on)—in sum, the entire pontificates of Paul VI and John Paul II.

Vatican II was the first ecumenical council that the Asian bishops took part in, though many of them were not Asian-born but expatriate missionaries. Nor did their voices carry much weight, since Vatican II—although it was the first general council truly represented by the *oikoumene*, hence ushering in what Karl Rahner famously called the "world church"—was still very much a European affair, dominated by European prelates and the preoccupations and agenda of the Western churches.[2] This lack of influence was due to the fact that the number of Asian bishops at Vatican II was relatively small and many Asian churches were at that time still in so-called mission lands.

The title of my essay contains two theologically significant terms, *reception* and *subversion*. The former has a respectable pedigree and constitutes an essential element in Catholic theology of tradition and the *sensus fidelium*. It refers to the ongoing process by which the community of faith makes that teaching or practice its own, acknowledging that a teaching or a practice enjoined by church authority is a genuine expression of the church's faith and is therefore true and binding. Contrary to conciliarism and Gallicanism, reception is not to be understood as a juridical ratification by the community of such a teaching or practice whose truth and validity would derive from such ratification. Rather, it is an act whereby the community affirms and attests that such teaching or practice really contributes to the building up of the community's life of faith.[3]

Such a process of reception, however, is not a simple act of obedience. It is not always an acceptance or at least a full acceptance of what is enjoined. At times it may involve rejection, either total or partial. At any rate, it is *always* a re-making, or to use the title of the book of one of our colleagues, an "inventing" of the tradition. As Terrence W. Tilley puts it, if *tradutore* is *traditore*, "it is not only necessary but good that, from one perspective, a *traditor* (i.e., the one handing on the tradition) is a traitor."[4] This second, inevitable aspect of reception is alluded to by the word *subversion*, which has gained currency in theological discourse on tradition by feminist, minority, and post-colonial voices. The question mark at the end of the title of my essay is not intended to convey a disjunction between "reception" and "subversion" of Vatican II by the Asian churches but rather to raise the question of how far these churches have *and* have not recognized the faith-building power of Vatican II and its aftermath in the last forty years, and in the latter case, what alternatives they have proposed for the life and mission of the church.[5]

Perhaps an anecdote will illustrate the two aspects of reception/subversion under discussion. At the end of the 1998 Special Assembly of the Synod of Bishops for Asia (the Asian Synod, for short), one frustrated participant complained that many of the issues and proposals broached by the Asian bishops in the discussion groups at the synod had not been incorporated into the final summary and that their ideas had been "filtered" by the Roman Curia. One Asian cardinal is said to have consoled him with the advice: "Don't worry about this filtering. When we go back to our churches, we will filter the official document ourselves."[6]

I will begin with a brief account of the contributions of the Asian churches at the Second Vatican Council. Next I present the current situation of the Catholic Church in Asia and examine the various areas of church life in Asia in which Vatican II has been positively received, with special reference to the activities of the FABC. In the third part I discuss the challenges as well as the contributions of the Asian churches to the church universal by focusing on the Asian Synod.

The Asian Churches at Vatican II

Announced by Pope John XXIII, to the consternation of his advisers, on January 25, 1959, and formally convoked on December 25, 1961, the Second Vatican Council, the twenty-first general council of the Catholic Church, opened on October 11, 1962. Suspended by Pope John's death on June 3, 1963, and continued by Pope Paul VI, the council met in four sessions and concluded on December 8, 1965. The council promulgated sixteen documents of various levels of authority (four constitutions, nine decrees, and three declarations).[7] Of these documents, it is generally agreed that in terms of dogma the most important is the Dogmatic Constitution on the Church (*Lumen Gentium*). In terms of immediate impact on church life, the Constitution on the Liturgy (*Sacrosanctum Concilium*) is the most significant; and in terms of the influence on the society at large, the Pastoral Constitution on the Church in the Modern World (*Gaudium et Spes*) is the most influential. In addition, in Asia, given its multireligious context and the Church's minority status, the Decree on the Church's Missionary Activity (*Ad Gentes*) and the Declaration on the Relationship of the Church to Non-Christian Religions (*Nostra Aetate*) are of particular relevance.[8]

In Preparation for Vatican II

As is well known, to prepare for the council and to minimize the Curia's opposition to it, John XXIII established an "antepreparatory commission" and assigned it not to the powerful Holy Office but to the Congregation for Extraordinary Ecclesiastical Affairs under the presidency of Cardinal Domenico Tardini.[9] The task of the commission was to consult with the episcopate worldwide, the Roman Curia, and Catholic universities to draw up a broad outline of the subjects to be discussed at the council, and to suggest membership of the preparatory groups. Tardini sent a letter to the bishops eligible to attend the council, asking them to send to the commission "critiques, suggestions, and wishes" that had to do with "points of doctrine, the discipline of the clergy and Christian people, the manifold activities of today's Church, matters of greater importance with which the Church must deal nowadays, or, finally, anything else" the bishops thought it good to discuss and clarify.[10]

Of the 2,594 bishops sounded out, 1,998 replied (77%), an astonishing response rate for any poll.[11] Of all the continents, Asia produced a relatively weak response (70.2%), lower than Central America (88.1%), Africa (83.3%), Europe (79.9%), although higher than Oceania (68.5%). Several factors accounted for the weak response from Asia: many of the Asian churches were still in mission territories;[12] responses had to be in Latin;[13] and in countries such as China, North Korea, and Vietnam, the bishops were silenced by communist regimes.

While many responses from Asia were short and formal, there were happy exceptions: Cardinal Valerian Gracias of Bombay (India) sent two rather lengthy replies; Cardinal Thomas B. Cooray of Colombo (Sri Lanka) did the same. Many bishops objected to the use of Latin as the official language of the council. Bishop Louis M. La Ravoire of Krishnagar (India) bluntly stated (in Italian!) that Latin was no longer the unifying element of the Church. As expected, most Asian bishops, particularly the Chinese and the Vietnamese, strongly demanded an unequivocal condemnation of communism. Characteristically, many of these bishops asked for a stronger devotion to Mary and even a definition of certain Marian privileges such as Mary's spiritual motherhood and her role as co-redemptrix and co-mediatrix, and a greater devotion to St. Joseph.

Theologically, the Filipino bishops, mostly of Spanish origin, were more conservative, in contrast to the more open Indonesian episcopate, who were of Dutch origin, and the Indian episcopate, whose Cardinal Gracias wanted a fairly radical reform of the Roman system. The Indonesian bishops made wide-ranging proposals regarding the adaptation of church law and worship to the local situations, stronger collaboration among local churches, participation of the entire church in its central government, dialogue with the World Council of Churches, more active roles for the laity, and reform in liturgy, law, and catechesis. Another interesting suggestion, which reflected the religious situation of Asia, concerned the need for dialogue with Buddhism. Archbishop Victor Bazin of Rangoon (Burma), proposed that the council not regard Buddhism as an atheistic religion but as an incomplete religion.[14]

Asian Presence at Vatican II

When the council opened on October 11, 1962, of the 2,449 participants of the first period (October 11-December 8, 1962), 298 came from Asia. In the second period (September 29-December 4, 1963), of 2,488 council fathers, 302 came from Asia.[15] In the third period (September 14-November 21, 1964), of 2,466 council fathers, 297 came from Asia. In the fourth period (September 14-December 8, 1965), of 2,625 participants, 311 came from Asia.[16] Given the preponderant number and role of European bishops and *periti* at the council,[17] Vatican II was essentially a European council. As Bishop Vicente Zazpe of Argentina noted in his diary: "The Church and the Council have remained in the hands of Central Europe. The only thing that counts is what they say. On the other hand, there is no current of thought or any group to hold them back or provide a balance. Even the pope is not a containing force. Neither America nor Africa nor Italy nor Spain counts."[18] That Zazpe did not even mention Asia in his list of insignificant voices at the council confirmed the fact the Asian bishops did not exercise a noticeable influence on it.

This does not mean, however, that the Asian bishops did not have their own contributions to make to the council. A survey of their interventions shows that consistent with their pragmatic outlook, their main concern was not with doctrinal issues but with practical church reforms. One area to which they contributed significantly is liturgy.[19] Cardinal Gracias asked that local episcopal conferences be given sufficient authority to implement liturgical reform.[20] A Chinese bishop requested the inclusion of St. Joseph in the eucharistic prayer.[21] Bishop Nguyen Van Hien of Saigon (Vietnam) asked on behalf of the Vietnamese bishops that episcopal conferences be permitted to introduce liturgical feasts on certain civil feast days in order to give them a Christian dimension and to show non-Christians that Christians respect ancestral traditions. He also requested permission to celebrate Asian martyrs with a liturgical feast in order to hold them up as models of Christian life appropriate to the Asian context.[22] Bishop Yoshigoro Taguchi of Osaka (Japan) pointed out that the splendor of the liturgical vessels gave offense in Japan because the Japanese love simplicity. He added that his people had trouble understanding certain Western rituals such as putting on and taking off the miter, kneeling to kiss the bishop's ring, and so on. He also proposed that liturgical vestments conform to local tastes and customs.[23] Along the same line, Bishop Paul Seitz of Kontum (Vietnam) said that sacred art should be marked by simplicity, integrity, and poverty.[24]

Another area on which the Asian bishops focused their attention was inculturation. Bishop Stanislaus Lokuang of Tainan (Taiwan) emphasized that every people has its own culture and that the Church must respect all of them and use them as a means for evangelization.[25] As we will see in detail below, the Asian bishops energetically initiated this process of inculturation in liturgical matters immediately after the promulgation of the Constitution on the Liturgy (*Sacrosanctum concilium*) at the end of the second period (December 4, 1963). Given the fact that Asian Catholics live in the midst of other religions, two of the central concerns of the Asian bishops during the council were interreligious dialogue and religious freedom.[26]

Furthermore, since the Asian churches were in mission lands, the Asian bishops showed a marked interest in mission. Here the greatest contribution was made by Bishop Lokuang, vice president of the Commission for the Missions. After the schema on mission by the Congregation for the Propagation of the Faith (whose prefect was Cardinal G. Agagianian) was rejected by the council fathers, in spite of Paul VI's appearance in person to the 116th general congregation on November 6, 1964, to publicly support it, a five-member editorial team was selected to do the revision, with Lokuang receiving the most votes. With Lokuang's shepherding of the revised document on mission, it was eventually approved by the council.

Another practical matter that drew the attention of the Asian bishops was priestly training and mandatory celibacy. During the fourth period of the council, the Indonesian bishops challenged the statement that "major seminaries are necessary for priestly formation" and suggested that new organizations, more suitable to contemporary needs, be adopted. In addition, they urged a reconsideration of the requirement of priestly celibacy.[27]

In sum, the contributions of the Asian bishops to Vatican II, while not as extensive as that of other bishops, were not insignificant. They focused less on doctrinal formulations than on how the Christian faith can be practiced effectively in their socio-political and religious locations. It is in this pastoral direction that their reception of the council must be evaluated.[28]

The Asian Churches: With and Beyond Vatican II

Before discussing how the Asian churches received Vatican II, it would be useful to take a brief look at the current situation of the Catholic Church in Asia. In Asia, Catholics (105.2 million in 1997) represent only 2.9 percent of the nearly 3.5 billion Asians. Moreover, well over 50 percent of all Asian Catholics are found in one country—the Philippines. Thus, if one excludes the Philippines, Asia is only about one percent Catholic. Despite its extreme minority status, the Catholic Church in Asia continues to grow. In 1988 there were 84.3 million Catholics. By 1997 the number had reached 105.2 million (an increase of 20.9 million or 25 percent). It is also interesting to note that most of the Asian clergy and religious are indigenous: In 1997 Asia had 617 bishops (out of 4,420 bishops in the world) and 32,291 priests (17,789 diocesan and 14,502 religious). Two-thirds of all religious priests are Asian; the vast majority of religious sisters (88 percent) are also Asian.[29] This minority status and the attendant lack of resources of all types no doubt limited the scope of Vatican II's influence on the Asian churches. However, this situation did not deter the Asian churches from immediately implementing the council.

Immediate Implementation of Vatican II

The first way in which the Asian churches received the Second Vatican Council was to translate its sixteen Latin documents into their own languages. While this task was somewhat easy for countries where English is by and large the second language (such as the Philippines and India), it posed formidable challenges for languages in which even a basic Christian vocabulary was not yet available, let alone highly technical theological and canonical terms, and where experts in both theology and the local languages were in short supply. For example, Chinese translation of such basic terms as "God" was a matter of serious and prolonged controversy, as is well known from the seventeenth-century disputes among missionaries.[30] Thus, the translation of Vatican II documents constitutes a major theological achievement of the Asian churches and was in itself an appropriation and inculturation of the theological orientations of the council.

It is universally agreed that the most immediate and visible impact of Vatican II was its liturgical reforms, not only with its encouragement of the use of vernaculars in liturgical celebrations but also thanks to a slew of new postconciliar liturgical books (such as the missal, liturgy of the hours, sacramentary, and *pontificale*) composed by the Concilium for the Implementation of the Constitution on the Liturgy established by Pope Paul VI in 1964. The goal of the reforms is to promote a "full, conscious, and active participation in liturgical celebrations."[31] Once again, the task of translating these liturgical books was a daunting one, but there is no doubt that with the use of vernaculars and the new rites, the faithful in Asia were enabled to achieve a full, conscious and active participation in the liturgical celebrations that had not been possible before the council.

The reception of Vatican II's liturgical reforms in Asia, however, went far beyond the translation of the liturgical books into vernaculars. It also included an explicit effort toward liturgical inculturation by bringing elements of the local cultures into sacramental and liturgical celebrations. This inculturation occurs at many levels. On a more superficial level, it includes the use of local music and songs, vestments, gestures, rituals, sacred objects, architecture, and so on. On a deeper level, it involves the composition of new sacramental rituals for significant events in a person's life, such as marriage and funerals. It sometimes includes the use of sacred texts of other religions in addition to the Christian Scriptures. In some countries, sacred rituals such as the cult of ancestors are incorporated into the liturgy.

This process of liturgical inculturation in Asia began even before the end of Vatican II. During the intercession after the council's second period (December 1963-September 1964), following the promulgation of the Constitution on the Liturgy (*Sacrosanctum concilium*), various Asian churches initiated new models of liturgical celebration. In India, under the dynamic leadership of Bishop Patrick D'Sousa, liturgical inculturation was vigorously pursued in different areas. In Sri Lanka, as part of liturgical innovation, Catholics collaborated with Protestants on a translation of the Bible into Sinhalese. In Japan, the bishops did away with the genuflection to bishops and the kissing of episcopal rings and replaced the genuflection before the Blessed Sacrament with a deep bow. In Taiwan, a study was made of the feasibility of introducing some Chinese feasts and usages into the liturgical year. In Hong Kong, work was done on liturgical hymns based on traditional Chinese music. In Vietnam, an attempt was made to incorporate the rites of ancestor and hero veneration into the liturgy. The Indonesian episcopate was the first to issue a decree on the implementation of

Sacrosanctum concilium, and during Holy Week in 1964 the Indonesian language was used in the chants, readings, and prayers.[32]

The Federation of Asian Bishops' Conferences (FABC)

These liturgical reforms, albeit still superficial and piecemeal, helped Vatican II have an immediate and extensive impact on the Asian churches. Nevertheless, the reception of Vatican II in Asia was not undertaken systematically and comprehensively until after 1972 when the Federation of Asian Bishops' Conferences was brought into being. In a sense, it was Vatican II that made the FABC possible, and, in turn, as will be shown, it is mainly through the FABC that Vatican II's reforms—and much more—were implemented in Asia. Prior to the council, the Asian bishops had more relationships with Rome than with one another. Vatican II brought them together and gave them a corporate identity as bishops of the "Asian Church," impressing upon them that to be pastorally effective they needed a structure like that of the Consejo Episcopal Latino-Americano.

It was during Pope Paul VI's visit to Manila in November 1970, where one hundred eighty Asian bishops had gathered for what was then called "the Asian Bishops' Meeting," that the idea of a federation of Asian bishops' conferences was broached. Two years later, on November 16, 1972, the structures and statutes of the FABC were approved. These were later amended and approved by Rome.[33] The FABC's stated purpose is "to foster among its members solidarity and co-responsibility for the welfare of Church and society in Asia, and to promote and defend whatever is for the greater good." However, the decisions of the Federation are "without juridical binding force; their acceptance is an expression of collegial responsibility."[34] In terms of the reception of Vatican II, it is interesting to note that among the FABC's manifold functions, one is "to study ways and means of promoting the apostolate, especially in light of Vatican II and post-conciliar official documents, and according to the needs of Asia."[35]

The FABC works through a series of bodies consisting of the Plenary Assembly (which meets every four years), the Central Committee (which meets every two years), the Standing Committee (which meets once a year), and the Central Secretariat with seven offices, each responsible for a particular area of Christian life.[36] The Plenary Assembly is the supreme body of the FABC, and so far there have been eight plenary assemblies, at the end of which a Final Statement was issued. Each assembly focused on a theme, and a look at these themes will give a sense of the major concerns of the Asian churches: evangelization in modern Asia, prayer as the life of the Church in Asia, church as a community of faith in Asia, the vocation and mission of the laity in the Church and in the world of Asia, the emerging challenges for the Church of Asia in the 1990s, discipleship as service to life, renewed Church—mission of love and service, and the Asian family—toward a culture of integral life. In addition to the authoritative Final Statements of the Plenary Assemblies, over a hundred papers of various length and importance by the FABC's seven offices and individual Asian theologians, published under the auspices of the FABC, bear witness to the emergence of a vigorous Asian theology during the postconciliar era.[37]

How has the FABC, itself the most important product of Vatican II, contributed to the reception as well as subversion of the council? Perhaps the best way to answer this question is to examine how well the Federation has fulfilled the principal functions it has set for itself. Besides the one already mentioned above, namely, to study ways and means of promoting the apostolate, the other functions include: "to work for and to intensify the dynamic presence of the Church in the total developments of the peoples of Asia; to help in the study of problems of common interest to the Church in Asia, and to investigate possibilities of solutions and coordinate action; to promote inter-communion and cooperation among local Churches and bishops of Asia; to render service to episcopal conferences of Asia in order to help them to meet better the needs of the People of God; to foster a more ordered development of organizations and movements in the Church at the international level; to foster ecumenical and interreligious communication and collaboration."[38]

"A New Way of Being Church": The Reign of God and a Triple Dialogue

These seven functions contribute to forming what the FABC calls a "new way of being church,"[39] an ecclesial mode of being that is inspired by Vatican II's vision and at the same time goes beyond it to respond to the various contexts of Asia. While taking a cue from Vatican II's self-understanding in *Lumen Gentium*, the FABC has expanded and, in a sense, subverted it, by replacing the council's potentially self-absorbing focus on intra-church matters with a consistent and thoroughgoing concern and, one might say, obsession with the kingdom of God.[40] While the theme of rule or kingdom of God is not absent in Vatican II, especially in *Gaudium et Spes*, nowhere in the council has it achieved the kind of theological and pastoral preeminence that it has with the FABC. Indeed, it is interesting that no document of the FABC or of its various offices in the last three decades has ever focused on the institutional elements of the church such as the papacy or canon law that have consumed much of the theological energy in the Western churches and that, albeit legitimate, run the risk of ecclesiastical narcissism.

This Copernican revolution—placing the kingdom of God rather than the church at the center of the Christian life and letting the *basileia* determine the shape and mission of *ecclesia*—is no abstract theological musing but has radical implications for the church's mission and its *modus operandi*, implications that were not anticipated, at least not fully, by Vatican II. This reversal of theological hierarchy is reminiscent of liberation theologies of all stripes,[41] but in Asia it was fueled principally not by politico-economic considerations but by the confluence, peculiar to Asia itself, of three intimately intertwined factors: massive poverty, cultural diversity, and religious pluralism.

Asian Christianity is present in the midst of a teeming mass of people worn down by dehumanizing poverty yet immensely rich in diverse and ancient cultures and religions that continue to give them dignity and freedom. Because of this, the mission of the church, contrary to some, even official, interpreters of Vatican II's decree on mission *Ad gentes*, can no longer be conceived as saving souls (*salus animarum*) and planting the church (*plantatio ecclesiae*).[42] Not that soul-saving and church-planting have ceased playing a role in the church's mission; rather, they no longer occupy the central position they enjoyed in mission theology and practice from the time of Augustine to Vatican II.[43] Nor is conversion eliminated as a possible response to evangelization.[44] However, soul-saving, church-planting, and conversion cannot and must not constitute the goal and objective of the church's mission.[45]

Rather they are only means to the church's end, which is the establishment of God's reign. As the FABC's Fifth Plenary Assembly states: "Our challenge is to proclaim the Good News of the Kingdom of God: to promote justice, peace, love, compassion, equality and brotherhood in these Asian realities. In short, it is to work to make a Kingdom of God a reality."[46]

Making the reign of God the sole *raison d'être* of the church entails important changes in the way the church carries out its mission. Here, going further than Vatican II, the FABC makes dialogue the comprehensive *modus operandi* of the church in Asia. It is vitally important to note that for the Asian churches dialogue is not simply one activity among many others that the church performs, but rather the basic and overarching *modality* in which the church's entire mission with all its manifold and complex activities—witness, proclamation, conversion and baptism, building up local churches, forming basic ecclesial communities, catechesis, worship, incarnating the Gospel in peoples' cultures, promoting social justice and peace, interfaith dialogue, theologizing, to name a few—are carried out.

Furthermore, this dialogue is not primarily an intellectual exchange among experts and religious leaders of various religions, as the term "dialogue" often suggests. Rather, it involves a fourfold presence, a presence demanded by the fact Asian Christians live as a minuscule minority among other Asians:

> a. The *dialogue of life*, where people strive to live in an open and neighborly spirit, sharing their joys and sorrows, their human problems and preoccupations. b. The *dialogue of action*, in which Christians and others collaborate for the integral development and liberation of people. c. The *dialogue of theological exchange*, where specialists seek to deepen their understanding of their respective religious heritages, and to appreciate each other's spiritual values. d. The *dialogue of religious experience*, where persons, rooted in their own religious traditions, share their spiritual riches, for instance, with regard to prayer and contemplation, faith and ways of searching for God or the Absolute.[47]

This fourfold presence takes place, according to the FABC, in three dialogues, corresponding to the three contexts of Asia mentioned above: massive poverty, cultural diversity, and religious pluralism. Again, with but moving far beyond Vatican II, the FABC insists repeatedly on the necessity of a threefold dialogue—with the Asian poor, with their cultures, and their religions.[48] Conceiving Christian mission as a deeply intertwined and simultaneous threefold dialogue, the affirmation of which has become something of a mantra among Asian theologians, is no doubt unique to the Asian churches. These three dialogues—liberation, inculturation, and interreligious dialogue—were at first conceived and practiced as three distinct activities. Gradually, by 1990, at the fifth Plenary Assembly in Bandung, Indonesia, it became clear that these three dialogues form but a three-pronged single approach to Christian mission in Asia.

The necessity of undertaking these three dialogues *together* has been argued most forcefully by Asian theologians such as Sri Lankan theologian Aloysius Pieris and Indian theologian Michael Amaladoss and has been repeatedly affirmed by the FABC. These three dialogues must be practiced together; only then can each guarantee the authenticity and success of the others. Indeed, theoretically, it is impossible to draw a clear dividing line among these three dialogues, since not rarely it is, as Jesus' ministry has made abundantly clear, the poor and marginalized people who are most religious and most attached to their cultures.

What kind of Christianity, then, would emerge from this new way of being church? At the Seventh Plenary Assembly in 2000, the Asian bishops took a retrospective glance at the FABC's teachings and activities in the previous three decades. They noted that the Asian churches have adopted "eight movements that as a whole constitute an Asian vision of a renewed Church": a movement toward a church of the poor and a church of the young; a movement toward a truly local church; a movement toward deep interiority; a movement toward an authentic community of faith; a movement toward active integral evangelization; a movement toward the empowerment of lay men and women; a movement toward active service of life; and a movement toward the triple dialogue with the poor people of Asia, with Asian cultures, and with Asian religions.[49]

In these eight movements the influence of Vatican II can easily be discerned. At the same time, it is no less clear that the Asian churches have done more than just receive the council. In many ways they have moved beyond it, precisely because they want to be not simply churches *in* Asia but churches *of* Asia, that is, truly and authentically local communities, radically committed to making the reign of God present in Asia through the triple dialogue.[50]

The Asian Synod: The Asian Church Brings Gifts Back to Rome

One of the signs that guests are on an equal footing with their hosts is that they can return the hospitality by bringing gifts of their own to their hosts. They no longer just receive favors but also give back something of their making, a dish of their own recipe, a bouquet of rare flowers, or perhaps an exotic bottle of wine, something different that would add beauty to their hosts' home and enliven the time spent together. Better still, the guests will in turn become hosts, inviting the friends who have entertained them into their own home and share with them their own food and drink.

In the post-Vatican II era, for almost three decades the Asian churches functioned mainly as unequal guests. For the most part, they received what Vatican II offered, in doctrines as well as in practical reforms. But because they carefully attended to the specific contexts of Asia, the Asian churches could not but adapt, modify, go beyond, and even subvert Vatican II in order to meet the needs of Asia, just as any American tourist would find that McDonald hamburgers and Coke do not taste the same in Beijing as in Mobile, Alabama, because these foods have to be modified to please the Chinese palate.

The Asian Synod

Sooner or later, however, the guests will feel confident enough to invite their former hosts into their own homes. The occasion arose for the Asian churches when Pope John Paul II convoked a Special Assembly of the Synod of Bishops for each of the five continents to celebrate the coming of the third millennium of Christianity. A special theme was chosen for each, the one for Asia being "Jesus Christ the Savior and his mission of love and service in Asia." According to Cardinal Jan Schotte, the General Secretary of the Synod of Bishops, this theme was supposed "to respond to the unique set of circumstances within the Church in

Asia as well as to address the actual state of affairs affecting all the peoples and cultures on the Asian continent. In highlighting the centrality of the Person of Christ, his Mission as Mediator and One and Only Savior in God's Eternal Plan of Salvation, the Church in Asia and all Her members will be better prepared to fulfill Christ's Evangelizing Mission of love and service in Asia."[51]

At times, hosts, sensitive to the dietary needs of their guests, would ask in advance what they like to eat and cannot eat. In preparation for the Asian Synod, no such sensitivity seemed to be uppermost in the minds of the Roman organizers. They thought that making the person of Christ and his mission as "mediator and one and only savior" central to the work of the synod would respond to "the unique set of circumstances within the Church in Asia" and would prepare Asian Christians "to fulfill Christ's Evangelizing Mission of love and service." This imposition of Christology with its claim of Jesus as the "mediator and one and only savior" on the Asian Synod's agenda and conceiving it as the panacea for what may ail the Asian churches constitute, to judge from all the documents of the FABC, a massive misdiagnosis of the situation of Asian Christianity. As we have seen above, neither Christology nor ecclesiology is at the center of the Asian churches' concerns; the primary concern is God's reign or a new way of being church. It is most interesting that the FABC's Seventh Plenary Assembly, which took place shortly after the synod on January 2-12, 2000, adopted the second part of the theme of the synod, "mission of love and service," but replaced the first part "Jesus Christ the Savior" with "A Renewed Church," thereby subtly but unmistakably subverting the Roman-imposed focus on Christology.[52]

Part of the preparation for the synod included the drafting of a document called the *Lineamenta* (Outline), which laid out the themes for discussion at the synod. True to the intention of the Roman organizers, the *Lineamenta* focused on Christology. While appreciative of various Asian Christologies intended to make Jesus relevant to the sociopolitical and religious situation of Asia, the document warned against the danger of partial Christologies, especially those that raised questions about the "uniqueness of Jesus Christ in the history of salvation."[53]

The *Lineamenta* was then sent to the Asian episcopates for responses and suggestions. Unlike the anemic reactions of their predecessors prior to Vatican II, this time the Asian bishops went into full action. Despite the shortness of time and numerous difficulties of various sorts, the Asian bishops' conferences took the task of responding to the *Lineamenta* very seriously. They organized study sessions and discussion groups to ponder over this preparatory document and provided lengthy and detailed answers to its questions. Besides offering helpful thumbnail sketches of the Asian churches, these responses highlighted the real concerns confronting Asian Christians, sometimes in contrast to those perceived by the Roman Curia. Again and again, almost *ad nauseam*, under various guises, the inculturation of the Christian faith into Asia emerged as the central and neuralgic issue: How can Asian Christians present Jesus Christ and the Church with an authentic Asian face? Or, to put it in the words of the Catholic Bishops' Conference of India, how can the church become "truly Indian and Asian"?

Even a cursory reading of these responses demonstrates that the uniqueness and universality of Jesus as the Savior was never placed in question by the Asian churches. Rather, the burning issue for the Asian churches, a tiny minority in Asia, is *how* to proclaim this truth about Jesus credibly in the midst of crushing poverty, competing religious systems, and cultural diversity. The unanimous answer to this problem was found to be dialogue: dialogue with the Asian poor, with their religions, and with their cultures. As the Indian bishops put it, "This dialogal model is the new Asian way of being Church, promoting mutual understanding, harmony and collaboration." The Asian bishops' reports were surprisingly frank. While humbly recognizing their churches' strengths, the bishops bluntly highlighted their weaknesses, which revolved around the absence of genuine inculturation by means of the triple dialogue mentioned above.

With regard to interreligious dialogue, many Asian episcopal conferences called for not only a respectful dialogue with non-Christians but also an explicit recognition of the salvific value of non-Christian religions, not as independent from or parallel to Christ, but in relation to him. The Indian bishops affirmed: "For hundreds of millions of our fellow human beings, salvation is seen as being channeled to them not in spite of but through and in their various socio-cultural and religious traditions. We cannot, therefore, deny a priori a salvific role for these non-Christian religions."

The Korean bishops asserted: "We have to study and re-evaluate the meaning and role of the great traditional religions in Korea. They too play a part in the salvific economy of God. This understanding is essential for the inculturation of the Gospel." The Filipino bishops urged an exploration "in an open and humble way" of the " 'revelatory' nature of the great ancient religions in Asia and its impact on the church's proclamation of the truth of Jesus." In this connection, the Japanese and the Vietnamese bishops found the Christology of the *Lineamenta* with its insistence on the uniqueness and universality of Christ too defensive and apologetic.[54]

Concerning the dialogue with the poor, the Asian bishops pointed out that Asia is a continent of massive poverty and systemic oppression and that the church cannot fulfill its evangelizing mission unless it walks with the poor. The Indian bishops put it starkly: "Clearly India's Christian Community is now being called to an ecclesial conversion: to be a Church of the Poor." In particular, the bishops call for an end to the discrimination against women, both in society and church.

Regarding the dialogue with Asian cultures, the Asian bishops decried the foreignness of Christianity to Asia and urged a systematic inculturation of the Christian faith in all its aspects, from worship to theology to ministerial formation. The Sri Lankan bishops called for a "divesting of the Western image of the Church in the liturgy, style of life, celebrations, and trying to overcome the present image of a powerful, affluent and domineering institution."

In order to carry out this triple dialogue with Asian peoples successfully, the Asian bishops believed that a certain degree of autonomy and freedom for the local churches was necessary. They lamented a lack of dialogue and even trust between the Asian churches and Rome. This lack was exemplified, according to some episcopal conferences, in the composition of the *Lineamenta* itself. The Japanese bishops spared no words to express their deep disappointment with the eurocentric focus of the *Lineamenta* and the lack of serious consultation in the way the synod was planned: "Since the questions of the *Lineamenta* were composed in the context of Western Christianity, they are not suitable. Among the[se] questions are some concerning whether the work of evangelization is going well or not, but what is the standard of evaluation? If it is the number of baptisms, etc., it is very dangerous. From the way the questions are proposed, one feels that the holding of the synod is like an occasion for the central office to evaluate the performance of the branch offices. That kind of synod would not be worthwhile for the church in Asia. The judgment should not be made from a European framework, but must be seen on the spiritual level of the people who live in Asia." Speaking of the goal of the synod, they said: "We do not hope for a Synod aiming at discovering how the Asian Church can be propped up by the Western Church, but one where the Bishops of Asia have an honest exchange and learn how they can support and encourage one another."[55] True to Asian hospitality, several episcopates suggested that the synod be held on their continent, with Roman representatives coming as guests.

All in all, the responses of the Asian episcopal conferences to the *Lineamenta* evinced a remarkable sense of collegiality and maturity. The Asian bishops appreciated the pope's convocation of a special synodal assembly for Asia but they made it clear that they wanted an *Asian* synod. As the bishops of the Philippines put it: "Ensure that the Synod is truly Asian, with an Asian reflection, with an Asian output, reflecting the Asian perspective of evangelization."[56]

As the result of the Asian bishops' responses, the *Instrumentum laboris* (Working Document) of the synod was composed in such a way as to reflect the pastoral concern for a new way of being church in Asia. Despite its title, "Jesus Christ, the Savior and His Mission of Love and Service in Asia," the central focus of the *Instrumentum laboris* was not Christology but how the church must carry out the mission of Jesus today in Asia.[57]

The Church as Communion of Local Churches

During the synod, which began on April 19 and concluded on May 14, 1998, there were 191 "interventions" on the floor, of eight minutes each. Needless to say, there is a great diversity in the contents of these mini-speeches as they represented the vastly different faces of the church in the immense continent of Asia. Nevertheless, on the whole, the Asian bishops did speak with a remarkably consistent voice about the basic needs and tasks of Christianity in Asia. As the FABC has repeatedly insisted, Christian mission in Asia can only be carried out in the form of dialogue in three intimately interrelated areas: with Asian cultures, Asian religions, and the Asian poor. Furthermore, to perform this dialogue successfully, the Asian bishops believed that a legitimate autonomy of the local churches, which is proper to and required by the principle of subsidiarity, is necessary. This autonomy enables the local churches to decide, in consultation with the other churches of the same region, what pastoral policies and practices are most effective for their evangelizing mission and for the life of Christians, without undue control by or interference from the Roman Curia. This autonomy, the Asian bishops believed, is not opposed to the supreme authority of the bishop of Rome. On the contrary, it promotes collegiality and communion among the bishop of Rome and the other bishops and thus brings forth the manifold riches of the universal church.

Another oft-repeated point in the interventions refers to the need to expand the roles of the laity, especially women, in the life of the church. The ecclesiological model that the Asian bishops tried to promote is what has been called the "participative church," namely, a church in which all members are fundamentally equal in dignity and share responsibility for the whole church, though with different functions and duties.

Gifts given by guests to their hosts are of course not always welcome, perhaps because they do not fit the hosts' tastes, or because they may be positively dangerous to the hosts, as the warning "Beware of Greeks bearing gifts" testifies. Some of the theological gifts the Asian bishops brought back to Rome were regarded as the Trojan horse. One of these was the contribution of Francis Hadisumarta, the Carmelite bishop of Manikwari, Indonesia. Referring to Vatican II's ecclesiology of communion, Hadisumarta said that "the Catholic Church is not a monolithic pyramid. Bishops are not branch secretaries waiting for instruction from headquarters! We are a communion of local churches." He pointed out the absurdity of the practice of having the liturgical translation and adaptation of the Asian churches approved by Roman officials, "who do not understand our language."[58] In the English-speaking discussion group, Hadisumarta later said quite bluntly: "The attitude of the Roman Dicasteries in regard to the inculturation of liturgy is not all positive. The Latin liturgy is a purely westernized liturgy translated verbatim into the local languages. Even the translations are to be approved by the said Dicasteries, which sounds paradoxical."[59]

Another gift, intimately related to the way of being church based on communion and solidarity, is collegiality rooted in the ancient tradition of patriarchate. Again it was Hadisumarta who was the bearer of the gifts. After speaking on behalf of the Indonesian Bishops' Conference on collegiality and the synodal nature of the church, Hadisumarta urged that the church "move from adaptation to inculturation and create new, indigenous rites." He went on to suggest that "in many crucial pastoral areas we need to adapt church law. We need the authority to interpret church law according to our own cultural ethos, to change, and where necessary, replace it." To achieve this inculturation, the bishop asked pointedly:

> Do we have the imagination to envisage the birth of new patriarchates, say the Patriarchate of South Asia, of Southeast Asia, and of East Asia? These new patriarchates, conciliar in nature, would support, strengthen, and broaden the work of individual episcopal conferences. As the episcopal conferences, in communion with neighboring conferences in the same (new) patriarchate, move forward in mission, new Catholic Rites would come into existence. Thus, we envisage a radical decentralization of the Latin Rite—devolving into a host of local Rites in Asia, united collegially in faith and trust, listening to each other through synodal instruments at parish, deanery, vicariate, diocesan, national/regional, continental, and international levels. Then, almost four decades after the Second Vatican Council, we would truly experience a "great synodal epoch."[60]

Using the traditional language of "patriarchate" and "rite," what Hadisumarta, and with him many Asian bishops, were driving at is a "radical decentralization" of the Roman Catholic Church. As has been remarked by several church historians and ecclesiologists, whereas during its first millennium the ecclesial paradigm was bearing faithful witness to the apostolic tradition with collegiality and communion as the modus operandi, in the second millennium this paradigm shifted to that of actively shaping the church tradition by means of a monarchical papal supremacy.[61] The names of popes such as Gregory VII, Innocent III, and Pius IX immediately come to mind. The affirmation of the papal *plenitudo potestatis* reached its apogee at Vatican I, where papal primacy and infallibility were defined as dogmas over against conciliarism, Gallicanism, control by the state, and the threats of modernity. While re-affirming the two papal dogmas, Vatican II made collegiality and communion its central ecclesial vision. However, during the post-conciliar years, church leaders bent on centralizing power in the papacy and the Roman Curia gained the upper hand and have successfully prevented the implementation of collegial structures.

What is urgently needed now, according to the Indonesian episcopate, is a radical decentralization, and one way to initiate this process is by organizing what Hadisumarta called new "patriarchates." This church structure, Hermann Pottmeyer points out, is rooted in three theological principles—catholicity, collegiality, and subsidiarity—and implements the triadic church organization of the first millennium: the particular church with its bishop; the regional ecclesiastical units, especially the patriarchal churches with their patriarchs; and the universal church with the pope as its head.[62] The importance of the "ancient patriarchal Churches" was recognized by Vatican II when it said: "It has come about through divine providence that, in the course of time, different Churches set up in various places by the apostles and their successors joined together in a multiplicity of organically united groups which, whilst safeguarding the unity of faith and the unique divine structure of the universal Church, have their own discipline, enjoy their own liturgical usage and inherit a theological and spiritual patrimony" (*Lumen Gentium*, 23).

Unfortunately, when in the West there was only the Latin patriarchate of the bishop of Rome, this triadic structure was lost, resulting in the dual structure of the local church/bishop and the universal church/pope and the eclipse of the character of the church as a communion of churches. As a result, the roles of the pope as the patriarch of the Latin West and the pope as the head of the universal church were fused together. Given the merging of the two roles of the bishop of Rome and the current excessive centralization of power in the papacy and the Roman Curia, it is high time to separate clearly the competencies of the bishop of Rome as the patriarch of the Latin West and the universal pastor and to create new patriarchates and separate them from the Latin church. This is exactly what Joseph Ratzinger strongly suggested shortly after the council as the "task for the future," namely, "to separate more clearly the office proper to the successor of Peter from the patriarchal office and, where necessary, to create new patriarchates and separate them from the Latin church." The reason for creating new patriarchates is that "a uniform canon law, a uniform liturgy, a uniform filling of episcopal sees by the Roman central administration—all of these are things that do not necessarily accompany the primacy as such, but result only from this close union of two offices."[63]

When Pope John Paul II came to New Delhi to promulgate his Apostolic Exhortation *Ecclesia in Asia* on November 6, 1999,[64] the churches to which he brought the final gift of the Asian Synod were no longer guests of Rome. Now they played hosts to the Patriarch of the West and the Universal Pastor. Almost forty years had elapsed between Vatican II and the Asian Synod, and a lot of water had passed under the ecclesiastical bridge since the time the Asian bishops as timid participants in Vatican II demanded a condemnation of communism and a greater devotion to Mary and St. Joseph to the beginning of the third Christian millennium when their successors proposed a new way of being church, with self-confidence and boldness, in front of the pope and the Roman curia.

"If the Asian Churches do not discover their own identity, they will have no future."[65] So declared the Asian Colloquium on Ministries held in Hong Kong on March 5, 1977. This search for self-identity, the Colloquium went on to suggest, consists in "the process of re-discovering that the individual Christian can best survive, grow, and develop as a Christian person in the midst of a self-nourishing, self-governing, self-ministering, and self-propagating Christian community."[66] This self-discovery by the Asian churches as *Asian* churches capable of self-government, self-support, self-propagation, and self-theologizing was achieved by both "receiving" and "subverting" Vatican II, by following the council's inspiration *and* going beyond it, under the guidance of the FABC.

The Asian Synod was the first official recognition that the churches of Asia have come of age. To Rome the Asian bishops came back as a body after Vatican II, this time to teach, and not only to learn from, Rome and the universal church, from their rich and diverse experiences of being church in Asia, with surprising boldness and refreshing candor, with what the New Testament calls *parrhsia* (freedom of speech). Things have come full circle: the Asian churches were guests *and* hosts, learners *and* teachers, receivers *and* subverters at the same time.[67]

Notes

[1]For a history of the Federation of Asian Bishops' Conferences, see Edmund Chia, *Thirty Years of FABC: History, Foundation, Context and Theology*. FABC Papers, no. 106 (16 Caine Road, Hong Kong: FABC, 2003). The associate members joined the FABC in 1998. On the history and contribution of the FABC to the reception of Vatican II, see the second section of the essay below.

[2]Indeed, the ten-volume *The Men Who Made the Council*, edited by Michael Novak (Notre Dame, Ind.: University of Notre Dame Press, 1964) does not mention any bishop from Asia.

[3]On reception, see the classic by Yves Congar, *Tradition and Traditions: An Historical and a Theological Essay*, trans. Michael Naseby and Thomas Rainborough (New York: Macmillan, 1967). Other useful works include Robert Dionne, *The Papacy and the Church: A Study of Praxis and Reception in Ecumenical Perspective* (New York: Philosophical Library, 1987); Hans Robert Jauss, *Toward an Aesthetic of Reception* (Minneapolis: University of Minnesota Press, 1982); Edward J. Kilmartin, "Reception in History: An Ecclesiological Phenomenon and Its Significance," *Journal of Ecumenical Studies* 21 (1984): 34-54; and Dale T. Irwin, *Christian Histories, Christian Traditioning: Rendering Accounts* (Maryknoll, N.Y.: Orbis Books, 1998).

[4]Terrence Tilley, *Inventing Catholic Tradition* (Maryknoll, N.Y.: Orbis Books, 2001), 10.

[5]I have done an extensive bibliographical survey of post-Vatican II developments in Asia in "Reception of Vatican II in Asia: Historical and Theological Analysis," in Peter C. Phan, *In Our Own Tongues: Perspectives from Asia on Mission and Inculturation* (Maryknoll, N.Y.: Orbis Books, 2003), 201-14. Some of the materials of this survey will be incorporated in this essay.

[6]Apparently this filtering by the Roman Curia was a common practice. Brazil's Cardinal Paulo Evaristo Arns said in a recent interview: "In 1983 and for the next eight years, I was the secretary of the Synod of Bishops in Rome. It was my responsibility to write down the conclusions of one synod and to draft the documents in preparation for the next synod. Nothing of what we prepared was ever taken into consideration. Very competent people carried out the whole process, but the texts were never used. At that time, the pope, or whoever he delegated, drafted the conclusions of the synod. The conclusions were formulated in such a way that they no longer reflected what had been said in the discussions" (*National Catholic Reporter* [March 4, 2005], 6.

[7]For an English translation, see *Vatican Council II*, New Revised Edition, ed. Austin Flannery (Collegeville, Minn.: Liturgical Press, 1975). English translations of Vatican II's documents in this essay are taken from this work.

[8]For a history of Vatican II, see the projected five-volume *History of Vatican II*, ed. Giuseppe Alberigo (English edition, ed. Joseph A. Komonchak), all published by Orbis Books (Maryknoll, N.Y.) and Peeters (Leuven, Belgium). So far, four volumes have appeared in English: vol. 1: *Announcing and Preparing Vatican II—Toward a New Era in Catholicism* (1995); vol. 2: *The Formation of the Council's Identity—First Period and Intersession October 1962-September 1963* (1997); vol. 3: *The Mature Council—Second Period and Intersession September 1963-September 1964* (2000); vol. 4: *Church as Communion—Third Period and Intersession September 1964-September 1965* (2003); vol. 5: *A Transition's Council—The Fourth Period and the End of the Council (1965)* is in preparation. Historical information on the council is taken from these five volumes.

[9]On the antepreparatory commission, see *History of Vatican II*, vol. 1, 44-60.

[10]*History of Vatican II*, vol. 1, 94.

[11]Over 95,000 proposals or *vota* were sent in to the antepreparatory commission.

[12]It was only at the beginning of 1961 that John XXIII established native hierarchies in Vietnam, Korea, and Indonesia.

[13]Even the Italian bishop Aloysius Scheerer of Multan (Pakistan) had to admit in his response: "I have lost the ability to write in Latin." See *History of Vatican II*, vol. 1, 103, note 72.

[14]For a study of the *vota* of the bishops, see *History of Vatican II*, vol. 1, 98-132.

[15]Note that the entire episcopates of China, North Vietnam, and North Korea could not attend the council.

[16]See *I Padri presenti al Concilio Ecumenico Vatican II*, ed. Segretaria Generale del Concilio (Vatican City: Tipografia Poliglotta Vaticana, 1966), 353.

[17]Of the 224 council "experts" appointed on September 28, 1962, only one was from East Asia (India), whereas 59 came from various European countries. On the council experts, see *History of Vatican II*, vol. 1, 448-62.

[18]Quoted in *History of Vatican II*, vol. 4, 631.

[19]There were 37 interventions by Asian bishops during the debate on the constitution on the liturgy.

[20]See *History of Vatican II*, vol. 2, 120.

[21]See ibid., 126.

[22]See ibid., 145.

[23]See ibid., 146.

[24]See ibid.

[25]See *History of Vatican II*, vol. 4, 315.

[26]See ibid., 126. It was in defense of religious freedom that several Asian bishops, especially the Chinese and the Vietnamese, advocated a forthright condemnation of atheistic communism described as "the culmination of all heresies." See ibid., 288-89.

[27]See *History of Vatican II*, vol. 5, chapter three, by Mauro Velati. This volume, not yet published, is available to me only in manuscript form. I will cite it not by page but by chapter.

[28]For an evaluation of the impact of Vatican II on the Asian churches, see the articles in *Asian Pastoral Review* 42, nos. 1/2 (2000).

[29]For resources on statistics of the Asian churches, consult *Catholic Almanac* (Our Sunday Visitor, Inc.), *Statistical Yearbook of the Church* (Vatican Press), and "Annual Statistical Table on Global Mission," in the first number of each volume of *International Bulletin of Missionary Research*. For statistics of Catholics in individual countries belonging to the Federation of Asian Bishops' Conferences, the following data are given for the year 2000, with the name of the country followed by its estimated general population in millions and the percentage of Catholics in brackets: Bangladesh (145.8/ 0.27%); Bhutan (1.8/0.02%); Burma/Myanmar (48.8/1.3%); Cambodia (10.3/0.02%); China (1,239.5/0.5%); Hong Kong (6.9/4.7%); India (990/ 1.72%); Indonesia (202/2.58%); Japan (127.7/0.36%); North Korea (22.6/ ?); South Korea (47.2/6.7%); Laos (6.2/0.9%); Macau (0.5/5%); Malaysia (22/3%); Mongolia (2.5/?); Nepal (23/0.05%); Pakistan (142.6/0.8%); Philippines (74.8/81%); Singapore (3.1/6.5%); Sri Lanka (20.8/8%); Taiwan (22.1/1.4%); Thailand (61.6/0.4%); Vietnam (78.2/6.1%). I am grateful to Rev. Dr. James H. Kroeger, MM, for information on these statistics. For a popular presentation of the Asian churches, see Thomas C. Fox, *Pentecost in Asia: A New Way of Being Church* (Maryknoll, N.Y.: Orbis Books, 2002).

[30]The question was whether the Chinese terms of *taiji* (supreme ultimate), *li* (principle), *tian* (heaven), and *shangdi* (lord on high) can be used to translate "God." Matteo Ricci thought that the first two were inappropriate and the latter two acceptable, although he preferred the newly coined term *tianzhu* (lord of heaven). In 1693, Bishop Charles Maigrot, vicar apostolic of Fujian, decreed that all the first four terms were incorrect and that the only acceptable term was *tianzhu*. His decision was ratified by Pope Clement XI (*Ex illa die*, 1715) and Pope Benedict XIV (*Ex quo singulari*, 1742). Today, Chinese Catholics use *tianzhu*, whereas Protestants prefer *shangdi* and *shen* (spirit, deity).

[31]*Sacrosanctum Concilium*, no. 14.

[32]For a detailed bibliographical survey of liturgical reform in Asia, especially in India and the Philippines, see Peter C. Phan, "Reception of Vatican II in Asia: Historical and Theological Analysis," in Phan, *In Our Own Tongues*, 204-06.

[33]See *Statutes of the Federation of Asian Bishops' Conferences* (Hong Kong: FABC Central Secretariat, 1992). The statutes were amended in 1974, 1990, and 1995.

[34]Article 1, A and B of the Statutes.

[35]Article 2, A of the Statutes.

[36]The seven offices are: Office of Human Development, Office of Ecumenical and Interreligious Affairs, Office of Evangelization, Office of Education and Student Chaplaincy, Office of Social Communications, Office of the Laity, and Office of Theological Concerns.

[37]For a list and analysis of these papers, see James H. Kroeger, *FABC Papers Comprehensive Index: Papers 1-100 (1976-2001)* (Hong Kong, FABC, 2001). For the documents of the FABC and its various institutes, see Gaudencio B. Rosales & C. G. Arévalo, eds., *For All the Peoples of Asia: Federation of Asian Bishops' Conferences: Documents from 1970 to 1991* (Maryknoll, N.Y./Quezon City, Philippines: Orbis Books/Claretian Publications, 1992); Franz-Josef Eilers, ed., *For All the Peoples of Asia: Federation of Asian Bishops' Conferences. Documents from 1992 to 1996* (Quezon City, Philippines: Claretian Publications, 1997); and Franz-Josef Eilers, ed., *For All the Peoples of Asia: Federation of Asian Bishops' Conferences. Documents from 1997 to 2002* (Quezon City, Philippines: Claretian Publications, 2002). These will be cited as *FAPA*, followed by their years of publication in parentheses.

[38]Article 2, A-G of the Statutes.

[39]*FAPA* (1992), 287; (1997), 3.

[40]On Asian theology of the kingdom of God, see Peter C. Phan, "Kingdom of God: A Theological Symbol for Asians?" in Peter C. Phan, *Christianity with an Asian Face: Asian American Theology in the Making* (Maryknoll, N.Y.: Orbis Books, 2003), 75-97.

[41]On the method of liberation theologies, see Peter C. Phan, "A Common Journey, Different Paths, the Same Destination: Method in Liberation Theologies," in Phan, *Christianity with an Asian Face*, 26-46.

[42]There are still traces of this double concern as the central aims of mission in Pope John Paul II's encyclical *Redemptoris missio: On the Permanent Validity of the Church's Missionary Mandate* (1990). See, for example, §49.

[43]For a comprehensive presentation of mission theology, see David Bosch, *Transforming Mission: Paradigm Shifts in Theology of Mission* (Maryknoll, N.Y.: Orbis Books, 1991); Jean Paré, *Défi à la mission du troisième millénaire* (Montreal: Missionaires de la Consolata, 2002); and Stephen Bevans and Roger Schroeder, *Constants in Context: A Theology of Mission for Today* (Maryknoll, N.Y.: Orbis Books, 2004).

[44]On conversion as response to evangelization, see Peter C. Phan, "Conversion and Discipleship as Goals of the Church's Mission," in Phan, *In Our Own Tongues*, 45-61.

[45]For a discussion of the goal of mission, see Peter C. Phan, "Proclamation of the Reign of God as Mission of the Church: What For, To Whom, By Whom, With Whom, and How?" in Phan, *In Our Own Tongues*, 32-44.

[46]*FAPA* (1992), 275.

[47]The Pontifical Council for Interreligious Dialogue and the Congregation for the Evangelization of Peoples, *Dialogue and Proclamation*, 42 (19 May, 1991). The English text is available in William Burrows, ed., *Redemption and Dialogue: Reading* Redemptoris Missio *and* Dialogue and Proclamation (Maryknoll, N.Y.: Orbis Books), 93-118. See also *FAPA* (1997), 21-26. It is to be noted that even though the text was first formulated in a Roman document, it is rooted in the Asian experience of being church, since the ghost author of this document was Jacques Dupuis, one of the main theologians of the FABC, who drafted it out of his decades-long work in India. At any rate, this fourfold presence has been repeatedly proposed by the FABC.

[48]On this threefold dialogue, see Peter C. Phan, "Christian Mission in Asia: A New Way of Being Church," in Phan, *In Our Own Tongues*, 13-31.

[49]See *FAPA* (2002), 3-4.

[50]On this theme, see the following works by James H. Kroeger, *Living Mission: Challenges in Evangelization Today* (Quezon City, Philippines: Claretian Publications, 1994); *Asia-Church in Mission* (Quezon City, Philippines: Claretian Publications, 1999); *Becoming Local Church* (Quezon City, Philippines: Claretian Publications, 2003).

[51]Quoted in Peter C. Phan, ed., *The Asian Synod: Texts and Commentaries* (Maryknoll, N.Y.: Orbis Books, 2002), 2.

[52]The full theme of the Seventh Plenary Assembly reads: "A Renewed Church in Asia: A Mission of Love and Service." On this "absence" of Christology at the FABC's Seventh Plenary Assembly, see Edmund Chia, "The 'Absence of Jesus' in the VIIth FABC Plenary Assembly," *Vidyajyoti* 63 (1999), 892-99. For the Final Statement of the Seventh Plenary Assembly, see *FAPA* (2002), 1-16.

[53]No. 23 of the *Lineamenta* says: "While Asian Christologies must interpret Jesus for Asians, as has been done by others during the twenty centuries of the Church's existence, all Christologies must be measured against the faith of the Apostles, the apostolic Church and the testimony of the New Testament. No sectarian or partial Christology can do justice to the true Jesus Christ of the Gospels. He is more than a social reformer, a political liberator, master of spirituality, champion of human rights, or savior of the marginalized." See Phan, *The Asian Synod*, 13-14.

[54]On interreligious dialogue from the Asian perspective, see Peter C. Phan, *Being Religious Interreligiously: Asian Perspectives on Interfaith Dialogue* (Maryknoll, N.Y.: Orbis Books, 2004).

[55]Phan, *The Asian Synod*, 27.

[56]For the Asian bishops' responses to the *Lineamenta*, see Phan, *The Asian Synod*, 17-51.

[57]For an analysis of the *Intrumentum laboris*, see Phan, *The Asian Synod*, 73-82.

[58]Phan, *The Asian Synod*, 119.

[59]Ibid., 10.

[60]Ibid., 120-21.

[61]See Hermann Pottmeyer, *Towards a Papacy in Communion: Perspectives from Vatican I & II* (New York: Crossroad, 1998).

[62]See ibid., 132.

[63]Joseph Ratzinger, *Das neue Volk Gottes: Entwürfe zur Ekklesiologie* (Düsseldorf: Patmos, 1969), 142. Cited by Pottmeyer, *Towards a Papacy in Communion*, 134.

[64]For the English text of *Ecclesia in Asia*, see Phan, *The Asian Synod*, 286-340. On the challenges of *Ecclesia in Asia*, see Peter C. Phan, "*Ecclesia in Asia*: Challenges for Asian Christianity," in Phan, *Christianity with an Asian Face*, 171-83.

[65]*FAPA* (1992), 70.

[66]Ibid., 77.

[67]A discussion of the reception and subversion of Vatican II by the Asian churches cannot omit their reactions to the Declaration of the Congregation of the Doctrine of the Faith *Dominus Iesus* (August 6, 2000), especially because it is rumored that it targeted some Asian Christologies. The FABC's Office of Ecumenical and Interreligious Affairs organized formation institutes for interreligious affairs on October 3-10, 2000 (at Jenjarom, Malaysia) and on August 20-25, 2001 (at Pattaya, Thailand). In the Final Statements of both institutes, reference was made to *Dominus Iesus*. The first stated that it found the Declaration "highly ambiguous in its message on interreligious dialogue" (*FAPA* [2002], 136). The second affirmed that the Declaration contains "quite a number of positive elements" but questioned "its tone, which is perceived as tending towards the dogmatic and authoritarian." It also found that "the various subtle distinctions between the Catholic Church and other churches as well as other religions—such as distinctions between faith and belief, inspired texts and sacred writings, and Churches and ecclesial communities—are areas that tend to offend other Churches and believers of other religions." Finally, it asked whether "important documents, such as *Dominus Iesus*, should not undergo a process of broader consultation before their publication, particularly with local ordinaries and Episcopal Conferences" (*FAPA* [2002], 143-44). Again, here, there has been a process of reception and subversion. For a fuller critique of *Dominus Iesus* from the Asian perspective, see Edmund Chia, "Towards a Theology of Dialogue: Schillebeeckx's Method as Bridge between the Vatican's *Dominus Iesus* and Asia's FABC Theology," Ph.D. dissertation, University of Nijmegen, 2003.

The Laity and Catholic Action in John Courtney Murray's Vision of the Church

Christopher D. Denny

Roman Catholic theologians who would envision the church of the future forty years after the close of Vatican II do well to note the caution of Karl Rahner: "How can a Church of the future be conceived? In view of the openness of the future and the impossibility of planning it, this question in the last resort is obviously unanswerable."[1] Since the church and its members face this open future, for the most part, bereft of prophetic powers that could predict what is yet to come, Rahner's question can be rephrased as "How can the church of today prepare for the incomprehensible mystery we call the future?" The church of the future is therefore not the church as it exists in some time that has not yet arrived. Rather, the church of the future is the church of the present open to the possibilities that await it within the developments of history.

The Second Vatican Council, with its program of *ressourcement* and *aggiornamento*, was a momentous event that tried to prepare the church for this mystery in a world that had been buffeted and transformed by the rapid changes of modernity. As contemporary Catholic theologians look back at Vatican II forty years after its close, they can profit greatly by heeding the work of the theologians from the middle of the twentieth century whose research laid the groundwork for the events from 1962 to 1965. Even though the future of these theologians is now our past, studying the hopes this earlier generation of scholars had for the church may rejuvenate our own quest for a community that continues to exist, in the words of *Lumen Gentium,* "in Christ as a sacrament, or sign and instrument, both of intimate union with God and also of the unity of the human race."[2]

John Courtney Murray, arguably the finest theologian the American Catholic Church has produced, devoted much of his work in the 1940s to appropriating a theology of church history and the church of the future in the light of the needs of his own times.[3] It is Murray's later writings on the relationship between church and state and his influence on Vatican II's "Declaration on Religious Freedom" that have drawn the lion's share of scholarly attention paid to his oeuvre. Controversies that persist today regarding his defense of "the American proposition" are a second-generation outgrowth of the controversies that flared between Murray and the editors of the *American Ecclesiastical Review* when Murray first advanced his revolutionary interpretations of the political doctrines in the encyclicals of Leo XIII.[4] A review of Murray's early lectures, however, reveals that his later interest in church-state relations and religious freedom arose from his concern about the ability of the Catholic Church to present a traditional yet timely message to the modern world. The lay movement Catholic Action played a pivotal role in Murray's understanding of the future of the church. While teaching at Woodstock College in the mid-1940s, Murray stated that Catholic Action "solves [the] ancient problem of civilization, [namely the] spiritual direction of [the] temporal order without violating [the] transcendence of [the] spiritual or [the] autonomy of [the] temporal" (MP).[5]

Borrowing from a 1935 article by Henri Carpay, Murray understood Catholic Action as part of the emerging sixth epoch of church history, one in which lay Catholics would undertake a new form of apostolate. In this present article I will trace both the characterization of these epochs in Murray's thought and Murray's conception of the transformative role Catholic Action was playing in the church in the generation before Vatican II. For Murray, each of these historical periods is defined by a distinctive relationship between the temporal and spiritual orders. Looking at Catholic Action through this historical prism, one discovers how Murray's hope for the church of the future shaped his evaluation of the church's apostolic mission in the generation preceding the Second Vatican Council.

From this introduction, I will proceed in three stages. First, I will outline Murray's understanding of the epochs of church history, using the schema he took from Henri Carpay. Second, I will discuss Murray's understanding of Catholic Action and its mission in the sixth epoch of church history, an age in which the Catholic laity would take the initiative in reforming the temporal order. Finally, I will conclude with some comments on how examining the supernatural significance of Catholic Action in Murray's vision of the future church might augment our contemporary understanding of Murray's significance and improve our ecclesiological approaches.

The Two Orders in Murray's Theology of Church History

In constructing an understanding of the church's past, present, and future, various Christian theologians have worked with a sixfold division of history, ever since the competing interpretations of the book of Revelation offered by Tyconius and Augustine.[6] Augustine's partition of history into six periods mirroring the six biblical days of creation, a schema with which he concluded the *City of God*, served as the origin for a tradition of exegesis taken up by Joachim of Fiore, Bonaventure, and Peter Olivi.[7] In Augustine's judgment, all six of these "days" of the *saeculum* of history are characterized by the opposition of two cities, the *civitas terrena* and the *civitas Dei.* Maintaining and refining Augustine's distinction after the final collapse of the Western empire later in the fifth century, Pope Gelasius I (r. 492-496) ushered in a new epoch in political theory with his letter "*Duo sunt*" to the Byzantine emperor Anastasius, in which Gelasius defined the two powers ruling the world as the power of kings and the sacred power of bishops.[8]

The sixfold division of church history that Murray employs is not directly dependent upon this long Augustinian and medieval tradition. Pope Gelasius's differentiation between the two powers, however, would prove increasingly important in Murray's thinking from 1949 onwards.[9] Yet earlier in 1942 Murray simply described the two orders of society as "the eternal and the temporal, the order of the specifically secular and the order of the specifically religious" (JTS).[10] Murray's immediate source for the sixfold division of church history is a 1935 article in the *Nouvelle Revue Théologique*, entitled "La Nouveauté de L'Action Catholique," written by Henri Carpay and published while Murray was studying at the Pontifical Gregorian University in Rome.[11] Carpay expanded upon the article in a 1948 book, *L'Action Catholique,* which Murray would praise the following year.[12]

According to Carpay, Christian history could be divided into six epochs, epochs not based upon biblical typologies but upon the relationship of the "two societies" he calls the spiritual and the temporal, without giving a general definition of these two terms. Carpay held that the two societies must be in a relation to each other while remaining distinct. The proper social apostolate of the church in every era is to reform both of these societies while maintaining and promoting their distinctiveness. Within these historical delineations, Carpay's theology of history was structured around one recurring theme: the church's evangelization of the temporal society. In each epoch the church adopted an apostolate for evangelizing the temporal society with varying degrees of success. These epochs and the corresponding apostolates are as follows.

The first epoch is coterminous with the pre-Constantinian era, in which the church's apostolate took the form of martyrdom. The church fostered and actively promoted the cult of martyrdom to inspire the temporal society with its commitment to the gospel. This was perhaps the only option available for influencing a pagan world bent on persecution of Christians. Carpay referred to it as a "purely spiritual" apostolate.

In the second epoch, from Constantine to the medieval age, the church was able to penetrate the temporal society due to the end of Christian persecutions and the political establishment of Christianity. Carpay censured the church's apostolate during this era because the two societies became confused with each other, as the temporal society was placed at the service of the spiritual society. He admitted that the church did gain influence, even if much of this influence was only superficially realized in the lives of many nominal converts.

The Middle Ages constituted the third epoch, which Carpay evaluated as one of stable equilibrium between the two societies. The church was able to use its established position within the temporal society for spiritual advantage.

The fourth epoch of church history, termed "the crisis" by Carpay, was ushered in at the Council of Vienna in 1311. The church, realizing that its spiritual mission was blunted by too great an entanglement with the temporal, reformed itself. This internal reform would itself prove to be the apostolate in this stage of church history. The temporal order, on the other side, began its long march away from the spiritual order with the advent of humanism. Although humanism originally aimed at simply distinguishing between the spiritual and the temporal—a healthy goal that insisted upon untangling the preceding confusion of the two societies—it was taken to a point where it ended in revolution. The Reformation and its aftermath, along with the French Revolution, brought about a reversal of history. After 1789 the church found itself once again facing a hostile temporal society, just as in its early centuries.

The nineteenth and early twentieth centuries composed the fifth epoch of church history, in which the church, divested of temporal power, again aimed at a purely spiritual penetration of the temporal order. According to Carpay, the church was able to recover its spiritual insights from the reign of Pius IX onwards, and so the clergy were "purified." A key development of this era, one of the positive changes in the newly pagan temporal society, was material progress, which, while sterile in itself, made possible the rise of a "lay elite."

The sixth epoch of church history began in 1922 with the accession of Archbishop Achille Ratti of Milan to the See of Peter as Pope Pius XI. By this time material progress, although unevenly distributed, had increased literacy and economic opportunities. Writing within this generation of history, Carpay claimed that "the question of an *accord between the church and the state* will decide the future of the world."[13] Murray later characterized this theo-political tension as "the deepest social problem of our contemporary age" and "the issue of human society on which all the future hangs" (JTS). The state could either be obstinate or turn toward the church to promote the work of education and world civilization.

This is the world that the Catholic Action movement faced from the 1920s through the 1940s. Although Pius XI's 1922 encyclical *Ubi Arcano* and his later papal statements built upon Pius X's earlier promotion of Catholic Action, Yves Congar echoed Carpay's appreciation of Pius XI's formative role in the movement when he wrote in *Lay People in the Church:* "Up to his time there had been very many active Catholics . . . there had been activity of Catholics, and in this sense Catholic action (with a small 'a,' as Jacques Maritain says): but Catholic Action was created by Pius XI."[14] Carpay claimed that this marked the beginning of the church's modern apostolate, as Pius "definitively liquidates the power of the popes and enjoins the clergy to retire from the political parties."[15]

Into this vacuum, Catholic Action entered. Pius XI defined it as "the participation of the Catholic laity in the hierarchical apostolate (*participation des laïcs catholiques à l'apostolat hiérarchique*)."[16] Catholic Action is for Carpay "the modern form of the official relation between the church and the state." In Carpay's estimation, Catholic Action aims at a "*reconstitution of a 'Christian temporal,'* " but it does this spiritually, with due concern that church and state remain two societies perfectly distinct yet sharing a common "Christian spirit."[17] Catholic Action is at once lay, universal, social, and spiritual, but also hierarchical insofar as the hierarchy directs the activity of the Catholic laity.

In 1942, seven years after the publication of Carpay's article in the *Nouvelle Revue Theologique*, Murray was invited to give a series of lectures at the Institute for Religious Studies at the Jewish Theological Seminary in New York City on the theme "Religion and Society." In the fourth and final lecture in this series, given on March 10, Murray outlined what he termed "the Catholic social program." Without making mention of Carpay and at times translating directly from him, Murray proceeded to outline the six periods of the history of the church as they had appeared in Carpay's article. Two years later, in 1944, Murray taught a course at Woodstock College entitled "*Conspectus Quaestionum de Munere Sociali Ecclesiae*" (Survey of the Questions of the Church Concerning Social Duty), this time with explicit reference to Carpay. Notes from the Murray archives at Georgetown University indicate he probably offered this course at Woodstock more than once. In Murray's lecture notes, Carpay's outline of church history appears under the heading, "Theory of Social Reform [that] Raises the Problem of the Supernatural" (MP).

In his lectures at the Institute for Religious Studies, Murray expanded upon the later epochs of Carpay's historical outline in important respects. First, Murray made it clear that the historical development of the church is the result of practical and concrete changes within history, rather than the predetermined unfolding of an abstract dialectic. Returning to the crisis of the late medieval church in Carpay's fourth stage of history, Murray insisted that the medieval theory delineating the proper relationship between the temporal and spiritual orders, a term he substitutes for Carpay's "societies," was different from what actually occurred in history. As Murray noted, authorities such as Aquinas went unheeded by religious and political leaders:

> The theory whereby the temporal had its own particular validity and was adequately distinct from the spiritual had been formulated already by St. Thomas Aquinas, but, as you

> know very well, it is a long step from the formulation of an idea in theory to its reduction in practice. . . . In a dialectic of history that would be purely abstract, the next step in human progress would have been the strengthening of the Christian unity and the Christian order by a progressive differentiation of its two elements, the spiritual and the temporal. That was indicated, and that was to have been desired. The theory that would preside over that development had already, I say, been formulated. . . . However, the differentiation of those two orders, like any great social movement, did not progress without checks and without excesses. (JTS)

By sounding this note of caution, Murray let it be known that a theology of church history must be more than dialectical philosophy or political theory. A theology of history must be based upon critical historiography and historical particularities. The church of the future does not come into being as a result of a seamless evolutionary process.

Murray's second expansion of Carpay's historical outline, building on this differentiation between theory and actuality, is an important distinction dealing with the long period of church crisis from the late Middle Ages to the French Revolution. While Murray holds that the distinction between the temporal and the spiritual orders is desirable, he condemns the actual manner in which this distinction came about in history. In 1942 Murray said to his audience:

> The aim was distinction between the two. What actually came about, however, was their separation, a rupture, and there ensued that very painful period in Christian history. . . . [T]here took place also a disruptive process in the temporal order. Its motive, of course, was the same, a desire for autonomy, a desire in itself legitimate, but in its realizations excessive. (JTS)

As an example of historical divergence between the ideal and the real, Murray mentioned to his predominantly Jewish audience the French Revolution, which, in overthrowing the Catholic establishment, ushered in what Carpay defined as the fifth stage of church history:

> [I]t constituted the principle of a certain separation of the spiritual and temporal order. Insofar as it did that, it did a good thing, and a thing that we would wish to be done, because the temporal and the spiritual order [sic] are distinct and, as I said, in the logic and dialectic of history they should have progressively become distinct. Therefore, that was real progress. On the other hand, the French Revolution in its principles consecrated the principle of the divorce of the temporal and the spiritual and brought them into hostility to each other, and in that was its sin. So far as it did that, it was evil. However, it did those two things, and once a thing is done it is done and that is the end of it. You cannot undo history. (JTS)

For Murray, a theology of church history is more than simply sacralizing the historical exigencies of past events. His ecclesiology does not presume that the history of the relationship between the temporal and spiritual orders is one of unmitigated progress. In his later Woodstock lectures, Murray characterized the "borderland" between the spiritual and temporal orders as an area of "spiritual crisis" (MP). Faced with such a crisis, the church moves into the future, and theologians must discern what are the positive developments in the church's history and what forces oppose these advances.

To summarize this first section of the present article, one can say that Murray, in borrowing from Carpay, is careful to stress both determinant historical particularities in the church's history and the distinction between theo-political goals and historical reality.

Catholic Action in the Sixth Epoch of Murray's History of the Church

It is possible here to give only a brief introduction to the Catholic Action movement. Its prehistory can be traced to the late 1860s and 1870s in Italy, where opposition movements such as the *Società della Gioventù Cattolica Italiana* and the *Opera dei Congressi e dei Comitati Cattolici* were organized by Catholic laity resisting political integration with the newly created Italian state.[18] Giuseppe Sarto, the future Pope Pius X (1903-1914), applied the specific term "Catholic Action" to a broad social movement undertaken by the laity and coordinated by the clergy. The aim of this social movement was made clear in a speech that Sarto gave while patriarch in Venice in which he characterized Catholic Action's goal as follows:

> Catholic Action consists especially in affirming the rights of Jesus Christ who is truly our King.
>
> Because Jesus Christ is represented by His Church, Catholic Action consists in being affectionate children of this perfect society. . . . Because, moreover, this Church is not built in the air . . . but does her work in this our sublunar world, having a Supreme Head, Bishops and Priests, Catholic Action is directed towards the defence of and to the revindication of the rights of the Roman Pontiff, who is to the Church of Christ what the head is to the body . . . for where the Pope is there is the Church. . . . The more open the war against the Pope is, the more open, the more active, the more resolute should Catholic Action be in defending and maintaining the inviolable rights of the Sovereign Pontiff.[19]

In this model, Catholic Action's platform was dedicated to a restoration of the church of the past. This restoration involves a public defense of the prerogatives of the church's hierarchy and the papacy.

In Sarto's thinking a restoration of the church in society necessarily entailed a restoration of its past position in the temporal order. Catholic laity were to lead in this effort. In the same speech, he continued:

> Catholic Action is properly lay in character for another reason also, which is obvious even to the most undiscerning, but which must not therefore be forgotten. At one time the rights of Jesus Christ, of the Church and of the Pope entered into the legislation of all Christian states, and no one dared to deny to the hierarchy, the Church and the Pope those immunities and those privileges which they have received from Christ, and have been recognised by so many centuries of State laws. Now it is no longer so. The Church, the Pope, are no longer recognised as such and no longer form part of the social organism; they are relegated to the sphere of common rights; nay, they are even considered as enemies; they are ranked with evildoers. Since these things are so, who

> is it that must bestir himself to defend the violated rights and insulted dignity of the Pope, the Church and the Bishops? . . . today it must be the children who will rise up in defence of their Father, the laity in defense of the Hierarchy.[20]

When Sarto referred to the "social organism" in this context, it is plain that he was using this term in a univocal sense, one that encompassed both the political-temporal order, with its capacity for making and enforcing the laws of a nation, and the spiritual order.

Upon his election to the papacy in 1903, under the papal motto "*Instaurare omnia in Christo*," Pius X became the first pope to use the precise phrase "Catholic Action (*Azione Cattolica*)."[21] Pius's 1905 encyclical *Il fermo proposito,* described by one writer as "the first complete treatise on Catholic Action," was dedicated to the movement, which Pius defined as "anything, in any manner, direct or indirect, which pertains to the divine mission of the church."[22] Pius acknowledged that Catholic Action was not one organization gathered into a singular juridical entity, but rather a lay movement that could take a variety of forms depending on the social context. Murray judged that *Il fermo* made "the social question" the principal part of Catholic Action (MP). Groups contemporary with the pontificate of Pius X, such as the *Jeunesse Ouvrière Chrétienne* (the "Jocists" or the "Young Christian Workers"), established in Belgium by Joseph Cardijn, and the *Association de la Jeunesse Française* in France, are particular examples of so-called "specialized Catholic Action movements" taking different forms in response to different social contexts.[23]

In the pontificate of Pius XI, the "Pope of Catholic Action," the Vatican's approach to Catholic Action changed markedly, even before the signing of the concordat with Italy in 1929. In 1928, Pius XI wrote a letter to the president of the International Union of Catholic Women's Associations in which he defined Catholic Action in the following terms, making no mention of a restoration of the Catholic political establishment from the past: "Participation of the Catholic laity in the hierarchical apostolate, for the defense of religious and moral principles, for the development of a sound and charitable social action under the direction of the ecclesiastical hierarchy, outside of and above all the political parties, in order to institute the Catholic life in the family and in society."[24] In a letter written to Cardinal Adolf Bertram of Breslau that same year, Pius indicated that approval given by the hierarchy to the social activity of laity working in Catholic Action would be a way to ensure coordination of lay and clerical efforts.[25] Both article 43 of the 1929 concordat and a subsequent agreement between the Italian government and the Holy See in 1931 ironed out a shared platform that stated that Catholic Action would be outside all political parties and that no person hostile to the Italian state would be a director of any Catholic Action apostolate.[26] In the 1931 encyclical letter *Quadragesimo Anno* ("On Reconstruction of the Social Order") Pius XI wrote that Catholic Action "excludes strictly synodal or political activities from its scope."[27]

In the wake of these developments of the late 1920s and early 1930s, Murray could say in his 1942 Institute for Religious Studies lecture that a "Christian temporal order" is "simply a social order in which a man can be a man without having to be a hero," omitting any reference to the past political privileges of the Catholic Church and its hierarchy (JTS). On the one hand, Murray did acknowledge Catholic Action's connection with the church's hierarchy, a point Pius X made emphatically. Murray here followed Pius XI's oft repeated definition of Catholic Action as lay participation in the hierarchical apostolate and said, "[T]he Catholic undertakes his Catholic Action not as a private individual, but as a member of the Church; and he conceives of his work as a participation in the total work of the Church" (JTS). On the other hand, Murray's exposition of Catholic Action had moved far beyond the restorative social and political project of Pius X. For Murray, unlike Pius X, did not tie the lay efforts of Catholic Action to the pursuit of the clerical political privilege sought by Pius X. In Murray's words, the laity help construct a social order, for "the creation of those earthly conditions which will be favorable to the growth of the divine life" (JTS). This creation does not take place in a supernatural order. Murray held that the task of the laity indirectly aims at the goal which the clergy themselves pursue directly, as the clergy attempt to sanctify souls through preaching, administering sacraments, and instilling moral discipline.

Indeed, for Murray the entire project of Catholic Action now presumed a distinction between the two orders of society. Assuming this dyarchy was an essential characteristic of Murray's exposition of the movement, Murray told his audience, "To realize that spiritual communication between two orders of human society: that is the special task of what we call Catholic Action, and it is that task which gives it its novelty [note here the use of Carpay's term from his article title], its distinctiveness, its appropriateness to the modern context" (JTS). Although his mention of restoring society echoed past magisterial themes, namely Pius X's papal motto and Pius XI's *Quadragesimo Anno*, Murray has a singular interpretation of the significance of Catholic Action.

Indeed, Carpay and Murray completely inverted what Cardinal Sarto had in mind for Catholic Action in the late 1800s. Cardinal Sarto, the future Pius X, wanted the Catholic laity to resurrect the union of "altar and throne" present in the Catholic confessional state, which had been the church's preferred relationship for the temporal and spiritual orders since the post-Napoleonic restoration. Such a relationship persisted in Spain under Franco at the time Murray addressed his audiences at Woodstock and the Institute for Religious Studies.[28] By contrast, Carpay and Murray defined Catholic Action as a forward-looking movement ushering in a new stage of history in which the proper distinction between social orders would be respected, unlike Carpay's second and third eras of history, late antiquity and the Middle Ages respectively, in which the two orders were improperly mixed. Murray did not see this necessary distinction as a Christian retreat from the demands of modern discipleship. In 1944 at Woodstock Murray told his students that the logical differentiation between grace and nature means that a natural order is inherent in human society and that this natural order is to be perfected by grace.

Yet logical development was not enough in Murray's mind to ground the vocation of the laity in the modern world. Just as Murray distinguished between abstract dialectic and concrete historical developments in the theology of church history, he also distinguished between abstract and historically informed justifications for Catholic Action. In the third lecture of his Woodstock course, he referred to these justifications as the "systematic" and "genetic" approaches. A systematic justification for Catholic Action simply defined the movement in terms of its constituent elements: lay, apostolate, organized, mandated. Murray judged this justification doctrinaire and problematic because it ignored the historical reality that Catholic Action grew organically out of a concrete situation. A "genetic" justification for Catholic Action moved "from situation, needs, etc. to concept," and properly realized that Catholic Action was related to the particular needs of its times and could only be understood in light of that history (MP). Murray quoted Pius XI, who followed this genetic approach in a February 1931 letter to the Argentine bishops: "The necessities of the times demand that, following *variations* in manners and customs, the clergy and the laity should create *new forms* of the Christian apostolate. . . . The experiences and the daily practices of the vast ministry which we exercise have long ago convinced us that the apostolate exercised by the laity is the form of apostolate that best suits the *needs* of these latter days" (MP).[29]

Indeed, Murray's exposition of Catholic Action to the Jesuit seminarians presumed that a genetic approach to the movement would take into account that Catholic Action presently faced a world in crisis, a "world relapsed into paganism," as Murray put it. To denounce this world in the midst of the Second World War was easy enough, but Murray credited Pius XI with a constructive response rather than mere denunciation. "Pius XI," Murray noted, "saw that [the] key to [the] modern problem was *organization.* [He] saw too, who had to be organized—laity." Murray judged that priests were numerically insufficient and an improper instrument for the work "of recapturing [the] direction of society and reforming social institutions." He believed this organization of lay people would be pursued "with a view (1) to their spiritual formation into interior Christian life, [and] (2) their mission to [the] work of fashioning society (domestic, civil, interior) according to Christian principles. [This] work opens vast perspectives" (MP). In other words, Catholic Action entrusts the laity with both a "spiritual" and a "social" apostolate, to use Murray's terms.[30] Murray refused to privilege either of these qualities over the other, and he interpreted their interplay as a dialectical circle. Without the aid of a concerted apostolate, Murray claimed that this dialectical circle would degenerate into a vicious circle, claiming: " 'Institutions deform men' equals 'men deform institutions.' [The] way out of [the] circle is Catholic Action, [which] takes hold of both ends at once by seizing man in [the] milieu, responsible to and for [the] milieu" (MP).

Nevertheless, the pragmatic and particular goals of the Catholic Action movement within the context of the early twentieth century did not preclude a theoretical understanding of Catholic Action's significance. Murray urged his Woodstock students to study the encyclicals of Pius XI, "See how his theory of society leads logically to [the] theory of Catholic Action as [a] means of realizing this theory" (MP). Looking back at Murray, present-day theologians can recognize that such logical development signals an awareness of the presence of the Holy Spirit at work in the history of the church. Indeed, in a 1927 address Pius XI himself claimed that he formulated the very definition of Catholic Action—the participation of the laity in the hierarchical apostolate of the church—with the aid of divine inspiration.[31]

At the close of this article's second section, one should note there is still ambiguity in Murray's exposition of the two orders of society and the place of the supernatural in them during the early- and mid-1940s. Indeed, in his Woodstock survey course syllabus, the final section described Catholic Action as a movement that served as "the means of injecting [the] supernatural into society thus effecting reform," despite Murray's claim that the lay apostolate only served as an indirect means for reforming the temporal order (MP). Direct sanctification of society was reserved for the clergy. As mentioned above, Murray's entire presentation of Catholic Action in this course followed Carpay's outline of church-state history, which Murray introduced under the heading, "Theory of Social Reform [that] Raises the Problem of the Supernatural." It is toward this issue of the supernatural and its place in the church's apostolate of the future that I would like to turn in the final section of this article.

Murray's History of the Supernatural and Contextualizing the Church's Apostolate

In the second installment of a 1944 two-part article in *Theological Studies* entitled "Towards a Theology for the Layman," Murray wrote that the specialized training that the modern Catholic laity required "should start with intensive research in the papal theory of Catholic Action. . . . In no other way can one learn exactly what a layman is and what the Church today wants to make of him."[32] While lay education should begin with this papal teaching, Murray made a deliberate distinction between "Catholic Action" in the strict sense employed by Pius XI, with its specific norms and its mandates, and the broader meaning of "Catholic action," which he termed "the laity as called to support and prolong the apostolate of the hierarchy" without reference to organizational structures.[33] With this distinction in place, Murray chose to concentrate on the broader definition, and left the specific discussion of Catholic Action behind him, proceeding to outline the type of theology that the laity should study in the emerging church of his day. Never again in his published writings would Murray offer such a detailed presentation of his views on Catholic Action, and by the late 1940s his efforts had turned to the issues of religious freedom and intercreedal cooperation that would lead to his censure in 1955.[34] One should note that the general line of development in Murray's thinking on Catholic Action moved from the theoretical and dialectical delineation of the two orders of society in church history towards the practical concern for what kind of lay person could effectively carry out the church's apostolate in the mid-twentieth century and what kind of education this lay person should receive.

We are left then with an abrupt hiatus in Murray's writings on Catholic Action. Forty years after the close of Vatican II, how should theologians evaluate Murray's understanding of the relationship between the two orders of society and the lay apostolate? Since his death in 1967, Murray's entire project has been the subject of spirited debate, but how does his vision of Catholic Action relate to the church's apostolate years later?

During the quarter-century after Vatican II, Christian theology in certain quarters turned against the distinction of temporal and spiritual orders that Murray and others of his generation presumed. In *A Theology of Liberation* Gustavo Gutiérrez criticized the debilitating effect that "the distinction of planes model" had on the Catholic Action movements and he criticized their "indirect" efforts at social change. In Gutiérrez's judgment, the dyarchy of orders or societies hindered these movements in their attempts to assume more specific political commitments, as Catholic Action's "spiritual apostolate" could not successfully penetrate the alleged temporal order. Gutiérrez held that the distinction of temporal and spiritual must be abandoned and the category of the supernatural reconceived and expanded.[35] Clodovis Boff seconded Gutiérrez's motion to abolish the distinction between two orders or societies.[36] Even among defenders of a new integralism, there is no consensus on how to proceed, as John Milbank's partiality for Maurice Blondel's thought and Milbank's accompanying criticisms of the socio-political mediating theologies of Gutiérrez and Boff demonstrate.[37]

It would be a logical move at this point to discuss the influence competing theories of nature and grace play in this dispute about the church's apostolate, but that will not be the move I will take. Instead, I would suggest that we pay attention to Murray's initial concern—the church's evangelization of the world and the concrete organization that movement would take. In other words, let us appreciate Murray's writings on Catholic Action and church history as primarily a functional ecclesiology rather than a theoretical one. The temporal and the spiritual orders do not exist as merely abstract, static, and dogmatic constructions in Murray's presentations. There is no mention of a "purely temporal" or "purely natural" society or order in his outline. In the fifth lecture of his Woodstock course, Murray insisted that without a pastoral effort of "moral renewal" even the natural order could not be fully established (MP). At each stage of its history, the church is always working to spread the supernatural gospel message within the temporal order, and this effort is constitutive of church history. Before he wrote about intercreedal cooperation and long before he wrote about religious freedom, Murray proved himself an insistently concrete thinker, with a practical concern for Christian witness.

Much of the current controversy regarding Murray centers upon the exegetical and philosophical strengths and weaknesses of Murray's grasp of his sources. Yet we would do well to examine how Murray read the signs of the times in his own day, specifically in regard to the major shift he observed in the twentieth century. Murray judged that the world in his lifetime had ushered in a new social order, an order that distinguished the church from antiquity through the First World War, on one hand, and the church of the generation before Vatican II, on the other hand. Murray made the provocative claim that the accession of Pius XI to the papal throne in 1922 and his promotion of the lay movement of Catholic Action marked an epochal shift in the social context of the church, analogous to the changes wrought by Constantine's Edict of Milan and the French Revolution. This new social order demanded a new response from the church, one that took the form of Catholic Action. Given the scope of Murray's social claims, his attentiveness to his own social context is as important for understanding his ecclesiology as are his political theories and his textual interpretations. Murray interpreted these particular events as more than historical occurrences. He interpreted them as stages in the evolution of the relationship between temporal and spiritual orders of society and, by extension, the unfinished process by which Catholic Christians learn to discern the movement of the supernatural in the world and the church. Yet Murray did not simply consecrate the differentiations of church history as the inevitable development of dialectical forces. On the contrary, he held that it is possible to determine both progress and setbacks in the church's pilgrimage toward the kingdom of God, and this possibility opens space for a future church that is more than a predetermined function of the past church.

Murray's lectures remind us to begin our contemporary ecclesiologies at the level he did, the functional and historical. Keeping Rahner's caution about the indeterminacy of the future in mind, we should hope that in a polarized church, currently riven by ideologies of left and right, the appeal to the present is where reflection on the church of the future should begin. Murray himself worked in a polarized church and strove to overcome this division with relentless attention to history. Where his opponents saw timeless political truths in papal encyclicals, Murray chose to reconstruct the development of theological history because the social activity of that changing history was where he saw "the problem of the supernatural" emerging. Following Murray in this functional approach would mean that contemporary ecclesiologies would begin not with reflections on the theoretical relationship between the church and the state, the church and the world, the temporal and spiritual orders, dualism and integralism, or public philosophy and public theology. We would begin our ecclesiologies by attentiveness to the communities and apostolates necessary for spreading the gospel message. Debates and disagreements about Catholic Action and the base communities of Latin America should be understood as debates about the types of praxis and apostolates in which we want lay Christians to engage. Our attempts to understand the mystery of the church should begin with the lived experiences of Christians in these movements.

In our present, forty years after Vatican II, the church does have a problem. It is the problem of the supernatural and where to find it, and we are very fortunate to have such a problem. For Murray, the problem of the supernatural in the twentieth century was increasingly a lay problem to which Catholic Action was the practical solution. Murray's theology of church history, however, teaches us that this supernatural problem is never solved once and for all. Recalling Rahner, the church should be thankful for this, because openness to the mysterious problem of the supernatural is necessary for the church to have any future at all. As history and society change, the supernatural needs to be discovered in changing historical guises and constantly reconceived. While Murray was concerned to bring the lay apostolate to the forefront of the church's evangelization, he also teaches us that for the laity, or any group within the church, to regard itself as the terminal point in the historical evolution of ecclesiology is presumptuous.

In considering these less-studied contributions of John Courtney Murray, theologians should note that his later concern for religious freedom, which Vatican II's "Declaration on Religious Freedom" embodied, is not simply the result of a theory about two distinct orders of society. It is also a consequence of Murray's vision of a Catholic Church that exhibits the proper respect for both its own identity and mission and that of the world. Forty years after Vatican II, as Catholic theologians examine the state of the church, we should note that at the heart of Murray's vision of the church of the future was the church's recognition of the value of the lay apostolate of Catholic Action, a movement that Vatican II's "Decree on the Apostolate of the Laity" described as yielding "abundant fruit for the kingdom of Christ."[38]

Notes

[1]Karl Rahner, *The Shape of the Church to Come,* trans. Edward Quinn (New York: Seabury Press, 1974), 92.

[2]*Lumen Gentium* (Dogmatic Constitution on the Church), 1, in *Decrees of the Ecumenical Councils,* vol. 2, *Trent to Vatican II,* ed. Norman P. Tanner (Washington: Georgetown University Press, 1990), 849. Translations from Vatican II documents in this article are my own based upon the Latin text in the Tanner edition.

[3]In using the phrases "church of the future" and "future church" in connection with Murray, I am aware that these phrases are not present in Murray's writings, at least to my knowledge. My intent here is to examine how Murray's theology of church history is relevant to the theme of this present volume, the possibilities facing the church forty years after Vatican II.

[4]For the state of the controversy from Murray's day, see Leo XIII, *Immortale Dei* (November 1, 1885), ASS 18:161-80; *Libertas Praestantissimum* (June 20, 1888), ASS 20:593-613. English translations of both encyclicals are found in *The Great Encyclical Letters of Pope Leo XIII* (Rockford, Ill.: TAN Books and Publishers, 1995), 107-63. Also see John Courtney Murray, "Freedom of Religion: The Ethical Problem," *Theological Studies* 6 (June 1945): 229-86; "Contemporary Orientations of Catholic Thought on Church and State in the Light of History," *Theological Studies* 10 (June 1949): 177-234; "The Problem of 'The Religion of the State,' " *American Ecclesiastical Review* 124 (May 1951): 327-52; "The Church and

Totalitarian Democracy," *Theological Studies* 13 (December 1952): 525-63; "Leo XIII on Church and State: The General Structure of the Controversy," *Theological Studies* 14 (March 1953): 1-30; "Leo XIII: Separation of Church and State," *Theological Studies* 14 (June 1953): 145-214; "Leo XIII: Two Concepts of Government," *Theological Studies* 14 (December 1953): 551-67; "Leo XIII: Two Concepts of Government: Government and the Order of Culture," *Theological Studies* 15 (March 1954): 1-33; "On the Structure of the Church-State Problem," in *The Catholic Church in World Affairs,* ed. Waldemar Gurian and M. A. Fitzsimons (Notre Dame: University of Notre Dame Press, 1954), 11-32; "Leo XIII and Pius XII: Government and the Order of Religion," in *Religious Liberty: Catholic Struggles with Religious Pluralism,* ed. Leon J. Hooper (Louisville: Westminster/John Knox, 1993), 49-125; Francis J. Connell, "Christ the King of Civil Rulers," *American Ecclesiastical Review* 119 (1948): 244-53; Joseph C. Fenton, "The Status of a Controversy," *American Ecclesiastical Review* 124 (1951): 451-58; and George W. Shea, "Catholic Doctrine and the Religion of the State," *American Ecclesiastical Review* 120 (September 1950): 161-74. For more recent evaluations of the "Murray Project," see David Hollenbach, "Public Theology in America: Some Questions for Catholicism after John Courtney Murray," *Theological Studies* 37/2 (June 1976): 290-303; Michael J. Schuck, "John Courtney Murray's Problematic Interpretations of Leo XIII and the American Founders," *The Thomist* 55 (October 1991): 595-612; Keith J. Pavlischek, "John Courtney Murray, Civil Religion, and the Problem of Political Neutrality," *Journal of Church and State* 34/4 (Autumn 1992): 729-50; Michael J. Himes and Kenneth R. Himes, *Fullness of Faith: The Public Significance of Theology*, Isaac Hecker Studies in Religion and American Culture (Mahwah, N.J.: Paulist Press, 1993), 8-15; and Michael J. Baxter, "The Non-Catholic Character of the 'Public Church,' " *Modern Theology* 11/2 (April 1995): 243-59.

[5]Source material in this article regarding this course can be found in the Woodstock College Archives, Murray Papers, Box 5, File 381, Mark Joseph Lauinger Library, Georgetown University, Washington, D.C. The materials are in the form of lecture notes and outlines. There are no finished lectures in this file, but the handwritten notes are extensive and offer a detailed presentation of the course's content. While a typed page outlining the course is dated Sept./Oct. 1944, numerous erasures in the handwritten pages and the presence in the file of excerpts from a 1946 *Life* article by Winthrop Sargeant entitled "The Cult of the Love Goddess in America" indicate that Murray probably gave these lectures more than once. One sheet has what could be "1947" in the upper left-hand corner, but the number is partially obscured and cannot be considered as a certain date. In this present article, references to Murray's papers from this file in the Woodstock Archives will be abbreviated in the text as MP.

[6]For the Latin text of Tyconius with translation, see *Tyconius: The Book*

of Rules, trans. William S. Babcock, Texts and Translations (Atlanta: Scholars Press, 1989), 91. Also see Auguste Luneau, *L'Histoire du Salut chez les Pères de l'Eglise: La Doctrine des Ages du Monde,* vol. 2 of Théologie Historique (Paris: Beauchesne, 1964), 283-383.

[7]See Augustine *De Civitate Dei* 22.30; E. Randolph Daniel, "Joachim of Fiore: Patterns of History in the Apocalypse," in *The Apocalypse in the Middle Ages,* ed. Richard K. Emmerson and Bernard McGinn (Ithaca: Cornell University Press, 1992), 72-88; David Burr, "Mendicant Readings of the Apocalypse," in *The Apocalypse in the Middle Ages,* 89-102.

[8]The Latin text of Gelasius's letter "*Duo sunt*" is in Migne PL 59:42. A translated excerpt with commentary is found in Aloysius K. Ziegler, "Pope Gelasius I and His Teaching on the Relation of Church and State," *The Catholic Historical Review* 27/4 (January 1942): 412-37.

[9]See Murray, "Contemporary Orientations," 16, 39-41; "Problem of 'The Religion of the State,' " 327, note 2; "Church and Totalitarian Democracy," 556-59; "Structure of Church-State Problem," 12, 24-25; *We Hold These Truths: Catholic Reflections on the American Proposition* (Kansas City: Sheed & Ward, 1988), 202.

[10]See Augustine, *De Civitate Dei* 14.28-15.4. These phrases of Murray's are taken from the fourth and final lecture in a series entitled "Religion and Society," which Murray gave at the Institute for Religious Studies at the Jewish Theological Seminary in February and March of 1942. Transcriptions of these unpublished lectures are in the archives of the Jewish Theological Seminary, New York City, record group 16, Institute for Religious and Social Studies box 2, folder 16-2-1. I thank Joseph Komonchak for providing me with typescripted copies of these lectures, corrected with Murray's lecture notes in the Woodstock College Archives. Murray's notes for these lectures are in Box 6, File 419 in the Murray Papers of the Woodstock Archives. References to these transcriptions in the present article will be abbreviated in the text as JTS.

[11]See Henri Carpay, "La Nouveauté de L'Action Catholique," *Nouvelle Revue Théologique* 52 (1935): 477-95. As a point of contrast, in 1938 Luigi Sturzo published a detailed historical synthesis of what he called the two "principles," rejecting the framework of two "societies" as found in Carpay's article, as *Church and State,* 2 vols., trans. Barbara B. Carter (Notre Dame: University of Notre Dame Press, 1962). Also see Jacques Maritain, *Integral Humanism: Temporal and Spiritual Problems of a New Christendom*, trans. Joseph W. Evans (New York: Charles Scribner, 1968).

[12]See Carpay, *L'Action Catholique: Essai de Justification Historique et de Précision Doctrinal* (Tournai: Casterman, 1948); Murray, "Contemporary Orientations," 55, note 123.

[13]Carpay, "Nouveauté de L'Action Catholique," 488.

[14]Yves Congar, *Lay People in the Church: A Study for a Theology of Laity,* 2nd ed., trans. Donald Attwater (Westminster, Md.: Newman Press, 1965), 361.

[15]Carpay, "Nouveauté de L'Action Catholique," 489.

[16]Congar, *Lay People in the Church*, 362; Pius XI, "La Relation" (July 30, 1928), in *L'Action Catholique: Traduction Française des Documents Pontificaux (1922-1933)*, Editions de la "Documentation Catholique" (Paris: Maison de la Bonne Presse), 40. Another collection of papal statements on Catholic Action, with commentary, is Émile Guerry, *L'Action Catholique: Textes Pontificaux,* rev. ed., Cathedra Petri (Paris: Desclée de Brouwer, 1936).

[17]Carpay, "Nouveauté de L'Action Catholique," 491, 489.

[18]A summary of the early history of these movements is found in J. Carroll-Abbing, "Catholic Action in Italy: The Beginnings of Italian Catholic Action," in *Restoring All Things: A Guide to Catholic Action*, ed. John Fitzsimons and Paul McGuire (New York: Sheed & Ward, 1938), 98-106; and Gianfranco Poggi, *Catholic Action in Italy: The Sociology of a Sponsored Organization* (Stanford: Stanford University Press, 1967), 14-18.

[19]To my knowledge this address has not been published. Carroll-Abbing offers a translation based upon manuscript notes (Carroll-Abbing, "Catholic Action in Italy," 107).

[20]Quoted in Carroll-Abbing, "Catholic Action in Italy," 108.

[21]The papal motto is from Ephesians 1:10 in the Vulgate, "to restore all things in Christ."

[22]Raymond F. Cour, "Catholic Action and Politics in the Writings of Pope Pius XI" (Ph.D. Diss., University of Notre Dame, 1952), 42; Pius X, *Il fermo proposito* (June 11, 1905), ASS 37: 741-67, translated as *All Things in Christ: Encyclicals and Selected Documents of Saint Pius X*, ed. Vincent A. Yzermans (Westminster, Md.: Newman Press, 1954), 60.

[23]For an analysis of the specialized Catholic Action movements in the United States during the 1930s and 1940s and their role in fostering lay participation in the church's apostolate, see Dennis M. Robb, "Specialized Catholic Action in the United States, 1936-1949: Ideology, Leadership, and Organization" (Ph.D. Diss., University of Minnesota, 1972).

[24]Pius XI, "La Relation," in *L'Action Catholique*, 40.

[25]See Pius XI, "Quae Nobis" (Nov. 18, 1928), AAS 20:385. In a 1944 article in *Theological Studies* entitled "Towards a Theology for the Layman: The Problem of Its Finality," Murray referred to this letter as "one of the two most fundamental pontifical documents on the subject [Catholic Action]." Murray, "Towards a Theology for the Layman: The Problem of Its Finality," *Theological Studies* 5 (March 1944): 67. The other was a 1929 letter, "Laetus Sane Nuntius" (November 1929) to Cardinal Segura of Toledo. See AAS 21:664-68.

[26]See Carroll-Abbing, "Catholic Action in Italy," 119-20.

[27]Pius XI, *Quadragesimo Anno*, II.96 (May 15, 1931), AAS 23:208, in *The Papal Encyclicals 1903-1939*, ed. Claudia Carlen (Ann Arbor, Mich.: Pierian Press, 1990), 430; and see Cour, "Catholic Action and Politics," 78-80.

Despite Pius XI's assurances, in 1938 Mussolini threatened Italian Catholic Action for its opposition to the government's anti-Semitic laws excluding Jews from administrative positions (see Sturzo, *Church and State*, vol. 2, 534-35). Sturzo here insisted that certain political options, including Fascism and Nazism, were unacceptable for members of Catholic Action. Compare Maritain, *Integral Humanism*, 268-70, 291-308.

[28]Murray later indicted this "union" for allying the church with the "capitalist bourgeoisie." See Murray, "Leo XII: Separation of Church and State," 202; and Murray, "Contemporary Orientations," 42.

[29]Emphasis is Murray's. Based upon his lecture notes, it appears Murray is translating from the collection of papal documents in *L'Action Catholique*, 399. An abbreviated English translation of this letter can be found in Luigi Cavardi, *A Manual of Catholic Action*, trans. C. C. Martindale (New York: Sheed & Ward, 1943), 259-62. The letter was eventually published by the Vatican as "Vos Argentinae Episcopos" (December 4, 1930), AAS 34:242-46.

[30]In a passage in his 1937 encyclical *Divini Redemptoris*, cited by Murray in his Woodstock lecture notes, Pius XI described Catholic Action along the same lines: "Catholic Action is in effect a *social* apostolate also, inasmuch as its object is to spread the Kingdom of Jesus Christ not only among individuals, but also in families and in society. It must, therefore, make it a chief aim to train its members with special care and to prepare them to fight the battles of the Lord. This task of formation, now more urgent and indispensable than ever, which must always precede direct action in the field, will assuredly be served by study-circles, conferences, lecture-courses and the various other activities undertaken with a view to making known the Christian solution of the social problem" (Pius XI, *Divini Redemptoris*, 64, (March 19, 1937), AAS 29:99-100, trans. by the Vatican Press as *Atheistic Communism* (Washington, D.C.: National Catholic Welfare Conference, 1937), 29.

[31]Pius XI, "Discourse to the Young Women's Section of Italian Catholic Action" (March 19, 1927), in *L'Action Catholique*, 118.

[32]Murray, "Towards a Theology for the Layman: The Pedagogical Problem," *Theological Studies* 5 (September 1944): 346-47.

[33]Murray, "Theology for Layman: Pedagogical Problem," 64.

[34]See Joseph A. Komonchak, "The Silencing of John Courtney Murray," in *Cristianesimo nella Storia: Saggi in onore di Giuseppe Alberigo*, ed. A. Melloni et al. (Bologna: Il Mulino, 1996), 657-702; "Catholic Principle and the American Experiment: The Silencing of John Courtney Murray," *U.S. Catholic Historian* 17 (1999): 28-45.

[35]See Gustavo Gutiérrez, *A Theology of Liberation: History, Politics, and Salvation*, rev. ed., trans. Matthew J. O'Connell (Maryknoll, N.Y.: Orbis Books, 1988), 39-46.

[36]See Clodovis Boff, *Theology and Praxis: Epistemological Foundations*, trans. Robert R. Barr (Maryknoll, N.Y.: Orbis Books, 1987), 93-100.

[37]See John Milbank, *Theology and Social Theory: Beyond Secular Reason* (Malden, Mass.: Blackwell, 1993), 206-55; Maurice Blondel, *Action (1893): Essay on a Critique of Life and a Science of Practice*, trans. Oliva Blanchette (Notre Dame: University of Notre Dame Press, 1984).

[38]*Apostolicam Actuositatem* (Decree on the Apostolate of the Laity), 20, in *Decrees of Ecumenical Councils*, 994.

Vatican II and the Role of Women

Harriet A. Luckman

More than forty-five years ago, an excited energy coursed through the world-wide community of the Roman Catholic Church. The tall, aristocratic Pope Pius XII was succeeded by the very different Pope John XXIII. Not unlike our own times, with the passing of the charismatic Pope John Paul II and the election of the relatively introverted Benedict XVI, there was a sense of real difference between the two men. John XXIII, against all odds, opened the windows of the Roman Catholic Church to the twentieth century. The optimistic excitement and sense of the Spirit's active workings within the inner circles of the Roman Catholic Church's power structures were almost palpable, and the documents that came out of Vatican II released a spirit of hope and optimism as to where the church could go in the years and decades to come. Gone, it was thought, were the suspicions against the modern world that had dominated theology and ministry for so many decades. Gone, it was thought, were the suspicions against the hard sciences such as medicine and astronomy, and the social sciences such as psychology, sociology, anthropology, and politics. Gone, it was thought, was the mentality of rule books and catechisms, where the big questions of humanity's search for meaning, for moral guidance in a complex world, and about God, were answered in simple black and white that left little if anything to ambiguity, question, or historical development. With the "Decree on the Apostolate of the Laity" (*Apostolicam Actuositatem*), it was also thought, gone was the notion that only those in holy orders would carry the burden of responsibility for directing the church and discerning the movement of the Spirit.

I was young at the time, but I still remember the parish conversations and excitement that the church would now belong to the faithful and would become a credible voice not only for religion, but also for secular morality and political structures. We were also still giddy from the fact that the new president of the United States was a handsome, educated, wealthy New England Roman Catholic. We were on the verge of a heady new epoch, and the Spirit was spreading the wings of the Church, preparing for it to soar high in the world of a new Christendom. Since then, the world has known four popes, eight American presidents, at least four wars, the fall of communism in Soviet Russia, and major cultural and communication changes, not only in the United States but world wide. Since then, the roles of women in industrialized democracies have multiplied and the status of women, in general, has become the focus of careful study and intense debate.

In its process of updating the church, the Second Vatican Council often retrieved forgotten or neglected aspects of the witness of scripture and the early church. My task in this essay is to examine whether the leaders of the church, both at Vatican II and in subsequent years, succeeded in fully utilizing the witness of the early church as a resource for re-thinking the roles of women in the contemporary church or whether they recalled in only a partial manner the often dangerous memory of the praxis of the early Christian communities.

Vatican II and the 1960s

Providentially or inspired as it was, the Council fathers of Vatican II were working on their documents at the same time the world at large was on the verge of massive cultural changes. Liberation movements, be they in South America in the form of liberation theology, in Poland as Solidarity, or in the United States as the civil rights and women's liberation movements, would all find echoes in the documents of Vatican II. Following the question of Cardinal Suenens of Belgium, who asked at the end of the second session of the Council why they were discussing the church when half of the people of God were not represented there with a voice, the Council made history when it then appointed twenty-three women as auditors at the Council and as participants in the theological commissions.[1] While women remained largely marginalized despite their inclusion in the commissions, there were signposts that seemed to point toward women's fuller participation in the church. These signposts of participation, however, rested more in the Council's expanded teaching on a number of traditional theological themes rather than explicitly on women's inclusion in active leadership roles within the church. These themes included the definition of the church, the renewed emphasis on baptism as a commissioning sacrament, ecumenism, and the role of the church in the modern world to eradicate injustice and discrimination. The theological commissions also did not address specifically the theology of what it meant to be female in the Roman Catholic Church.[2]

In sections 1 through 11 of *Lumen Gentium* ("Dogmatic Constitution on the Church")[3] the Council restored the biblical proclamation of the church as mystery and as the "People of God." Paul VI would say of the church, "it is a reality imbued with the hidden presence of God. It lies, therefore, within the very nature of the church to be always open to new and greater exploration."[4] By returning to this biblical and early Christian understanding of the church, the Council promoted a more dynamic understanding of the church. The restored understanding was marked by a long-forgotten openness to growth and change, and by a mission for all its members to be signs of God's inclusive love.[5]

Of course, such a restored understanding of church led to a deeper sense of mission as it was embodied in the early Christian communities. The understanding of ministry as belonging only to the male ordained clergy reflected the medieval European understanding of church in the twelfth century. Later, ministry exercised by what the medieval church began to refer to as "the laity," including women in religious communities, was called the apostolate and understood as deriving its grace or power from the clergy under the leadership and approval of the bishop.[6] By recovering the biblical and early Christian notion that all are called to build up the church by reason of the gift of baptism and confirmation, Vatican II instigated what should have been a profound shift in the church's self-understanding of ministry, a shift back to the original understanding of the first Christians themselves and an understanding adopted by the Protestant Reformation. Following the definition of ministry expressed by the Council, Roman Catholics came to understand that all the members of the body of Christ are called to ministry, so directed by their participation in the life and ministry of Jesus Christ through the sacrament of baptism and the reception of the gifts of the Holy Spirit.

Vatican II, with its renewed emphasis on baptism as the primary sacrament of the church, returned this sacrament—along with confirmation and the Eucharist—to a commissioning and empowering sacrament and gift from God for the people of God.[7] The theology of baptism now moved away from the Augustinian, almost exclusive focus on remission of the stain of original sin to include a commissioning of the Christian man or woman for active contributions to the body of Christ according to their individual gifts and opportunities.[8] However, despite the obvious call to "return to the sources," the Council nevertheless maintained the church's medieval hierarchical character and the lay-clergy distinction.[9] This contradiction between what the Council seemed to suggest and what, in fact, the reality of its practices and the succeeding documents from later commissions would have to say provoked heated and painful exchanges between the church's theological commissions and the voices of women in Europe, the United States, and South America.[10]

Women and the Church

It would seem, following the resurfacing of the notion of baptism as a commissioning event and the Council's expressed wish to uncover the early church's experience and practice, that women would see a historical and theological reappraisal of their position in the church. Along with the renewed emphasis on baptism, another conciliar document, "The Pastoral Constitution on the Church in the Modern World" (*Gaudium et Spes*), should have affected the role and status of women in contemporary Catholicism. This document renewed the gospel imperative for justice when it condemned all forms of discrimination regardless of "sex, race, color, social condition, language, or religion" because it "is contrary to God's intent."[11] *Gaudium et Spes*, historically concurrent with society's growing need to address women's issues and racial issues in forming a more just society, should have opened the door for the church to encounter the wisdom of the times with regard to women and the church. As Mary Ellen Sheehan has commented, this meant the church had to acknowledge new cultural and social interpretations—quite in line with the gospel imperatives of justice that the Council itself had highlighted—emerging from the feminist identification of the extent of sexism and discrimination so long legitimated in cultures of the world. It meant that the church's own preaching concerning the eradication of all forms of discrimination came under social and theological scrutiny. If the church chose to challenge societal and political injustice, the church also needed to look inside itself, at its theology, institution, and practices. Doing so would expose the church's long-standing theological and pastoral tradition of subordinating women and their gifts in the life of the church.[12]

The Council's commitment to ecumenical dialogue should have also opened the door for granting women positions of greater leadership, responsibility, and authority within the Roman Catholic Church. Through ecumenical dialogues, fostered by the mandates of Vatican II, members of the Roman Catholic community came into contact, theologically and socially, with research and discussions on women and church ministry already occurring in many Christian denominations. At the time of Vatican II, the World Council of Churches had established a Commission on the Life and Work of Women in the Church[13] and the Anglican Church had begun theological reflection on the ordination of women.[14] As more and more non-Catholic churches opened their doors to the ordained ministry of women, Roman Catholics thereby gained knowledge and experience of women serving as ordained leaders in neighboring Christian communities. This contact led some to believe that the Vatican would eventually lift the bar to women's ordination in the Catholic Church.

But despite what seemed obvious to many in the conciliar teachings on the church, on the ministry of the laity, on the critical relationship of the church with culture in the pursuit of justice, and on ecumenism, the Catholic hierarchy did not move church practice in the direction many thought was required by those teachings. While a consciousness of new positions for women in society expanded and deepened in European and North American cultures and scholarly writing, the Vatican's theological reflection and pastoral practice with regard to women changed little. How did the Council and subsequent popes understand the nature and role of women? Why didn't Vatican II's enlarged understanding of the church and the role of the laity have a more decisive impact upon the status and role of women in the church? I turn to these questions in the next section of this essay.

Vatican II and the Laity

In considering Vatican II's understanding of women's roles in the church, we need first to examine the Council's understanding of the laity.[15] Vatican II's understanding of the role of laypeople in the church is articulated primarily in three documents: *Lumen Gentium* (Dogmatic Constitution on the Church), *Apostolicam Actuositatem* (Decree on the Apostolate of the Laity), and *Gaudium et Spes* (Pastoral Constitution on the Church in the Modern World).[16] Chapter 4 of *Lumen Gentium* lays out a foundational understanding of the lay state, in which both the similarities and differences between the lay and clerical vocations are clearly articulated. The "Decree on the Apostolate" builds upon this foundation, and the "Pastoral Constitution" develops the theme of the laity's role in consecrating the world to God.

Lumen Gentium emphasizes four principal theological ideas concerning the laity: the priority of baptism, the priesthood of the laity or of all the faithful, the specific character of lay ministry, and the solidarity of laity and pastors. These four elements are to be interpreted in the context of three overarching theses of the document: 1) the image of the church as the people of God, 2) the universal call to holiness, and 3) the understanding of the church as a pilgrim.

Because the discussion of the laity cannot be separated from that of the guiding image of the church as the people of God, and because the image of the people of God is so absolutely central to the Council's ecclesiological vision, it is also true to say that the developing theology of the laity at the time of the Council documents is a central and crucial element of the legacy of Vatican II. Any ecclesiology is an implicit theology of the laity and any theology of the laity contains within it a specific vision of the church.

Vatican II's ecclesiology entails a theology of the laity quite different from the Counter-Reformation ecclesiology that permeated the Catholic Church's life from the sixteenth to the twentieth century. Robert Bellarmine defined the church as "The society of men on the way to the Fatherland above, united by the profession of the same Christian faith and participation in the same sacraments, under the authority of lawful pastors and principally of the Roman Pontiff."[17] Under this Tridentine definition, the layperson is deprived of any active role in the life of the church and is defined by his or her beliefs and obedience to hierarchical authority structures. The ecclesiology of Vatican II, however, changed this and charged the layperson with the additional responsibility of exercising ministry to the church both internally and externally. Chapter 4 of *Lumen Gentium* affirms that the laity, like the clergy and vowed religious, share, by virtue of baptism, in the priestly, prophetic, and kingly functions of Christ. This means that lay ministry involves an ecclesial responsibility within the community and an apostolic and missionary responsibility outside it, in the secular sphere, which has always been the domain of the laity so defined.

While it seems the document moved past the notion of the non-ordained as passively reactive or responsive to the direction of the clergy, it must be said that there remains a separation between the kinds of pastoral responsibilities proper to the ordained ministry and those proper to the non-ordained. Yet it is implied for the first time since the first Christian centuries that there is a truly apostolic role for both, and both are vital for the well-being and "reality" of the church.[18]

The last document to come out of Vatican II, *Gaudium et Spes,* presupposing what had already been stated in the documents preceding it, concerned itself with two primary issues. The first part looked at the nature of the church/world relationship, and the second part addressed the urgent concerns in marriage and family, economics, politics, culture, and international relations. I wish to focus on the former because it reveals the underlying ambiguity of the document as a whole, an ambiguity that persists in the church today: the division into sacred and profane. This dualism asserts that the inner life of the church or the Christian believer—prayer, ritual, contemplation, and so on—is "sacred" and that the "world" of work, entertainment, and culture is "profane." This dualism, I would argue, is at the root of the current discontinuity between the early Christian world, in which such a distinction was largely alien, and the post-Enlightenment world of Western Europe. This dualism also determines the "location" of women. Because family and home have been the "locations" to which women have traditionally and "naturally" been assigned, women are automatically placed in the "secular" world.

Such a distinction between sacred and profane helps to support a theory of complementarity, according to which the roles of men and women—both in church and in society—are strictly differentiated without implying necessarily that the roles of one gender are more important or necessary than those of the other gender. In the wake of Vatican II, church leadership, and others, have endorsed this theory of complementarity and, consequently, they have affirmed the beauty and value of motherhood as the special vocation of women (for example, in *Dignitatem Mulieris* (1988), on the one hand, while on the other denying women access to ordination, which, according to *Ordinatio Sacerdotalis* (1994) Christ intended for males only.

Oppositional dichotomy—sacred vs. profane, men vs. women—is in tension with the incarnation, a foundational doctrine of Christianity. If we truly believe in the reality of the incarnation, in the sacredness of all creation redeemed by Christ, then all of human life and activity can be sacred and redemptive. If we can manage to see sacredness in everything, we may be less inclined to distinguish so sharply between the roles of clergy and laity or between the roles of men and women.

Vatican II and Women

At the close of the Council in 1965, special words of encouragement were given to several groups of people, including women. The intention of the Council fathers was doubtless to acknowledge publicly the contributions of women in all states and ages of life. They identified women as girls, wives, mothers, consecrated virgins, and single women living alone. They officially exhorted these women to share responsibility for humanity's future. What is curious is that no such message of encouragement was given to men, identifying them as boys, husbands, fathers, consecrated eunuchs, and so on. One reason for this curiosity is perhaps that even though the church is composed of men and women, it has been the false belief that only men are authorized to speak for the People of God as pastors and teachers. Women are generally presumed to constitute a "class" united by a common "nature" in a way that men are not. Men are regarded either as identical with the ideal of humankind—with the male Christ—or as members of subgroups differentiated on some basis other than sex.[19] When speaking about women and the church, official church documents maintain an understanding of a woman's status, vocation, and mission in the church and society based primarily upon her relationship with men, and this relationship is determined by her "nature."[20] While the three major "waves" of feminism have swept the world in varying degrees, the very question of what constitutes a woman's "nature" has often been central in the discussion of women's rights and opportunities. It is not possible to deal in depth with each stage of feminism and the response of the Roman Catholic Church to these stages within the space of this essay. A short examination of the "Second Wave" of modern feminism, however, is important because it was concurrent with Vatican Council II.

The "Second Wave" of Modern Feminism and Vatican II

In the 1960s feminism emerged as a profoundly influential social and intellectual movement.[21] At the beginning of this so-called "Second Wave," many Catholics expected to see the church as a champion of women, primarily on account of the Council's strong defense of human rights. Disagreement over what women's rights required in practice—a divergence based on different philosophical and theological understandings of human nature and the meaning of human sexuality—led to divisions among feminists themselves, as well as among Catholic women, Catholic feminist theologians, and between some Catholic women and their male pastors.

This second wave of feminism, termed by some "Liberal Feminism," gave urgency to the question of women's sense of identity. Betty Friedan's book *The Feminine Mystique* (1963) provided a popular impetus to women's demands for a life and an identity of their own, separate from their roles as daughters, wives, or nuns. Feminism at this time rejected the sex/gender-role stereotyping that limited women's access to public life by appealing to their supposedly "innate feminine gifts" or "female character traits" that made them ideally, if not exclusively, suited for roles as wives, mothers, and homemakers. This wave of feminism initially emphasized legal rights, equal pay for equal work, and equal access to education and all professions. Some years later, feminism expanded its range of personal rights and campaigned for reproductive rights and access to family planning services, the right to a legal, safe abortion, and the right to bear a child outside of marriage.

As a result of the feminist movement at this time, many Catholic women and men began to raise critical questions about Roman Catholic teachings concerning women and their "roles" and "nature." Some saw the prohibition of contraception and the exclusion of women from ordained priesthood as a sexist refusal to acknowledge women as truly equal to men in every reasonable way. These prohibitions seemed to question the ability of women to act on their own behalf as moral agents with respect to their own bodies, as well as their ability and right to participate in deciding moral teachings that would affect them in many important ways. Many women also saw themselves as competent to function in ordained ministry, and they pointed to the biblical and historical scholarship that disclosed no compelling reasons to ban them from such ministry.[22] The topic of women's ordination was added to the feminist agenda after the initial meeting of the Women's Ordination Conference (1975). Fuel was added to the flame when, after a long debate, the Episcopal Church began to ordain women to the priesthood in 1976. The Vatican responded to this move with the promulgation of the Declaration *Inter Insigniores* in 1977, which reiterated the Catholic Church's traditional ban on female ordination.[23]

During this same period, religious congregations of women were also moving to reclaim the charisms of their foundresses and stood firm in their self-determination in matters of corporate renewal. This often led to tensions between religious congregations of women and the Vatican officials who felt it their duty to regulate the rules and constitutions of women religious. Again, it is noteworthy that such tensions did not exist, or at least were relatively minimal, between the Vatican and congregations of religious men who had always known self-determination and relative autonomy compared to the religious congregations of women. These prolonged struggles between the Vatican and women religious further fanned the flames of feminism.[24]

Magisterial teaching concerning women and their rights in the 1970s presents a mixed picture. Pope Paul VI's encyclical *Humanae Vitae* underlined the Council's teaching on the equal personal dignity of husband and wife within the union of marriage, while condemning all forms of artificial contraception. Pope Paul advocated the social advancement of women in his apostolic letter "A Call to

Action" in 1971 and in several addresses in connection with the United Nation's International Women's Year in 1975. During the 1971 Synod of Bishops, he taught that women's advancement in the social order must have as its counterpart their fuller integration into the church's life and mission. The Study Commission on Women in Society and in the Church, convened in response to this synod, recommended women's inclusion in church advisory bodies at all levels, and their access to theological education and to nonordained ministries, as well as participation in some forms of ecclesiastical jurisdiction. Those recommendations were published in 1976.[25] As optimistic as this sounded, however, Paul VI reserved installation of the minor orders of lector and acolyte to men, with *Inter Insigniores* upholding the tradition of reserving the ministerial priesthood to men. The Vatican, unlike many feminists, did not see this restriction as a matter of injustice to women. The restriction, so the document made clear, derives from the fact that the call to priesthood is a gift from God to men, who are called to represent Christ in the church and to act *in persona Christi*. *Ordinatio Sacerdotalis* repeats this restriction, insisting that the church has no authority to ordain women since that would violate Christ's intention.[26]

Pope John Paul II continued to advocate the teaching of his recent predecessors: women have equal dignity with men and play an important role in the life of society and the church, but are not permitted to be ordained. Addressing the women of the world on the occasion of the Fourth World Conference on Women in 1995, John Paul II reaffirmed the church's desire to promote and defend women. He wrote that justice for women required "equal pay for equal work, protection for working mothers, fairness in career advancement, equality of spouses with regard to family rights, and the recognition of everything that is part of the rights and duties of citizens in a democratic state."[27] In his apostolic letter "On the Vocation and Dignity of Women," John Paul II applied to women the Council's teaching on the dignity of the *person*: a person, made in the divine image, is "the only creature on earth willed by God for its own sake."[28] According to John Paul II, a woman, no less than a man, is a person endowed with intelligence and freedom and capable of self-determination. Because he saw as deplorable the victimization of women by a mentality that reduces a human being—man or woman—to the level of an "object" to be used, bought, and sold as an instrument for hedonistic pleasure, John Paul II came to the conclusion that in order to avoid such exploitation, and to safeguard the sanctity of life, contraception and abortion should be banned.[29] In John Paul's thinking, such things did not add to the dignity, freedom, or self-determination of women, but only enslaved them and degraded them to the status of "objects of pleasure." Interestingly enough, John Paul II did not appear to recognize that by simply banning contraception and abortion the issue of abuse would not come to an end. Whether a pregnancy was involved or not, abusive men would continue to harm women. Contraception and abortion were not the real issue. The real issue was abuse.

As was the case with his teaching concerning the role of women in society, Pope John Paul II's teaching concerning women's status and role in the church was also mixed. During his pontificate, the Second Vatican Council's teaching on the baptismal equality of women with men was confirmed and developed in the 1983 Code of Canon Law and in the post-synodal apostolic exhortation *Christifideles Laici* of 1988. The basis for distinctions among the Christian faithful in the new code was not sex or gender, but "condition and function." Women were now recognized as having the same juridical rights, status, and obligations as laymen. Previous canons that had discriminated against women on the basis of their gender/sex were omitted or changed. In addition, certain functions and offices previously reserved to ordained men were opened to the laity—both men and women.[30] *Christifideles Laici* stated that laypersons could now serve as chancellors and censors and as defenders of the bond and collegiate judges in church tribunals. They could preach—though not the homily—in church, cooperate in the pastoral care of parishes, exercise the ministries of lector and acolyte, administer sacramentals, and if necessary confer baptism and lead liturgical services. Women could be consulted and involved in the process of coming to pastoral decisions, in transmitting the faith as pastoral and academic theologians not only within the family but also to the larger community, and in the evangelization of the culture.[31] Yet in his 1994 apostolic letter concerning the question of the ordination of women (*Ordinatio Sacerdotalis*), John Paul II insisted the church did not have the authority to change the tradition of reserving the ministerial priesthood to males.[32] The reason given is again based on the belief that

Christ chose only men as apostles and that the Last Supper was indeed an ordination event. Scant, if any, attention is given to the evidence and arguments that seem to demonstrate that women held leadership roles—even ordained positions—in the early church.[33]

In his "Letter to Women" (1995), John Paul II continued the tradition of thanking women—mothers, wives, daughters, sisters, women who work, consecrated women—for their contributions and "for the simple fact of being a woman." Addressing all the women of the world, he proclaimed the power of the gospel to emancipate them and uphold their dignity and rights as being made in the image of God. Citing ways in which women had been treated unjustly, John Paul II offered an apology for the way members of the Roman Catholic Church may have contributed to this injustice and called the entire church to renewed fidelity to the gospel vision. He praised women "who have devoted their lives to defending the dignity of womanhood by fighting for their basic social, economic, and political rights," and he described the process of women's liberation as "difficult," "complicated," and "unfinished," but "substantially positive."[34]

John Paul II also called for an end to discrimination so that humanity could benefit from the contributions women would make—spiritual, cultural, sociopolitical, and economic—to the solution of contemporary problems in the life of societies and nations. In his 1995 encyclical *Evangelium Vitae* (The Gospel of Life), he wrote that it depended on women to promote a "new feminism" that would transform culture to support life.[35]

Clearly to some, it seemed as if the post-Vatican II years did indeed promote the equality of women in society and church. Yet, the question of what that equality really means still remained. Some Catholic women, such as Sara Butler, Elizabeth Fox-Genovese, Mary Ann Glendon, and Alice Hitchcock, argue that the writings of John Paul II and the current understanding of women in the church do "elevate" women to a rank of dignity never before experienced. It is a dignity based on the traditional assumption that women find their highest fulfillment in traditional roles of wife, mother, daughter, and consecrated virgin, and that the self-determination won by the work of feminists prior to 1980 should be applied to their right to choose and advocate goals such as premarital chastity, traditional marriage, motherhood, unpaid work in the home, volunteerism, and solidarity with the poor.[36]

Others would argue, however, that official church teaching and practice since Vatican II have done little to challenge the "traditional" teachings on the nature of women (the "Eternal Feminine") and their proper role in church and society. Among these many theologians and scholars one could cite such well-known women as Elisabeth Schüssler Fiorenza, Elizabeth A. Johnson, Rosemary Radford Reuther, and Sandra Schneiders, to name just a few.[37] I would agree that the writings of Vatican II and of John Paul II spoke on behalf of woman's rights and dignity as creatures made in God's image.[38] Yet John Paul II locates this right and dignity of woman in her "essential nature," which consists not only in her ability to bring forth life and to nurture and care for it, but also in her activities as man's "helper."[39] While it is not my purpose in this paper to critique or support any form of feminism, yet it must be acknowledged that many women today who stand vehemently against the "feminist movement" nonetheless have gained the freedom to speak, to become educated, and to "choose" how they are going to live their lives because of those very feminists who went before them.[40] It is also important to point out that what was once considered radical and unacceptable oftentimes is taken for granted generations later as acceptable. This was true concerning women's right to vote and be educated. Perhaps the next step, following the trajectory of Vatican II and related documents, is to move beyond the idea that biological maleness is the only or most appropriate way to image Christ. The church of the future faces the challenge of making real Paul's words, "in Christ there is neither male nor female" (Gal 3:28).

Conclusion

After this brief look at Vatican II and women, what can we say about how Vatican II affected women and where Vatican II should have led us? What implications does Vatican II's shift in focus concerning baptism, affirming it as a source of mission as well as transformation, have not only for the dignity and responsibility of the individual Catholic, but also for the entire structure of the church? If we return to the early Christian notion that baptism helps us grow in our likeness of Christ and transforms us into vehicles of the divine in service to others, we will see that baptism itself is the empowering event, the commissioning event, the ordaining, the setting apart, event in the life of the Christian. Baptism, confirmation, and Eucharist, as they were originally combined, initiate the believer into the community of faithful, into the body of Christ. It is because of one's baptism that one is adopted as a son or daughter of God and bears the likeness of the death and resurrection of the Christ. Baptism commissions one to "go into all the world and preach the good news in the power of the Spirit," be that as a homily from some pulpit on Sunday morning or in the board room of a major corporation. Empowered to speak for God does not mean speaking only of theology and church matters, but to speak to society and to confront injustice in all its forms.

Taking seriously its appeal to return to the sources (scripture and the witness of the early church), Vatican II should remind us of the days when everyone was responsible for the well-being of the church, even in such matters as voting to depose an unworthy guardian (bishop or priest) or electing to "ordain" someone of virtuous life (ordination by acclamation).[41] Along with this memory, we should recall that, prior to the restriction of liturgical and ecclesiastical leadership roles to monks and celibate male priests, women too had active roles in running churches, discussing doctrine, selecting community church procedures, and participating in a shared diaconate.[42] Once women were taken out of the inner circle through the imposition of a celibate all-male clergy, they were looked to, if at all, as examples of such virtues as meekness, long suffering, humility, and obedience. These were women's "special gifts," and Jesus' mother Mary became the model for this type of silent, hidden, unassuming and submissive woman.[43]

As we envision the church of the future, we should recall that as long as we continue to separate this world into spheres of the sacred and profane, we also separate the activities of the members of the body of Christ into "sacred" and "profane." As a result, we tend to think we are not working in the church unless we wear a stole and preside at a liturgy. While those roles should not be withheld from the worthy petitioner, man or woman, married or single—if indeed we were to recover the practice of the early church—we need to remember they are not the only ways Christ is made present on earth. In fact from what we know, the closest Jesus came to official ritual service in the synagogue was reading the words of the prophet Isaiah.

We would also do well to recall that while the Spirit leads the church, many of its laws and structures are human-made to fit a particular need for a particular time and culture. They can and have been changed over the centuries and will continue to change as the church continues to live and grow. How are the laity—a modern concept after all—empowered for mission? Simply by being reborn into the risen Christ. As transformed individuals of faith, the baptized are given the commission to transform the world for Christ, and part of that world includes the body of Christ, the church. As the "sense of the faithful" has throughout the centuries shaped doctrine, church practice, and devotion, so the laity, the body of the faithful, will continue to be empowered by the Spirit to build up the body of Christ as they have been doing in the church from the beginning.

The situation of women within the Roman Catholic community also has seen much growth and change since 1963. While official Vatican documents and papal encyclicals continue to advocate the complementarity model of male and female, with special areas reserved for each sex/gender, this can lead to a path of true equality, provided one gender is not seen as superior or more "Christ-like" than the other. Vatican II also opened the door to discussion of what it means to be a baptized member of the body of Christ and what constitutes personhood in the image of Christ. This allowed the question of women's roles and their imaging of Christ to become a topic of discussion and theological reflection, a discussion that doubtless will continue and develop.

Whatever direction society, public intellectuals, theologians, scientists, and the hierarchical church take in the years to come concerning the question of man and woman, one thing is certain at this point in time: the vision and accomplishments of Vatican II would have seemed outlandish and perhaps radical, if not also heretical, to Roman Catholics during the modernist crisis of the early 1900s. Perhaps an equally radical church will emerge from the post-Vatican II struggles of the twentieth and twenty-first centuries.

Notes

[1]See Mary Luke Tobin, "Women in the Church: Vatican II and After," *Ecumenical Review* 37 (1985): 295-305; Carmel McEnroy, *Guests in Their*

Own House: The Women of Vatican II (New York: Crossroad, 1996); and Mary Ellen Sheehan, "Vatican II and the Ecclesial Ministry of Women," *Toronto Journal of Theology* 16/1 (2000): 51-61. Sheehan notes that while significant at least for breaking the barrier that excluded women from universal church gatherings, in actual fact the women's participation in the council remained marginalized and largely invisible.

[2]While not the work of a theologian or historian, the recent book *Good Catholic Girls: How Women Are Leading the Fight to Change the Church* by Angela Bonavoglia (New York: Regan Books, 2005) is a wonderful collection of stories of contemporary Catholic women and how they view their lives within the Roman Catholic Church.

[3]All citations from the Vatican II documents are taken from *Vatican Council II: The Conciliar and Post Conciliar Documents*, ed. Austin Flannery, rev. ed. (Leominster: Fowler Wright, 1988).

[4]From Paul VI's address at the opening of the Council's second session in 1963, as cited in *The Documents of Vatican II*, ed. Walter M. Abbott (New York: America Press, 1966), 15.

[5]Two of the oldest though most influential documents on the early church, *The Shepherd of Hermas* and *The Didache*, both speak of the church as the community of faithful which utilizes the gifts of all its members according to the collective discernment and wisdom of all. The *Didache*, which includes the oldest eucharistic prayer we have, described the eucharistic bread as the gathering of wheat together from distant hilltops to form the bread as the church was gathered together from many distant places. *The Shepherd of Hermas* spoke of the community discerning who should and should not teach or hold positions of responsibility in the community. For both of these early documents and the oldest post-New Testament understanding of church, see *The Apostolic Fathers: Greek Texts and English Translations of Their Writings*, 2nd ed., ed. Michael W. Holmes, trans. J. B. Lightfoot and J. R. Harmer (Grand Rapids: Baker Books, 1992).

[6] The historical development of the notion of the laity is concisely covered by Paul Lakeland in *The Liberation of the Laity: In Search of an Accountable Church* (New York: Continuum, 2003). His bibliography is a valuable resource for major works on the topic.

[7]Vatican II, in its discussion of baptism, described the sacrament as one of the three sacraments of initiation, together with confirmation and the Eucharist. The doctrine of Christian initiation is summed up in the 1972 *General Introduction to the Rite of Christian Initiation* in the revised Roman Ritual.

This represents a major shift in theological and pastoral understanding from the sacramental theology and liturgical practice of the pre-Vatican II church. Vatican II returned to the early Christian notion that baptism is not meant only for the recipient but it also discloses something fundamental about the church as a whole. Baptism incorporates the believing person into the church, associates one with the death and resurrection of Christ into new life "in the Spirit," effects a forgiveness of sins, and orients one to the worship of God and the wider mission of the church. In baptizing its faithful, the church shows itself to itself and to the rest of the world primarily as a community, the body of Christ, and only secondarily as an institution. Ideally, the church identifies itself with the sufferings and death of Christ and so points the way to a share in his resurrection and glorification. It shows itself as a forgiving community and at the same time as a community itself in need of forgiveness. The whole life of the church is directed to the glory of God which is achieved in and through the humanization of the world. According to the rite of baptism, the church that baptizes and is baptized has been given a "new birth by water and the Holy Spirit" and as such is a "holy people anointed with the chrism of salvation just as Christ was anointed Priest, Prophet, and King" for everlasting life.

[8]*Apostolicam Actuositatem,* "The Decree on the Apostolate of the Laity," was solemnly promulgated by Pope Paul VI on November 18, 1965.

[9]For an excellent study of ministry, see Edward P. Hahnenberg, *Ministries: A Relational Approach* (New York: Crossroad, 2003).

[10]Concerning Vatican II, I refer the reader to the five-volume work *History of Vatican II*, edited by Joseph Komonchak and Guiseppe Alberigo. For any serious student of this Council, this work is invaluable, even amidst the immense volume of published works on the Council.

[11]*Gaudium et Spes,* 29.

[12]See Mary Ellen Sheehan, "Vatican II and the Ecclesial Ministry of Women," 53.

[13]World Council of Churches, *Uppsala to Nairobi* (New York: Friendship Press, 1975).

[14]This commission was appointed by the archbishops of Canterbury and York, and the proceedings were published as *Women and Holy Orders* (London: Church Information Office, 1966). For later developments between Roman Catholicism and Anglicanism, see "The Vatican and Canterbury Exchange of Letters," in *Origins* 16 (1985-1986): 153-60.

[15]For an excellent study on the laity see Lakeland, *The Liberation of the Laity.* I am indebted to this work for this section.

[16]Initially, the schema on the laity produced by the preparatory commission had been intended to gather together in one place all that the bishops would have to say about laypeople, but as the Council sessions came and went, pieces of the document were moved to places that seemed more appropriate. While this was unsatisfactory to many Council fathers for a variety of reasons, it made particularly good sense to place the theological treatment of the lay state within the central document on the church. The second draft of the document on the church included a third chapter entitled "The People of God and in particular the Laity," but this was soon divided into two, and the section on the People of God became the opening chapter of the document, ahead of the chapter on the hierarchy.

[17]Lakeland, *The Liberation of the Laity*, 81.

[18]Ibid., 82.

[19]See Sara Butler, "Women and the Church," in *The Gift of the Church*, ed. Peter C. Phan (Collegeville: Liturgical Press, 2000), 415.

[20]It is beyond the scope of this paper to enter into a discussion of the notion of a woman's essential "nature," particularly as defined by John Paul II. This philosophical issue is taken up in numerous recent works including those by such outstanding women theologians as Sandra Schneiders, *Beyond Patching: Faith and Feminism in the Catholic Church* (Mahwah, N.J.: Paulist Press, 1991); Rosemary Radford Ruether, *Sexism and God-Talk: Toward a Feminist Theology* (Boston: Beacon Press, 1985); Elizabeth A. Johnson, *She Who Is: The Mystery of God in Feminist Theological Discourse*, 10th anniv. ed. (New York: Herder and Herder, 2002); Rebecca Chopp, *Horizons in Feminist Theology: Identity, Tradition, and Norms* (Minneapolis: Fortress Press, 1997); and Grace Jantzen, *Becoming Divine: Toward a Feminist Philosophy of Religion* (Bloomington: Indiana University Press, 1999), to name just a very few.

[21]I am indebted to Sara Butler's research in her article "Women and the Church" (419-32) for this section. While she is not usually considered a "feminist" by most, it should be mentioned that women on both sides of the debate concerning the identity and definition of the "nature" of womanhood consider themselves feminists. The question is simply what type of feminist. I have chosen Sara Butler's work for this section in order to include a feminist voice from what many consider the more conservative theological understanding.

The "Three Waves of Feminism" are usually divided historically as the First Wave from 1848 to 1920, the Second Wave from 1960 to 1982, and the Third Wave from 1982 into our own time. The First Wave concerned itself with women's suffrage and anti-slave movements, the Second Wave concerned economic, professional, legal, and educational equality as well as reproductive rights and freedoms. The Third Wave consists of young women who grew up with the rights and privileges achieved by the First and Second Wave and are defining their feminism as the right to choose their lifestyles and choices of how to live as women. For more information on the feminist movements, see Nancy F. Cott, *The Grounding of Modern Feminism* (New Haven: Yale University Press 1987); Willian O'Neill, *Everyone Was Brave: The Rise and Fall of Feminism in America* (Chicago: Quadrangle Books, 1969); and Leila Rupp and Verta Taylor, *Survival in the Doldrums: The American Women's Rights Movement: 1945 to the 1960s* (New York: Oxford University Press, 1987).

[22]Scholarship on women's roles in the early Christian community and modern biblical scholarship have proven the existence of women in the diaconate and even ministerial priesthood and episcopacy during the first centuries of Christianity. An excellent source of early epigraphical and

literary studies can be found in Ute E. Eisen's *Women Officeholders in Early Christianity* (Collegeville: Liturgical Press, 2000). The scriptural question has been discussed well by Sandra M. Schneiders in her work *Beyond Patching; Faith and Feminism in the Catholic Church* (Mahwah, N.J.: Paulist Press: 1991), chap. 2, "Scripture: Tool of Patriarchy or Resource for Transformation."

[23]See "Vatican Declaration: Women in the Ministerial Priesthood" and commentary in *Origins* 6 (February 3, 1977).

[24]The struggles between bishops and religious communities of women in their renewal processes following Vatican II are too numerous to document here, however I would refer the interested reader to one of the most poignant and well-documented struggles over renewal following Vatican II. The work, *Witness to Integrity: The Crisis of the Immaculate Heart Community of California* by Anita Marie Caspary (Collegeville: Liturgical Press, 2003), puts into focus how such struggles were the fare of women religious especially in the United States.

[25]*Crux of the News Special* (September 20, 1976).

[26]This certainty about the intention of Jesus concerning the ordination of only men rests upon the interpretation that the Passover meal celebrated by Jesus with his disciples before his passion was an ordination event and that only the twelve male apostles were present at this meal. This interpretation, however, leaves out the important scriptural account that the one Jesus commissioned to be the first to proclaim the "good news/Gospel" was Mary Magdalene who was the first to speak to the risen Christ.

[27]"Letter to Women," *Origins* 25 (July 17, 1995); see also the collection *The Genius of Women* (Washington, D.C.: United States Catholic Conference, 1997).

[28]"On the Vocation and Dignity of Women," 6-7, and *Gaudium et Spes*, 24.

[29]See *Familiaris Consortio*, 28-33.

[30]See Rose McDermott, "Women in the New Code," *The Way Supplement* 50 (Summer 1984): 27-37.

[31]*Christifideles Laici*, 23. "The Ministries, Offices, and Roles of the Lay Faithful" (December 30, 1988).

[32]"Apostolic Letter on the Ordination of Women," *Origins* 24 (June 9, 1994).

[33]The papal insistence on this point has often been debated as relying on outdated historical and biblical scholarship, as well as refusing to acknowledge that these same arguments were long ago abandoned by the Anglican and other Christian denominations as no longer theologically valid or historically accurate. Numerous works on early Christianity have concluded that women were an intimate part of the early church community and exercised roles and responsibilities together with men. Ute Eisen's work alone has provided much evidence in support of the reality of women's ordination to the

diaconate, the priesthood, and even to the episcopate in the first centuries of Christianity. Nevertheless, the debate on this issue continues. For just a few works on women's roles in the early Christian period, see Ute E. Eisen, *Women Officeholders in Early Christianity: Epigraphical and Literary Studies* (Collegeville: Liturgical Press, 2000); Lavinia Byrne, *Woman at the Altar: The Ordination of Women in the Roman Catholic Church* (Collegeville: Liturgical Press, 1994); Karen Jo Torjesen, *When Women Were Priests: Women's Leadership in the Early Church and the Scandal of Their Subordination in the Rise of Christianity* (San Francisco: HarperSanFrancisco, 1993); Elisabeth Schüssler Fiorenza, *In Memory of Her: A Feminist Theological Reconstruction of Christian Origins* (New York: Crossroad, 1983); and Susanna K. Elm, *Virgins of God: The Making of Asceticism in Late Antiquity* (Oxford and New York: Oxford University Press, 1994).

[34]See "Letter to Women," 6.

[35]*Evangelium Vitae*, 99.

[36]Some articles along this line include Mary Ann Glendon, "A Glimpse of the New Feminism," *America* 175 (July 6-13, 1996); Elizabeth Fox-Genovese, *Feminism without Illusions: A Critique of Individualism* (Chapel Hill: University of North Carolina Press, 1991); and Elizabeth Fox-Genovese, *Feminism Is Not the Story of My Life* (New York: Doubleday, 1996).

[37]The list of their works as well as the works of other prominent women theologians and scholars who share their views is immense and most are already cited in this paper. Some additional works include Anne Carr and Elisabeth Schüssler Fiorenza, eds., *Motherhood: Experience, Institution, Theology* (Edinburgh: T&T Clark 1989); Anne E. Carr and Mary Stewart Van Leeuwen, eds., *Religion, Feminism, and the Family* (Louisville: Westminster John Knox Press, 1996).

[38]Unfortunately this paper could not address women of color or women in Third World countries whose experience of injustice and discrimination are doubled by their race, ethnicity, or culture. I refer the interested reader to the large body of work done by African American, Latin American, and Asian feminist theologians for a clearer understanding of their plight. Two excellent resources for such works are *Feminist Theology in Different Contexts*, ed. Elisabeth Schüssler Fiorenza and M. Shawn Copeland (London: SCM Press, and Maryknoll, N.Y.: Orbis Books, 1996) and Rosemary Radford Ruether, ed., *Gender, Ethnicity, & Religion: Views from the Other Side* (Minneapolis: Fortress Press, 2002).

[39]John Paul articulates this notion of woman's glory being that of serving or helping men in his "Letter to Women," 10-11.

[40]I always enjoy asking traditional-aged undergraduate women if they consider themselves "feminists." Almost without exception they respond vehemently that they are not feminists, until they are asked if they believe they should not be in school, they should not choose their career paths, they should not vote or be allowed to choose their husbands if they decide to marry, and

so on. When they are reminded that it was "radical" just a few decades ago to want these choices and status, they are often less vehement "anti-feminists."

[41]One needs only to recall the teachings of the *Didache* and *Didascalia* with regard to the worthiness of those serving in ministry, including deaconesses.

[42]Again, I would refer the reader to Ute Eisen's work on the early church, as well as the surviving accounts of pre-Carolingian Benedictine abbesses such as Hilda of Whitby as recorded in Bede's *Ecclesiastical History of the English People*, and the medieval roles of Benedictine abbesses in Germany prior to the Gregorian reforms of the late eleventh century. An interesting phenomenon occurred in the European church of the early medieval period once Gregory VII imposed his reforms on ecclesiastical governance and life. Not only were priests now required to practice mandatory celibacy, but the influence and voice of women within the structures of the church were soon to be silenced with very few exceptions, those few exceptions being women such as Saint Catherine of Siena who would advocate for Gregory's understanding of a centralized Roman Catholic Church.

[43]It must be added, however, that this image of Jesus' mother Mary has undergone tremendous change over the past decades thanks to the scholarship of such women theologians as Elizabeth A. Johnson, Elizabeth Schüssler Fiorenza, Sandra Schneiders, again to name just a few. Historical and biblical scholarship has revealed Miriam of Nazareth as a far more complex woman than she has been portrayed in much of the Roman Catholic tradition. I would refer the reader particularly to Elizabeth A. Johnson's most recent works, *Dangerous Memories: A Mosaic of Mary in Scripture* (New York: Continuum, 2004) and *Truly Our Sister: A Theology of Mary in the Communion of Saints* (New York: Continuum, 2003) for excellent studies on Mary.

Scripture after Vatican II

Revelation and Symbol, History, and Postmodernism

Alice Laffey

A document issued by Vatican II, *Dei Verbum* (Dogmatic Constitution on Divine Revelation), speaks of scripture and tradition—Tradition as distinct from traditions—as together comprising the privileged medium of God's revelation to humankind. In response to the Council's call to "return to the sources," Vatican II lay Catholics began to read, to pray, and to study biblical texts in a new way. The trajectories through which Catholics gained new access to the scriptures were at least five: 1) the readings proclaimed at mass, now in the community's vernacular; 2) the "homilies" (as opposed to "sermons" that the liturgical celebrants were meant to preach); 3) personal Bible reading; 4) parish "Bible study groups"; and 5) the formal and more scholarly pursuit of biblical study in the academy.

The first four of these trajectories derive naturally from Vatican II because each presupposes a context of faith. The fifth trajectory, however, is a bit more complicated. While the goal of the intellectual pursuit may well be in keeping with our faith tradition of "faith seeking understanding,"[1] the methodologies employed in the academy deliberately bracketed faith.[2] And so the methodologies adopted by Catholic biblical scholars from their Protestant colleagues also bracketed faith. The dominant methodology, of course, has been historical criticism. It has been successful insofar as it has helped believers to understand the cultural and social worlds that produced the texts, thus providing some level of increased understanding of the texts themselves. We know infinitely more than we did forty years ago about the complexities of both the texts' composition and their redaction, and we better understand the diverse settings that produced the different types of literary genres that the Bible contains. We better understand the presence and function of etiological narratives. Indeed, we have grown our knowledge. But to what extent, one might ask, have we grown our faith? Nurturing faith, of course, was never the primary intent of the historical-critical method.

In *Beyond New Testament Theology*,[3] Heikki Raisanen criticizes biblical scholars who, when writing syntheses, that is, New Testament theologies, *compromise*, as he sees it, the results of their historical research on individual biblical passages or books. Influenced by and respecting the faith context of the popular audience for whom their syntheses are intended, these scholars deliberately deprive their audience of the sometimes jarring results of historical inquiry. For Raisanen, these scholars err when they compromise the truth for the sake of faith.[4] The trajectory of his thinking leads in many instances, however, to the severe critique, even rejection, of certain biblical texts by the faithful.[5]

At the other end of the spectrum, when Adelphi University held a conference to celebrate the twenty-fifth anniversary of Vatican II, scripture was nowhere to be found on the first drafts of the program. The theologians planning the conference, representing a scholarly voice of the implementation of Vatican II, apparently did not find the work of most biblical scholars relevant to the theological enterprise.[6] And even more recently Linda Maloney, biblical editor for Liturgical Press, commented that most of the monographs authored by biblical scholars are not brought to the annual meeting of the Catholic Theological Society of America because few theologians attending the meeting would buy them.[7] The Catholic Biblical Association has maintained its identity as a scholarly society separate from the Catholic Theological Society of America[8] even though, according to Rome, the study of scripture is a theological discipline.[9]

Even before Catholic scholars began to be educated in the methods of historical criticism, certain Protestant biblical scholars had begun to see the method's insufficiency. They realized that the texts, regardless of the worlds that produced them, are literature. In the same way that those who study the *Iliad* and the *Odyssey* are better versed in the epics themselves than in the circumstances leading to their production, so scholars of the Bible should be more knowledgeable of the biblical texts than of the worlds that produced them. Some biblical scholars, therefore, insisted that the sacred texts should contain some contemporary relevance for believers.[10] Structuralism, post-structuralism, deconstruction, the hermeneutical theories of Ricoeur[11] and Gadamer[12] came to the fore for these biblical scholars. As a result, they used literary criticism to assist in the interpretation of texts. Whereas historical criticism seeks the meaning of the text in the cultural and social worlds that produced the texts and identifies a text's meaning with the intention of its author, literary criticism focuses on the text itself and is open to a text having multiple, even contemporary meanings.

Although some might infer from the breadth of topics identified in the title that this essay will provide only superficial treatment of those topics, I have chosen such a broad title in order to explore and to express seemingly disparate ideas that for a long time now I have intuitively experienced as being interwoven and interconnected.

Vatican II had considered scripture to be revelation. Such an understanding was consistent with the pre-modern interpretation of scripture, which assumed the faith of the scholars—most of whom were churchmen, bishops, and ministers—who studied the scriptures. But Vatican II has also been described as the church coming to terms with the modern world (see, for example, the Pastoral Constitution on the Church in the Modern World, the Decree on Ecumenism, and so on). For Catholic scripture scholars, coming to terms with the modern world translated into the appropriation of the biblical findings and methodologies of their Protestant counterparts, findings that included the history of ancient Israel and the social worlds of ancient Palestine, Antioch, and Rome, and methodologies, whether historical criticism or literary criticism, that had, for valid historical reasons, deliberately bracketed faith.

I submit, however, that literary criticism, as a method, can be more amenable to faith than historical criticism. While its practice in the academy is independent of faith, literary criticism's openness to multiple interpretations is more conducive to some connection with the multiple interpretations that are, de facto, produced in churches whenever the texts are proclaimed and elucidated. Bible study groups also produce multiple interpretations. Interpreting texts in such a way that they can have contemporary relevance is more easily accomplished using literary criticism, and is also more amenable to faith, to prayer, and to transformation.[13] While the methods of literary criticism themselves may, like those of historical criticism, be independent of and even bracket faith, still, the understandings they produce, because of the possibility of contemporary insights and the consequent possibility of transformation, are more conducive to faith development. Literary criticism examines the Bible as the foundation of Christian revelation.

The previous contextualizing brings us from 1962[14] (or even 1943)[15] to the world of Catholic biblical studies in 1993 and the publication by the Pontifical Biblical Commission (PBC) of its document "The Interpretation of the Bible in the Church."[16] While the document affirms all modern methodologies, including historical criticism,[17] as instruments that have led to a greater understanding of the Bible, it nevertheless places these methodologies at the service of faith. No one methodology can be an end in itself.[18] The document insists that the fruit of any or even of all methods of scholarly biblical study is insufficient insofar as it is independent of faith.[19]

Some of the contemporary scholars whose work is attuned to the admonition and guidance of the PBC document include Sandra Schneiders,[20] Luke Timothy Johnson,[21] William Kurz,[22] Ben F. Meyer,[23] John L. Topel,[24] and the members of the Feminist Hermeneutics Task Force of the Catholic Biblical Association, especially Carol Dempsey and Mary Margaret Pazdan,[25] and Barbara Green.[26] These have been important voices of Catholic biblical scholars who have "stood out from the crowd." Though their perspectives can be critiqued,[27] their importance individually and collectively[28] has been to challenge the almost exclusive use of historical criticism by Catholic biblical scholars.[29] From among the various recent attempts to unite historical scholarship and the nurturance of faith, I would like to highlight three: Peter Williamson's *Catholic Principles for Interpreting Scripture*,[30] David Williams's *Receiving the Bible in Faith*, [31] and Mary Ann Pelletier's *D'âge en âge les Ecritures.*[32] All three try to wrestle with the tensions between modern biblical methodologies and the faith assumed in the Dogmatic Constitution on Divine Revelation of Vatican II.

Williamson's Principles

After an extensive introduction, Williamson sets out twenty principles that are present in the Pontifical Biblical Commission's document. I have condensed them as much as possible and have also rearranged them, collecting the principles into four categories: 1) the affirmation of modern methods of biblical interpretation and then expressions of their insufficiency; 2) the assertion that interpretation should include a contemporary focus; 3) scripture as the word of God as well as the word of human beings; and 4) the essential roles of the believing community and tradition in interpretation.

Modern Methods

- Because the human authors were limited by their personal abilities and by their historical and social contexts, Catholic exegesis uses scientific methods to better grasp the texts' meanings;
- Because of the historical character of biblical revelation, Catholic exegesis is concerned with history;
- The historical-critical method can be used because it helps to ascertain the literal sense of a text; it must not be used with philosophical presuppositions that are contrary to Christian faith. Despite its importance, the historical-critical method has limits and cannot be granted a monopoly in the interpretation of the Bible.
- The Old Testament is one stage in the history of salvation as well as a preparation for the coming of Christ;
- Because the word of God has been expressed in writing, Catholic exegesis is concerned with philological and literary analysis;
- Catholic exegesis interprets individual texts in the light of the whole canon of scripture;
- Catholic exegesis is characterized by openness to a plurality of methods and approaches.

Contemporary Focus

- The literal sense of scripture is that which has been expressed directly by the inspired human authors; the literal meanings of many texts possess a dynamic aspect that enables them to be reread later in new circumstances;

- Because Christians seek the meaning of ancient biblical texts for the present, literary and historical criticism must be incorporated in a model of interpretation that overcomes the distance in time between the origin of the text and our contemporary age;
- The primary aim of Catholic exegesis is to explain the religious message of the Bible, in others words, its meaning as the word that God continues to address to the church and to the entire world for today;
- Actualization, which involves the rereading of biblical texts in the light of new circumstances and applying the texts to the contemporary situation of the people of God, includes three steps:
  —to hear the word of God from within one's own concrete situation;
  —to identify the aspects of the present situation highlighted or put in question by the biblical text;
  —to draw from the fullness of meaning contained in the biblical text those elements capable of advancing the present situation in a way that is constructive and consonant with the saving will of God in Christ;
- Interpretation occurs in all the ways in which the church uses the Bible—in the liturgy, *lectio divina*, pastoral ministry, and ecumenism.

Scripture as the Word of God

- Sacred scripture is the word of God expressed in human language; the thoughts and words of scripture belong both to God and to human beings;
- The *sensus plenior* is a deeper meaning of the text, intended by God but not clearly expressed by the human author;
- Biblical knowledge must seek to arrive at a transcendent reality, God; the light of the Holy Spirit is needed to interpret scripture correctly;
- The spiritual sense of scripture is the meaning expressed by the texts when they are read under the influence of the Holy Spirit in the context of the paschal mystery and the

new life that flows from it; continuity and conformity between the literal and the spiritual sense are necessary.

Tradition and the Believing Community

- Because sound interpretation requires a lived affinity with what is studied and requires the light of the Holy Spirit, full participation in the life and faith of the believing community provides the truly adequate context for interpreting scripture;
- Catholic exegesis deliberately places itself within the stream of the living tradition of the church, and seeks to be faithful to the revelation handed on through the tradition; interpretation must remain faithful to the gospel and the tradition;
- The relation between the word of God and the human cultures it encounters is one of mutual enrichment.

The principles that Williamson condenses from the Biblical Commission's document highlight both how biblical scholarship has succeeded and also how it has failed to appropriately implement the interpretation of scripture as envisioned by Vatican II. Catholic scholars have excelled in modern methodologies that have bracketed faith. They have not, however, done as good a job of developing sufficiently new methodologies to which the presumption of faith is integral or of exploiting the symbolism contained in the Bible.

The Approach of David Williams

Receiving the Bible in Faith: Historical and Theological Exegesis is David Williams's revised dissertation. Williams sets out two representative figures from what he identifies as the classic period of biblical interpretation and six scholars from the modern period. While many centuries separate Origen (ca. 185-253) and Thomas Aquinas (1224-1274), and while the approaches they take to biblical interpretation are clearly different—God as the author of scripture for Origen, and the Holy Spirit as the principal author and humans as the instrumental authors for Thomas—Williams highlights their essential points of agreement. They share a belief in the inspiration of scripture, they presume the importance of the spiritual sense of scripture, and they assume that the text speaks to the present and contains insights beneficial for contemporary thinking and behavior.

Williams then investigates six biblical scholars of the modern period. Two early scholars, Spinoza and Troeltsch, regard history, not God, as the ultimate source of the biblical texts. They see the Bible as an assemblage of diverse texts from diverse historical circumstances that convey the concerns and thoughts of their authors from within their own particular situations. Understanding a biblical passage, according to Spinoza and Troeltsch, depends on the ability to recover its historical context and to read the text in that light, just as one does with any other historical text. For Spinoza not only is scripture not privileged,[33] it is better replaced by a rationalist philosophy that focuses on the eternal principles of Nature. For Troeltsch scripture is better replaced by the ideal of progress and development within history.

Williams then turns his attention to four biblical scholars from the later portion of the modern period: Raymond Brown, Brevard Childs, Juan Luis Segundo, and Henri de Lubac. These men share the following characteristics or commitments: they consider the scriptures as privileged media of divine revelation; they acknowledge the importance and usefulness of modern biblical scholarship, especially historical criticism; and they are themselves men of faith. Williams affirms the contributions of each of these interpreters while also pointing out the inadequacies in their approaches. Although Childs locates the proper object of biblical study in the canon—rather than in the history behind the text or in the multiple parts that comprise the text—still, *in Williams's view*, Childs fails to show explicitly how and why the canon makes an interpretive difference.[34]

While Williams supports Segundo's liberation perspective, at the same time he criticizes Segundo's work for not being sufficiently grounded in the historical particulars of Jesus as these are made known through the biblical accounts.[35] Williams is less critical of Brown, lauding him for his commitment both to historical criticism and to Roman Catholicism. He quotes an article that Brown co-authored with Sandra Schneiders;[36] he credits Brown with asserting that no one methodology is sufficient, and he praises

Brown's ongoing interest in the difference between what scripture meant and what scripture means. For Williams, Henri de Lubac is the most successful of the modern interpreters. According to Williams, he is able to affirm both the indispensable role of history and to defend the traditional approach to biblical interpretation that makes the Bible a unique voice in a new time. In point of fact, Brown is more weighted toward history, especially in his later scholarly work, while de Lubac's scholarly work is more focused on "spiritual exegesis."

I wish to commend Willliams for his scholarly efforts. As a theologian, he struggles to study those modern biblical scholars who have self-consciously tried to bring together their historical scholarship and their faith. It is unfortunate that Williams did not have many scholars from whom to choose.[37] While there are many excellent Catholic biblical scholars who are both *historical critics* and people of faith, rarely do they bring these two dimensions of their lives together formally in their scholarly work. The tragedy for me is that Williams had only four modern representatives, only three of whom are Catholic (Childs is not), one of whom is not trained as an exegete (Segundo), and one who is not really contemporary with the others (de Lubac).

Pelletier's Assessment

The third monograph I wish to consider is Anne-Marie Pelletier's *D'âge en âge, les Ecritures: La Bible et l'herméneutique contemporaine.* In this volume Pelletier deals with contemporary hermeneutics and faith, detailing the contributions of each of the modern methodologies to interpretation that are both intellectually reputable and spiritually life-giving. The monograph traces the history of biblical scholarship in the modern period. Chapter 1 provides a brief history of the origin of historical criticism to the present. Chapter 2 chronicles the return to reading the *text itself* under the influence of both philosophy and literature. Chapter 3 shows how contemporary philosophical and poetic hermeneutics contribute to scriptural interpretation that approaches ancient exegesis. Chapter 4 deals with the essential role of tradition in biblical interpretation, and chapter 5 tackles what Pelletier considers contemporary challenges. For her, tradition is important because it reasserts the text as privileged, legitimates the history of interpretation, and takes seriously the role played by faith in interpretation.

Among the challenges she sees for contemporary hermeneutics are the plurality of interpretations and the collapse of alterity. With multiple individuals acting autonomously and "merely out of curiosity" to arrive at multiple interpretations—welcome to postmodernity—the danger is that such interpretations have no authority and ignore the past, with its essential relationship to God and to prayer.

Pelletier also argues that the biblical text must preserve its otherness; it must not become so domesticated in its interpretation that it no longer confronts the hearer or the reader with the unexpected and the demanding. Too much attention to the hearer or reader (again postmodernism, wherein the world in front of the text, the social location of the interpreter, is emphasized) can allow the text too easily to confirm the hearer or reader's own context, making it all too likely that the text will *conform* rather than *transform*.

For me, Pelletier's book is significant because: 1) It is respectful of the thinkers and exegetes whom it represents, even as it sometimes takes issue; 2) it is comprehensive; 3) even as it places the contributions of others into historical context, its own historical context provides a vantage point for elucidating the hermeneutics practiced by Roman Catholic biblical scholars since Vatican II. Setting forth the "non-negotiable" role of tradition in the interpretation of scripture, it allows the best of contemporary hermeneutics to be placed at the service of faith.

Where do we go from here? The reason I ended with Pelletier's work is because I believe we must take the past, the journey of biblical interpretation that she has outlined, with us. Holding firm to the assumptions and principles of Vatican II's *Dei Verbum*, reiterated and amplified in the Biblical Commission's document, we must embrace the modern methodologies as valuable but insufficient. As we move into the future, we must put the knowledge gained from the application of historical and literary-critical methods at the service of faith[38] and, even as we bracket faith in parts of the process of interpretation, we must consciously reclaim scripture as a theological discipline.

Notes

[1]Augustine, *Sermon* 43.7, 9.

[2]This had been the response of Protestant ministers and scholars to challenges made to the credibility and reliability of the biblical texts in the Enlightenment, but most especially since Darwin.

[3]First published by Trinity International Press (Philadelphia, 1990). A second edition, published by SCM Press (London), appeared in 2001.

[4]Raisanen himself becomes an object of criticism when he equates the hypotheses generated by historical reconstruction with truth.

[5]This differs from some feminist scholarship that minimizes the revelatory value of texts judged not to be, because of a contemporary more egalitarian consciousness, "helpful for salvation."

[6]The sharp contrast depicted here is not meant to imply that all theologians twenty-five years after Vatican II found biblical scholarship irrelevant. That is surely not the case. One notes, for example, the contributions of Hans Küng, Edward Schillebeeckx and others. Still, the history of the Adelphi Conference confirms that a respected group of American theologians, those who constituted the Conference's Planning Committee, did not originally include in the program the contributions of Roman Catholic historical critics since the Council.

[7]This information comes from a private communication to me at the annual CTSA convention, June 2003.

[8]The reasons for maintaining this separation are several, including the size of the respective memberships and the ethos and logistics associated with the execution of the meetings.

[9]"Being itself a theological discipline, '*fides quaerens intellectum*,' exegesis has close and complex relationships with other fields of theological learning" (The Pontifical Biblical Commission, "The Interpretation of the Bible in the Church," III.D. *Origins* 23/29 [January 6, 1994]: 518). The Catholic Biblical Association has also maintained its identity as a separate scholarly society distinct from the Society of Biblical Literature by usually including an afternoon panel presentation that in some way explicitly acknowledges the accountability of Catholic biblical scholars to the church.

[10]The work of Walter Wink (such as *The Bible in Human Transformation: Towards a New Paradigm for Biblical Study* [Philadelphia: Fortress Press, 1973]) and of Walter Brueggemann (such as *The Land*, 2d ed. [Minneapolis: Fortress Press, 2002]) come readily to mind.

[11]See, for example, Paul Ricouer, *Interpretation Theory: Discourse and the Surplus of Meaning* (Fort Worth: Texas Christian University Press, 1976).

[12]See, for example, Hans-Georg Gadamer, *Truth and Method* (New York: Seabury Press, 1975).

[13]Though less frequently and less obviously than with literary interpreta-

tion, historical-critical interpretation of biblical passages can also have important contemporary relevance. A case in point is the historical and cultural circumstances surrounding the origin of Genesis 19 and Leviticus 18:22. In some cases a historical-critical interpretation fosters authentic faith and provides a necessary corrective to literalist-fundamentalist interpretation.

[14]The Second Vatican Council opened during this year.

[15]The encyclical, *Divino Afflante Spiritu,* was published during this year.

[16]*Origins* 23/29 (January 6, 1994).

[17]The PBC document explicitly affirms the value of historical criticism. "A second conclusion is that the very nature of biblical texts means that interpreting them will require continued use of the *historical-critical method*, at least in its principal procedures. The Bible, in effect, does not present itself as a direct revelation of timeless truths but as the written testimony to a series of interventions in which God reveals himself in human history . . . the biblical writings cannot be correctly understood without an examination of the historical circumstances that shaped them" (Conclusion, 524).

[18]"Each sector of research (textual criticism, linguistic study, literary analysis, etc.) has its own proper rules, which it ought follow [sic] with full autonomy. But no one of these specializations is an end in itself" (ibid.).

[19]"Through fidelity to the great tradition, of which the Bible itself is a witness, Catholic exegesis should . . . maintain its identity as a *theological discipline*, the principal aim of which is the deepening of faith" (ibid.).

[20]Especially *The Revelatory Text: Interpreting the New Testament as Sacred Scripture* (Collegeville, Minn.: Liturgical Press, 1999). (A Benedictine seminarian at St. John's, Collegeville, in the early nineties did a paper in a course I was teaching comparing the assumptions and work of Sandra Schneiders to those of then Cardinal Ratzinger.)

[21]For example, *The Real Jesus: The Misguided Quest for the Historical Jesus and the Truth of the Traditional God* (San Francisco: HarperSan Francisco, 1996) and *Religious Experience in Earliest Christianity: A Missing Dimension of New Testament Study* (Minneapolis: Fortress Press, 1998).

[22]With Timothy Luke Johnson, *The Future of Catholic Biblical Scholarship: A Constructive Conversation* (Grand Rapids, Mich.: Eerdmans, 2002).

[23]*The Aims of Jesus* (London: SCM Press, 1979).

[24]*Children of a Compassionate God: A Theological Exegesis of Luke 6:20-49* (Collegeville, Minn.: Liturgical Press, 2001).

[25]Co-editors of and contributors to *Earth, Wind and Fire: Biblical and Theological Perspectives on Creation* (Collegeville, Minn.: Liturgical Press, 2004). Other contributors to the volume include Barbara Bowe, Joan Cook, Mary Ann Donovan, Mary Catherine Hilkert, Alice Laffey, Sheila McGinn, Kathleen O'Connor, Barbara Reid, Judith Schubert, and Tatha Wiley.

[26]See especially the Interfaces Series (Collegeville, Minn.: Liturgical Press, 2000) of which, with Carleen Mandolfo and Catherine Murphy, she is co-

editor, and her volumes in the series, *Jonah's Journeys* and *King Saul's Asking*.

[27]In my opinion, Johnson and Kurz, for example, do not find sufficient value in the modern methodologies; I would prefer a constructive tone that is less negative.

[28]One might speculate on the social locations of the authors cited in notes 13-22, almost all of whom either are or were in religious life. Their identification with religious life indicates that they have had formal ecclesial training as well as academic training.

[29]Luis Alonso Schokel (for example, *The Inspired Word: Scripture in the Light of Language and Literature* [New York: Herder & Herder, 1972]) used his own training in literature to produce commentaries on the books of the Bible, though much of his work still has not been translated into English.

[30]Rome: Pontifical Biblical Institute, 2001. See also his essay, "Defining the Spiritual Sense for Catholic Exegesis Today," that he presented in one of the Task Forces at the annual meeting of the Catholic Biblical Association, 2003.

[31]Washington, D.C.: Catholic University of America Press, 2004.

[32]Editions Lessius, 2004.

[33]The position of Heikki Raisanen (see above, page 101) conforms to that of Spinoza and Troeltsch with regard to understanding scripture as a non-privileged historical text.

[34]See, however, Brevard Childs's *Introduction to the Old Testament as Scripture* (Minneapolis: Fortress Press, 1979) and his *Biblical Theology of the Old and New Testaments: Theological Reflection on the Christian Bible* (Minneapolis: Fortress Press, 1993).

[35]To my knowledge, Juan Luis Segundo was not trained as a biblical exegete.

[36]"Hermeneutics," in *The New Jerome Biblical Commentary*, ed. Raymond E. Brown, Joseph A. Fitzmyer, and Roland E. Murphy (Englewood Cliffs, N.J.: Prentice Hall, 1990).

[37]He might have included Sandra Schneiders and/or Timothy Luke Johnson, or other scholars whose use of the insights of Ricoeur and Gadamer has contributed to their integration of modern methodologies and faith.

[38]There are broad implications here for teaching and pedagogy as well as for textbooks and other materials used for teaching.

Dei Verbum

Its Historic Break from Curial "Theology" and Its Subsequent Official Use

Francis Holland

This paper seeks to evaluate *Dei Verbum* (Dogmatic Constitution on Divine Revelation) forty years after the Second Vatican Council (1962-1965).[1] To do so I will first situate *Dei Verbum* in the context of the breakthrough that it represents from curial theology.[2] I will establish this breakthrough by comparing the Vatican II text with relevant magisterial texts and previous conciliar documents, especially *Dei Filius* (Dogmatic Constitution on Catholic Faith) from the First Vatican Council in 1870. Having determined the significance of *Dei Verbum*, we can then judge whether its spirit and dynamic are maintained in subsequent ecclesial texts. In particular, attention will be paid to its use and role in the *Catechism of the Catholic Church*.

The thesis proposed here is that the promise of *Dei Verbum* has failed to be fulfilled, not because of its high ideals but because its vision and intention have been officially thwarted. Although others have asserted that the official interpretation of *Dei Verbum* has been regressive, I intend to substantiate and validate that judgment. A brief comment on method: I have chosen to proceed historically and diachronically, first treating the build-up to *Dei Verbum*, then examining the final text, and finally describing its reception. This method, a type of historical-critical approach, respects the dynamic of pre- and post-Vatican II theology. The alternative approach is synchronic, commenting thematically and topically. This latter orientation may be more user-friendly but it is at the expense of a preferred organic approach.

History of the Text

In the context of Vatican II, *Dei Verbum* is significant for a number of reasons. First, only four Council documents are called a "constitution," and only two are "dogmatic": *Dei Verbum* and *Lumen Gentium* (Dogmatic Constitution on the Church). Second, the history of the development of *Dei Verbum* parallels the course of the Council itself. Archbishop Florit stated on September 30, 1964, "Because of its inner importance, as well as the many vicissitudes that it has undergone, the history of the draft of the Constitution on Divine Revelation has fused with the history of the Council into a kind of unity."[3] This comment suggests that *Dei Verbum* is a mirror of the whole Council and thus its subsequent treatment is an indication of a more general attitude toward Vatican II and the so-called "spirit" of Vatican II. Third, as René Latourelle notes, "This is the first time that a Council has studied the *fundamental and absolutely primary categories* of Christianity in such a deliberate and methodical way: Revelation, Tradition and Inspiration."[4]

The preparations for the Council were apologetic. Before the Council convened, the Holy Office had sought a clear and emphatic statement on inspiration and the inerrancy of scripture, together with an emphasis on the historicity of the gospels. An attack was launched in December 1960 against the Biblical Institute because of its use of modern critical approaches to the Bible, and in 1961 the Holy Office informed the general superior of the Jesuits that two professors at the Biblical Institute, Stanislas Lyonnet and Maximilian Zerwick, were to be removed from the faculty.[5] The Holy Office apparently continued to feel that innovations—deviations from a fixed scholasticism—were expressions of modernism. Thus the historical-critical method was viewed with suspicion. The Theological Commission, with Cardinal Ottaviani as president and Sebastian Tromp as secretary, reflected this cautious attitude. Tromp proposed an initial text[6]—*de deposito fidei pure custodiendo* (concerning the deposit of faith to be preserved authentically)—which comprised a list, as it were, of nonnegotiables.[7] This document set the parameters for orthodoxy. Topics therein were "supported" by magisterial statements mainly from Vatican I, Pius X, and Pius XII. Ultimately a text[8] emerged faithful to the limits of the Tromp text.

The fourth chapter was on revelation and faith. There, revelation was defined as *locutio Dei attestantis* (the documented speech of God). Revelation was viewed largely as doctrine, comprising objective abstract statements distinguished from their subjective experiential effect. There was also a warning against questioning the permanence and adequacy of traditional doctrinal concepts. For example, monogenism, the doctrine that Adam and Eve were the first humans created by God and the biological "parents" of all subsequent humans, was under assault from science and critical biblical interpretation. Henri de Lubac perceived that his theology fell under such a warning. But neither he nor Yves Congar could prevent this from happening. Positions of Teilhard de Chardin were also targeted, although de Lubac succeeded in not having de Chardin directly named.

De Lubac, though hardly a neutral observer, made the following comment about the spirit that animated the Theological Commission:

> They knew their craft, but little else. . . . They are, it seems, too certain of their own superiority; their practice of judging does not incline them to work. It is the milieu of the Holy Office. . . . The result is a little academic system, ultra-intellectualist but without much intellectual quality. The Gospel is folded into this system, which is the constant *a priori*.[9]

The schema evolved and was titled *Schema Constitutionis dogmaticae de fontibus Revelationis* (Dogmatic Constitution on the Sources of Revelation). It was presented to the Central Preparatory Commission[10] on October 4, 1961, and then sent to the Council fathers in the summer of 1962. It comprised five chapters: The Twofold Source of Revelation; Inspiration, Inerrancy, Literary Genre; Old Testament; New Testament; and Sacred Scripture in the Church.[11] Cardinal Ratzinger[12] makes the following observation on this early schema:

> All the relevant questions were decided in a purely defensive spirit: the greater extent of tradition in comparison with Scripture, a largely verbalistic conception of the idea of inspiration, the narrowest interpretation of inerrancy ("*in*

> *qualibet re religiose vel profana*"),[13] a conception of the historicity of the Gospels that suggested that there were no problems etc.[14]

Opening the debate, Cardinal Ottaviani began by discounting alternative, less defensive, schemata that were being circulated, largely prepared by committees of French, German, and Dutch theologians. The response to his official schema was negative, with Cardinal Liénart asserting "*Hoc schema mihi non placet*" (This schema is not acceptable to me). He was supported by Cardinals Frings, Leger, König, Alfrink, and Suenens among others. Concerns were raised about the notion of a twofold source of revelation and the text's ecumenical insensitivity.[15]

More offensively, the mode of voting on the draft used a technical device designed to override the Council fathers' opposition to the schema. Instead of a regular *placet* (an affirmative) vote, where a two-thirds acceptance of the schema was necessary to save the unpopular schema, a vote was proposed on interrupting the discussion. Apart from the considerable confusion it generated, it also gave the minority the *status quo* so that now a two-thirds majority was necessary for those who opposed the schema. A two-thirds majority was not achieved. Thus the original schema appeared safe.

To offset such blatant manipulation of the process by Curia officials, it was announced on November 21, 1962, that Pope John XXIII had the text removed and handed over to a specially created mixed committee. This committee represented both the views of the Theological Commission and the less defensive Secretariat for Christian Unity.[16] Latourelle notes that this action by the pope "was a turning point in the Council."[17]

The new committee was inclined toward consensus and dodged disagreement among its members. They agreed upon a new title—*De Divina Revelatione* (On Divine Revelation). The thorny question of the material sufficiency of scripture arose, in other words, what tradition had to offer over scripture. After taking a vote, the committee decided to leave this question open. Ratzinger suggests that the draft was a "product of resignation" and was perceived as such.[18] In that same spirit there was a move to incorporate the text into the "Constitution on the Church." Pope Paul VI, however, indicated that it should remain an independent text. Ratzinger suggests that such incorporation into the "Constitution on the Church" would run the risk of "ecclesio-monism"[19] by subsuming revelation into and under the church. The Central Preparatory Commission accepted the text on March 27, 1963. The text was then printed and presented to the Council fathers in April of that year.

Written responses to the schema were submitted from June 1963 to January 31, 1964. On March 7, 1964, a special sub-committee of the Theological Commission was established and worked on the draft in the light of these submissions.[20] Revelation was understood more as God's self-disclosure and moved beyond an intellectualist approach. Revelation was by words and deeds, and was progressive. However, again the material completeness of scripture remained the problem. This was pertinent to the controversial second chapter, "The Transmission of Revelation," which passed by a 17-7 vote. Here scripture and tradition were not viewed as two sources but they were viewed as a "mirror" in which the pilgrim church contemplates God. It was again agreed to leave open the question of the material sufficiency of scripture.

Fidelity to the April 1963 draft and the subsequent, more progressive responses to it caused a division within the committee. Given this division, two reports were presented to the Council fathers. Karl Rahner drafted the majority report and Archbishop Floret, generally viewed as a traditionalist, presented it to the Council. Archbishop Franić presented the minority report. This minority report gave greater emphasis to word over deeds in revelation, had a more intellectualist view of revelation, and was suspicious of the notion that "tradition grows."[21] The minority wanted the constitutive function of tradition firmly expressed.[22] The minority report was nonetheless unable to demonstrate that the schema contained error; rather it displayed "*defectum notabilem*" (remarkable weakness).[23]

From September 20 to 22, 1965, twenty votes were taken in the plenary assembly of the Council with a large number of amendments being submitted. Alarm ensued when the Theological Commission at a number of its meetings, after angry debate among its members, refused to consider these amendments, although submitted by the majority. Finally the pope intervened and the amendments were heeded. The controversial issues were inerrancy, tradition, and historicity. Some wished to return to the language of two sources and to insist upon the idea of absolute inerrancy. The phrase "saving truth" was adopted instead. This phrase did not require inerrancy in matters not pertaining to salvation. Some wished the pope to remove the schema, fearing its progressive elements. Others wanted to strongly reassert the role of the magisterium, desiring "an excessive esteem for the ecclesiastical magisterium, which is treated as having an almost constitutive part to play in faith."[24] On November 21, 1964, the schema was printed and distributed to the Council fathers. It would be dealt with finally in the last session. With most of the difficulties already resolved, 2,344 bishops voted in favor and 6 against the document in that last session on November 18, 1965.

Selected Commentary on *Dei Verbum*

The Preface

The preface of *Dei Verbum* situates itself in the "steps of the councils of Trent and of Vatican I." This reference arose fairly late in the development of the text, something of a concession to the conservative group, who wanted the mention of these councils to suggest the perspective from which *Dei Verbum* ought to be interpreted.[25]

But, as we shall demonstrate, in comparing selected texts from *Dei Verbum* with these earlier councils, one notes a considerable, albeit subtle, distancing from the earlier texts. Thus, reference to the Councils of Trent and Vatican I, in Ratzinger's view, does not indicate enslavement to these previous Councils but rather is more of a "*relecture*" of the corresponding texts from the Councils of Trent and Vatican I.[26] Moreover, *Dei Verbum* mentions these earlier councils, but within the context of its dominant focus upon the word of God. As Ratzinger notes,

> If sometimes it might appear that the Council was tending towards an ecclesiological mirroring of itself, in which the Church moved completely within its own orbit and made itself the central object of its own proclamation, instead of constantly pointing beyond itself, here the whole of the life of the Church is, as it were, opened upwards and its whole being gathered together in an attitude of listening, which can be the only source of what it has to say.[27]

In *Dei Verbum* the Council offsets any temptation to ecclesial priority by setting as its first response a "reverent attention" (*religiose audiens*) to the word of God and only thereafter faithful proclamation of that which it has heard. This attitude is further emphasized by the cited text from 1 John 1:2-3, which speaks of proclaiming what already was with God and has become manifest. The introduction in *Dei Verbum*, starting with divine revelation and receptive listening, which presumably does not prejudge or predetermine what is heard, contrasts with the corresponding text from Vatican I (in particular *Dei Filius*).

Dei Verbum *and* Dei Filius

The evolution of *Dei Verbum* from previous councils becomes evident if one compares Article 2 in *Dei Verbum* with the relevant text from Vatican I. *Dei Filius*, in its chapter on revelation, opens with the following statement:

> The same holy mother church holds and teaches that God, the source and end of all things, can be known with certainty from the consideration of created things, by the natural power[28] of human reason: *ever since the creation of the world, his invisible nature has been clearly perceived in the things that have been made* [Rom 1:20]. It was, however, pleasing to his wisdom and goodness to reveal himself and the eternal laws of his will to the human race by another, and that a supernatural, way. . . .[29]

Thus Vatican I begins from a natural knowledge of God and only then considers supernatural revelation, and thereafter treats of its transmission in scripture and tradition.

By contrast, in *Dei Verbum* the issue of natural knowledge is put at the *end* and *Dei Verbum* begins with a view of revelation as God's self-disclosure in the context of salvation history. While in Vatican I the view of God is somewhat abstract and impersonal—"It was, however, pleasing to his wisdom and goodness to reveal himself and the eternal laws (*decreta*) of his will. . . ."[30]—*Dei Verbum* adopts a more personalist approach. God's goodness is mentioned before his wisdom, and there is a strong dialogical tone: God speaks to humanity as "friends" and invites them into fellowship with God. The Vatican I reference to *decreta* is replaced by the Pauline notion of *sacramentum/mysterium*. Thus the human in this context is, as Ratzinger notes, "the creature of dialogue who, in listening to the word of God, becomes contemporaneous with the presentness of God and in the fellowship of the word receives the reality which is indivisibly one with this word: fellowship with God."[31]

Revelation is "through deeds and words bound together by an inner dynamism" (*DV* 2). This formulation overcomes the "neo-scholastic intellectualism," which gave words a priority over deeds and saw faith as an assent to supernatural insights transmitted in propositions.[32] On the other hand, revelation is not reduced to deeds, favoring the locus of revelation as prior to its formulation in scripture. *Dei Verbum* does not side with either of these positions, but rather presents revelation as comprising both. The text will subsequently elaborate on how deed and word are related.

An overview of salvation is offered beginning in paragraph three. The created order offers a testimony to God (Rom 1:19-20) and God manifested Godself to "our first parents." At this point Ratzinger picks up a motif that he will repeat, a certain caution if not pessimism. He asks as to "whether the Council did not start from an over-optimistic view in its account of revelation and salvation history, losing sight of the fact that divine salvation comes essentially as a justification of the sinner."[33] Ratzinger notes that the broader context of the quote from Romans, which is not referenced in *Dei Verbum*, is the indictment of universal sinfulness. *Dei Verbum* does use the phrase *lapsus* (*post eorum lapsu*—after their [humanity's] fall), which is then immediately softened by reference to "the hope for salvation." Thus Ratzinger suggests that the notion of law, sin, and the anger of God is "given neither its full weight nor is it taken seriously enough. The pastoral optimism of an age that is concerned with understanding and reconciliation seems to have somewhat blinded the Council to a not immaterial section of the testimony of Scripture."[34] Ratzinger prefers that in this outline of Christian revelation the double nature of gospel and law should be accorded more attention. The hope of the gospel should be taken together with law. Ratzinger understands law in the Pauline sense of "the punitive function of the Old Testament."[35] In contrast, he suggests that *Dei Verbum* here understands law "in the more friendly light of modern pedagogics."[36]

This note of pessimism by Ratzinger is significant on two counts. First, within the context of *Dei Verbum*, it allows Ratzinger to appreciate and endorse God's revelation as sovereign, which situates the church then as dependent on it and also its servant. In this regard ecclesial traditions are not absolute but may be distortions of revelation. Second, in the context of Ratzinger's theology, it suggests that what is perceived as his "later" disillusionment with Vatican II is rather an application of that pessimism voiced already in regard to *Dei Verbum*, but now transposed more broadly to Vatican II and beyond.[37]

On a more positive note, Ratzinger observes how *Dei Verbum* departs from the previous conciliar treatment of revelation in that it has a Christocentric and personalist emphasis. Christ takes the place given to the magisterium in the previous documents. Also *Dei Verbum* emphasizes more the giver and the recipient of revelation—the "who"—rather than the propositions that have been revealed—the "what." Thus, Ratzinger affirms Latourelle's observation that when "Vatican I speaks of the Church as a testimony of revelation, it uses formulations that are similar to those employed by Vatican II when it talks of the function of Christ."[38] While this may not have been intentional, the "centring of everything on Christ, which leaves any ecclesio-monism far behind it, is very clear."[39]

Article 5 again corresponds to a text from Vatican I. However, there is a shift of focus arising from a different context and a contraction of the Vatican I text. As has been noted, the context of *Dei Verbum* is largely Christocentric. In reference to the arising of faith, *Dei Verbum* takes up Vatican I's view of the assistance of the Holy Spirit and prevenient grace. It omits, however, Vatican I's "outward indications of his revelation, that is to say divine acts, and first and foremost miracles and prophecies. . . ."[40] Thus *Dei Verbum* omits the positivism of Vatican I. *Dei Verbum* is here again more personalist: faith is given to God who reveals, while in Vatican I faith is that "we believe to be true what he has revealed."[41] In *Dei Verbum* "who" seems to have primacy over "what." The last sentence in Article 5 speaks of the Holy Spirit who brings faith to completion (*perficit*).

Article 6 once more picks up on Vatican I but re-contextualizes it. Instead of Vatican I's simple use of *revelare* (to reveal), *Dei Verbum* replaces it with *manifestare et communicare* (to manifest and communicate), which moves beyond an understanding of revelation as intellectual. In a similar vein, Vatican I's affirmation of the ability of natural reason to arrive at certain knowledge of God's existence is now read after revelation is expressed as God's free self-disclosure. *Dei Verbum* ends at the point from which Vatican I sets out (natural knowledge) and by so doing, in its opening chapter, has literally overturned Vatican I. While the possibility of "natural" revelation is not discarded, it is certainly thus minimized. Even the technical term *supernaturalis* (supernatural) is studiously avoided. Such technical terms were under increasing suspicion as they were taken to suggest a two-tiered view of reality, the natural and the supernatural, with the insinuation that the natural was not graced. Avoidance of these terms then obviated tendencies toward dualism with an extrinsic view of grace. The omission of these terms was more consistent with an organic view of revelation associated with Henri de Lubac, Yves Congar, and others.

Revelation

Chapter II, "The Transmission of Divine Revelation," was *Dei Verbum*'s most contested chapter. The opening article (*DV* 7) adapts, with significant alterations, a text from Trent concerning canonical scriptures. Whereas Trent speaks of our Lord Jesus who "promulgated" the gospel, *Dei Verbum* speaks of Christ first fulfilling (*adimplevit*) the gospel. That Christ fulfills and not just promulgates the gospel diminished the legal tone of Trent. Trent interpreted the gospel more as a new set of laws/commandments, whereas Vatican II interpreted the gospel primarily as a gift of new relationship with God. This greater focus on Christ himself as the fulfillment of the gospel is strengthened by another addition. The apostles are not just to preach the gospel to all, but also to communicate to them heavenly gifts (*eis dona divina communicantes*). This additional phrase (communicate heavenly gifts) reintroduces the notion of grace and dialogue. In this perspective, transmission means something different than before. What is being emphasized again is revelation as a divine personal self-disclosure rather than as mediating something extrinsic, such as law, commandments, or the like. These later aspects have their foundation and meaning as expressions of interpersonal disclosure.

Apart from that context, revelation is simply reduced to upholding prescribed morality.

Next, *Dei Verbum* describes more concretely the process of transmission. If Trent speaks of the preaching of Christ and the apostles, *Dei Verbum* fills in with the apostles' examples (*exemplis*) and observances (*institutionibus*), which the apostles gained "from the Christ's lips, his way or life or his works, or had learned by the prompting of the holy spirit" (*DV* 7). The Tridentine phrase *Spiritu Sancto dicante* (at the utterance of the Holy Spirit), suggesting an instrumental, passive model, is here replaced with *Spiritu Sancto suggerente* (at the prompting of the Holy Spirit). Moreover, the commission in *Dei Verbum* is not just fulfilled by the apostles, but also fulfilled by "apostolic men" (*virisque apostolicis*) who committed the message of salvation to writing. These "apostolic men" as distinguished from the apostles leaves open the question of the authorship of the scripture and implicitly respects the task of exegetes.

Tradition

Dei Verbum presents an organic, dynamic, and evolving notion of tradition, illustrated by its consistent use of the singular term *traditio*. The significance of this use of the term is that Vatican II is referring conceptually to the *process* of "handing on" the faith, whereas when it uses the term "tradition," Trent is generally referring to the *content* of what is handed on—that is, already existing traditions that may need to be justified or defended.[42] *Dei Verbum's* more dynamic understanding of tradition also includes an eschatological dimension, expressed in the image of tradition as a mirror in which the pilgrim church on earth looks at God. Ratzinger sees in this metaphor a "gentle note of criticism of tradition" for a mirror may yield distortions and shifts of emphasis.[43]

Article 8, added relatively late to the document, grew out of the desire for a clearer account of tradition. Latourelle declares that here "is the first time any document of the extraordinary Magisterium has proposed such an elaborate text on the nature, object and importance of Tradition."[44] Ratzinger perceives here the influence of Congar's dynamic view of tradition, influenced by German Romanticism as represented by the Catholic Tübingen

School of the nineteenth century. Although Article 8 states that "what has been handed down from the apostles" includes "everything that helps the people of God to live a holy life and to grow in faith," Ratzinger, echoing a concern already expressed by Cardinal Meyer in the debate on this text, explains that

> not everything that exists in the Church must for that reason be also a legitimate tradition; in other words, not every tradition that arises in the Church is a true celebration and keeping present of the mystery of Christ. There is a distorting, as well as a legitimate, tradition. . . . Consequently, tradition must not be considered only affirmatively, but also critically; we have Scripture as a criterion for this indispensable criticism of tradition, and tradition must therefore always be related back to it and measured by it.[45]

Article 8 also asserts that "the tradition which comes from the apostles progresses (*proficit*) in the church" and that there is "a growth in the understanding (*crescit . . . perceptio*) of what is handed on, both the words and the realities they signify." Some opposed this formulation because it did not view revelation as concluding with the death of the last apostle. The notion of a growing knowledge was considered a type of theological evolutionism and, when linked with experience, was deemed a form of modernism. Significantly, *Dei Verbum* does not cite Vincent de Lérins, as did Vatican I: "May understanding, knowledge, and wisdom increase as ages and centuries roll along, and greatly and vigorously flourish, in each and all, in the individual and the whole church: but this only in its own proper kind, that is to say, in the same doctrine, the same sense, and the same understanding."[46]

This citation from de Lérins is used to fortify the Vatican I statement: "Hence, too, that meaning of the sacred dogmas is ever to be maintained which has once been declared by holy mother church, and there must never be any abandonment of this sense under the pretext or in the name of a more profound understanding."[47] *Dei Verbum*, however, reverses Vatican I's static and defensive understanding. Vatican II is no doubt aided by the distinction between the meaning of a doctrine and how that meaning is expressed. Indeed, in Pope John XXIII's speech opening the Council he acknowledges such a distinction:

> The substance of the ancient doctrine of the deposit of faith is one thing, and the way in which it is presented is another. And it is the latter that must be taken into great consideration with patience if necessary, everything being measured in the forms and proportions of a Magisterium which is predominantly pastoral in character.[48]

Thus fidelity does not necessarily imply "sameness," since the means by which something is expressed legitimately changes.

So *Dei Verbum* allows for growth in tradition, which happens "through contemplation and study by believers . . . and through the preaching of those who, on succeeding to the office of bishop, receive the sure charism of truth." Since the role of the magisterium is found in Article 10, the ordering in Article 8 is important: it begins with believers. As Robert Murray states: "[I]t is important that their activities [bishops] are mentioned *among* the others: they have a special charism, but they are not said to be the only teachers. The 'study' on the part of others which is mentioned may reasonably be understood to imply also communicating the fruits of study."[49] What is noteworthy is not just at what point the magisterium is mentioned, but also that the role of the magisterium is more limited and circumspect. While Article 10 grants to the magisterium only (*soli*) the task of authentic interpretation, this exclusive role of the magisterium is to be understood in the broader setting of Article 8.

Article 9 considers the controversial relationship between scripture and tradition. Its major contribution is a rejection of a "two sources" theory of revelation. The subtext here is a contentious debate at Trent on this matter. J. R. Geiselmann[50] had argued that the original words at Trent—*partim in libris . . . partim in . . . traditionibus* (partly in books . . . partly in traditions) —had been changed at the last minute[51] to *in libris scriptis et sine scripto traditionibus* (contained in the written books, and the unwritten traditions). Geiselmann had concluded that the new formulation *et* (and) was deliberately intended to avoid the issue of the relationship between scripture and tradition and thus left open the question of the material completeness of scripture.[52] This seems also to be the intention of *Dei Verbum*. Nonetheless, some advocated a *partim . . . partim* approach, which a few believed to have been the position of Trent,[53] but others argued that it was, instead, a post-Tridentine distortion.[54] The next sentence in *Dei Verbum*, "Consequently, the church's certainty about all that is revealed is not drawn from holy scripture alone," is the result of a *modus* suggested by one hundred and eleven Council fathers. Then the following sentence from Trent is tagged on, "[B]oth scripture and tradition are to be accepted and honoured with like devotion and reverence (*pari pietatis affectu ac reverentia*)."[55]

Dei Verbum seems thus to be affirming a single source (*fons)* of revelation, without taking a position on the sufficiency of scripture yet noting a divine basis for tradition.[56] In trying to interpret *Dei Verbum* here, one might observe about this, and many other Roman Catholic documents, that they exhibit a desire to have it both ways, to please various views and groups. As a Protestant commentator has noted, "the genius of Rome, unlike Wittenberg and Geneva, has always been its ability to hold opposite tendencies together."[57]

The ambiguity of *Dei Verbum's* statements about the relationship between scripture and tradition allows different interpretations. Latourelle, for example, interprets the text as maintaining parity between scripture and tradition: "Scripture is the word of God insofar as it is consigned to writing under the inspiration of the Holy Spirit. Tradition is also the word of God entrusted by Christ and the Holy Spirit to the apostles. . . ."[58] Ratzinger's interpretation, however, is more circumspect: "It is important to note that only Scripture is defined in terms of what it *is*: it is stated that Scripture *is* the word of God consigned to writing. Tradition, however, is described only functionally, in terms of what it *does*: it hands on the word of God, but *is* not the word of God."[59] In general, I find Ratzinger's approach more viable.

Biblical Interpretation, the Role of the Magisterium, and the Centrality of the Bible

Dei Verbum promotes several other themes that demonstrate that Vatican II was moving in a direction different from previous councils. It teaches that the magisterium is the servant of God's word, rather that its master. It acknowledges that the human authors of scripture were not passive instruments of God but genuine authors. Consequently, the document recognizes that biblical exegetes have a necessary and positive role in understanding the context in which those authors wrote and in interpreting what their words mean. *Dei Verbum* concludes by affirming the ultimate goal of service to the word and its careful interpretation: The functions of reading and studying, and the pertinent roles of the magisterium and theologian are to allow "the treasure of revelation [to] fill human hearts more and more" (*DV* 26).

Article 10, the last article of chapter II, deals with the issue of authentic interpretation. Footnotes here are to Vatican I, Pius XII's *Munificentissimus Deus*, and *Humani Generis*. However, consistent with Article 8, *Dei Verbum* begins again with the people of God as a whole, not merely with the hierarchy. The strident *Humani Generis* statement—"The task of interpreting the deposit authentically was entrusted by our divine Redeemer not to the individual Christian, nor even to the theologians, but only to the Church's teaching authority"[60]—has been softened to "the task of interpreting the word of God, whether written or handed on, has been entrusted exclusively to the living teaching office of the Church, whose authority is exercised in the name of Jesus Christ." Gone now are the negatives from *Humani Generis* and its parallel "not even to the theologians, but only to. . . ." Also the "exclusively" of *Dei Verbum* does not bear the same constriction and prohibition as the "only" of *Humani Generis*. Neither here does *Dei Verbum* say that the teaching office of the church is restricted to the pope and bishops.[61] At a minimum one could infer that the magisterium is encouraging itself toward a more attentive and inclusive listening disposition, paralleling the model of church vis-à-vis the word of God expressed in the Preface. Moreover, this modified *Humani Generis* position is now sandwiched between the broader context of the church—the entire holy people who are involved in the study of scripture—and the affirmation that the magisterium is not above the word of God. To this last point, Ratzinger notes,

> For the first time a text of the teaching office expressly points out the subordination of the teaching office to the word, i.e. its function as a servant. . . . One can hardly deny that the point which sees only Scripture as what is unclear, but the teaching office as what is clear, is a very limited one and that to reduce the task of theology to the proof of the presence of the statements of the teaching office in the sources is to

> threaten the primacy of the sources which . . . would ultimately destroy the serving character of the teaching office.[62]

These words, situating the magisterium as servant of the word, were "intended to reassure the separated brethren about the nature of the authority claimed for the *magisterium* in the Catholic Church."[63] Frères Roger Schutz and Max Thurian, founders of the ecumenical Taizé community and invited non-Catholic observers at the Council, welcomed this sentiment.

The subsequent articles of Chapter III reflect insights from modern biblical scholarship, such as a rejection of narrow, simplistic notions of inspiration and inerrancy, the active contribution of the human authors of the Bible, and the literary and historical embodiment of scripture. With regard to Article 11, Alois Grillmeier notes, "The development of the text shows that teaching on inspiration was to be purified of certain mechanistic ideas."[64] Hence, there is a rejection of the phrase "living instruments" in regard to the biblical human authors, who are now called "true authors" (*veri auctores*). Concerning inerrancy, the phrase *sine errore* (without error) is to be read in the context that truth is "for the sake of salvation." A previous draft on inerrancy had stated, "[I]t is completely forbidden to admit that the sacred authors could have erred, since divine inspiration of its very nature precludes and rejects all error in everything, both religious and profane."[65] Article 12 gives hermeneutical rules to guide the work of exegetes.[66] And although this article affirms, like Vatican I, that the exegetes' work is "ultimately subject to the judgment of the church,"[67] *Dei Verbum* does not identify "church" explicitly with the magisterium.

Chapter IV deals with the Old Testament, and Article 15 notes that books therein "contain some things that are imperfect and of merely temporary value." An earlier draft of this text stated that this incompleteness "must be finally compared with the Gospel of Christ preached by the Apostles, and its correct interpretation must be duly submitted to the living magisterium of the Church."[68] However, in successive drafts, this statement with its call to submit to the magisterium was deleted.

The Historicity of the Gospels

Chapter V, entitled "The New Testament," in large part takes up the controversial issue of the historical reliability of the gospels. In many ways, on a micro-level it illustrates the history of *Dei Verbum*. The heart of the chapter is Article 19, of which José Caba notes, "[i]ts development was painful."[69] The historicity of the gospels had been assiduously defended in previous magisterial documents.[70] The encyclical *Divino Afflante Spiritu* (1943), however, gave evidence of a greater openness to biblical scholarship. The encyclical encouraged exegetes to examine the issue of historicity rather than simply, as previously, mandating the acceptance of historicity. *Divino Afflante Spiritu* also gave as a rule of interpretation "what the writer meant." There was a rapid growth in critical biblical scholarship as a result of this greater freedom. Yet some were troubled by the direction and speculations of this research. The alarm was sounded by a *Monitum* of the Holy Office (June, 1961), admonishing opinions that challenged the historicity of scripture.

The history of the drafting of Chapter V reflects this concern. The first schema, *De Fontibus Revelationis*, affirmed the historical value of the gospels and included a condemnation of positions that denied the historicity of the gospels. This schema was rejected as a whole and a new one was formulated. The second schema, *De Divina Revelatione*, excluded the condemnation of the previous one and received numerous comments from the Council fathers. Schema III benefited much from the comments of the Council fathers, largely in reference to the structure of the chapter,[71] and from an instruction issued by the Pontifical Biblical Commission, *Sancta Mater Ecclesia* (made public May 14, 1964). The instruction had a significant impact in two ways. First, while continuing the encouraging tone toward biblical research of *Divino Afflante Spiritu*, it cautioned against exaggerating the creative power of the Christian community. Second, it posited the three stages in the formation of the gospels, what will be accepted as a) the Jesus stage, b) the kerygmatic stage, and c) the composition of the gospels stage. Article 18 of *Dei Verbum* synthesized stage one; Article 19, the other stages.

This schema was discussed in the Council assembly from September 30 to October 6, 1964. A number of fathers wished greater affirmation of the historicity of the gospels. In the light of this discussion, a fourth schema was presented to the Council fathers on November 20, 1964. Apart from improvements in style, there were two significant omissions. First, reference to the creative power of the community was omitted in deference to *Sancta Mater Ecclesia* because it suggested an exaggerated (Bultmannian) role of the Christian community. Second, the phrase *non facta* (not fabricated/invented) was omitted. This phrase had been attached to the adjectives *vera et sincera* (true and sincere) in reference to the account of Jesus that had been transmitted. It was omitted as being already implied by *vera et sincera*. Furthermore, the terms "historical" and "history" were avoided because of their ambiguity in the then current biblical scholarship.

On September 22, 1965, a vote was taken on Article 19. The affirmative vote was 2,162, while 61 voted against and 10 votes were void. The opposition felt that *vera et sincera* was too weak. Although two-thirds affirmed the text, Pope Paul recommended to the Theological Commission (October, 1965) that *vera et sincera* be replaced by *vera seu historica fide digna* (true, worthy of historical belief). The commission rejected this suggestion on grounds previously mentioned, the ambiguity of the term "historical" linked with faith. But in deference to the suggestion, after reference to the gospels in Article 19, the following phrase was added: "whose *historicatem* (historicity) [the church] unhesitatingly affirms." A final text incorporating these changes was presented to the Council on October 29, 1965, and overwhelmingly accepted.

As Béda Rigaux notes, this chapter seeks a balance between two dangers: first, an excessive clinging to literal, historical meaning; and, second, the risks involved in questioning the historical reliability of the gospels.[72] Historical reliability is affirmed in the use of such phrases as *vera et sincera* with reference to the transmission of the account of Jesus; *reapse* (actually) in reference to communicating what Jesus did and said; and *historicatem* (historicity) with regard to the final version of the gospels. Yet the chapter does not affirm a crass historicism. The historical reliability of the gospels is affirmed precisely in the context of those insights gained from modern biblical scholarship. In the spirit of *Divino Afflante Spiritu* and drawing from *Sancta Mater Ecclesia*, at times verbatim, *Dei Verbum* expresses respect for literary genres, the three stages in the coming to be of the gospels, and the editorial activity of the evangelists. This is evident in Article 19, which speaks of those "inspired writers [who] composed the four gospels, by various processes . . . [who] selected some things. . . . Other things they synthesized, or explained with a view to the needs of the churches. . . . They preserved the preaching style, but worked throughout to communicate to us a true and sincere account (*vera et sincera*) of Jesus." Solid biblical methodology and analysis enabled the balancing act of avoiding both historicism and historical minimalism. As we shall shortly observe, such balance is less evident in the *Catechism of the Catholic Church*.

Scripture in the Life of the Church

Chapter VI, the final chapter, deals with "Holy Scripture in the Life of the Church." Some non-Catholic observers at the Council, such as Max Thurian, saw in it "a key for the understanding of the whole Constitution."[73] Lyonnet describes the evolution of the text in this way: earlier texts consider "mainly what the Church has done for Scripture, whereas the successive versions consider exclusively what the Church owes to Scripture."[74] Thus the "church has kept and keeps the scripture, together with tradition, as the supreme rule (*supremam . . . regulam*) of its faith" and all the preaching of the church "must be nourished and ruled by holy scripture" (21). This is indeed strong language and there was an endeavor to weaken it by the elimination of the notion of rule (*regula*). But this assertion that the church is bound by and indebted to revelation was already sounded in the preface and marked there, as Ratzinger noted, a rejection of the temptation toward "ecclesiomonism." Article 23, which repeats the rules for interpretation already expressed in Article 12, gives further evidence of Vatican II's new direction. Whereas a previous version of the text had asserted that Catholic exegetes work under the *regulation* of the church's teaching authority (*sub duce magisterii*), the final version affirms that "Catholic exegetes and other theologians should work together, under the *eye* of the church's teaching authority (*sub vigilantia sacri magisterii*)." Whereas an earlier version of the text identified scripture and tradition jointly as the soul of theology,[75] the final version ascribed this position to scripture.

Not just is the church bound by the word, it is also obligated to share the word. Thus Article 22 in encouraging "[E]asy access to the holy scripture to all the Christian faithful" represents, as Ratzinger notes, "the final and definitive overcoming of the restrictions set up in the various forms of the index of Paul IV, and from Pius IV, Sixtus V, Clement VIII down to Gregory XVI, and proves itself here to be a revision of the Tridentine decisions."[76] In fact, Article 25, the penultimate article, places Bible-reading "in the centre of Christian life."[77] Whereas the earliest draft of this text insists that translations must receive the approval of the bishops and be accompanied by explanations in accordance with "the mind of the Church, whose living magisterium is for the faithful the first rule of faith,"[78] the final version of the text encourages all Christian faithful to learn by frequent reading of the divine scriptures and directs bishops to give suitable instruction in the right use of the divine books. As Lyonnet notes: "Today, we may find it embarrassing, or indeed scandalous, to read the restrictions the hierarchy imposed on reading the Bible by all Christians in the past."[79] Ratzinger concludes his commentary on this article with a quote indicating the spirit of openness evident here: "It seems to me incontestable that with this statement of the Council the Church has more or less renounced the monopoly of alone being able to read and 'be in charge of the Bible.' In this simple way it has provided a yardstick for the renewal that it introduced in the incredibly short period of three years."[80]

The Reception of *Dei Verbum* in the *Catechism of the Catholic Church*

But have the gains made by *Dei Verbum* found expression in post-conciliar documents? In this regard I wish to comment on the *Catechism of the Catholic Church*.[81] My remarks on the *Catechism* will largely make use of two commentaries published in 1994.[82]

An initial question is the appropriateness of reading the *Catechism* in the context of *Dei Verbum* and vice versa. While it is of course true that the *Catechism* is not a conciliar document, both *Dei Verbum* (in the context of the purpose of Vatican II) and the *Catechism* are pastoral in intent. Furthermore, as Peter Phan notes, with "regard to Vatican II, it is obvious that the *Catechism of the Catholic Church* depends extensively upon the conciliar texts. All sixteen conciliar documents are cited, with those on the liturgy, the church, revelation, and the church in the modern world taking the lion's share of attention."[83] Also Pope John Paul II, in his concluding sentence promulgating the *Catechism*, links it to both Vatican II and his own pontificate by dating it to the "thirteenth anniversary of the opening of the Second Vatican Eceumenical Council, in the fourteenth year of my Pontificate."[84]

The *Catechism* sees itself as instructional rather than theologically declarative.[85] But in regard to the distinction between catechesis and theology, given the *Catechism*'s widespread use for instruction, it nonetheless may represent "theology" to a large number of Catholics, who may not distinguish catechesis from theology. Also, for many Catholics, the *Catechism* may well provide their primary or only contact with Vatican II.

The Role of the Bible in the Catechism

In assessing the *Catechism* and its use of the Bible, I wish to turn initially to an essay by Gerard Sloyan.[86] I find his interpretation substantially valid. His evaluation of the *Catechism* is largely negative. First, he is disturbed that the encouragement to Catholics to read the Bible is given so belatedly in the *Catechism*, toward the end of 2653 out of 2863 sections.[87] One may ask whether this is evidence of at least an implicit ecclesial control over the Bible from which *Dei Verbum* sought to break free.

Second, Sloyan notes that while the *Catechism* mentions the principles for interpreting the Bible given in *Dei Verbum* 8 and 10, these are then "conveniently forgotten."[88] Sloyan argues that in Parts One and Two of the *Catechism,* which deal with the creed and the sacraments, the sense of scripture used tends to be allegorical, moral, or anagogic rather than literal. By "literal" Sloyan means what the author intended to say with deference to the mode by which the author wrote. The impact is that the Bible is seen as "an oracular source that can justify whatever is previously known from doctrinal and ethical sources, rather than the other way around."[89] Such a use of the Bible by the magisterium is commonly called "proof-reading." But it is precisely the "other way around" that *Dei Verbum* sought to encourage exegesis over eisegesis. Also this bypassing of the "literal" meaning of the text dangerously leaves the reader of the *Catechism* with the impression that Genesis and the Apocalypse are to be read in a literalist fashion. On this basis, those instructed by the *Catechism* are ill-prepared to engage with creationists, "end of the worlders," and their like. In short, the *Catechism* fails to follow up and adhere pedagogically to the principles of reading the Bible stated in *Dei Verbum.* As Sloyan summarizes, "the Catechism appears to be embarrassed by the study of the Bible in the west of the last two hundred years."[90]

Third, Sloyan is critical of the sectarian assumptions of the *Catechism*. Thus he argues that the *Catechism* was blithely written as if "there ain't nobody here but Catholics."[91] In addition Sloyan charges that the *Catechism* is "supersessionist": "As the Catechism views things . . . this Spirit of God employed the biblical writers for no other purpose than to prepare for Christ"; and "But the bland assumption that the biblical history of Israel was but a typology of the antitype who is Christ—and this Catechism affirms it many times—can only mean trouble for Christians no less than for Jews. It simply is not true."[92] In contrast, one recalls how *Dei Verbum* was conscious of its ecumenical obligations and indeed won praise in this regard.

Finally, Sloyan is critical of the relationship between scripture, tradition, and the magisterium. Of the *Catechism*'s view of the relationship between scripture and tradition, Sloyan notes that it "goes about it in such a way as to create the impression that scripture and tradition are two sources of revelation rather than witnesses, of unequal importance, to the apostolic tradition. This was the very thing *Dei Verbum* sought to express, whether it was successful in doing so or not."[93] Such a view of the relationship, in the context of a failure to give weight to principles of biblical interpretation, favors a magisterial, post-biblical interpretation of the Bible. This last criticism merits further elaboration.

Scripture and the Magisterium in the Catechism

Robert Murray, in his commentary on the *Catechism* (in particular on sections 26 through 141), exposes an encroachment of the magisterium into spheres previously left to the wider church at Vatican II.[94] For his exposé, *Dei Verbum* is the most relevant conciliar document and he compares the *Catechism*'s treatment of themes found in *Dei Verbum.*[95] In reference to the first theme, "the analysis of how divine revelation reaches its human addressees," Murray suggests that the *Catechism* adopts the more negative Augustinian legacy: the section in the *Catechism* headed "Ways of Coming to Know God" begins with "proofs for the existence of God"; the section headed "The Knowledge of God according to the Church" opens with Vatican I's assertion of the possibility of knowing God with certainty by natural reason, and the limitations of human reason are underlined by the following severe passage from *Humani Generis*, not quoted in *Dei Verbum*:

> Though human reason is, strictly speaking, truly capable by its own natural power and light of attaining to a true and certain knowledge of the one personal God, who watches over and controls the world by his providence, and of the natural law written in our hearts by the Creator; yet there are many obstacles which prevent reason from the effective and fruitful use of this inborn faculty. For the truths that concern the relations between God and man wholly transcend the visible order of things, and, if they are translated into human action and influence it, they call for self-surrender and abnegation. The human mind, in its turn, is hampered in the attaining of such truths, not only by the impact of the senses and the imagination, but also by disordered appetites which are the consequences of original sin. So it happens that men in such matters easily persuade themselves that what they would not like to be true is false or at least doubtful.[96]

Thus the opening chapter in the *Catechism* places into the foreground Vatican I's view of revelation, which theoretically is more abstract and intellectualist than that of *Dei Verbum*. Chapter I in the *Catechism* does not even mention the Holy Spirit, let alone the prevenient action of the Holy Spirit. In sum, Murray states, "The *Catechism*, both by omissions and by its order [of *Dei Verbum*], tends to underplay the importance of personal experience and the presence of the Holy Spirit to all members of the Church, and to put greater stress on obedience to external authority."[97] This indeed is a consistent trend. In the *Catechism*, the emphasis "on every believer's growth in faith, through the Holy Spirit, is replaced by an extra stress on control by church authority."[98]

As we have seen, *Dei Verbum* does not restrict the teaching function of the church to the pope and bishops. This is not to say that *Dei Verbum* states that theologians and the Christian faithful share in the official teaching office (*de iure*); nonetheless, theologians and the Christian faithful minimally augment and assist that office. But the *Catechism* (85) in quoting *Dei Verbum* (10/2) strengthens a *de iure* focus with the following—this "means that the task of interpretation has been entrusted to the bishops in communion with the successor of Peter, the Bishop of Rome." This addendum and assertion is restrictive of the scope of the teaching office compared with *Dei Verbum*. The *Catechism* then has a succession of paragraphs that are not from *Dei Verbum*, whose effect "is to add enormous weight to that of the magisterium" (85).[99] In developing the relationship among scripture, tradition, magisterium, and the Holy Spirit, Murray makes the sobering comment: "[I]n this the *Catechism*, while aiming to interpret *Dei Verbum*, sometimes echoes earlier tones of warning and calling to submission which were muted or even absent in [*Dei Verbum*]."[100] His concluding comment is, "The activity of the Holy Spirit among all the members of the Church is underplayed in comparison with *Dei Verbum*, particularly as regards scholars and teachers, whose role is only grudgingly mentioned; *magisterium* as centralised authority is emphasised far more than in *Dei Verbum*."[101]

In the same commentary, Gabriel Daly offers an even more negative appraisal, citing the church historian, Giuseppe Alberigo:

> Recent years have seen a surprising revival of positions that were characteristic of more conservative circles of the Roman Curia and the episcopate in the 1960s. There has been, in other words, a clear return to attitudes that Vatican II unequivocally disavowed and overcame, attitudes that found refuge in tiny groups of nostalgic individuals. A pessimistic vision of history, poisoned by Manichaeism, seems to be spreading abroad. There is a rejection of the Council's call to the churches to become once again pilgrims and missionaries, as though it implied the abandonment of tradition, and finally, a revival of the "closed" ecclesiology of the post-tridentine period in which the Church is a fortified castle, jealous of its own purity and bristling with condemnations.[102]

Moreover, the tone and approach that exemplifies the *Catechism*'s handling of revelation appear in its interpretation of other topics. An example is the *Catechism*'s treatment of Christology as found in sections 512 through 570. In his handling of this section, Gerard O'Hanlan notes that, in part stemming from a descending Christology, there is a tendency to produce a rather "spiritual" portrait of Jesus, such that the *Catechism* runs the "risk of presenting a rather one-sided, pious image of Jesus, not well rooted in the social context of his day, and without much challenge to the *status quo* of our day."[103] But if one minimizes an historical critical approach to the Bible, one invariably is going to produce a one-sided Christology, namely, the spiritualized, sanitized one that O'Hanlan speaks of. Consistent with this, formulations concerning church authority, he notes, also "are extremely eirenic in tone."[104]

To move to a wider context, John Donahue has offered a sobering comment on Catholic biblical scholarship fifty years after *Divino Afflante Spiritu*.[105] Many of his observations coincide with our examination of the use of *Dei Verbum* in the *Catechism*. Among his major concerns are, first, despite the acceptance of historical-critical method in official magisterial documents and its widespread productive use, nevertheless its leading practitioners "are subject to constant attacks from 'neo-integrist' writers who label historical criticism as modernist or too concerned with the human elements in the Bible."[106] Second, Donahue laments that "30 years of biblical research [after Vatican II] have been virtually ignored in official statements." In regard to the *Catechism*, Luke Timothy Johnson is quoted by him as stating "how completely this Catechism ignores the results of biblical scholarship."[107] This appraisal suggests a post-conciliar retreat from the gains achieved by *Dei Verbum*.

Conclusion

I began this essay by highlighting two pivotal comments, among others, from Joseph Ratzinger, namely that all traditions, simply as traditions, are not to be affirmed; there is a distorting, as well as a legitimate, tradition. Second, and as a corollary from the first, we have heard his positive evaluation of the significance of placing the magisterium under the word.[108] The history of the development of the text of *Dei Verbum* demonstrates how this represented a hard-won breakaway from curial theology.[109] But the subsequent reception of *Dei Verbum* suggests it is being interpreted regressively by those forces it had temporarily escaped.[110] As Archbishop Christopher Butler, a *peritus* at Vatican II, later stated, "It is all very well for us to say and believe that the Magisterium is subject to holy Scripture. But is there anyone who is in a position to tell the Magisterium, 'Look, you are not practicing your subjection to Scripture in your teaching?' "[111]

Notes

[1]Unless otherwise stated or unless already embedded in a quotation, church documents will be cited from Norman Tanner, *Decrees of the Ecumenical Councils*, vols. 1 and 2 (London/Washington: Sheed & Ward/ Georgetown University Press, 1990). Parallel reference will also be provided to Henricus Denzinger and Adolfus Schönmetzer, *Enchiridion Symbolorum* (Freiburg: Herder 1963), henceforth DS.

[2]From the outset I wish to acknowledge my indebtedness to Herbert Vorgrimler, ed., *Commentary on the Documents of Vatican II*, 5 vols. (New York: Herder & Herder, 1969). In the third volume, the relevant commentators on *Dei Verbum* are Joseph Ratzinger, Alois Grillmeier, and Béda Rigaux. (Citations from this work will be identified by the commentator's last name, the shortened form of *Commentary*, and the volume number.) I also rely on Giuseppe Alberigo and Joseph A. Komonchak, eds., *History of Vatican II,* vols. 1-4 (Maryknoll, N.Y.: Orbis Books, 1995-2003).

[3]As quoted in Ratzinger, *Commentary*, vol. 3, 155.

[4]René Latourelle, *Theology of Revelation* (New York: Alba House, 1966), 484.

[5]See Xavier Rynne, *Vatican Council II* (Marynkoll, N.Y.: Orbis Books, 1999), 35.

[6]Information about this text relies heavily on Komonchak, *History of Vatican II*, vol. 1, 240-46.

[7]Nine topics were proposed: 1) the notion of objective truth, 2) the existence of a personal God and apologetic demonstrations, 3) cosmic evolution, 4) monogenism, 5) a true concept of revelation, 6) certitude of revelation, 7) a notion of faith, 8) the distinction and harmony between the natural and supernatural, and 9) no new revelation after the close of the deposit. To these nine topics, five further questions were added: 1) biblical inspiration and inerrancy, 2) original sin, 3) the real presence of Christ in the Eucharist, 4) the sacrificial character of the mass, and 5) the Blessed Virgin Mary.

[8]This text comprises eleven chapters.

[9]As quoted in Komonchak, *History of Vatican II*, vol. 1, 245-46.

[10]The Central Preparatory Commission was effectively the steering committee of the Council. It could establish specialized commissions and committees, such as the Theological Commission, that submitted their work to the Central Commission, which coordinated such input and disseminated the outcome to the Council at large.

[11]Latourelle, *Theology of Revelation*, 453.

[12]Reading Cardinal Ratzinger's commentary on *Dei Verbum* is rewarding on at least three levels: First, it is a classical and brilliant commentary; second, one can trace themes that endure into his later theology, such as a certain

pessimism; and, third, it is illuminating in the context of his election in 2005 as Pope Benedict XVI.

[13]"In whatever matter, religious or profane"—translation mine.

[14]Ratzinger, *Commentary*, vol. 3, 159.

[15]Bishop De Smedt of Bruges from the Secretariat on Christian Unity noted: "The schema is a[n ecumenical] step backwards, a hindrance, it does damage . . ." (quoted in Ratzinger, *Commentary*, vol. 3, 160).

[16]Cardinals Ottaviani and Bea were the chairmen, with Tromp and Willebrands as secretaries. Other members were Cardinals Liénart, Frings, Ruffini, Meyer, Lefèbvre and Browne (Ratzinger, *Commentary*, vol. 3, 161).

[17]Latourelle, *Theology of Revelation*, 454.

[18]Ratzinger, *Commentary*, vol. 3, 161.

[19]Ibid., 162.

[20]See Hanjo Sauer in Komonchak, *History of Vatican II*, vol. 4, 195ff.

[21]See Rynne, *Vatican Council II*, 305ff.

[22]Franić's presentation was somewhat counter productive, as peritus Semmelroth noted in his diary, "The debate on the revelation schema began. Franić was first with a negative report. He is a true reactionary. . . . It was very good, psychologically, that it was he who gave the negative report, because the fathers already know it. The positive report of Florit was far more effective and will be influential" (in Komonchak, *History of Vatican II*, vol. 4, 209).

[23]See Ratzinger, *Commentary*, vol. 3, 163.

[24]Hanjo Sauer in Komonchak, *History of Vatican II*, vol. 4, 228.

[25]See Ratzinger, *Commentary*, vol. 3, 168.

[26]Ibid., 168-69.

[27]Ibid., 167.

[28]Tanner (*Decrees of the Ecumenical Councils*) translates *lumine* with "by the power." The more literal translation is "by the light."

[29]*Dei Filius*, Tanner, *Decrees of the Ecumenical Councils*, 806; see also DS 3004.

[30]DS 3004.

[31]Ratzinger, *Commentary*, vol. 3, 171.

[32]Ibid., 172.

[33]Ibid., 173-74.

[34]Ibid., 174.

[35]Ibid.

[36]Ibid.

[37]John Allen, in his popular biography, perceives that "there is a bedrock conviction that has remained constant in Ratzinger from the council to the present: a pessimistic view about the relationship between church and culture." This pessimism, one may speculate, has pre-conciliar influences, such as growing up in Nazi Germany; being formed by his scholarship on Augustine; and the impact of Luther on German theology. This outlook

appears to have solidified from the latter part of the Council onwards, through the student riots in Tübingen and in the experience of theological turmoil in the post-conciliar period (*Pope Benedict XVI* [New York: Continuum, 2000], 78).

[38]Ibid., 176.

[39]Ibid., 176.

[40]Vatican I, *Dei Filius*, in Tanner, *Decrees of the Ecumenical Councils,* 807; DS 3009.

[41]Ibid.

[42]See Ratzinger, *Commentary*, vol. 3, 184.

[43]Ibid., 182.

[44]Latourelle, *Theology of Revelation*, 476.

[45]Ratzinger, *Commentary*, vol. 3, 185. This quotation by Ratzinger was used in the Catholic Theological Society of America's document in response to the Vatican prohibition against female ordination based on the argument from tradition.

[46]*Dei Filius,* in Tanner, *Decrees of the Ecumenical Councils*, 809; DS 3020.

[47]Ibid.

[48]Given by John XXIII on October 11, 1962, on the opening day of the Council as cited from http://www.rc.net/rcchurch/vatican2/j23open.txt.

[49]Robert Murray, "The Human Capacity for God, and God's Initiative," in Michael J. Walsh, ed., *Commentary on the Catechism of the Catholic Church* (Collegeville, Minn.: Liturgical Press, 1994), 15.

[50]J. R. Geiselmann, "Das Konzil von Trient über das Verhältnis der Heiligen Schrift und der nicht geschriebenen Traditionen" in Michael Schmaus, ed., *Die Mündliche Überlieferung* (Munich: Max Hueber Verlag, 1957).

[51]The change was made on April 7, 1546, and the decree was promulgated the next day. But knowledge of this change was not widely disseminated. Thus Geiselmann, "Das Konzil von Trient," indicates that the protocol annotating the deliberations was placed in a private collection and was largely unknown. Hubert Jedin notes a similar inattentiveness to protocol: "[U]nbelievable as it must appear, up to this time [March 27, 1546] the leaders of the Council had neglected to take one of the most elementary measures to assure an orderly business procedure, namely, that of having minutes of the negotiations of the general congregations drawn up" (*A History of the Council of Trent*, vol. 2 [Edinburgh: Nelson, 1961], 79).

Such an attitude prevailed and M. Schmaus notes, "According to Geiselmann, the intention of the council was to a great extent misunderstood in the theology which followed the council, because the first draft [*partim . . . partim*] had not been published, and the change [*et*] made by the council went unnoticed" (*Dogma: God in Revelation*, vol. 1 [New York: Sheed & Ward, 1968], 218).

[52]In reference to the last-minute change, Geiselmann asks, "*Was hat also das Konzil mit dem 'et' über das Verhältnis von Schrift und Tradition*

entschieden? Die Antwort kann nur lauten: nichts, gar nichts. Mit dem 'et' ist das Konzil einer Entscheidung ausgewichen, weil diese Frage noch nicht entscheidungsreif war" (What therefore did the Council decide about the relationship between scripture and tradition by *et*? The answer can only be: nothing, nothing at all. With this *et* the Council avoided a decision because this question was not ripe for decision.—translation mine) ("Das Konzil von Trient," 163).

[53]Jedin, *A History of the Council of Trent*, 75: "There can be no doubt that though the majority of the theologians of Trent may not have approved the formula *partim-partim*, they approved the thing itself, that is, the statement that dogmatic tradition was a channel of revelation which supplemented the Scripture." Yves Congar concurs with Geiselmann's interpretation of Trent that the *et* formulation was a decision not to decide the issue of scripture and tradition (*Tradition and Traditions* [New York: Macmillan, 1967]). Thus he notes:

> Faced with two opposing currents of opinion among the Catholic theologians—the one, perhaps the stronger, in favour of *partim . . . partim . . .*, the other in favour of the sufficiency of Scripture—the council, seeing no adequate solution and ever careful to express itself only where Catholics were in agreement, contented itself, by juxtaposition and with no precision of their interrelation, the *two forms* under which the Gospel of Jesus Christ is communicated, in its plenitude and purity, as the source of all saving truth and of Christian discipline (165).

And, "It is quite possible that *partim . . . partim . . .* really expressed the thought of the Council Fathers, for they were concerned to reaffirm that truths existed which had not been formulated in Scripture."

[54]This latter group will appeal to the phrase *pari pietatis affectu* (with equal reverence) in reference to scripture and tradition (Trent, *Decretum de libris sacris*, DS 1501).

[55]Trent, *Decretum de libris sacris*, DS 1501. The Council was unsure how to express the reverence to be accorded toward scripture and tradition. It wavered between the word *pari* (with equal) or *simili* (with similar). Eventually *pari* was accepted, though not without protest. Jedin notes that the bishop of Chioggia, instead of voting against *pari*, rather states, *obediam*—"I will obey" (*A History of the Council of Trent*, 93).

[56]*Dei Verbum* here then is following Trent as understood by Geiselmann and Congar. According to Geiselmann the *misunderstanding* of Trent was that neutrality of *et* was read in a *partim . . . partim* way, a two-source theory of revelation. This understanding is not surprising as it was the pre- and post-Tridentine position. Congar has a similar judgment. Thus in reference to the view leading up to the decree, he notes: "The expression *partim . . . partim*

. . . is already found in the speech of Cardinal Cervini, the second legate. There were, therefore, grounds for believing—and fearing—that the council might proceed to present the unwritten traditions and Scripture as two independent and parallel sources of the rule of truth which is the Gospel" (*Tradition and Traditions*, 64).

On the post-Tridentine reception, Congar notes: "[Q]uite a few Catholic apologists presented Scripture and tradition as two complementary principles. It is, moreover, certain that the controversialists who wrote on the subject after the council, generally did so along the lines of the *partim . . . partim* . . . distinction [a footnote cites, among others, Robert Bellarmine]. This was so right into the nineteenth century, and indeed even up to our own day" (*Tradition and Traditions*, 165-66).

[57]As quoted from http://www.sounddoctrine.net/LIBRARY/Modern%20Day%20Reform%20Teaching/Sinclair%20Ferguson/scripture_tradition_Ferguson.htm.

[58]Latourelle, *Theology of Revelation*, 479-80.

[59]Ratzinger, *Commentary*, vol. 3, 194.

[60]Translation from Jacques Dupuis, ed., *The Christian Faith* (New York: Alba House, 2001), 331, #859; DS 3886.

[61]See Murray, "The Human Capacity for God, and God's Initiative," 15.

[62]Ratzinger, *Commentary*, vol. 3, 197.

[63]Murray, "The Human Capacity for God, and God's Initiative," 15.

[64]Grillmeier, *Commentary*, 3:228

[65]As quoted in John Donahue, "A Journey Remembered: Catholic Biblical Scholarship 50 Years after *Divino Afflante Spiritu*," in *America* 169, no. 7 (September 18, 1993).

[66]Reference is to scriptures in "human fashion"; literary forms; attention to be paid to the time of the sacred author; the unity of the whole scripture; the living tradition of the whole church.

[67]*Dei Filius*, "[T]hat in matters of faith and morals, belonging as they do to the establishing of Christian doctrine, that meaning of holy scripture must be held to be the true one, which holy mother Church held and holds, since it is her right to judge of the true meaning and interpretation of holy scripture" (DS 3007).

[68]Stanislas Lyonnet in René Latourelle, *Vatican II: Assessment and Perspectives* (Mahwah, N.J.: Paulist Press, 1988), 1:171.

[69]Analysis of this chapter relies much on José Caba, "Historicity of the Gospels (DV 19)" in Latourelle, *Vatican II: Assessment and Perspectives*, 1:299-320.

[70]The follows documents, among others, are significant: the *Syllabus* (1864) repeated by Vatican I (1870); the decree *Lamentabili* (1907) linked questioning of the historicity of the gospels with modernism; the encyclical *Pascendi* (1907) made the same association; the Pontifical Biblical Commission in a series of pronouncements (1911-1912) affirmed the historicity of the

synoptic gospels; the encyclical *Spiritus Paraclitus* (1920) proclaimed the historicity of all four gospels.

[71]While the chapter was entitled "The New Testament," the primary focus was the gospels. To be more faithful to the chapter title, a new paragraph was added (17) giving a broader background to the gospels in the context of God's revelation. This paragraph consciously opens with "The Word of God," as does the Preface. However the Latin word order is inverted: *Dei Verbum* and *Verbum Dei* respectively.

[72]Rigaux, *Commentary*, 3:257.

[73]As quoted by Lyonnet, in *Vatican II: Assessment and Perspectives,* 1:177.

[74]Ibid., 176.

[75]Lyonnet, in *Vatican II: Assessment and Perspectives,* 1:196.

[76]Ratzinger, *Commentary,* 3:264.

[77]Ibid., 3:270.

[78]As quoted by Lyonnet, in *Vatican II: Assessment and Perspectives*, 1:199.

[79]Ibid., 187.

[80]As quoted in Ratzinger, *Commentary*, 3:272.

[81]*Cathecism of the Catholic Church* (New York: Doubleday, 1995). Henceforth reference will be to the *Catechism.*

[82]Bernard Marthaler, ed., *Introducing the Catechism of the Catholic Church* (New York: Paulist Press, 1994), and Michael J. Walsh, ed., *Commentary on the Catechism of the Catholic Church* (Collegeville, Minn.: Liturgical Press, 1994).

[83]Peter Phan, "What Is Old and What Is New in the Catechism?" in Marthaler, ed., *Introducing the Catechism of the Catholic Church*, 61.

[84]However, as Phan remarks: "Indeed, while Vatican II is copiously cited, its spirit, as many commentators have lamented, is conspicuously absent" (ibid.).

[85]The preface to the *Catechism* is rather restrained, stating that the pope does "declare it to be a sure norm for teaching the faith and thus a valid and legitimate instrument for ecclesial communion" (3). The pope also refers to it as this "reference text."

[86]Gerard Sloyan, "The Role of the Bible in Catechesis According to the Catechism," in Marthaler, ed., *Introducing the Catechism of the Catholic Church*, 32-42.

[87]Ibid., 34.

[88]Ibid., 35.

[89]Ibid.

[90]Ibid.

[91]Ibid., 37.

[92]The quotations are found on ibid., 39 and 40 respectively.

[93]Ibid., 38.

[94]Robert Murray, "The Human Capacity for God, and God's Initiative" in Walsh, ed., *Commentary on the Catechism of the Catholic Church*, 6-35.

[95]These are 1) the analysis of how divine revelation reaches its human addressees; 2) the balance, maintained by the Holy Spirit, between the total church's response to revelation and the role of episcopal authority; 3) the relationship of scripture, tradition, magisterium, and the Holy Spirit; 4) the various modes in which God speaks through scripture; 5) the value of the OT in the church; 6) how the NT uses the OT; and 7) holy scripture in the life of the church.

[96]*Humani Generis* 561, DS 3875.

[97]Murray, "The Human Capacity for God, and God's Initiative" in Walsh, ed., *Commentary on the Catechism of the Catholic Church*, 13.

[98]Ibid.

[99]Ibid., 17.

[100]Ibid., 16.

[101]Ibid., 28.

[102]Gabriel Daly, "Creation and Original Sin," in Walsh, ed., *Commentary on the Catechism of the Catholic Church*, 109, quoting Giuseppe Alberigo et al., eds., *The Reception of Vatican II* (London: Burns & Oates, 1987), 21-22.

[103]Gerard O'Hanlan, in Walsh, ed., *Commentary on the Catechism of the Catholic Church*, 140.

[104]Ibid., 139.

[105]Donahue, "A Journey Remembered."

[106]Ibid.

[107]Donahue, quoting Johnson from *Commonweal*, May 7, 1993.

[108]Elsewhere Ratzinger stated: "Criticism of papal pronouncements will be possible and even necessary, to the degree that they lack support in Scripture and the Creed, that is, in the faith of the whole Church. When neither the consensus of the whole Church is had, nor clear evidence from the sources is available, a definitive decision is not possible. Were one formally to take place, while conditions for such an act were lacking, the question would have to be raised concerning its legitimacy" (*Das Neue Volk Gottes*, as quoted in Francis A. Sullivan, *Magisterium: Teaching Authority in the Catholic Church* [New York: Paulist, 1983], 209).

[109]A similar approach could be applied to other ecclesial documents. A good comparison would be Vatican II's *Nostra Aetata* (Declaration on the Relation of the Church to Non-Christian Religions) with *Dominus Iesus* (Declaration on the Unicity and Salvific Universality of Jesus Christ and the Church).

[110]There has been a tendency to argue that the differing interpretations of the Council may be traced to those who sought a return to sources approach (*ressourcement*) and a modernizing approach *(aggiornamento*). While this distinction and its application have occasional merit, I do not think that the reception of *Dei Verbum* may be justified by either approach.

[111]Donahue, quoting from J. J. Miller, ed., *Vatican II: An Interfaith Appraisal* (Notre Dame: University of Notre Dame Press, 1966).

Vatican II's Ecclesiology and the Sexual Abuse Scandal

Jason King

For the last forty years, interpretations of Vatican II have been mired in a liberal and conservative dichotomy. Conservatives believe that the documents of Vatican II were valid, yet were poorly interpreted and implemented, thereby leading the church to too great a capitulation to the modern world. Liberals believe that the documents of Vatican II inaugurated a momentous and positive change in the church's response to the modern world, but that their great reforming impetus was squandered by subsequent papacies and curial officials. From this perspective, the church is now languishing because the hierarchy has hindered the full implementation of the needed reforms.[1]

Each of these perspectives on the Council entails a concomitant ecclesiology. The conservative interpretative framework views Vatican II's ecclesiology as one that intended to enhance the role of the clergy, especially as a continuation and fulfillment of Vatican I's teaching on the powers of the papacy. This interpretation was lost after the Council and a renewal of it is the best response to the modern world. The liberals contend that Vatican II's ecclesiology is one that reformed church authority. It abandoned the primacy of the hierarchical understanding of the church and replaced it with one that made the laity a constitutive part of church governance. Yet, this reform has been held up by popes and other church officials.

As has been noted by countless theologians, these categories are inadequate.[2] Not only are they inadequate for interpreting the complexity of Vatican II and its ecclesiology, they also fail to offer an understanding of the church that can address the complexity of the contemporary world. These two problems are interrelated. In focusing on certain aspects of the Council and neglecting others, conservatives and liberals do not utilize all the resources the Council has to offer the church today.

The sexual abuse scandal provides evidence of these limitations. It began in January 2002 with the *Boston Globe*'s story about Fr. John Geoghan. This story revealed that not only had Geoghan sexually assaulted over 130 people, but that Cardinal Bernard Law had kept him in ministry for more than ten years, even though he was apparently aware of the priest's problem. Law moved him from parish to parish and permitted him to reenter ministry after four separate trips to treatment centers. The response to the *Globe*'s article was not only horror at Geoghan's actions, but visceral anger at Law's decision to return him to ministry when he repeatedly demonstrated he would abuse again.

The *Globe* followed this initial story with approximately 250 more stories on various Boston priests, their sexual abuses, and the bishop who allowed them to continue in ministry. As the stories in Boston broke, other newspapers across the country investigated their local dioceses and uncovered similar types of sexual abuse and cover-ups. Yet, the stories were often unintentionally misleading. People assumed that the reporting coincided with the abuse when in fact the abuse usually happened twenty to forty years earlier.

The full story of the sexual abuse only began to be clarified with John Jay College's *A Report on the Crisis in the Catholic Church in the United States*, published in 2004. The report was commissioned as part of the *Charter for the Protection of Children and Young People* adopted by the U.S. Catholic bishops in 2002 at their Dallas meeting. The report did extensive research on the number of incidents of abuse and the associated costs. What the researchers found was that between 1950 and 2002, 4,392 clergy (approximately 4 percent of all Catholic clergy) were accused of sexually abusing 10,667 people, mostly (80 percent) boys ages 11 to 14. The majority (75 percent) of these incidences occurred between 1960 and 1984. While over 50 percent of the perpetrators had only one victim, just 3 percent of the perpetrators accounted for over 25 percent of the victims.[3]

The acts tended to follow a general pattern. Most of the victims were post-pubescent boys, the abuse was usually a serious sexual offense, and the abuse often happened in the clergy's own house. The resulting settlements cost dioceses approximately $573 million dollars, and insurance companies covered about $219 million. The report notes that these financial figures cover only the years from 1950 to 2002 and hence do not include all settlements, especially the more recent ones (for example, the $85 million dollar settlement in the Boston diocese in 2003).

Several authors have covered these facts, yet they differ in their analyses. They tend to offer a liberal or conservative ecclesiology for fixing the problems that gave rise to the abuse and cover up. As Peter Steinfels notes, "Although [the sexual abuse scandal] temporarily united left and right, liberals and conservatives, in criticism of the bishops, ultimately it supplied the polarized camps in the Church with new reserves of outrage to fuel their conflicting outlooks."[4] These outlooks, which have been in place almost since the close of the Council, fail to adequately address the ecclesiological issues arising from the sexual abuse scandal.

In this paper, I intend to focus on this last point. I analyze three of the many works on the sexual abuse scandal that together are representative of the literature. One approaches the sexual abuse scandal from a liberal Vatican II ecclesiology, a second uses a conservative one, and the third a combination of the two. While noting their relative merits, I discuss their two major limitations. First, the ecclesiologies address only a part of the problems arising from the sexual abuse scandal, that of accountability, and neglect issues of healing and reconciliation. Second, the authors neglect at least one very key aspect of Vatican II that would seem to be extremely relevant for dealing with the sexual abuse crisis, that of the "pilgrim church." The conclusion is thus twofold: not only do the commentators on the sexual abuse crisis rest on inadequate ecclesiologies, but their ecclesiologies also rest on an incomplete appropriation of Vatican II. After critically analyzing the deficient ecclesiological interpretations of Vatican II by both conservatives and liberals during the past forty years, I offer a proposal for the church of the future.

Sexual Abuse Literature

A number of books have been published on the sexual abuse crisis.[5] Yet, they all seem to fall somewhere along the liberal and conservative spectrum. They advocate various forms of lay participation or increased episcopal authority or some mixture of the two. I have selected three works out of this literature as representative of the whole. The first two are the clearest examples of the liberal and conservative views respectively. The third is an attempt to navigate a middle course between the left and the right. While they have merits, I ultimately believe they are inadequate for addressing the sexual abuse scandal.

Paul Dokecki's The Clergy Sexual Abuse Crisis

In *The Clergy Sexual Abuse Crisis*, Paul Dokecki analyzes the sexual abuse crisis from a number of different perspectives including psychology, sociology, ethics, and ecclesiology. His chapter on the ecclesiological problems and solutions is one of the best representatives of the liberal approach to the sexual abuse crisis. Dokecki argues that there is a tension in Vatican II between the hierarchical model and the "people of God" model of the church. He argues that the latter should be prioritized because it was intentionally placed before the hierarchical model in Vatican II's central document on the church, *Lumen Gentium*.[6] Dokecki contends that the hierarchical model, however, continued to dominate church thinking since the end of the Council and thus contributed to the scandal. It generated an insulated clerical culture that made leaders suspicious of rather than open to the voices of the laity, the victims, and their families.[7] It also gave Rome a definitive role in determining the response.[8]

According to Dokecki, the hierarchical model of the church failed miserably in dealing with the scandal and thus needs to be replaced by the "people of God" model. He believes that

> [h]ad the Church functioned more as the People of God, had the Church been more open and transparent by virtue of the *laity being more involved in the everyday life of the Church and its governance*, opportunities for abuse would have been greatly reduced, and the Church's response would have been more charitable and pastoral and less obsessed with avoiding scandal. Further, *if the hierarchy would share its power and meaningfully join with the laity in dealing with clergy sexual abuse and other matters of Church governance*, great strides

would be made toward preventing future abuse and restoring trust and rebuilding the credibility of the Church.[9]

Thus, according to Dokecki, if church leaders had operated with the "people of God" model, they would have included the laity in their decision-making and thus there would have been fewer incidents of abuse, less cover-up, and a greater chance of avoiding a future recurrence of these acts.

Dokecki's perspective captures the essential features of the liberal perspective. It argues that Vatican II established lay involvement in church governance. It states that church leaders abandoned this trajectory in favor of a hierarchical approach. It concludes by insisting that the sexual abuse crisis could have been avoided and can be avoided in the future if the church responds to the true intention behind Vatican II.

George Weigel's The Courage to Be Catholic

George Weigel offers the quintessential conservative perspective. In his *The Courage to Be Catholic*, Weigel argues that the sexual abuse crisis "has everything to do with the authentic implementation of Vatican II, and with the failure of the Church's leadership to do just that."[10] Weigel contends that church leaders implemented the "spirit of Vatican II" instead of its authentic teaching. According to this "spirit," leaders were to be people chosen democratically, not individuals marked and set apart because of their priestly role.[11] The result was a loss of the distinctiveness of the clergy. Priests no longer saw themselves as "living icons of the eternal priesthood of Jesus Christ,"[12] but people who "in dress, lifestyle, and habits of association and recreation" were almost indistinguishable from the laity.[13] Bishops viewed themselves as administrators instead of leaders. They understood their job as "discussion-group facilitation" instead of "teaching and sanctifying."[14]

Weigel believes that this "spirit," which is ultimately a misreading and misapplication of the Council, is one of the major causes of the sexual abuse scandal.[15] Because priests and bishops were no longer understood as distinct from the laity, priests were no longer properly screened,[16] formed,[17] or disciplined[18] as priests should be and consequently had little hindering them from engaging in sexual abuse. The bishops' abdication of their leadership responsibilities led first to failing to protect people from sexually abusive priests, then to trusting therapists who advocated rehabilitation over a theology that finds sexual abuse incompatible with the priesthood, and finally to bowing to the media-generated "one-strike-you're-out" criterion instead of showing genuine concern about the priests in their dioceses. [19]

For Weigel, the solution to the sexual abuse crisis is thus a recovering of the proper role and authority of priests and, especially, bishops. Weigel believes that bishops need to recover the true understanding of the nature of their office. They must

> come to know, again, that they are genuine vicars of Christ, not vicars of the pope or vicars of their national conference. Bishops must come to think of themselves, again, as men to whom the Holy Spirit has given the fullness of the sacrament of Holy Orders, not a promotion in a corporate structure. That the word "bishop" derives from the Greek word for "overseer" must never blind the bishop to his basic apostolic responsibilities, which are to be a teacher and a pastor. A bishop, as the Catholic Church understands it, is a successor of the apostles.[20]

Weigel insists that this understanding of bishops is precisely what the documents of Vatican II imply.[21] Far from indicating a loss of clerical identity or democratization as the advocates of the "Spirit of Vatican II" propose, "[t]he Second Vatican Council made a serious effort to lift up the supernatural vocation and real pastoral authority of the local bishop." [22] For Weigel, increasing episcopal strength and authority or, in other words, authentically implementing Vatican II's teachings, will result in bishops taking their positions more seriously and, thus, being less complicit in the abuse and covering up of sexual abuse.

Weigel is arguing for a particular understanding of the Council, one that exemplifies the conservative perspective. He argues that the Council addressed the needs of the church in the modern world by emphasizing the role of bishops and priests in church governance. The failure to heed these teachings led to the current crisis. A return to the genuine teachings of the Council documents will lead to a stronger church that will not tolerate either sexual abuse or its cover-up.

Peter Steinfels's A People Adrift

In *A People Adrift*, Peter Steinfels tries to steer a middle course between these two extremes. His interpretation of Vatican II[23] consists of two parts. First, Steinfels believes that the Council's full call for reform has been hindered by "curial conservatives." By "bottling up legitimate change and provoking overreactions," by creating an environment of frustration and obstructionism, these officials hindered the necessary reforms the Council set in motion: dialoguing with the modern world, recognizing the historical and mutable nature of the church, and organizing the church more communally and locally.[24] The most obvious example of resistance to change came with *Humanae Vitae*. This reassertion of the church's ban on artificial contraception caused numerous laity and clergy to feel frustrated at the lack of change and, consequently, to disregard church authority.[25] Many religious and priests left their ministry, and Catholic institutions started to distance themselves from their Catholic identity.[26] Second, Steinfels also thinks that the church regretfully lost much of its distinctiveness and many of its practices in order to adapt to the modern world, all in the name of the "spirit of the Council": "Hierarchy was to give way to democracy, traditional morality to current opinion, established doctrines to the latest consensus of theologians and biblical scholars."[27]

The result of both of these trends has been a dearth of effective leadership.[28] On the one hand, curial conservatives and their obstructionism and procrastination have generated a "habit of subservience" to Rome. [29] Bishops appear afraid of any displeasure coming from Vatican officials and retract whatever generates such a response. On the other, excessive adaptation to the modern world has generated a bureaucratic structure in the United States Conference of Catholic Bishops that is so concerned with consensus and avoiding public disputes that it sacrifices "honest debate and respectful but frank disagreements."[30]

According to Steinfels, the U.S. bishops' fear of Rome and a push for conformity among themselves led to their failure in the handling of the sexual abuse scandal. The bishops lacked focus. They were pressured by Rome to act on other concerns, includinkg removing Fr. Charles Curran from his teaching position, stripping Archbishop Raymond Hunthausen of his powers, and forcing a pullback on the bishops' statement on combating AIDS, and thereby neglected issues connected to sexual abuse.[31] "Dealing with sexual abuse, in short, was anything but high among Vatican priorities."[32] The bishops did not adequately inform parishioners of the abusive history of some priests because of the desire to avoid public scandal and the standard practice of covering up the incidents. They underestimated the gravity, danger, and effects of the sexual abuse and thus were slack in implementing procedures for stopping it in the future.[33]

Since Steinfels believes that a lack of leadership led to the sexual abuses crisis, he concludes that the solution is the emergence of authentic leadership in the episcopacy. In defining the kind of leadership needed, Steinfels attempts to bridge the gap between conservatives and liberals by drawing on elements from both of their arguments. On the one hand, Steinfels agrees with conservatives that the bishops need to live up to the true nature of their office and thereby help preserve the Catholic tradition. In the sexual abuse scandal, the bishops behaved more like managers and thus failed to lead the church to an authentic Catholic response to the abuse.[34]

On the other hand, Steinfels agrees with the liberals that authentic episcopal leadership necessarily includes consultation with the laity. An authoritarian form of episcopal leadership, Steinfels believes, not only does not work (because there are not enough clergy)[35] but also led to some of the worst atrocities of the sexual abuse scandal (for example, those of Cardinal Law).[36] The consultative approach, however, would have greatly reduced the incidents of abuse and the propensity for covering them up.

Steinfels offers the example of the late Cardinal Bernardin to establish his claim. "Bernardin believed in collegial decision making and in strengthening the bishops' conference. He believed in consultation. He believed in mediating different points of view."[37] The result was that the diocese of Chicago had already taken measures to stop sexual abuse before the 2002 scandal broke. It had established a diocesan committee to find and remove abusers as well as a lay-dominated committee to handle accusations.[38]

Thus, bishops who want to be true and effective leaders must consult with, direct, motivate, trust, listen to, and learn from the laity.[39] They need to be people who are open to and capable of sustained, honest, and open discussion of ideas—all ideas. Steinfels thereby weds his conservative concern for the preservation of tradition to the liberal concern for bishops' accountability to the laity. He maps out an ecclesiology in which bishops lead by both handing on the Catholic tradition and consulting with others, particularly, the laity.

The Need for Healing

As representative works, these three texts reveal two inadequacies of the literature analyzing the sexual abuse crisis. First, the focus on church governance is inadequate because it only addresses one of the needs of victims: the need for changes in church structure to prevent the abuse and cover up from happening again. Questions about why and how it happened and the means for dealing with the resulting psychological, emotional, sexual, spiritual issues—basically questions about healing—are left unaddressed by focusing predominantly on governance. These questions are not just personal ones, but social ones as well. The church as a whole was wounded, the laity was betrayed, the reputations of innocent priests and responsible bishops were tarnished, and the ability of the church to effectively encourage others to follow the gospel was weakened.

Even the proposed changes in church structure—the liberal advocacy for lay involvement and the conservative argument for increased episcopal authority—do not inherently guarantee protection from new sexual abuse scandals. In the 1993 scandal, it was the waning of lay interest subsequent to the false accusation against Cardinal Bernardin that relieved the bishops from the pressure to fully implement child-protection procedures.[40] Moreover, qualified lay people, those with degrees in psychology, therapy, and pastoral counseling, advised bishops to return abusing priests to the ministry.[41] Hence, lay voices, even qualified lay voices, are not necessarily a perfect protection for individuals.

To be sure, the conservative perspective has its weaknesses in preventing sexual abuse. While a strong sense of clerical identity can make people accountable to higher standards, it can also lead to a greater effort to cover up scandalous behavior in order to protect the strong sense of one's self. Millions of dollars are spent each year to protect a particular image or feeling about a product. Companies bring lawsuits to protect their names and logos. Thus, it is no surprise to find bishops who went to similar extremes to protect their own self-image and who became extremely reticent to acknowledge anyone or anything that might tarnish or jeopardize it.

The focus on accountability in these two models of change is inadequate without a deeper institutional commitment to healing and reconciliation. Healing would require the institution to help victims overcome the effects of the abuse, to seek to alleviate the betrayal felt by those not physically victimized, to form leaders sensitive to these issues and willing to address them, and, finally, to facilitate the repentance and therapy of victimizing priests while assuring that they are never in a position to repeat their crime.

The commitment to reconciliation is a more difficult task because it commits the institution to trying to keep all of these groups—abused, non-abused, innocent priests and bishops, and guilty priests and bishops—together and foster, without forcing, forgiveness. This commitment implies a richer notion of church, one not captured by the liberal and conservative concepts. Thus, the second inadequacy of literature on the sexual abuse crisis is its appropriation of Vatican II: the conceptions of the Council and its ecclesiology miss valuable resources needed to sufficiently address the sexual abuse scandal. The most obvious example of this is that the literature on the sexual abuse scandal neglects what should be one of the most relevant ecclesiologies from Vatican II, the "pilgrim church" model.

The Pilgrim Church

Chapter Seven of *Lumen Gentium* presents a model of the church as a pilgrim church. This model is marked by four characteristics that make it extremely applicable to addressing the issues raised by the sexual abuse scandal: 1) its imperfection, 2) its striving for perfection, 3) its sense of solidarity, and 4) its accountability to Christ.

First, the pilgrim church acknowledges its own imperfection. Vatican II said that the church does not reach the fullness of its perfection until the eschaton and that, even though it is marked by real holiness, it is also an imperfect holiness (*LG* 48). These statements indicate that not only are people imperfect, but that the church as a social body is not perfect. Recognition of this reality requires the church to change in the understanding of itself as a social institution. These changes are particularly suited to address the challenges and consequences brought about by the sexual abuse scandal. By acknowledging that the church is imperfect, the church hierarchy would be more willing and ready to seek out weaknesses and breakdowns. The hierarchy would not be so constrained by fear that the revelation of failures would necessarily bring scandal. Rather, it would be more open to those who discover or point out failings in the life of the church. On the other hand, acceptance by the faithful of an imperfect church might prepare them in a more realistic way for addressing church deficiencies.

Once the church recognizes that it is imperfect, then it must conclude that it is also in need of repentance. This can and should be true at an institutional level. The church as a whole body needs to confess its wrongs, express sorrow, commit itself not to repeat its wrongs, and carry out some penance to help rectify the wrongs. The church needs the sacrament of reconciliation expanded to cover social sin and social repentance.

Many theologians in the discipline of social ethics have been examining just how institutions in general can repent and mediate forgiveness.[42] These works provide examples of what a social sacrament of reconciliation might look like. Let me draw on two examples. First, in his essay "Mediating Repentance, Forgiveness, and Reconciliation: What Is the Church's Role?" Robert Schreiter notes that reconciliation on an institutional level involves an apology for the actions, repentance and reparation for what happened, and an act of forgiveness from the victims.[43] He continues by saying that the church can contribute to this process by creating safe places for people to talk about what happened, providing rituals and symbols that can express the injury and forgiveness in ways words cannot, and reconnecting victims to the larger community. Second, William Bole, Drew Christiansen, and Robert Hennemeyer articulate what is needed for institutional healing in their book *Forgiveness in International Politics*.[44] They contend that the key characteristics of institutional healing are: truth about what happened, forbearance from revenge, empathy for opposing sides, commitment to repair the damage, and recognition that reconciliation is a process. Either of these examples supplies a framework for conceptualizing a social sacrament of reconciliation.

A social sacrament of reconciliation could have addressed two problems that emerged out of the scandal. It could have helped to mitigate the alienation from the church felt by most victims. People felt harmed and betrayed not just by individual clergy members, but by the church as an institutional community. Hence, many in the Catholic community desired apologies and penance not just from the perpetrators, but from the institution that had failed and wounded them. Without replacing individual repentance, a social sacrament of reconciliation provides a ritual whereby the institution itself can confess its sin and ask for forgiveness for the damage and marshal its resources for reform.

This sacramental notion of institutional forgiveness is also a way in which the pilgrim church model can sublate the insights of the conservative understanding of the church. The conservatives called for bishops to heed their true calling as leaders of their dioceses. In the pilgrim church model, episcopal authority is not dictatorial but reconciling. The bishops' "ministry of alleviation and reconciliation" (*LG* 28) becomes key. The response of Cardinal Bernardin toward his accuser and John Paul II toward his assassin are examples of this kind of reconciling leadership. Martin Luther King, Jr., and Archbishop Oscar Romero are also models for leading by calling for repentance and acting in ways that would foster healing and reconciliation.

A corollary of this recognition of the church's imperfection is the awareness that the church should be striving for perfection, the second characteristic of the pilgrim church. The pilgrim church "groans . . . to be with Christ" and is constantly "urged to live more for Him" (*LG* 48). This desire for perfection comes from the recognition of imperfection. Thus, a church that recognizes officially and ritually its imperfection will (or should) also strive to become more perfect. In the example of a social sacrament of reconciliation, this striving is inherently part of the process. The recognition of the imperfection elicits a cry of sorrow from the institution. The striving for perfection, however, transforms this cry into action. It makes the cry sincere by engendering a commitment to repair the damage.

In the sexual abuse scandal, this striving would have flowed naturally from repentance. It would have sought the nature of the problem and the means to resolve it. It would have sought more than financial help for victims from the beginning and done more to protect innocents from abusing priests. As the problem became more widespread, the church would have addressed it more readily and effectively. In short, the church would have acted more expeditiously. As it was, the recognition of the scandal and the need for change seemed to come slowly and grudgingly, thereby exacerbating the wounds of the faithful, abused and non-abused alike.

Third, the pilgrim church is also a church of solidarity. It recognizes that its members who are currently alive are just one part of the church, which extends from the past and into the future. The pilgrim church is thus in solidarity with the believers on earth, the dead in purgatory and heaven, saints, martyrs, the blessed Virgin Mary, and all who are bound by mutual charity and praise the Trinity (*LG* 49-50). Thus, there are bonds that connect all members of the church, past, present, and future.

Lumen Gentium recognizes that if this solidarity were taken seriously, the devotion to the saints would become a high priority of all believers. The devotion would not take on the veneer of superstition that it so often does (burying a St. Joseph statue upside down in a lawn to sell a house, for example), but rather would be an act of getting to know a fellow member of the church (*LG* 51). It would be like cultivating a friendship. The logical extension, though, of devotion to the saints is devotion to Christians in the pews. Solidarity for the pilgrim church is not just devotional practices to the dead, but devotional practices to the living as well. Just as we are to cultivate friendships or, at least, familiarity with the saints, we are called to develop companionships with and compassion for other members of the church. Thus, it is a solidarity that connects the faithful to each other as well as to believers of the past and the future.

This practice of solidarity has great potential in fostering healing in the church, a healing greatly needed as a result of the sexual abuse scandal. If people recognized their devotion to one another and the demands of solidarity in a community, there would have been greater efforts on the part of the whole church community to reach out to victims. So often, it was left in the hands of the bishops, and their ability to reach out was usually compromised by the fact that they were involved in settlement processes. The community, though, could more readily reach out by providing safe spaces for victims to talk about what happened, thus helping victims feel accepted by the community.

The welcoming of conversation by members of the parish would also foster greater solidarity. Healing is a process and it is not completed with a financial settlement or even an apology. Rather, the process takes some time. If the community had an on-going conversation with victims, it would not only help the victims heal, but also bring the suffering of the victim to the whole community. The community would be able to share some of the victims' sufferings, grow in empathy toward them, and thereby become a community that better embodied solidarity. Moreover, the church could hardly slacken its efforts to protect its members, if the whole community shared in the suffering of the victims.

The last characteristic of the pilgrim church would be its accountability to Christ. Granted, the church is always accountable to Christ, yet the pilgrim church, focused as it is on its imperfection and striving for perfection, must confront the impending judgment of Christ in a unique way. The church must bear in mind that since it does not know the day or the hour of the judgment, it must remain "constantly vigilant" in its efforts toward perfection (*LG* 49). Moreover, because the judgment is a real judgment, issuing in rewards and condemnations, people must acknowledge and repent of their sins. Since the pilgrim church is also filled with imperfection, it must, before the judgment, seek to acknowledge its faults and rectify them. Finally, the hope is that if the church both repents of its imperfections and is vigilant toward perfection, it will not be condemned but rewarded. It will be "glorified" and "refashioned" and "conformed to Christ" (*LG* 49).

The pilgrim church's accountability to Christ thus takes on certain characteristics. The church must be honest in what it has done well and done poorly. This honesty will spur the vigilance toward perfection. The acknowledgment of failures is just the beginning of repentance, which ends in actions and reform. Finally, this practice of honesty also is a foretaste of the eschaton. It is the partial emergence of the church conformed to the God who is truth.

This notion of accountability is also where the pilgrim church model can sublate the insights of the liberal understanding of the church. While lay accountability does not inherently guarantee the prevention of abuse or the healing of victims, it greatly helps to ensure that any decisions made are public and not concealed. Lay involvement means there is less chance of quiet settlements and covering up for abusing priests. It makes it more likely that the church will be honest in its dealings with abused, abusers, and parishes where abusive priests served.

While this understanding of the pilgrim church is just a sketch of what an institution committed to healing and reconciliation might entail, I believe it shows that while the liberal and conservative perspectives have valuable insights that can help the church, their approaches are not expansive enough. They leave out valuable aspects of Vatican II, aspects that are extremely fruitful for dealing with the sexual abuse crisis.

Conclusion

I have argued in this paper that the commentators on the sexual abuse crisis fall into conservative or liberal perspectives on Vatican II and that these perspectives are inadequate for addressing the wounds caused by the scandal. I have proposed that an understanding of the church as a pilgrim church is not only more adequate for the task of healing, but one that can move us beyond the liberal and conservative dichotomy by incorporating the better insights of both. The need for this move is expressed well by Peter Steinfels, who declares: "Liberals and conservatives raise the same fears, make the same complaints, offer the same arguments as they did twenty years ago. Has the world stood still, one wonders, since the Second Vatican Council?"[45] I propose the pilgrim church model as an understanding of the church that, because of its dual emphasis upon recognition of its own imperfection and its firm commitment to strive to be more and more the sacrament of Christ's presence in the world, can help the church better address the issues of the contemporary world—issues like the sexual abuse crisis, but also the ethnic and religious wars around the world and other issues that desperately need healing and reconciliation. I propose the pilgrim church as a way of envisioning the church of the future.[46]

Notes

[1]My summaries are indebted to Peter Steinfels's liberal and conservative categories. See his *A People Adrift: The Crisis of the Roman Catholic Church in America* (New York: Simon & Schuster, 2003), 32-36.

[2]For works criticizing the limitations of conservative and liberal

ecclesiologies, see Dennis Doyle, *Communion Ecclesiology: Vision and Versions* (Maryknoll, N.Y.: Orbis Books, 2000) and Ormond Rush, *Still Interpreting Vatican II: Some Hermeneutical Principles* (Mahwah, N.J.: Paulist Press, 2004).

[3]For the basis of these statistics, see John Jay College of Criminal Justice's *The Nature and Scope of the Problem of Sexual Abuse of Minors by Catholic Priests and Deacons in the United States*, 2004. Available on-line: www.usccb.org/nrb/johnjaystudy/index.htm, downloaded 10/20/05. For a brief summary of these statistics see "Four Percent of Priests Accused Over 52 Years," *America* (March 15, 2004), 5-6.

[4]Steinfels, *A People Adrift*, 41.

[5]For standard books about the sexual abuse scandal, see Paul Dokecki, *The Clergy Sexual Abuse Crisis: Reform and Renewal in the Catholic Community* (Washington: Georgetown University Press, 2004); Donald Cozzens, *Sacred Silence: Denial and the Crisis in the Church* (Collegeville, Minn.: Liturgical Press, 2002); David Gibson, *The Coming Catholic Church: How the Faithful Are Shaping the New American Catholicism* (San Francisco: HarperSanFrancisco, 2003); Paul Lakeland, *Liberation of the Laity: In Search of an Accountable Church* (New York: Continuum, 2003); Francis Oakley and Bruce Russett, eds., *Governance, Accountability, and the Future of the Catholic Church* (New York: Continuum, 2004); Stephen Pope, ed., *Common Calling: The Laity and Governance of the Catholic Church* (Washington: Georgetown University Press, 2004); Peter Steinfels, *A People Adrift*; and George Weigel, *The Courage to Be Catholic* (New York: Basic Books, 2002). For a survey of most of the articles on the sexual abuse crisis, see James Keenan, "Notes on Moral Theology: Ethics and the Crisis of the Church," *Theological Studies* 66 (2005): 117-36.

[6]See Dokecki, *The Clergy Sexual Abuse Crisis*, 169, 198.

[7]Ibid., 204.

[8]Ibid., 170-76.

[9]Ibid., 204-205. Emphasis added.

[10]Weigel, *The Courage to Be Catholic*, 46-47.

[11]Ibid., 45.

[12]Ibid., 28.

[13]Ibid., 25.

[14]Ibid., 31.

[15]Ibid., 46. See also ibid., 93: "Just as priests who truly believe that they are what the Catholic Church teaches they are—living icons of the eternal priesthood of Jesus Christ—do not behave as sexual predators behave, so bishops who truly believe themselves to be what the Church teaches they are—successors of the apostles, who make present in the Church the headship of Christ the Good Shepherd—do not behave the way too many U.S. bishops have behaved: as managers, not as shepherds who are also authoritative teachers."

[16]See ibid., 151-55.

[17]See ibid., 155-66.

[18]See ibid., 191-96.

[19]See ibid., 29-32, 102-104.

[20]Ibid., 199-200.

[21]Ibid., 200.

[22]Ibid., 199. See also ibid., 97: "Each local bishop, the Council taught, exercises true headship in his diocese."

[23]See Steinfels, *A People Adrift*, 36. Steinfels indicates that of the four interpretative narratives of Vatican II—from ultra conservative to moderately conservative to moderately liberal to radical—he states that his position "would come closest to the third, with an admixture of the second, a touch of the fourth, and a whiff of the first."

[24]Ibid., 34.

[25]Ibid., 37.

[26]Ibid., 35.

[27]Ibid., 32.

[28]Ibid., 65.

[29]Ibid., 347.

[30]Ibid., 346.

[31]Ibid., 310.

[32]Ibid.

[33]Ibid., 309-12.

[34]Ibid., 313.

[35]Ibid., 341-42.

[36]Ibid., 353.

[37]Ibid., 353.

[38]Ibid., 46-47.

[39]Ibid., 342-45. Because of this stance, Steinfels is slightly suspicious of the "John Paul II" priests who, statistics indicate, are less consultative (see pages 321-22).

[40]On the waning interest in the sex abuse scandal of 1993 resulting from Bernardin's false accusation, see ibid., 60-61.

[41]See Weigel, *Courage to Be Catholic*, 102-104.

[42]For examples, see Robert Browning and Roy A. Reed, *Forgiveness, Reconciliation, and Moral Courage* (Grand Rapids: Eerdmans, 2004); Kay Carmichael, *Sin and Forgiveness: New Responses in a Changing World* (Burlington: Ashgate, 2003); Michael Duffey, *Sowing Justice, Reaping Peace: Case Studies of Racial, Religious, and Ethnic Healing around the World* (Lanham, Md.: Sheed & Ward, 2001) John Gruchy, *Reconciliation: Restoring Justice* (Minneapolis: Fortress Press, 2002); Raymond Helmick, Raymond Peterson, and Rodney Peterson, eds., *Forgiveness and Reconciliation: Religion, Public Policy, and Conflict Transformation* (Philadelphia: Templeton Foundation, 2001); Douglass Noll, *Peacemaking: Practicing at the Intersec-*

tion of Law and Human Conflict (Scottdale, Penn.: Herald Press, 2003); Stephen Pope, "The Convergence of Forgiveness and Justice: Lessons from El Salvador," *Theological Studies* 64 (2003): 812-35; Gerard Powers, Drew Christiansen, and Robert Hennemeyer, eds., *Peacemaking: Moral and Policy Challenges for a New World* (Washington: Georgetown University Press, 2004).

[43]Robert Schreiter, "Mediating Repentance, Forgiveness, and Reconciliation: What Is the Church's Role?" in *The Spirit in the Church and the Modern World*, ed. Bradford Hinze (Maryknoll, N.Y.: Orbis Books, 2004), 51-67. See pages 54-62 for his discussion of the institutional elements of forgiveness.

[44]William Bole, Drew Christiansen, and Robert Hennemeyer, *Forgiveness in International Politics: An Alternative Road to Peace* (Washington: United States Conference of Catholic Bishops, 2004).

[45]Steinfels, *A People Adrift*, 10.

[46]I would like to thank Christopher McMahon, Brian Doyle, Richard Gaillardetz, and two anonymous reviewers who all read drafts of this paper and offered extremely helpful suggestions.

Part II

THE CATHOLIC CHURCH ENGAGES THE MODERN WORLD

Straining toward Solidarity in a Suffering World

Gaudium et Spes "After Forty Years"

Christine Firer Hinze

> *The joys and hopes, the grief and anguish of the people of our time, especially of those who are poor or afflicted, are the joys and hopes, the grief and anguish of the followers of Christ as well. Nothing that is genuinely human fails to find an echo in their hearts. For theirs is a community of people united in Christ and guided by the Holy Spirit in their pilgrimage towards the Father's kingdom, bearers of a message of salvation for all of humanity. That is why they cherish a feeling of deep solidarity with the human race and its history.*[1]

"*Gaudium et spes, luctus et agor. . . .*" Looking back at a groundbreaking Catholic social document from the vantage point of forty years prompts thoughts of Pope Pius XI, who, in 1931, also looked back forty years to the 1891 encyclical of Pope Leo XIII, "On the Condition of the Working Class." Today we point to Leo's encyclical as marking the start of "official" modern Catholic social teaching—but that is in large part because, forty years later, Pius XI so powerfully remembered it. In 1891 Leo offered a Catholic response to the "new things," *rerum novarum*, economic, political, and cultural, in which people of the late nineteenth century were immersed, for good and ill. When, in 1931, Pius judged that it was time for another major social encyclical, the world was awash in a new set of "new things"—most of them troubling. Pius promulgated his letter "Forty Years After," or *Quadragesimo Anno*, in an atmosphere thick with economic and political crisis. With

Hitler's fascist Germany tightening an oppressive grip, Mussolini in power in Italy, and economic depression ravaging the world, things were very bad and were soon going to get worse. Pius's express purpose in *Quadragesimo Anno* was threefold: to *recall* the benefits and contributions of Leo's 1891 letter for a new generation, to *clarify and underline* its teachings concerning the church's social mission, and to *update* its message in light of changed historical circumstances. Pius also intended his letter to be a *call to action* to Catholic Christians, who were mandated to devote their heartfelt energies to "reconstructing the social order and perfecting it in conformance with the norms of the gospel."[2]

The Catholic social document whose fortieth anniversary we recall in 2005 is equally groundbreaking. The Pastoral Constitution on the Church in the Modern World was the last document approved by the Second Vatican Council, just days before its closing in December 1965. *Gaudium et Spes* is clearly in the tradition of modern Catholic social teaching inaugurated by Leo and affirmed by Pius. But it is also very different. *Quadragesimo Anno* was conceived and approved by the pope alone, after being drafted in secret by a lone consultant. *Gaudium et Spes* was not in the original plans for the Council and came about only because of spontaneous public interventions from the floor by three cardinals (among them Cardinal Montini of Milan who would soon become Pope Paul VI) who argued that the dogmatic constitution on the church, *Lumen Gentium,* needed to be complemented by a second document devoted to the relationship of the church to the modern world. After numerous drafts, much floor debate, four major rewritings, and thousands of amendments, the Pastoral Constitution on the Church in the Modern World was adopted on December 4, 1965, by 1,710 of the 2,200 bishops present, and approved by Pope Paul VI.[3]

Pius's 1931 letter was longer than its predecessor by a third, but *Gaudium et Spes* at seventy-two pages is much longer, "indeed the longest document ever produced by any of the 21 ecumenical councils in a 2000 year history!"[4] But it is the contrasting methods, tones, and emphases of the 1931 and 1965 documents that illustrate most dramatically that *Gaudium et Spes* has taken a new approach. Pius confidently underlined the supreme authority of the pontiff and the church's competence to instruct the world on the moral dimensions of economic and political life. *Gaudium et Spes* addressed the peoples of the modern world as a compassionate companion, eager to dialogue and to humbly share the wisdom about life's meaning afforded by the gift of faith. Pius XI addressed his letter to bishops, clergy, and Catholics; applied natural law categories to the social issues of the day; and envisaged phalanxes of the faithful joining in "Catholic action" associations that, under the clergy's guidance, would comprise a sort of spiritual militia to advance Christian social reforms. *Gaudium et Spes*, by contrast, spoke in biblical and personalist language and called on all people of good will to join in efforts to create social conditions consonant with the dignity of every person. In 1931 Pius represented a church that handed down the answers concerning social justice and spiritual well-being, which the faithful were to apply to the situations of daily life. In 1965 *Gaudium et Spes* attempted to correlate modern concerns, anxieties, and questions with a coherent and persuasive vision of human nature and destiny illuminated by the mysteries of faith, and courteously invited its listeners to discover the humanity and attractiveness of the moral and spiritual truths Christians treasure. Finally, Pius XI envisaged the good social order as explicitly Christian, indeed, Catholic. *Gaudium et Spes* emphasized the correspondence and interpenetration of authentically human and truly Christian values and practices. It affirmed that the sought-for social order may exist and even thrive in conditions where both religious freedom and the rightful autonomy of the secular sphere are respected.[5]

David O'Brien writes that while in 1931 Pope Pius XI "spoke for a more triumphal church to a world on the point of despair," Pope John XXIII "addressed a weary and worried world from the standpoint of a more humble and chastened church." In the Pastoral Constitution on the Church in the Modern World, "the church speaks to issues from a standpoint deeply within the society, winning support by persuasion and seeking common ground with others, including non-Christians."[6] Thus in *Gaudium et Spes* the Council realized John XXIII's and Paul VI's desire for a new posture toward the world that would be neither triumphalistic, isolationist, nor combative, but instead humble, engaged, and dialogical.

This essay attempts very modestly to emulate Pius's way of remembering in *Quadragesimo Anno* by lifting up a critical remembrance of the Pastoral Constitution on the Church in the Modern

World and its significance for subsequent Catholic ethics. My thesis is this: *Gaudium et Spes* introduced a particular way of framing social ethics, and enacting social mission; that is one of its most important, and (especially in the affluent North and West) still undeveloped, legacies. A scarlet thread running through this pastoral constitution is a growing recognition of *solidarity* or, as I will call it, incarnational solidarity, as an essential key for authentically Christian and human living in today's world. In a contemporary context wherein systemic human suffering bespeaks the critical need to recognize, confront, and work to transform killing ideologies and social structures, incarnational solidarity, as depicted in *Gaudium et Spes* and developed in the years since the Council, denotes the personal and communal virtue that the pursuit of justice entails.

I will offer, first, a précis of what *Gaudium et Spes* contributes toward this "new idea" of incarnational solidarity. I will then provide a glimpse at its post-conciliar reception and development in three theological loci. The final part of the essay focuses on challenges facing persons seeking to grasp and enact incarnational solidarity in affluent, first-world settings such as U.S. Catholic colleges and universities, and considers ways those working in Catholic academe might contribute to addressing those challenges.

Primary Contributions of *Gaudium et Spes* to a Catholic Ethic of Solidarity

Four interrelated features of *Gaudium et Spes* stake out the foundations for a theology and ethic of solidarity for contemporary Catholics and their neighbors.

Dialogical Engagement with the "Signs of the Times"

First we are struck by *Gaudium et Spes*'s inductive, empathetic, and dialogical attention to "the signs of the times" as the starting point for speaking of the relationship between church and society.[7] Following its famous opening affirmation of human and Christian solidarity, *Gaudium et Spes* reaches out to connect with its contemporary audience through a vivid portrayal of the panoply of good things and evils, discoveries and perplexities, triumphs and failures that mark the experiences and shape the mood of the late twentieth century, particularly in the modern West.

On the one hand, *Gaudium et Spes* describes an era marked by new and deeper understandings of the human mind and the laws of society, astonishing advances in science and technology, the spread of culture and abundance for many, and great inroads in freedom and unity. Simultaneously, there are persisting, often shockingly deteriorating, problems. Amid unprecedented wealth, "huge proportions of the world's citizens are still tormented by hunger and poverty." Economic disparities and illiteracy among the poor have increased at alarming rates. War and violence have ravaged the century. Political injustice and oppression mar the lives of millions. Social, cultural, and racial divisions and misunderstandings both result from and cause oppression, violence, and poverty (4). People experience confusion and anxiety as they struggle to make sense of this mélange of experiences and to respond in coherent and meaningful ways.

Adding to the pressure is a new, modern conviction: that humanity can, and therefore must, take action to establish social arrangements that respect the dignity proper to every person. "Now for the first time in history people are not afraid to think that cultural benefits are for all and should be available to everybody." These claims are symptomatic of a deeper longing: "Persons and societies thirst for a full and free life worthy of humanity; one in which they can employ for the common good all that the modern world can offer them so abundantly" (9).[8]

In the face of a heightened sense of capability and responsibility, coupled with perplexity about how to make good on the deeper desires of the human heart, many find themselves overwhelmed by a situation riven by "tensions, imbalances, and contradictions."[9] The modern world "shows itself at once powerful and weak, capable of doing what is noble and what is base, disposed to freedom and slavery, progress and decline, amity and hatred" (9). "Buffeted between anxiety and hope," people are driven to ask the most fundamental questions: "What is humanity? What is this sense of sorrow, of evil, of death, which continues to exist despite so much progress? What purpose have these victories purchased at so high a cost? What can people offer to society, and what can they expect from it? What follows this human life?" (10).

In a trope that recurs through the document, this crescendo of existential questioning draws a response that points to the God of

Jesus Christ. In Christ "can be found the key, the focal point and the goal of humanity, as well as of all human history." Beneath the swirls and surfaces of modern experience lie firm verities and values, and these too have God in Christ as their foundation. In *Gaudium et Spes,* therefore, the church proposes to enter into dialogue with the world "in order to help shed light on the mystery of humanity, and to cooperate in finding solutions to the problems of our time" (10).[10]

A Comprehensive Theological and Anthropological Framework for Articulating the Contemporary Christian Mission in the World

Second, *Gaudium et Spes* offers a comprehensive, biblically grounded, theological framework for the Christian mission in late modernity. It is a framework that boldly proclaims the confluence of the genuinely human and the genuinely Christian, articulated from the perspective of a religious faith that "throws a new light on everything."[11] Authentic faith "directs the mind to solutions that are fully human."[12] Christianity's holistic, faith-based response to the existential questions of our day lays bare the fact that "People of God and the human race in whose midst it lives are interdependent, and render mutual service to each other." Thus the mission of the church "shows its religious and by that fact its supremely human character" (11).[13]

The linchpin of *Gaudium et Spes*'s interpretive schema is a social anthropology focused on the God-given dignity of the human person. Human dignity, uniquely personal while grounded and realized in community, is the juncture at which the Christian message meets the world, and the world connects with the church. *Gaudium et Spes* depicts the human person and its inviolable dignity as socially embedded: my good and the common good—and conversely, my harm and the "common harm"—are inextricably meshed. This deep communal understanding of human nature and flourishing is distinctly Catholic; its significance cannot be overestimated.[14]

Gaudium et Spes's humanly focused message about the meaning of life is equally christological. Its affirmation of the human person as created in the image and likeness of God and destined for fulfillment in God goes hand-in-hand with an accessible description of sin and the fall's split or taint of the human heart as at the root of the evils, divisions, and destructive patterns in which contemporary people find themselves entangled. For Christians, human dignity, rooted in humanity's call to communion with God, is healed, restored, and supremely exemplified in the person, life, death, and resurrection of Jesus Christ.

Walter Kasper argues that

> The relationship between christology and anthropology in *Gaudium et Spes* can be . . . defined in three ways: as an affirmation of everything that is right, true, good, and lovely about human beings; as a prophetic criticism of all forms of alienation in human beings; and finally as the creative surpassing of everything that is possible in purely human terms, and thus as the completion and fulfillment of human beings in God.[15]

An oft-quoted passage in *GS* 24 affirms that "In reality it is only in the mystery of the Word made flesh that the mystery of humanity truly becomes clear." With Kasper, William McDonough cautions that a univocally christological interpretation of the document "forgets to start on modernity's turf—which is the turf of humanity and human experience," and in that way fails to keep the church *in* the modern world." Yet an exclusive focus on *Gaudium et Spes*'s personalism and moral message commits the opposite error by forgetting to "move beyond modernity's paralyzed anxiety in the face of death" and the other perplexities that confront it, and thus failing "to keep the modern world *in* some context that can give it a reason to go on."[16] It is by means of a christological move, but one engaged "from below," that *Gaudium et Spes* plants and keeps the church in its modern context.

Gaudium et Spes can so confidently tether the human to the Christian because of a shocking revealed truth—that the Divine, despite human depravity and failure, is not only *for* humanity, but has, in the person of Jesus of Nazareth, become completely and fully one with it and the human journey. This mystery of the incarnation grounds the Pastoral Constitution's affirmation of the worthiness of the human, the material, and the historical. In the incarnation we find solidarity's deepest theological ground and warrant. The redemptive economy of Christ's life, death, and resurrection, presently efficacious even as it awaits eschatological fulfillment in God's final kingdom "when every tear will be wiped away," blazes the path that disciples are invited to follow by emulating Jesus' loving solidarity with God and neighbor.[17]

Gaudium et Spes's depiction of the solitary Christian mission eschews complete continuity or discontinuity between the present order and the age to come, but focuses on their tension-yet-connection. From the point of view of this "incarnational humanism," writes John Courtney Murray, "The heavens and the earth are not destined for an eternal dust-heap, but for a transformation. There will be a new heaven and a new earth; and those who knew them once will recognize them, for all their newness."[18] Expectation of a new earth should not weaken, but rather stimulate, Christians' concern for cultivating this one. "For here grows the body of a new human family, a body which even now is able to give some kind of foreshadowing of the new age" (39).

Engagement with Concrete Issues in Family, Culture, Economy, and Politics

Third, *Gaudium et Spes* does not limit itself to theological generalities, but in Part II reaffirms and develops church teaching on particular facets of social life: marriage and family, culture, economy, political life, war and peace. By including the material in Part II, the Council bishops made it clear that, as fresh as its humanistic emphasis and conversational rhetoric might have been, *Gaudium et Spes* did not signal a retreat by the church from the risk of taking specific, and at times controversial, stands on real life matters across the gamut of societal spheres. Part II suggests ways that solidarity is to be envisaged and practiced in light of the particular, contemporary exigencies of these various spheres and relations.

A New and Thoroughgoing Christian Mandate: "Incarnational Solidarity"

Fourth, *Gaudium et Spes* presents solidarity as an urgent modern Christian moral and spiritual mandate. Starting with its emblematic opening words, as David Hollenbach notes, "this theme of solidarity is a *leitmotif* throughout the entire Pastoral Constitution."[19] Though nowhere systematically developed, the notion saturates the text. Solidarity emerges in the document as a fact, a norm, and an embodied vocation. [20]

Solidarity as fact. Solidarity is, first, the fact of human interconnection, the "is" of human interdependence that grounds the "ought" of an affirmative response to it.[21] We are in this together, *Gaudium et Spes* contends, and we each have things to give to and receive/learn from one another (40-45).[22] Though simple in concept—"because we belong to each other, we are called to live with and for one another"—the implications of *de facto* solidarity are far-reaching and complex. At root it is a traditional idea, a way of stating the basis of the Christian relation to the neighbor. Yet, in late modern circumstances, responding affirmatively to the fact of solidarity by living as if we truly belonged to one another is a radical prospect too often honored in the breach (4, 5).

Solidarity as norm and virtue. More than a fact to be recognized, solidarity is a norm whose realization requires appropriate dispositions and patterns of action. The spirit of interdependence and co-humanity that breathes through the pages of *Gaudium et Spes* bespeaks and urges a responsive way of seeing, judging, and acting in relation to these realities. It points, in short, to solidarity as a *virtue.*[23] The essence of this particular virtue is to recognize, to acknowledge, and to take appropriate responsibility for our *de facto* interdependence as human beings and as children of the same God. In Richard Rodriguez's terminology, this means waking up to our "we-ness" and living as if it were real.[24] *Gaudium et Spes* thus challenges its readers to transcend individualistic morality and embrace social responsibilities. "All must consider it their sacred duty to count social obligations among their chief duties today and observe them as such. For the more closely the world comes together, the more widely do people's obligations transcend their particular groups and extend to the whole world. This will be realized only if individuals and groups practice moral and social virtues and foster them in social living" (30).

For Christians, this socially responsible way of living is a way of love. God is love, and "the fundamental law of human perfection and consequently the transformation of the world is the new commandment of love." Christ assures those who trust in the love of God that "the way of love is open to all and that the effort to establish a universal communion will not be in vain"(27). This social friendship or love is expressed in occasions of "sincere self gift" for the sake of the neighbor and the common good (24). *Gaudium et Spes*'s insistence that the human person "can never discover oneself except through a sincere gift of self" illumines the inextricable bond between personal flourishing and loving, serving interrelation that the practice of solidarity honors.

Strikingly, solidarity enacted in love is reserved not only for important matters, but—and this is mentioned repeatedly—it must be exercised above all in the ordinary circumstances of daily life. Also mentioned repeatedly: this is a love that is to be directed particularly toward those most in need: the poor, the afflicted. And Christ's example of loving unto death teaches that a lifestyle of neighbor love will require that we carry the crosses "which flesh and the world inflict on the shoulders of any who seek after peace and justice" (38; see 30, 32).

Solidarity as incarnational. The solidarity *Gaudium et Spes* urges cannot remain simply an ideal, or an interior attitude.[25] It involves the immersion of bodies, the expenditure of time and energies in the midst of the blood, sweat, and tears of the real world, in practices of presence and service. Incarnational solidarity entails cultivating concrete, habitual ways of acknowledging our we-ness by being *with* the neighbor, especially the suffering and needy neighbor.

Two points about solidarity's incarnational character merit special emphasis. First, authentic incarnational solidarity differs from cheap "virtual" or sentimental forms of solidarity proffered by a consumerist culture and economy. As described in Vincent Miller's *Consuming Religion,* virtual solidarity substitutes sentimental gestures that are primarily acts of consumption for political action or actual encounter: "The uncomfortable, challenging, disruptive aspects of face-to-face, shoulder-to-shoulder solidarity are eliminated." Virtual solidarity "does not disrupt; instead it legitimates the subjectivity of the consumer through the payoff of moral sentiment." In contrast, incarnational solidarity is practical, embodied, and comes at a cost.

> Unlike the symbolic solidarity of consumption, real solidarity requires the effort of departing from the well-worn channels of our lifestyle niches. We must make time in our daily routines, travel to parts of town we do not frequent, struggle with language barriers, wrestle with just what we

> want from or for these other people who have their own lives and projects. This is both inconvenient and excruciating.[26]

Second, incarnational solidarity involves a humble, kenotic posture that can help traverse divisions caused by disparities of power. To truly be "for" in a way that avoids paternalism, sentimentality, or a protected and aloof throwing of alms to the poor, whom we want to keep their distance, requires a praxis of humble presence and collaboration. Practices of solidarity must honor what Peter-Hans Kolvenbach calls "the logic of the incarnation," whereby "Jesus did not cling to his divine station, but emptied himself of every privilege in order to be one of many." Such practices make the goal of doing "for" another the attainment of mutuality, of communion, or at least the potential thereof. [27] Thus understood, solidarity has a hierarchy-melting, deeply egalitarian thrust.[28]

The gracious, vulnerable, and courteous solidarity of God with and for humanity revealed in Jesus Christ, then, lays down the pattern of solidarity to which Christian disciples are also called. The devotional image of the sacred heart of Jesus offers another moving symbol of incarnational solidarity: the compassionate love of Jesus who invites followers to rest in and learn from the one who is "gentle and humble of heart" (Mt 11:28-30).[29]

Reception and Development of *Gaudum et Spes* on Solidarity

General Reception

From its promulgation, *Gaudium et Spes* has been hailed as a watershed document that repositioned the church in relation to the modern world as a dialogue partner and companion, eager to shoulder its part in the collaborative quest for social justice and human flourishing. It has also drawn criticism. Some have faulted the Pastoral Constitution for reflecting a predominantly first-world perspective and a concomitant tendency to sidestep strongly prophetic social positions. *Gaudium et Spes*'s genesis owed much to the presence and voices of bishops representing poor nations of the world. But for many, the Council document evinces a deep compassion *for* the poor but no clear indication of solidarity *with* the poor. Donal Dorr argues that only in the wake of the Council, with the rise of liberationist movements and theology, has the church become more aware that "it is not enough to be *for* the poor; one must discover what it means to be *with* the poor. Only then can one experience what it is like to be humanly weak and powerless, but still to be powerful in the awareness that God is on one's side."[30]

From another direction has come the charge that *Gaudium et Spes* takes a too irenic view of the modern world and of the compatibility between the gospel and the values of modern (Western) culture.[31] Joseph Komonchak sees this criticism as indicative of a post-conciliar ascendance of a more Augustinian interpretation of history and the church, as distinct from a Thomistic interpretation that predominated during the Council.[32] In fact, however, both Augustinians and Thomists participated in the drafting process, and the resulting document combines both optimism in tone about church-world compatibility and a more dialectical emphasis on the church and world in tension. Richard Schenk thus suggests that post-conciliar reception of *Gaudium et Spes* has developed in two waves, "beginning with a period of roughly two decades in which the more optimistic reading dominated its interpretation," followed by twenty years during which what Charles Moeller in 1969 described as *Gaudium et Spes*'s more "dialectical, even paradoxical aspect" has been brought to the fore.[33]

A third trajectory of criticism points out the relatively weak impact of conciliar social teaching, including its message of incarnational solidarity, on the lived practices of the faithful, particularly in the affluent West. Contributing to this is what we might call the "Teflon problem," the phenomenon wherein the "nice idea" of solidarity appeals, but seems to slide off its listeners leaving no noticeable scratches or marks. Developing a line of analysis found in the writings of Pope John Paul II, Vincent Miller and others trace Catholic social teaching's tepid impact to the logic and habits of interpretation inculcated by a consumer culture whose mode of existence is focused on "having" and consuming, rather than "being" or serving (see *GS* 35). Received in cultures formed by the overriding dynamics of commodification, Catholic social teaching's counter-messages often fall on well-meaning yet functionally deaf ears, blind eyes, and calloused hearts. Clearly this inefficacy is symptomatic of the need for conversion. But Miller contends, chillingly, that the pervasive, abstracting *habitus* of consumerist capitalism so badly gums up even the "conversion" works that Catholics' capacity to embrace and enact their own social teaching is grievously compromised.[34]

Three Nodes of Reception

Movement toward a church of incarnational solidarity has occurred fitfully in the four decades since the close of Vatican II. Three loci or "nodes" of reception help shed light on how this new way of conceiving and enacting social mission has been advancing, and on the obstacles it has encountered. These loci of reception are rooted in three different contexts: 1) Latin American liberation theology reflects the poverty-stricken majority or "two-thirds" world; 2) the writings of Pope John Paul II are shaped by his experience in what was till the 1990s known as the "second" world of communist eastern Europe; and 3) believers in western Europe and North America seek to grapple with solidarity while ensconced in affluent "first-world" circumstances.

Liberation Theology

The cause of solidarity has been developed most originally and powerfully in the movements and theologies of liberation that emerged first in Latin America in the 1960s, along with other liberationist movements and theologies (focused on gender and racial/ethnic, and later, ecological justice)[35] that have emerged in the decades since the Council. Inspired by the groundwork laid down in *Gaudium et Spes*, liberationist theologians and their communities have advanced an understanding of solidarity that accentuates the need to detect, analyze, and dismantle unjust structures and the ideologies that support them, with the concomitant recognition that combating these unjust structures requires facing conflict, struggle, and suffering.[36]

Liberationist movements and theologies have made at least five major contributions to a theology and ethics of solidarity over the past forty years, contributions that have directly influenced official teaching and Christian practice. First, liberation theologians have successfully advanced a hermeneutical and practical option for the poor as a constitutive feature of solidarity. While solidarity is fundamentally inclusive in its thrust, in a world riven by injustice, it requires in each particular instance active preference for, side-taking with, the poor, oppressed, or most vulnerable.[37] Second, solidarity entails recognizing and combating structures of sin. Liberation theology has offered the church a more profound apprehension of the social and structural nature of humanity and its embodiment in dynamic patterns of relationship for good or ill, patterns that exert influence and power to the benefit of some and the harm of others, and which become entrenched and difficult to change. Third, solidarity requires, but cannot stop at, ideology critique or consciousness-raising. It propels people into transformative action aimed at dismantling or reconstructing unjust social structures and relations, in the interest of creating conditions conducive to an inclusive common good in which members can not just survive, but flourish.

Fourth, as Gustavo Gutiérrez has written, "It is an oft-noted fact that *Gaudium et Spes* in general offers a rather irenic description of the human situation; it touches up the uneven spots, smoothes the rough edges, avoids the more conflictual aspects, and stays away from the sharper confrontations among social classes and countries."[38] Far more than the bishops at Vatican II, liberation theologians and movements have faced the fact that committing oneself to practices of solidarity will result in conflict. Conflict is not the goal of solidarity. But Roman Catholicism's great tradition of synthesis and perennial concern for social order have made it too eager to focus on organic unity and social harmony. Challenging and working to change an unjust status quo demands a tolerance for disagreement, resistance, and conflict—including among the very people one is working with and whose good one may seek to advance.[39]

Fifth, solidarity requires a spiritual and practical openness to accepting suffering and the cross. Those who take sides with the poor and the underdog will pay a price. Solidarity is not possible without a willingness to accept suffering for the sake of the kingdom in which Christians hope. Brazilian theologian Rubem Alvez writes: "The two, suffering and hope, live from each other. Suffering without hope produces resentment and despair. Hope without suffering creates illusions, naiveté, and drunkenness." The discipline of working for a more just world requires that we must live by the love of what we will never see. "Such disciplined love is what has given prophets, revolutionaries and saints the courage to die for the future they envisaged. They make their own bodies the seed of their higher hope."[40]

Post-conciliar Papal and Episcopal Teaching

A second major resource for Catholics' evolving understanding of solidarity since 1965 has been papal and episcopal teaching. The social teaching of Pope Paul VI, the Latin American and other regional bishops' conferences, and the pontificate of Pope John Paul II have both inspired and been nourished by on-the-ground solidary initiatives and theological reflections throughout the world. For reasons of space I will limit myself to brief comments on the contribution of Pope John Paul II.[41]

Pope John Paul sounded *Gaudium et Spes*'s theme of Christian-human solidarity as early as his first encyclical (*Redemptor Hominis*, 1979) where he identified the good news of the gospel with "amazement at human worth," stating that, "the name for that deep amazement at human worth and dignity is the Gospel, that is to say: the Good News. It is also called Christianity. This amazement determines the Church's mission in the world, and, perhaps even more so, in the modern world" (*Redemptor Hominis* 10). Repeatedly over the course of his pontificate, John Paul II invoked *GS* 22 and 24, texts that identify the authentically human with the authentically Christian, Christ the Incarnate Word as the fulfillment of human longings, and genuine self-realization as resting in "the sincere gift of self." Also frequently quoted is *GS* 27: "Everybody should look upon his or her neighbor without any exception as another self, bearing in mind especially their neighbor's life and the means needed for a dignified way of life, lest they follow the example of the rich man who ignored Lazarus, who was poor."

Pope John Paul's social writings from the late 1980s underscore the fact that solidarity comprises a preferential option for the poor.[42] His 1987 encyclical "On Social Concern" observes that the growing awareness of interdependence among individuals and nations today prompts a moral response (*Sollicitudo Rei Socialis* 37-38). When such interdependence becomes recognized, the proper, "correlative response as a moral and social attitude, as a 'virtue', is solidarity. This is not a feeling of vague compassion or shallow distress at the misfortunes of so many people, both near and far . . . but rather a firm and persevering determination to commit oneself to the common good . . . to the good of all and of each individual. . ." (*SRS* 39).

For John Paul II, solidarity involves active collaboration among rich and poor and among the poor themselves. In particular, Christians and the church are called to take their stand beside the poor—"to become a church of and for the poor . . . while keeping in mind the common good."[43] Ultimately, solidarity is a religious virtue, the "social face of Christian charity" (*SRS* 40). Solidarity, the late pontiff argued forcefully, is the primary antidote to and weapon for confronting and dismantling the sinful social structures and patterns that stunt and destroy the well-being and very survival of so many today.[44]

"First-world" Theology and Practice

Several important trajectories of reflection concerning solidarity have emerged in post-conciliar first-world regions of Europe and North America. In Europe, political theologians such as Johann-Baptist Metz offer trenchant criticisms of how bourgeois culture fosters mindsets and habits that shirk solidarity.[45] In the United States, indigenous liberationist theologies, African American, Hispanic/Latino American, feminist, and others, are giving voice to traditionally marginalized and oppressed communities and producing multitextured reflections on solidarity's promise and pitfalls. Another powerful form of Christian solidarity with the poor continues in communities of radical Catholic witness in the tradition of Dorothy Day and the Catholic Worker movement, and still others in the ongoing history of direct service to and advocacy for the poor in a range of Catholic institutions. Yet despite these important examples (each with its own strengths, problems, and critics), in the affluent West and North the growth of an ethic of incarnational solidarity remains stunted. One key reason for this has been mentioned: a consumer capitalist culture whose kudzu-like values and practices so crowd the landscape of daily lives that solidarity finds precious little ground in which to take root.

Gaudium et Spes and Solidarity Forty Years

Reading *Gaudium et Spes* in 2005 leads to an inescapable conclusion: the joys and hopes, griefs and anxieties, and the afflictions of the world community described by *Gaudium et Spes* forty years ago have changed far too little. In many cases, the problems it highlighted have only further deteriorated. Two glaring examples are the persistence of abject poverty and huge increasing economic disparities.

Even a glance at contemporary global economic and social conditions reveals a shameful picture of inequality and suffering. World Bank statistics indicate that, "each year 10 million children die before their fifth birthday. More than 100 million do not attend primary school. And more than a billion people lack access to a safe source of water." As many as 2.7 billion people, or 38 percent of the world's population, live on less than $2 day in a state of absolute poverty, defined as a situation in which the food for each day is constantly in doubt.[46]

The scandal of poverty decried in *GS* 27 and 29 persists today, as 2.7 billion people in absolute poverty suffer amid yawning global inequalities that have been visualized in the graphic known as "the champagne glass of world income." At the wide brim of the "glass," 20 percent of the earth's population is receiving and using 82.7 percent of the world's income. This leaves 17.3 percent for the other 80 percent of the world to share. The poorest 20 percent share only 1.4 percent of the world's income.[47]

This perverted edifice is secured and reinforced by twin ideological dynamics. In a first dynamic, ingrained habits of abstraction and "otherization" are sustained amid varying concatenations of racism, sexism, and classism. In a second, culture is permeated by the bewitching effects of commodification and the consumerist ethos. These criss-crossing influences gird and stabilize sinful social structures that enmesh both rich and poor. The resulting "champagne glass" of injustice imprisons its victims in one way, its beneficiaries in another (see *GS* 27).

This morally poisonous otherizing/consumerist mix (often cloaked by the rhetoric of "individual freedom") allows advantaged citizens to dismiss or ignore the suffering of people they are encouraged to regard as remote, different, or not as valuable as themselves. Consumerist culture uses seduction and misdirection to lay a soothing, obfuscating mantle over systemic injustices that solidarity would expose. Its participants are fitted with Oz-like lenses, fed a stream of distractions and novelties, and situated in a 24/7 schedule of work-spend-consume that virtually insures they will "pay no attention" to the suffering multitudes behind the curtain. As Miller's *Consuming Religion* details, an especially pernicious aspect of the consumerist *habitus* is its knack for cheerfully appropriating and commodifying, thereby disarming and domesticating its own opposition and critique—including religious critique. In analogous fashion, the practices, wisdom, and artifacts of other peoples are also appropriated, repackaged, and sold as cultural "experiences" so that, in bell hooks's pungent phrase, in place of respectful encounter and listening that marks solidarity, consumers end up simply "eating the other."[48] If this analysis is on target, and I believe it is, overcoming obstacles to incarnational solidarity will require systematic intellectual and practical attention to understanding and combating these powerful, too often invisible cultural dynamics.

Confronted with all this, what are Catholic Christians, academics, and citizens to do? Most fundamentally, I suggest, we face a choice between two postures for living in the interdependent and fractured world of the early twenty-first century. A first option is to withhold one's mind and heart from (or anesthetize them to) solidarity and its demands. There are many varieties of this "clenched" living. Hollenbach describes one common pattern in the United States wherein people attempt to construct isolated parallel universes, while civic life atrophies into "disengaged tolerance," and society is reduced to "regulated ways of leaving one another alone."[49] Juliet Schor, John Kavanaugh, and Vincent Miller elaborate consumer culture's role in fostering such delusory isolationism, in particular by alienating us from the flesh-and-blood connections that hide behind our commodified world, and by sucking time, attention, and energies into privatized, work-spend-consume patterns. In such a milieu, even those who do choose social engagement can fall prey to a more subtle version of clenched living that Sharon Welch describes as "an ethic of control"—a posture that limits "helping" to actions according to terms set by the more powerful "helper," who also has the luxury of exit at any point.[50]

The alternative, necessary for genuine solidarity, is to deliberately cultivate a posture of "unclenched living." Unclenched living makes possible the receptivity and initiative that building an equitable, inclusive common good requires. It includes a commitment to humble, dialogical listening and speaking across religious and cultural boundaries that Hollenbach calls intellectual solidarity.[51] Unclenched living shakes off fear and inertia to engage with others in what Welch calls an ethic of risk. Such an ethic embodies solidarity by envisioning and taking action meant not to "solve" overwhelming injustices, but to nurture hope by creating seedbeds and staging grounds for further transformative action.[52]

The incarnational solidarity adumbrated in *Gaudium et Spes* remains an urgent calling for Christians today. Walter Kasper's comment of fifteen years ago remains apt: "[T]oday the reception of the Second Vatican Council is by no means behind us but in many respects still before us."[53] Certainly the limited reception of *Gaudium et Spes*'s teaching on incarnational solidarity, especially among elites, has directly to do with its price—the cost of discipleship that confronts us today.[54] Faced with this cost, our contemporary hanging back at the invitation to solidarity evokes the excruciating ambivalence on the brink of moral conversion that Augustine dissects so dramatically in Book 8 of his *Confessions*.

What can be done to address this impasse? To employ Lonerganian language, it seems we must first attend to the unclenching of our spirits by opening ourselves to the dynamic of ongoing religious conversion, cultivating receptivity to the gift of the transforming love of God that floods our hearts through the Holy Spirit (Rom 5:3-8). Religious conversion orients and clarifies intellectual conversion, which consists in receptivity to seeking and discovering the truth. Religious conversion also orients and clarifies moral conversion, which consists in receptivity and commitment to living a life oriented by genuine value.[55] Grounded in the "de-clenching" pedagogy of these continuing conversions, advantaged first-worlders may then take the next step and approach the demands of solidarity using our God-given human capabilities to "be attentive, be intelligent, be reasonable, and be responsible-loving."[56] Attention to these imperatives can orient and empower efforts to advance incarnational solidarity, the virtue requisite to long-term commitment to social transformation, across familial, academic, pastoral, civic, economic, and cultural arenas.

Be attentive. Incarnational solidarity entails a way of attending to reality that resists the distraction, abstraction, alienation, and apathetic hedonism cultivated by late capitalist consumerism. Aided by concrete encounters and local engagement with the poor and vulnerable, a bedrock practice of solidarity can attune one's mind and heart to the *de facto* connections among human persons in contemporary social circumstances.[57] The discipline of attentiveness—intellectual, spiritual, moral—helps disclose bonds with others around the world, and the patterns of exploitation, oppression, and neglect in which those in advantaged situations are, if often unintentionally, implicated.

Be intelligent. Awakening to the social crisis of human suffering and to our spiritual, moral, and institutional connections with those who suffer can create a powerful temptation to flee or withdraw. Incarnational solidarity counters this "flight from understanding" by cultivating steady habits of asking questions, seeking information, and discovering insights that help clarify those connections and uncover avenues to their more just comportment. *GS* 31 speaks of the need for ongoing *education for solidarity*—above all, of the need to educate young people from all social backgrounds if we are to produce "the kind of great souled men and women so urgently needed today, men and women who are not only highly cultured but generous in spirit as well."

Be reasonable. Driving beyond understanding, incarnational solidarity entails discerning, in dialogue with others, what form justice and right-relations must take in changing social and temporal contexts. Judging solidarity's requirements calls for an intelligent assessment of the facts and values relevant to this particular situation and for practical wisdom that engages real possibilities while acknowledging limitations.[58] Enacting solidarity in one's particular context cannot mean deciding, doing, or changing everything; but neither does it mean deciding, doing or changing nothing. Coming to judgment is a crucial step, and it tests the presence of the virtue. Solidarity is only enacted in moving from awareness and understanding to conscientious judgments concerning what should be done and what one can do.

Be responsible. Responsibility is the crown of freedom, and it entails action. In the face of our interdependence in a suffering world, we must respond, even though our responses may be imperfect or later proved wrong. *Gaudium es Spes* wisely points out that responsibility requires lived circumstances that enable people to become conscious of their dignity and capable of rising to their destiny of love of God and neighbor. Both acute deprivation and excessive advantage undermine this capacity. "For freedom is often crippled by extreme destitution, just as it can wither in an ivory-tower isolation brought on by overindulgence in the good things of life. It can, however, be strengthened by accepting the inevitable constraints of social life, by undertaking the manifold demands of human relationships, and by service to the community at large" (31). Being responsible, then, means moving from judgment to embodied engagement, overcoming fear and inertia to risk solidarity's costs, and act.

Christian solidarity, according to Mexican theologian Javier Jímenez Limón, must above all be active solidarity with the victims of humanly caused socio-historical injustice. Solidarity "takes action against the technically avoidable sufferings of others without becoming paralyzed through fear of its own suffering, which such action may provoke." For, "if solidarity among human beings does not include the victims, it becomes perverted into a pact or an interested deal between the evildoers among themselves. . . ."[59] Rembert Weakland, speaking of Vatican II's legacy, adds: "We need to accept that if the future is going to be hopeful for all of us, then we have to indeed accept the Cross right now and suffering."[60]

The Next Forty Years

Along with a wealth of other contributions to the post-conciliar church, *Gaudium et Spes* bequeathed a daunting challenge: to discover and shape a way of life that actually incarnates the we-ness our human and Christian experience discloses. Why, then, forty years later, do Catholics so often fail to experience and enact solidarity as a live and practicable norm?

David O'Brien has posed the question more broadly, asking why modern Catholic social teaching has remained the church's "best kept secret." His answer gives pause: "The best kept secret remains secret because it is presented [either] under a guise that makes it so demanding that it negates lay life, or . . . so modest that it makes no real difference. Until a third way, at once demanding and responsible, emerges with greater clarity, the rich, vital body of Catholic social teaching will likely remain too little known"[61]—and solidarity too little enacted.

Articulating and modeling this third way, and deciphering tactics for overcoming obstacles to attaining it, are tasks that carry special responsibilities for those of us privileged to be working and ministering in North American Catholic colleges and universities. When our future colleagues gather in 2045 to recall *Gaudium et Spes* ("*octogesima adveniens*"), they will scrutinize our records to discover how well we met this responsibility. Here and now, our institutions, teaching, and scholarship embody either a commitment to incarnational solidarity or its absence. Unfortunately, best intentions notwithstanding, faculty, administrators, and students living and working in the relative lap of luxury of U.S. private academe are especially vulnerable to patterns of "clenched living" within an anti-solidary status quo.[62] Habituated consumerist egoism buttressed by conformist cultural norms, and the enormity and complexity of social and ecological problems, conspire to drag us down. Pleading realism, practicality, or lack of time and energy, we too easily lapse into a sophisticated way of copping out that Welch calls "cultured despair."[63] And in this era of furious globalization, political strife and economic distress, and mounting ecological crisis, despair (no matter how cultured) is truly a mortal sin; it is the last thing our suffering world can afford.

Catholic higher education has pedagogical, spiritual, and practical resources at its disposal for combating despair and fostering the solidarity that *Gaudium et Spes* endorses. As Lonergan's transcendental precepts suggest, promoting the knowledge and competencies necessary for intellectual and practical solidarity is an agenda deeply compatible with universities' truth- and value-seeking mission. Their explicitly religious identities also make the larger environs of Catholic colleges and universities apt loci for cultivating a mystical-political spirituality that connects prayerful living, thoughtful and intelligent living, and solidary living.[64] Traditional devotional, ascetic, and sacramental practices (for instances, ascetic disciplines of prayer and fasting; devotions to the Sacred Heart; and especially the eucharistic liturgy), engaged from within such a mystical-political spirituality, harbor wells of solidarity-nurturing insight, energy, and grace that await our drawing. Participating in these practices can generate powerful spiritual antidotes to the closing-off, hedonism, and security-mongering that commodity culture encourages.[65]

Certainly Christian tradition in its manifold expressions constitutes, in and of itself, a potent form of resistance to the solidarity-killing pretensions of consumerist culture. Certainly, too, these traditions ought never be reduced to instruments in service to a moral agenda. Today, however, commodification's capacity to infiltrate and subtly undermine religion makes it imperative that the inherently counter-cultural and socially transformative power of Christian belief, prayer, and practice be consciously evoked and deliberately articulated. Herein lies another important avenue for theological and pedagogical work.

Finally, along with honing the intellectual and spiritual competencies required for incarnational solidarity, Catholic colleges and universities should be sites where a vibrant *habitus* of action on behalf of justice is nurtured. Pius XI recognized in 1931 that the gospel would most effectively leaven the modern world through organized, communal forms of "Catholic action." Building on longstanding records of service, our institutions can contribute to an ethic of incarnational solidarity by working to shape community service activities in ways that can foster in us a deeper commitment to the struggle for justice for our most vulnerable neighbors.

Jon Sobrino has observed that practicing solidarity is like gospel living: "The gospel is a heavy light burden: the more one carries it on one's shoulders, the more one is carried by the gospel." "This," says Sobrino, "is how I see solidarity: a heavy light burden. The more we carry the church of the poor—a very heavy burden because the crosses of the people are in it—the more that church carries us."[66] Forty years after, *Gaudium et Spes* continues to invite us to pick up the "heavy light burden" and embody the good news in the world by living with, among, and for our sisters and brothers, in a concrete, messy, ever-threatened incarnational solidarity that immerses us in struggle for a world transformed according to God's justice. Though it enmeshes us too in the crushing *luctus et agor* of the cross, there is no doubt that such solidarity, the solidarity God shows toward us in Jesus, is the only way toward authentic joy and hope, and into lives that refract, imperfectly yet truly, the justice and *shalom* of God's reign.

Notes

[1]Translation from Austin Flannery, ed., *Vatican Council II: Basic Documents: Constitutions, Decrees, Declarations*, revised and inclusive language (Northport, N.Y.: Costello, 1996).

[2]For analysis and commentary on the background to *Quadragesimo Anno*, see Christine Firer Hinze, "*Quadragesimo Anno*," in Kenneth Himes et al., eds., *Modern Catholic Social Teaching: Commentaries and Interpretations* (Washington, D.C.: Georgetown University Press, 2005).

[3]Events during the Council leading up to the promulgation of *Gaudium et Spes* are detailed by Charles Moeller in Herbert Vorgrimler, ed., *Commentary on the Documents of Vatican II*, trans. W. J. O'Hara (New York: Herder & Herder, 1969), 1-76.

[4]Kenneth Himes, "The Church in the Modern World: A 30-Year Perspective," *Woodstock Report* 42 (June 1995), 3-8.

[5]The continuities between Vatican II's teaching and that of earlier popes, however, should not be forgotten. See Avery Dulles, S.J., "Vatican II: The Myth and the Reality," *America*, February 24, 2003. (Date of access for this and all following web citations:1 June, 2005) at http://www.americamagazine.org/gettext.cfm?articleTypeID=1&textID=2810&issueID=423

[6]David O'Brien, "A Century of Social Teaching, Contexts and Comments," in John A. Coleman, S.J., ed., *One Hundred Years of Catholic Social Teaching* (Maryknoll, N.Y.: Orbis Books, 1991), 23-24.

[7]Ratzinger, in Vorgrimler, ed., *Commentary on the Documents of Vatican II*, 117-19, avers that to present "genus humanum" as the interlocutor with "the church" is problematic, for "The Church itself is part of the genus humanum and cannot therefore be contradistinguished from it. . . . The Church meets its vis-à-vis *in* the human race, for example in non-Christians, unbelievers, etc. But it cannot stand outside the human race, and even for reasons of dialogue it cannot exclude itself from the human race and then artificially create a solidarity which in any case is the Church's lot." One reason for the lack of clarity is a historical tendency "to retreat into a special little ecclesiastical world from which an attempt is then made to speak to the rest of the world" (119).

[8]Translation taken from Walter M. Abbott, ed., *The Documents of Vatican II*, trans. and ed. Joseph Gallagher (Piscataway, N.J.: Association Press, New Century Publishers, 1966).

[9]So, for example, "Increase in power is not always accompanied by control of that power for the benefit of humanity. . . ." Some enjoy unprecedented levels of economic and material wealth and power while a huge proportion of the world's citizens are tormented by hunger, poverty, and illiteracy. "The world is keenly aware of its unity and of mutual interdependence in essential solidarity, but at the same time it is split into bitterly opposing camps" (4). "[T]he bonds uniting human beings multiply unceasingly, and *socialization* creates yet other bonds, without, however, a corresponding personal development, and truly personal relationships *(personalization)*" (6).

[10]"The Council brings to mankind light kindled from the gospel, and puts at its disposal those saving resources which the Church . . . receives from her

Founder. For the human person deserves to be preserved; human society deserves to be renewed. Hence the pivotal point of our total presentation will be man himself, whole and entire, body and soul, heart and conscience, mind and will. . . . Inspired by no earthly ambition, the Church seeks but a solitary goal: to carry forward the work of Christ Himself under the lead of the befriending Spirit. And Christ entered the world to give witness to the truth, to rescue and not to sit in judgment, to serve and not to be served" (3). See also Jn 18:37, Mt 20:28, and Mk 10:45.

[11]See 41: "But only God, who created humanity in his own image and ransomed humanity from sin, provides a fully adequate answer [to life's deepest questions]. This he does through what he has revealed in Christ his Son, who became human. Whoever follows after Christ, the perfect human being, becomes themselves more of a human being."

[12]Ratzinger, in Vorgrimler, ed., *Commentary on the Documents of Vatican* II, 117-18, speaks of the document's "anthropological theme and starting point," which "determines the whole theological conception of the text," and "probably represents its most characteristic option."

[13]This double affirmation reflects a way of holding together the particularity and universality of the church's message and mission that Hollenbach has called "dialogic universalism" (David Hollenbach, *Claims in Conflict: Retrieving and Renewing the Catholic Human Rights Tradition* [New York: Paulist Press, 1979], 131, and David Hollenbach, "Commentary on *Gaudium et Spes*," in Kenneth Himes et al., eds., *Modern Catholic Social Teaching*, at note 15).

[14]This distinctive viewpoint is elaborated, for example, in Severnie Deneulin, "Amartya Sen's Capability Approach to Development and *Gaudium et Spes*: On Political Participation and Structural Solidarity." Paper presented at the conference "The Call to Justice: The Legacy of *Gaudium et Spes* Forty Years Later," Vatican City, March 16-18, 2005. Accessed at http://www.stthomas.edu/gaudium/papers/Deneulin.pdf.

[15]A number of post-conciliar interpreters have emphasized "the christological anthropology" of *Gaudium et Spes*. See, for example, David Schindler, "Christology and the *Imago Dei*: Interpreting *Gaudium et Spes*," *Communio* 23:1 (1996): 156-84. Others caution that the inductive and anthropological starting point of *Gaudium et Spes* must neither be obscured, nor itself allowed to obscure the fact that Christology is a critical principle for evaluating particular anthropological schemes. "[Christology] therefore outbids anthropology" (Walter Kasper, *Theology and Church*, trans. Margaret Kohl [New York: Crossroad, 1989], 92, 108, quoted in William C. McDonough, "The Church in the Modern World," in Anthony J. Cernera, ed., *Vatican II: The Continuing Agenda* [Fairfield, Conn.: Sacred Heart University Press, 1997], 120).

[16]McDonough, "The Church in the Modern World," 120-21.

[17]Human solidarity is connected to Christology and to eschatological hope

in each section of Part One. See, for example, 22, 32, 38, and 45.

[18]John Courtney Murray, *We Hold These Truths: Catholic Reflections on the American Proposition* (New York: Sheed & Ward, 1960), 190.

[19]David Hollenbach, *The Common Good and Christian Ethics* (Cambridge: Cambridge University Press, 2002), 149.

[20]The term "solidarity" (the Latin *solidaritas*) appears in *GS* 4, 32, 57, and 90; terms such as mutual dependence and interdependence appear in sections 25, 26, 40, 42, 63, and 84.

[21]As William French's trenchant response to this essay underscores, *Gaudium et Spes* virtually ignores humanity's interdependence with its biological and material environment. Only in the later 1980s did this severe lacuna in Catholic social teaching begin, slowly, to be redressed. French's proposal, "no solidarity without sustainability," captures an indispensable dimension of a twenty-first-century Catholic ethic of solidarity.

[22]The "fact" of human solidarity expressed here is grounded in creation, broken and distorted due to sin, and renewed in the incarnate and redemptive mystery of Christ. As such it is simultaneously an anthropological-moral reality and a spiritual-Christological one (27).

[23]M. V. Bilgrien considers "solidarity" among the traditionally mentioned virtues in Marie Vianny Bilgrien, SSND, *Solidarity: A Principle, An Attitude, a Duty? Or the Virtue for an Interdependent World?* (American University Studies Series VII, vol. 204 [New York: Peter Lang, 1999], chap. 6), and argues, with Marciano Vidal, that solidarity is a form of general justice particularly suited to the contemporary era.

[24]Richard Rodriguez, unpublished lecture delivered September 25, 2003, at the conference, "The Church in the Modern World: Celebrating *Gaudium et Spes*," University of Dayton, Ohio.

[25]*GS* 30 states that today it is particularly urgent that "no one, ignoring the trend of events or drugged by laziness, content himself with a merely individualistic morality." The document singles out for special criticism "those who, while professing grand and rather noble sentiments, nevertheless in reality live always as if they cared nothing for the needs of society." *GS* 32 underscores Jesus' incarnational involvement in the daily realities of community and society in his day.

[26]Vincent J. Miller, *Consuming Religion: Christian Faith and Practice in a Consumer Culture* (New York: Continuum, 2005), 76, 134-35.

[27]Peter-Hans Kolvenbach, S.J., address delivered at the inauguration of the Semena Social [Social Week] organized by the Centro Gumilla, Fe y Algeria, and the Universidad Catholica Andreas Bello, Caracas, February 2, 1998. Typescript ms.

[28]See *GS* 29, which speaks of the essential equality of all as grounding universal human rights and as arguing against "excessive economic and social differences between the members of the one human family or population groups." Such excessive differences "cause scandal, and militate against

social justice, equity, the dignity of the human person, as well as social and international peace." Bilgrien (*Solidarity*, 131-33) elaborates relationships among solidarity, mutuality, and equality in *Gaudium et Spes* and in recent Catholic social teaching.

[29]The plenary address on which this essay is based was delivered at the College Theology Society annual meeting on June 3, 2005, the Solemnity of the Sacred Heart of Jesus.

[30]Donal Dorr, *Option for the Poor: A Hundred Years of Vatican Social Teaching,* rev. ed. (Maryknoll, N.Y.: Orbis Books, 1992), 165-66. See also Marvin L Krier Mich, *Catholic Social Teaching and Movements* (Mystic, Conn.: Twenty-Third Publications, 1998), 128-31.

[31]See, for example, James Hitchcock, "The End of *Gaudium et Spes*?," *Catholic World News*, May 2003. http://www.cwnews.com/news/viewstory.cfm?recnum=22816. Similar but more measured and subtle criticism of a tone of "optimism" in the text is offered by Joseph Ratzinger in Vorgrimler, *Commentary on the Documents of Vatican II*, 119-24, 136-40.

[32]See Joseph A. Komonchak, "Vatican II and the Encounter between Catholicism and Liberalism," in *Catholicism and Liberalism*, ed. R. Bruce Douglass and David Hollenbach (Cambridge: Cambridge University Press, 1994); see Hollenbach, "Commentary on *Gaudium et Spes*," at note 39.

[33]Richard Schenk, "*Officium Signa Temporum Perscrutandi.* New Encounters of Gospel and Culture in the Context of the New Evangelization." Unpublished paper presented at the conference "The Call to Justice: The Legacy of *Gaudium et Spes* Forty Years Later" (Vatican City, March 16-18, 2005), 4, 9. Accessed at http://www.stthomas.edu/gaudium/papers/Schenk.pdf.

[34]Miller, *Consuming Religion,* 19-20, 37-38; and see Christine Firer Hinze, "What Is Enough? Catholic Social Teaching, Consumption, and an Ethic of Sufficiency," in William Schweiker & Charles Mathewes, eds., *Having: Property and Possessions in Religious and Social Life* (Grand Rapids: Eerdmans, 2004), 162-88.

[35]A compendium of Latin American liberation theology is *Mysterium Liberationis* (Maryknoll, N.Y.: Orbis Books, 1993). On Catholic feminist theologians and *Gaudium et Spes,* see Anne Patrick, "Toward Renewing 'The Life and Culture of Fallen Man': *Gaudium et Spes* as Catalyst for Catholic Feminist Theology," in Judith Dwyer, ed., "*Questions of Special Urgency*": *The Church in the Modern World Two Decades after Vatican II* (Washington, D.C.: Georgetown University Press, 1986), 55-72. On North American liberationist theologies, see M. Shawn Copeland, "Black, Hispanic/Latino, and Native American Theologies" and Rebecca S. Chopp, "Feminist and Womanist Theologies," in David F. Ford, ed., *The Modern Theologians: An Introduction to Christian Theology in the Twentieth Century*, rev. ed. (Cambridge, Mass.: Blackwell, 1997), chaps. 19 and 20. On post-conciliar Catholic reflection on ecology, see Walter Grazer and Drew Christiansen, S.J., eds., *And God Saw That It Was Good: Catholic Theology and the*

Environment (Washington, D.C: United States Catholic Conference, 1996).

[36]Manuel Valesquez contends that *Gaudium et Spes*'s most significant contribution "was the impetus it gave to the liberationist themes that emerged in church documents during the late sixties and early seventies." Post-conciliar teaching amplified and extended the understanding of integral human fulfillment proposed in *Gaudium et Spes*. Further, "*Gaudium et Spes* . . . urged, cautiously but in unprecedented ways, that economic life and justice are essentially dependent on the social and economic structures within which individuals live, and that no important changes will take place unless these structures themselves are altered and reformed. Social structures shape human personalities so that 'men are often diverted from doing good and spurred toward evil by the social circumstances in which they live and are immersed from their birth' (*GS* 25)." This crucial recognition made it possible to begin to see critical social analysis and working for structural reform as congruent with, and even forms of, religious activity (Manuel Valasquez, "*Gaudium et Spes* and the Development of Catholic Social-Economic Thinking," in Dwyer, ed., *Questions of Special Urgency,* 187-89).

[37]See Douglas Hick's helpful treatment of preference in liberation theology in *Inequality and Christian Ethics* (Cambridge, Mass.: Cambridge University Press, 2000), 172ff.

[38]Gustavo Gutiérrez, *A Theology of Liberation* (Maryknoll, N.Y.: Orbis Books, 1971), 34.

[39]This aversion to conflict in Catholic social thought is elaborated in Hollenbach, *Claims in Conflict*, 118, 122, 161-66, and in Charles E. Curran, *Catholic Social Teaching: A Historical and Ethical Analysis* (Washington, D.C.: Georgetown University Press, 2002), 85-91.

[40]Alvez is quoted without attribution in Rembert Weakland, "Introduction: From Dream to Reality to Vision," in Pierre Hegy, ed., *The Church in the Nineties: Its Legacy, Its Future* (Collegeville, Minn.: Liturgical Press, 1993), xxviii. Miller (*Consuming Religion*, 134) cautions that "Suffering shares the same fate as other elements of culture in a commodified world. It becomes an abstract signifier, separated from its causes and valued for its intensity." The news media then acts as a "marketer of intensities, of which the suffering other is a best-selling variety. This irruption of suffering alterity [via the media] does indeed have [a] disquieting effect . . . but, in the absence of analysis of its causes and proposals to address it, it merely stupefies."

[41]Bilgrien charts Karol Wojtyla/John Paul II's use of "solidarity" from his 1969 work *Osaba I Czyn* (*The Acting Person*) through 1994 (*Solidarity,* chap. 2).

[42]Bilgrien suggests that John Paul II draws his understanding of the option for the poor not first from the Latin American context, but from *Lumen Gentium*, n. 8 (*Solidarity*, 135). In "One Church Many Cultures," the pope cites Vatican II as the foundation for his support of the contemporary option for the poor, and notes: "This 'option' is emphasized with particular force by

the episcopates of Latin America today; it has been repeatedly confirmed by me, after the example...of Pope Paul VI. . . . [T]he commitment to the poor constitutes a dominant motive of my pastoral action and the constant solicitude accompanying my daily service to the people of God" (Address to cardinals in Rome, December 21, 1984 [*Origins* 14:30, January 10 1985], 501).

[43]"[For John Paul II,] the practice of solidarity either begins with an option for the poor or ends with it. . . . It is not true solidarity if the poor are overlooked" (Bilgrien, *Solidarity*, 149).

[44]Dorr, however, criticizes Pope John Paul II's account of solidarity's "partisan" aspect as "somewhat bland, since he offers no strong social analysis and less theological emphasis than liberationists do on the role of the poor in God's liberation" (Donal Dorr, "Solidarity and Human Development," in Gregory Baum and Robert Ellsberg, eds., *The Logic of Solidarity* [Maryknoll, N.Y.: Orbis Books], 141).

[45]Metz argues that the dynamics of bourgeois culture promote a "cult of apathy," wherein people "do not want to take on dangerous responsibilities, they play possum, they stick their heads in the sand in the face of danger or they become voyeurs (spectators) of their own downfall" (J. B. Metz, "Theology Today: New Crises and New Visions," *Proceedings of the Catholic Theological Society of America* 40 [1985], 13, cited in Miller, *Consuming Religion*, 134).

[46]World Bank President James Wolfensohn's presentation of this information in the Foreword to *World Development Indicators 2000* is summarized at http://www.globalpolicy.org/socecon/bwi-wto/wbank/poverty.html. For a U.S. embassy summary of this same report see http://canberra.usembassy.gov/hyper/2000/0413/epf406.html.

[47]For one example of the "champagne glass of world income" chart, see Michael Naughton, "A Theology of Fair Pay," *Regent Business Review* 15. Accessed at http://www.regent.edu/acad/schbus/maz/busreview/issue15/fairpay.html.

[48]See Miller, *Consuming Religion*, 133-37.

[49]Hollenbach, *Common Good*, 138-46. See also Robert Putnam, *Bowling Alone: The Collapse and Revival of American Community* (New York: Simon & Schuster, 2000).

[50]Sharon Welch, *A Feminist Ethic of Risk* (Minneapolis: Fortress Press, 1990, 2000), 13-39.

[51]Hollenbach, *Common Good*, chap. 6, esp. 137-38, and see Jodi Dean's substantive contribution to this subject in *Solidarity of Strangers: Feminism after Identity Politics* (Berkeley: University of California Press, 1996); also M. Shawn Copeland, "The New Anthropological Subject at the Heart of the Mystical Body of Christ," *Proceedings of the Fifty-third Annual Convention of The Catholic Theological Society of America* 53 (June 11-14, Ottawa, 1998), 25-47.

[52]See Welch, *A Feminist Ethic of Risk*, chaps. 4 and 5.

[53]McDonough, 114, quoting Kasper, "The Theological Anthropology of *Gaudium et Spes*," *Communio* 22 (Spring 1996): 140.

[54]For, as Kolvenbach notes, solidarity with the poor, especially for the economically and socially advantaged, requires a "re-dimensioning of existence"—personal, ecclesial, and institutional—that will entail dispossession and loss of comfort and security (Address delivered at the inauguration of the Semena Social [Social Week).

[55]Also relevant here is what Robert Doran has described as "psychic conversion." See Robert Doran, *Subject and Psyche* (Milwaukee: Marquette University Press, 1994), especially chap. 5.

[56]See Bernard Lonergan, S.J., *Method in Theology* (New York: Herder & Herder, 1972). A helpful interpretation of Lonergan's thought focusing on social ethics is Kenneth Melchin, *Living with Other People: A Common Good Approach to Christian Ethics* (Ottawa: Novalis, 1998).

[57]Such attentiveness is nurtured in more local and personalized contacts. Hollenbach thus contends that "Civil society, not the state, is the primary locus in which human solidarity is realized. . . . [C]ivil society is the soil in which the seeds of human sociality grow. When communities are small or of intermediate size, they enable persons to come together in ways that can be vividly experienced. The bonds of communal solidarity formed in them enable persons to act together, empowering them to shape some of the contours of public life and its larger social institutions such as the state and the economy" (*Common Good*, 102).

[58]By habituating relationships to time, resources, acquisition, and consumption that obscure the reality of limits and the meaning of sufficiency, consumer culture works against the capacity for reasonable judgment described here. See Miller, *Consuming Religion*, 19-20, 37-38; and Christine Firer Hinze, "What Is Enough?" in Schweiker & Mathewes, eds., *Having: Property and Possessions in Religious and Social Life*, 162-88.

[59]Proclaiming hope to those experiencing suffering can become wrong if it accepts, through action or omission, the "untimely death of the great majority, which there is no doubt is the greatest and most mortal contemporary sin." Solidarity becomes universal and effective only through a liberating and cross-bearing siding with the poor (Javier Jímenez Limón, "Suffering, Death, Cross, and Martyrdom," in Ellacuría and Sobrino, eds., *Mysterium Liberationis*, 707).

[60]Weakland, "Introduction," xxviii.

[61]David O'Brien, "Catholic Social Teaching since Vatican II," in Cernera, ed., *Vatican II*, 146-47.

[62]This tendency may be subtly exacerbated in Catholic academe by the historically recent ascension to the upper-middle class of many of the Catholic families on whose support these institutions depend. bell hooks trains a race- and gender-sensitive lens on the moral and social ambiguities of class status

and mobility in the United States in *Where We Stand: Class Matters* (London: Routledge, 2000).

[63]Welch, *A Feminist Ethic of Risk*, 11-12.

[64]Dorothee Sölle, *The Silent Cry: Mysticism and Resistance* (Minneapolis: Fortress Press, 2001); Janet K. Ruffing, ed., *Mysticism and Social Transformation* (Syracuse: Syracuse University Press, 2001). And see Ian Bell, *The Significance of the Work of Bernard Lonergan for a Mystical-Political Theology and Ethics*. Unpublished Ph.D. dissertation, Marquette University, May, 2005.

[65]Miller suggests ways this might take place in *Consuming Religion*, chap. 7, such as through pedagogies of the eucharistic liturgy (201-203) and abstinence from consuming certain commodified cultural artifacts (207). See also Daniel J. Webster, "Praying Your Labels: One Response to Globalization," in the April, 2004 Anglican e-publication "A Globe of Witnesses" newsletter. Accessed at http://thewitness.org/agw/webster040804.html.

[66]Sobrino notes that solidarity in faith entails different things from people in different social locations. "The type of communion generated by the church of the poor is that of solidarity, of 'bearing one another.' This is . . . the communion of giving and receiving from one another the best that each has to give. . . . The faith of those who are below . . . better expresses the disconsolate suffering of the creature before God and the sense of a hidden and crucified God. . . . It better expresses the grace that is found in history, the capacity for celebration and joy in the midst of countless tribulations. . . . The faith of those who are above, but who lower themselves, better expresses conversion, the radical exchange of oppressive life for life in community with the oppressed. . . . It better expresses the love that sacrifices and takes risks that they could have avoided" (Jon Sobrino, S.J., "Communion, Conflict, and Ecclesial Solidarity," in Ellacuría and Sobrino, eds., *Mysterium Liberationis*, 632-33).

Greening *Gaudium et Spes*

William French

Forty years ago the Second Vatican Council promulgated a watershed document *Gaudium et Spes*, the Pastoral Constitution on the Church in the Modern World.[1] The document was, and remains, inspiring for its new sense of the dynamism of human history and the significance of the range of emergent global challenges. Against currents of thought that place the church in opposition to the world, *Gaudium et Spes* calls Catholics to a generally positive engagement with the world and with modern currents of culture, science, and thinking. It clearly notes emerging problems and sources of brooding anxiety, like the injustice of vast social inequity and the scourge of the destructiveness of war with greatly enhanced modern weaponry, but it generally affirms the world, its cultures, and modern history as a genuine sphere of Christian engagement, learning, and responsibility.

Religious communities sometimes get so bound up with keeping faith with tradition and custom that they fail to direct sufficient attention to the distinctive challenges emerging in the present age. Pope John XXIII often referred to the need to read the "signs of the times" and we are fortunate to have the Council pick up that phrasing in the Pastoral Constitution where it stresses the importance of "scrutinizing the signs of the times and interpreting them in light of the gospel" (*GS* 4). This is an important reminder that Catholic ethics and theological reflection must be developed through a method of critical correlation between the church's tradition and the realities of our contemporary situation.[2]

In many ways *Gaudium et Spes*'s call remains as fresh today as it did when it was first published. It notes how surging scientific and industrial advances are pushing the integration of the global human family through the promotion of increased economic alliances and an increased ease of transportation and communication. Likewise, this same dynamic of change poses new threats to the peoples of the Earth, threats that require a broadening sense of our responsibility to the entire global human community. An expanded range of our new-felt sense of community, the text suggests, must inspire a broadening of the sense of our obligations to live in solidarity with others. An important theme that resonates throughout the document is its stress on our interrelationality and sociality and on the foundational value of human dignity.

Christine Firer Hinze rightly argues that the Pastoral Constitution's central focus on and call for solidarity remains a powerfully relevant ethical and theological resource.[3] She is certainly right that this theme deserves to be lifted up and brought forward to inspire the next generation. My own view, however, is that for the vision of solidarity to be brought forward in a responsible way, it must first be disconnected from the personalist and historicist concentrations that govern the theological anthropology developed in the Pastoral Constitution and then re-envisioned inside a broader creation-centered, ecologically-informed frame of understanding. In what follows, I will offer a brief sketch of such an ecologically broadened understanding of human dignity, solidarity, and responsibility.[4]

In the forty years since *Gaudium et Spes* we have witnessed a steady rise of troubling ecological signs of the times and a church that has generally been slow to appreciate the range of implications of our emerging ecological crisis. A common reaction has been to note the degradation of ecosystems, the draining of aquifers, the rapid melting of ice fields and glaciers that sustain river flows in summer months, the worries about habitat destruction and rising rates of species extinction, the growing concerns about global warming and climate change, and then to cluster all these as a new sphere of concern to be added to the church's long list of moral concerns, like economic justice, international peacemaking, or sexual ethics. This view would hold that the Pastoral Constitution could be retrofitted with an ecological appendix.

This approach, I believe, simply fails to appreciate the significance of the paradigm shift required in our understanding of human nature, history, and God's ways of gracing the world. *Gaudium et Spes* employs a human-centered, personalist philosophical and theological lens that nicely highlights human sociality and our solidarity with other humans. It fails, however, to situate the social question inside the larger frame of the ecological question. Solidarity is a fine stance but the building evidence of forty years of ecological studies suggests the necessity of expanding our understanding of the community to which our solidarity is owed. Solidarity must be temporally expanded to a felt sense of communal relationship and responsibility for the needs of future generations, and ecologically expanded to a sense of kinship with the rest of "the whole community of the universe," to borrow Thomas Aquinas's wording.[5]

The Pastoral Constitution's stress on human dignity, the dynamism of history, the power of culture, human sociality, and the call for solidarity are all admirable elements. What I find troubling in the reflection about these elements is the imbalance that is caused by the dominant assumptions of the personalist frame of understanding. It is, of course, important to emphasize human dignity, but do not other life forms have "dignity" too? What is the proper standard for measuring "dignity?" Francis of Assisi preached to birds and to a wolf. He named the sun "Brother" and the Earth "Sister" and "Mother."[6] Was he confused? *Gaudium et Spes* rightly stresses that humanity is created in the "image" of God, but pays no heed to affirmations, like those of Thomas Aquinas, that all creatures are created in the "likeness" of God.[7]

An ecological frame entails no need for a loss of an emphasis on human dignity. But it does require an end to purchasing a celebration of human dignity by a sustained undercutting of any sense of the continuities between humanity and the other animal species, or by a loss of a sense of kinship with the Earth, or by an assumption that the nonhuman natural world is somehow lacking in its own distinct modes of dignity. The Pastoral Constitution exhibits a flat and unnuanced appeal to the doctrine of creation. We are offered an image of the nonhuman natural world as primarily a resource bank for human use. Human need and use are the "universal purpose for which created goods are meant" (*GS* 69). We are told that the human "is the only creature on earth which God willed for itself" (*GS* 24).

A human-centered theological anthropology guides the Council in its appeal to the Hebrew Bible. Human dignity is tied to an affirmation that "all things on earth should be related to man as their center and crown" (*GS* 12). Genesis 1:26 is cited to affirm that humanity was appointed by God "as master of all earthly creatures that he might subdue them and use them. . . ." Psalm 8:5-6 is quoted—"Thou hast made him a little less than the angels . . ." to reiterate humanity's function as the apex and master of all of the rest of creation (*GS* 12).

Gaudium et Spes's appropriation of the dominion theme found in Genesis 1 follows the historically dominant emphasis placed on humanity's privileged position vis-à-vis the rest of creation. The Priestly account of creation found in Genesis 1:1-2:4 has long served as the chief theological warrant for viewing humanity as ruling over the rest of creation. In Genesis 1:26-28 we are told of humanity's grant of "dominion" (*râdâ*) over the rest of creation and of our charge by God to "fill the earth and subdue (*kâbaš*) it." Down through the generations, the Priestly account's sequence of creation has generally been interpreted as further strengthening the case for humanity's superiority over the rest of nature, for God seems to build the order of creation from the lower to the higher elements, concluding with humanity as creation's crown. God first creates the heavens and the earth, the dry land and oceans—the environmental infrastructure. Then God begins to create life, vegetation on the third day, fish and birds "of every kind" on the fifth day, and all manner of land creatures on the sixth day. And then God caps off creation with humanity, his highest creation in the visible realm. Down through the centuries these prominent texts have served to buttress the dominant Christian emphasis on humanity's distinction from and superiority to the rest of the natural world.

But in the last fifty years growing appreciation for humanity's evolutionary history has sensitized many to the thick continuities between human life and the living history of the planet. Likewise, this growing awareness of humanity's intimate relationship with the rest of nature has been complemented by a deepening appreciation for how human flourishing is dependent on the ongoing vitality and well-being of Earth's ecosystems and Earth's full range of species. With eyes opened to these new understandings and with a sense of the ecological threat, an increasing number of Christians and Jews are moving beyond the historic fixation on Genesis 1:26-28 to examine the broad range of scriptural materials that deal with God's and humanity's relationships to the natural world.

Indeed, many note that even within the Priestly materials of

Genesis 1 there is a strong qualification regarding the range of humanity's "dominion." The authorization of rule by humans appears to be checked by a powerful vision of the original "peace of creation," in which, according to Genesis 1:29-30, God gave humans and other animals only plant matter for food. In this enchanting vision of the "peaceable kingdom," we are presented with a picture of vegetarian harmony, a world without predators, without the killing and eating of animal life. In the Genesis narrative it is only in Genesis 9:2-3, after the Fall and the banishment from Eden, after brother kills brother and wickedness grows, and after the ark stops bobbing on the waters of the great flood, that God establishes a new beginning. This beginning, however, is marked by the loss of the innocence of the "peaceable kingdom" and an explicit divine permission given to humanity to kill and eat animals. The harmony in Eden between humans and animals is lost and now, we are told in Genesis 9:2, the "fear of you and dread of you shall rest on every animal of the earth. . . ."[8]

Likewise, many now note that if the Priestly account of creation in Genesis 1 has tended to be read as highlighting humanity's superiority and dominion over the rest of nature, the Yahwist account found in Genesis 2:4b-3:24 offers a marvelously humble counterbalancing portrayal of humanity. God forms "man" or "human being" (in Hebrew, *'âdâm*) from ground or soil (in Hebrew *'ădâmâ*) by breathing into it the "breath of life." The man was set in the garden to "till and keep it." In a recent essay Theodore Hiebert argues that the Hebrew term *'âbad*, meaning "to till or to cultivate," is best understood as a call "to serve" the rest of creation even as Israel is meant to serve God.[9]

Much is at stake in the historic privileging of Genesis 1 over Genesis 2, a privileging strongly apparent in *Gaudium et Spes*. For Hiebert, the Priestly account of Genesis 1, with its stress on dominion, reflects the priestly elite's understanding of their honored role of mediating God's presence on earth, from which they generalize a model of humanity similarly mediating between God and the rest of creation. The Priestly account thus is grounded in a hierarchical image of humanity as the "master of the earth" that, in turn, is rooted in the societal experience of priestly privilege. Even though the dominion theme is understood to imply that humanity has stewardship obligations to protect the rest of creation, Hiebert rightly believes that the Priestly account's stress on hierarchy has helped justify an historic overemphasis on humanity's rights to use nature and a de-emphasis on our obligations to care for and protect nature. For Hiebert, the Yahwist account of creation offers an important resource to Jews and Christians, for it highlights humanity's close continuity with animals and the rest of the natural world. It views humans as made and sustained, like other animals, from the "arable soil." Where the Priestly account stresses humans' vocation of dominion, the Yahwist view, for Hiebert, presents a more humble and ecologically helpful portrayal of humanity's vocation of service to, and responsible use of, the natural world. It reflects, he believes, the experiential world of the ancient "subsistence farmer" of Israel's hill country, who does not see his or her role as lording over the land, but rather as working with the land to insure its well-being so as equally to secure the well-being of the farmer's family and community.[10] Agrarian societies—both ancient and contemporary—tend to be well aware of their dependency upon the land's capacities and their vulnerability to nature's degradation at human hands. And this understanding needs to be recovered by today's contemporary industrialized societies before it is too late. Similarly, this understanding needs to be retrieved into the mainstreams of Catholic theology.

Gaudium et Spes illustrates a wide-ranging and historically sustained paradigm in biblical text selection that needs to be deconstructed and challenged. It illustrates the circularity of how a personalist and human-centered theological lens too often guides the selection and highlighting of scriptural texts and themes and how these, in turn, are used to provide scriptural support to the theological anthropological assumptions derived on the basis of other grounds. We can see this dynamic at work in the early stages of liberation theology, which highlighted God's action in the sphere of human history but downplayed any notion of the importance of God's action in creating or sustaining nature. The Exodus story was lifted up as a key disclosure of God's saving works in history in covenanting with the people of Israel and in leading them out of slavery into freedom. Liberation theologians joined with mainstream biblical theologians to stress the "mighty acts of God" in history. As Gustavo Gutiérrez put it in his classic, *A Theology of Liberation*, "Other religions think in terms of cosmos and nature. Christianity, rooted in Biblical sources, thinks in terms of history."[11]

But, as Wendell Berry and others have reminded us, we need to pay attention to the role of land and nature in Israel's great Exodus. An ecologically informed reading of the Exodus narratives will help us to see the prominence of the role of the land as a conduit of God's blessings and curses to the people of Israel as they live out their new covenant. God, the texts suggest, acts fully in nature as in history and the Israelites do not just get something called "freedom" at the end of their journey, but more importantly a "gift of good land," a land "flowing with milk and honey."[12]

Freedom by itself does not guarantee the flourishing of a people. That requires also an ecosystem capable of providing sustenance. The covenant between God and Israel requires that Israel keep God's statutes and ordinances. If it does, God promises that Israel will enjoy prosperity in this new land. As God makes clear: "You shall keep all my statutes . . . so that the land to which I bring you to settle in may not vomit you out" (Lv 20:22). If Israel keeps faith with God, "I will give you your rains in their season, and the land shall yield its produce. . . . [Y]ou shall eat your bread to the full, and live securely in your land" (Lv 26:4-5). The mighty acts of God's saving grace, it seems, are found as fully in the sphere of nature as in the sphere of history for life is sustained simultaneously by energies from both spheres.[13] Happily in the last two decades a number of liberation theologians have begun to stress God's blessings in sustaining the natural world. These theologians have emphasized the need for an ethic of ecological sustainability to bring balance to their long-standing emphasis on God's action in the historical sphere and the need to end oppression and to promote justice.[14]

I share with Hinze the desire to have the Council's stress on solidarity be received and taught, but first it needs to be ecologically expanded into a creation-centered frame. Humanity, when understood in a creation-centered vision, retains dignity, indeed immense dignity, but it is not a dignity purchased by an explicit or implicit denigration of the dignity of the rest of God's creation. It would recall God's questions posed to Job that suggest that we humans are but a part of a grander community of creation. "Where were you when I laid the foundation of the earth? Tell me, if you have understanding. . . . Have you entered the storehouses of the snow . . . can you hunt the prey for the lion. . . . Who provides for the raven its prey. . . . Do you know when the mountain goats give birth? . . . Do you give the horse its might?" (Jb chaps. 38-40).[15]

Some church documents from the last twenty years give evidence of a developing sensitivity to ecological issues. In 1990 Pope John Paul II wrote an important letter, "The Ecological Crisis: A Common Responsibility," in which he calls our attention to the seriousness of ecological degradation and to the need to respect the order of the created world and "to care for all of creation."[16] While the pope's letter opened up new ground in its concern for ecological issues, still it remained largely wedded to a human-centered theological understanding. But John Paul's initiative helped prompt a number of national bishops' conferences around the world to write pastoral letters calling for new efforts at ecological responsibility. Many of these letters developed their account of human dignity and community in a genuine creation-centered frame.[17] The United States Catholic Conference, for example, promulgated a fine statement, *Renewing the Earth* (RE), in 1991 in which they systematically integrated social justice concerns into the frame of broader concerns about the integrity of creation and our ecological responsibilities. The American bishops employed a much broader array of scriptural texts to affirm "our kinship with all that God has made."[18] In eloquent terms they affirmed that we live in a "sacramental universe"—a universe saturated with holiness and dignity, a universe created and sustained by God's energies. They call us to awaken to the "sense of God's presence in nature" (RE 231). They look to the diversity of animal and plant species and ecosystems and affirm that, in addition to their value for humanity, the nonhuman created world possesses "an independent value worthy of our respect and care" (RE 232). The bishops note how ecological concerns force us now to be mindful of the "planetary common good." This expanded frame of reference requires an extension of love and solidarity both to future generations and to the "flourishing of all of earth's creatures" (RE 232-33, 238-39).

Sadly, even though other bishops' conferences around the world have also published a number of good, ecologically oriented pastoral letters,[19] it seems clear that the church has not made ecological concerns a top ecclesiastical or moral priority. A personalist-informed, anthropocentric theological anthropology still dominates Vatican thinking. The stress on humanity's mastery over nature, evident in the Pastoral Constitution and in many of Pope John Paul II's encyclicals, simply confirms the conventional beliefs of many.

In my view, the theological anthropology operative in *Gaudium et Spes* is simply inadequate. Perhaps after forty years it is time for a new effort to integrate more adequately notions of human dignity and the wider dignity of creation and to integrate sensitivities to the dynamism of history with an appreciation for how human history is an evolutionary outgrowth of natural history and an integration of Christology with the Hebrew Bible's prominent emphasis on the doctrine of creation. *Gaudium et Spes* reflects on the "Church in the Modern World," but after forty years perhaps we need a new document, a "Pastoral Constitution on the Church in a Post-Modern World." Perhaps a better title might be a "Pastoral Constitution on the Church in an Age of Emerging Global Climate Change" or maybe we could honor Thomas Berry and title it a "Pastoral Constitution on the Church Mourning the Passing of the Cenozoic Age and Hoping for the Emergence of an Ecozoic Age."[20]

What might an ecological, creation-centered frame do to our understanding of solidarity? It would, I believe, make more explicit that genuine solidarity requires sustainability. Without sustainable levels of consumption, energy and resource use, agriculture, modes of transportation, levels of human procreation, and population size, we will progressively undercut the abilities of the world's ecosystems to sustain healthy human communities. Ecosystem degradation is increasingly being recognized by base communities across the globe as a materially central component of the structural violence that so heavily hammers the poor.[21] Today's "signs of the times" suggest that a) habitat degradation equals structural violence, b) long-term justice requires eco-justice, and c) there can be no real solidarity without sustainability.

Gaudium et Spes deserves great respect for its careful stance of calling upon the church to engage the distinctive challenges of the contemporary world. This is a project that must be regularly revisited. Our task remains to "scrutinize the signs of the times" and to seek to empower an ethic of solidarity that is adequate to the challenge.

Notes

[1]"Concilium Oecumenicum Vaticanum II, Constitutio Pastoralis de Ecclesia in Mundo Huius Temporis," *Acta Apostolicae Sedis* 58 (December 1966):1,025-1,120. Among other places, this can be found in David J. O'Brien and Thomas A. Shannon, eds., *Catholic Social Thought: The Documentary Heritage* (Maryknoll, N.Y.: Orbis Books, 1992), 164-237. Hereafter, cited in text as *GS* with section numbers.

[2]For more on the method of correlation, see David Tracy, *The Analogical Imagination: Christian Theology and the Culture of Pluralism* (New York: Crossroad, 1981), 59-64.

[3]See Christine Firer Hinze's "Straining toward Solidarity in a Suffering World" in this book for her fine development of the importance of solidarity in *Gaudium et Spes*.

[4]See Christine Firer Hinze, "Catholic Social Teaching and Ecological Ethics," in *"And God Saw That It Was Good": Catholic Theology and the Environment*, ed. Drew Christiansen, S.J., and Walter Grazer (Washington, D.C.: United States Catholic Conference, 1996), 170. See also my essay "Ecological Dangers and Christian Response: Attending to Creation," *New Theology Review* 4, no. 2 (May 1991): 26-42.

[5]Thomas Aquinas, *Summa Theologica*, 5 vols., trans. Fathers of the English Dominican Province, (Westminster, Md.: Christian Classics, 1948, reprint 1981), 2:996; 1a, 2ae, q.91, art.1.

[6]See Regis J. Armstrong and Ignatius C. Brady, trans. and intro., *Francis and Clare: The Complete Works* (Ramsey, N.J.: Paulist Press, 1982), 37-39. See also Roger D. Sorrell, *St. Francis of Assisi and Nature: Tradition and Innovation in Western Christian Attitudes toward the Environment* (New York and Oxford: Oxford University Press, 1988) and Dawn M. Nothwehr, *Franciscan Theology of the Environment: An Introductory Reader* (Quincy, Ill.: Franciscan Press, 2002).

[7]Aquinas, *Summa Theologica* 1a, q. 57, art.2, 1:284 and q. 93, art.6, 1:473.

[8]See George L. Frear, Jr., "Caring for Animals: Biblical Stimulus for Ethical Reflection," in *Good News for Animals: Christian Approaches to Animal Well-Being*, ed. Charles Pinches and Jay B. McDaniel (Maryknoll, N.Y.: Orbis Books, 1993), 3-11. See also Karl Barth's commentary on these passages in his *Church Dogmatics*, III/4, trans. A. T. MacKay, T. H. L. Parker et al. (Edinburgh: T & T Clark, 1961), 351-56.

[9]Theodore Hiebert, "The Human Vocation: Origins and Transformations in Christian Traditions," in *Christianity and Ecology*, ed. Dieter T. Hessel and Rosemary Radford Ruether (Cambridge: Harvard University Press, 2000), 135-54. See also Theodore Hiebert, *The Yahwist's Landscape:*

Nature and Religion in Early Israel (New York: Oxford University Press, 1996).

[10] Hiebert, "The Human Vocation," 140-41.

[11] Gustavo Gutiérrez, *A Theology of Liberation*, trans. and ed., Caridad Inda and John Eagleson (Maryknoll, N.Y.: Orbis Books, 1973), 174.

[12] Wendell Berry, "The Gift of Good Land," in Wendell Berry, *The Gift of Good Land* (San Francisco: North Point Press, 1981), 267-81.

[13] See William C. French, "Chaos and Creation," *The Bible Today* 33:1 (January 1995): 9-15. See also James M. Gustafson, *Ethics from a Theocentric Perspective*, vol. 1 (Chicago: University of Chicago Press, 1981) and *A Sense of the Divine: The Natural Environment from a Theocentric Perspective* (Cleveland: Pilgrim Press, 1994).

[14] See, for example, Leonardo Boff, *Ecology & Liberation: A New Paradigm*, trans. John Cumming (Maryknoll, N.Y.: Orbis Books, 1995).

[15] See Bill McKibben, *The Comforting Whirlwind: God, Job, and the Scale of Creation* (Grand Rapids, Mich.: Eerdmans, 1994), 37.

[16] Pope John Paul II, "The Ecological Crisis: A Common Responsibility" (December 8, 1989), in Drew Christiansen, S.J. and Walter Grazer, eds., "*And God Saw That It Was Good,*" 215-22.

[17] See, for example, the Guatemalan Bishops' Conference letter of February 29, 1988, *The Cry for Land*; the letter of September 15, 1988 on *Ecology* by the Catholic bishops of Northern Italy; and the Filipino bishops' letter of January 29, 1988 *What Is Happening to Our Beautiful Land?*—all found in Drew Christiansen, S.J. and Walter Grazer, eds., "*And God Saw That It Was Good.*" Likewise, see the South African Catholic Bishops' Conference's *Pastoral Letter on the Environmental Crisis* published on September 5, 1999, as well as important letters offered by the Australian bishops, the Canadian bishops, and the bishops' conferences of a number of other countries. Helpful websites are: The United States Catholic Conference of Bishops' "Environmental Justice Program" page at http://www.usccb.org/sdwp/ejp/index.htm; the Catholic Conservation Center at http://conservation.catholic.org/; Marquette University's website titled "Catholic Church on Ecological Degradation" at http://faculty.theol.mu.edu/schaefer; and Catholic EarthCare Australia at http://www.catholicearthcareoz.net/index.html.

[18] U.S. Catholic Bishops, *Renewing the Earth: An Invitation to Reflection and Action on Environment in Light of Catholic Social Teaching* (November 14, 1991) (Washington, D.C.: United States Catholic Conference, 1992), in Drew Christiansen, S.J. and Walter Grazer, eds., "*And God Saw That It Was Good,*" 223-43. This quote is from p. 229. Hereafter, cited in text as RE with page numbers.

[19] See the documents listed in note 17.

[20] See Thomas Berry, *The Great Work: Our Way into the Future* (New York: Bell Tower, 1999), 1-8, 29-30, 196-201. The Cenozoic Era, beginning 65 million years ago, is our geological age. As Berry and others note, this is

the era when remarkable energies of life "flared forth" on Earth in a marvelous diversity of plant, tree, bird, fish, and animal species. It is this species diversity that is threatened today by humanity's increasing development and transformation of wild habitats and natural ecosystems. Earth has experienced five vast extinction events, and many biologists worry that today humanity's actions are pushing toward a tragic sixth such event. See, for example, Richard Leakey and Roger Lewin, *The Sixth Extinction: Patterns of Life and the Future of Humankind* (New York: Doubleday, 1995), and Edward O. Wilson, "Is Humanity Suicidal?" *The New York Times Magazine* (May 30, 1993), 24-29.

[21] See Alberto Múnera, S.J., "New Theology on Population, Ecology and Overconsumption from the Catholic Perspective," in Harold Coward and Daniel C. Maguire, eds. *Visions of a New Earth: Religious Perspectives on Population, Consumption, and Ecology* (Albany: State University of New York Press, 2000), 65-78; Heidi Hadsell, "Eco-Justice and Liberation Theology," in Dieter T. Hessel, ed., *After Nature's Revolt: Eco-Justice and Theology* (Minneapolis: Fortress Press, 1992), 79-88; and Leonardo Boff, *Cry of the Earth, Cry of the Poor* (Maryknoll, N.Y.: Orbis Books, 1997).

Changing Views on the Relation of Christ and the State

Vatican II and John Paul II

Victor Lee Austin

Gaudium et Spes (Pastoral Constitution on the Church in the Modern World) and *Dignitatis Humanae* (Declaration on Religious Freedom) show an attenuated perdurance of traditional political theology. In that tradition, the state is understood as an instrument of God's mediated governance of the world, and Christ is taken to be the ultimate ruler over all earthly rulers. Echoes of such traditional affirmations can be found in these Vatican II documents, but alongside them are more modern affirmations of subjective human rights. By contrast, Pope John Paul II's social encyclicals tend to be innocent of the traditional claims. In these writings, John Paul conceives the state not as God's instrument but as an instrument of a pre-existing, and thus pre-political, society. He similarly avoids attributing ultimate political rule to Christ. He does, however, continue and expand the social tradition's affirmation of human rights. And John Paul conceives the state's function as being to protect and promote human rights. In short, in this matter John Paul selects and develops further one aspect of the Council's teaching—its modern affirmations of subjective rights—while silently, as it were, editing out the elements of the Council's teaching that maintained traditional politico-theological claims.

Christ and the State in Vatican II

This paper postulates that an adequate grasp of "traditional political theology" is given by two claims, referenced as "A" and

"B": A) that the state is providentially instituted to provide a mediated form of divine rule for and over a given political society and its members; and B) that Christ holds a superior political authority over all humans who exercise political authority.[1] In these two claims, Christ and the state are mutually implicated. The providentially provided agents for political rule of earthly society have been placed under the higher yet still politically real rule of Christ. In this tradition, the state apart from Christ is thinkable only as idolatrous insurrection, and Christ is particularly identified by the political functions that the Father has given to him—victory over death, legislation of the new law, and final judgment.

Traditional political theology thus defined is present, although not without admixture of modern elements, in *Dignitatis Humanae* (*DH*). This document is structured as, first, a natural-law argument for religious freedom (sections 2–8), and second, an argument for the same from Christian revelation (9–15). The natural-law argument preserves the tradition of speaking of God as ruling the universe by divine law, in which human reason is capable of participating. "The highest norm of human life is the divine law—eternal, objective, and universal—whereby God orders, directs, and governs the entire universe and all the ways of the human community, by a plan conceived in wisdom and love" (*DH* 3).[2] However, in this section, *DH* does not claim that the state has a place in mediating God's ordering, directing, and governing of the universe. One must wait until *DH* turns to make an argument, on the basis of Christian revelation, for religious freedom to find an assertion of the traditional doctrine. "As the Master, so too the apostles recognized legitimate civil authority. 'For there exists no authority except from God,' the Apostle teaches, and therefore commands: 'Let everyone be subject to the higher authorities . . . he who resists the authority resists the ordinance of God' (Rom. 13:1-2)" (*DH* 11).

Thus the substance of Claim A is found in *DH*: God rules the universe and all humanity, and from God comes all civil authority. Nonetheless, it is the case that this claim of traditional political theology is considerably attenuated by the surrounding text. *DH* notes that although Christ asserted ultimate judgment—which would be Claim B—he declined to pronounce it during his life, leaving it, rather, for the future "day of judgment."[3] *DH* seems to equate the political with force (to the exclusion, one suspects, of law-giving and judgment), so that it interprets Christ's refusal of force as a refusal of the political ("He refused to be a political Messiah, ruling by force").[4] Still, it does acknowledge that Christ rules; by using love, by witnessing to the truth, by his death on the cross, he draws people to himself (*DH* 11). Moreover, the state's responsibility includes such matters as giving constitutional recognition to the human right to religious freedom (*DH* 2), acknowledging "the right of parents" to determine their children's education (*DH* 5), giving the church freedom to function (*DH* 13), and in general protecting and promoting "the inviolable rights of man" (*DH* 6).

In summary, it is clear that *DH* asserts Claims A and B, albeit in a diminished fashion. God does govern the universe, and Christ does have genuine rule. But the state here is not an agent of divine governance. Its duties lie in the protection and promotion of human dignity, particularly, subjective human rights.

Yet an understanding of the state and Christ is ancillary to the primary aim of *DH*, which is to shed light on religious freedom. Within *Gaudium et Spes*, however, lies a section whose explicit purpose is to give an account of political life ("The Life of the Political Community," *GS* 73–76).[5] This section reads the signs of the times in modern politics: a sense that the state should protect personal rights, including rights to civil and religious liberty, and the right to participate "in organizing the life of the political community" (*GS* 73).[6] It then gives an account of political community, which is said to be set up by people who see the insufficiency of families and associations to provide fullness of human life.[7] Despite this human origin, *GS* also says that since "political community and public authority are based on human nature," they are "divinely foreordained" (74). And, in a sense the state, like the family, is prior to the individual, having a "greater immediacy" to the human person's "inmost nature" than other elective forms of association (25).[8] Still, the choice of the form of government and the manner of selecting its officials remain in human hands. Thus *GS* gives an account of the state that is traditional in the manner of Claim A, in that it has a divine purpose.[9] Nonetheless, *GS* does not profess that in the state people experience a mediated form of divine rule.[10] Since the state serves the common good, given in human nature that is itself given by God, an obligation falls on citizens from their conscience to obey the juridical order of their state. This obligation may be suspended when the state ceases to serve the common good and abuses its power (74). It would be an excessively fanciful reading, however, to claim that the rule of God occurs in the state through the exercise of the citizens' conscience.[11]

In *GS*, Christ is given no direct connection to the state. He appears only when the discussion turns to the relationship of the political community to the church. *GS* assumes a pluralistic context of a variety of religions in various relationships in the states of the world. The Council is at pains to distinguish sharply the church from any political community on the grounds that the church is "founded on the Redeemer's love" and is "a sign and a safeguard of the transcendence of the human person." With a mission to proclaim Christ to all people and to proclaim to all people the dignity of the human person, the church transcends states, and thus "it is always and everywhere legitimate for her to preach the faith with true freedom, to teach her social doctrine, and to discharge her duty among men without hindrance." The church even has the right to pass judgments over the state "whenever basic personal rights or the salvation of souls make such judgments necessary." But her "helps" are only those means that are consonant with the gospel and the temporally conditioned general welfare (*GS* 76). Thus, when human dignity or evangelical freedom is at stake, the church may issue judgment upon the state. Although this judgment is not explicitly stated to be Christ's, it bears a kinship to the ultimate judgment of Claim B.

In summary: the teaching of Vatican II is that God does govern the universe through divine law, and that the state has a divine purpose given by natural law, namely, the rational requirements for fulfilling human nature. It also claims that the church may pass judgment upon the state when it impinges upon evangelical freedom or upon the transcendence of the human person. However, Vatican II does not say that the state is an instrument of God's mediate governance of the universe, nor does it say explicitly that Christ will pass ultimate judgment upon the actions of states.

Christ and the State in John Paul II

The change from Vatican II to John Paul II can be characterized generally as follows: those elements of traditional political theology that could be found in Vatican II are not present in John Paul II, although neither are they specifically denied. John Paul does not affirm Claim A or B. At the same time, those elements of the teaching of *DH* and *GS* that emphasize human dignity and human rights are further emphasized in John Paul, who gives them a distinctive christological interpretation: namely, that persons have human rights because of the union of Christ with all persons.[12]

John Paul's understanding of the state can be drawn from his social encyclicals.[13] *Laborem Exercens* (*LE*), a personalist analysis of the phenomenon of human work, contains the pope's famous central contention that through work a person not only creates a product (which is the work objectively considered), she also creates herself. This reflexive understanding of work as above all a subjective process shows the importance of work to human dignity and thus signals human dignity as a key theme of John Paul's political thought (see *LE* 6, 9-10).

Social life should be, according to John Paul, rich and multitextured, including organizations (such as labor unions) that perform socially useful tasks such as education and the encouragement of self-education (20.2, 20.6). These "intermediate bodies" (14.7) place limits upon the state's direct influence upon and control over the human person, while they express and foster the human person in her creative agency. Thus do the limitations placed upon the state flow from human dignity.

A limited state underlies two descriptions in *LE* of the levels or spheres of which society is composed. The first comes at the end of John Paul's discussion of the meaning and value of work. He identifies three "spheres of value" for work. First is the personal: the overriding importance of the self-creating, subjective value of work. The second sphere is family life: the formation and sustenance of which is founded in work, and which also has an educational function, "for the very reason that everyone 'becomes a human being' through, among other things, work, and becoming a human being is precisely the main purpose of the whole process of education" (10.1). The third sphere of value for work is "the *great society* to which man belongs on the basis of particular cultural and historical links" wherein, by combining "his deepest human identity with membership of a nation," the human person adds through work "to the heritage of the whole human family" (10.3).

The picture, then, is of a person, in a family, in a nation, somehow contributing through these spheres to the good of "the whole human family." A later section discusses the obligation to work, and discerns the following sources of that obligation: the Creator, the person herself, the family, the society to which she belongs, the country of which she is a child, and finally the whole human family (16.2). Here the obvious addition is of a divine sanction for the duty to work. And the order of *LE* 16 is significant: it moves from God to the human person, then outward to family, society, country, and the human "family" as a whole.

The state is extrinsic to the implicit taxonomy of society in *LE* 10 and 16. The state is not a sphere of value or a fount of obligation: it is not an element of society so much as an instrument employed by it. John Paul's lines of connection run directly from God to the person who has rights, and then from the person outwards to the family, then to the country or nation or society, and finally to the broad human "family."

Further in *LE* is the notable non-appearance of the state as a place where work is done. In *LE*, no political function is described as work. When John Paul discusses the spirituality of work he gives over two paragraphs to a celebratory listing of all the forms of work mentioned in scripture (26.2–3).[14] Yet he omits governing, judging, ruling, and political administration (all of which can be found instanced in scripture).[15] This is an odd omission, particularly given the pope's desire to make his list of work as inclusive as possible (and also given his broad definition of work as, essentially, any human activity).[16] Again the state is shown to be marginalized in the pope's thought.

In *Centesimus Annus* (*CA*) the pope declares that the state has an "instrumental character": "the individual, the family and society are prior to the State"; "the State exists in order to protect their rights and not stifle them" (11.2). It has a limited role that can be seen, for instance, in the pope's discussion of unemployment. While the state has an important role in "protecting the worker from the nightmare of unemployment," either through economic policies aimed at full employment or through unemployment insurance and retraining programs, this is a role shared by both "society and the State" (15.2). Indeed, "primary responsibility" for guaranteeing the right to employment "belongs not to the State but to individuals and to the various groups and associations which make up society" (48.2). It falls to the state *along with* "the forces of society" to control the market appropriately "so as to guarantee that the basic needs of the whole of society are satisfied" (35.2).

Hence, in John Paul's handling, the oversight function of the state is disbursed beyond the state to society's various elements. Thus John Paul widens the responsibility for the common good and shrinks the role of the state. The state's fundamental *raison d'être* is to protect and promote human rights. "The recognition of these rights [of conscience] represents the primary foundation of every authentically free political order" (29.1). Democracy must have "an authentic and solid foundation through the explicit recognition of [human] rights." The "source and synthesis of these rights is religious freedom, understood as the right to live in the truth of one's faith and in conformity with one's transcendent dignity as a person" (47.1). The root error of totalitarian regimes is their "denial of the transcendent dignity of the human person who, as the visible image of the invisible God, is therefore by his very nature the subject of rights which no one may violate—no individual, group, class, nation or State. Not even the majority of a social body may violate these rights" (44.2).

Thus John Paul does not describe the state as instituted by God, as having a divine or sacred character, or as providing a mediated form of God's rule over a political society (Claim A), nor does he ascribe to Christ a position of authority when he is speaking of the state (Claim B). The state is rather extrinsic to society, not a place where humanly-fulfilling or subjectively self-creating work is done; an instrument of a pre-existing society, the state should defer to, protect, and promote human rights. And as the chief right is the right to religious freedom, the state should make room for the church, which proclaims the truth about the human person (cf. *Sollicitudo Rei Socialis* [*SRS*] 41.1). John Paul makes a connection explicit which was implicit in Vatican II: that the source of human rights is Christ's anthropological solidarity with each person.[17] And thus the implied logic of his position is that the state should see Christ, not as its higher judge and the ultimate political authority, but as the one in solidarity with its citizens, particularly the poor.

John Paul is reluctant to apply political language to Christ. In his social encyclicals, he never calls Christ a king, nor does he ascribe to Christ a political function. In fact, he tends to abbreviate biblical quotations—and even on occasion emends a quotation from Vatican II—in order to avoid political language for Christ. At the same time, he emphasizes Christ's anthropological solidarity.

For an example of the pope's treatment of this point in scripture, one may look to his two references in his social encyclicals to that portion of 1 Corinthians 15:24 in which St. Paul writes that Christ will turn over the kingdom to the Father (*SRS* 31.4, *CA* 62.2). In neither case does the pope quote the entire verse, and he passes over what St. Paul states as necessarily preceding this transference of "the" kingdom—namely, Christ's political victory as, in Paul's words, "destroying every rule and every authority and power." Nor does the pope quote at any place in his social encyclicals the subsequent verse: "For he [Christ] must reign until he has put all his enemies under his feet" (1 Cor 15:25). John Paul thus avoids depicting Christ as a ruler or as a victor over political authorities.

An example of the pope's change from Vatican II is provided at *SRS* 48.2, where the pope quotes *Gaudium et Spes* 39. *GS* 39 writes of that future time "when Christ presents to the Father a kingdom eternal and universal." *GS* then quotes from the proper Eucharistic Preface for the feast of Christ the King. *GS* 39 urges the careful distinction of earthly progress and the progress of "Christ's kingdom." In *SRS*, John Paul urges the same distinction and makes generally the same points as *GS* 39, but he avoids calling the kingdom "Christ's."[18]

He avoids depicting Christ not only as a king but also as a judge. Matthew 25:31–46 is referenced at *SRS* 13.2, where John Paul writes that to bring about a commitment to the development of all peoples, in the face of "tragedies of total indigence and need, . . . it is the Lord Jesus himself who comes to question us." Although his reference to this pericope is brief, John Paul makes two moves that hide its political character. First, he does not pick up the titles for Christ—"the Son of man," "the King"—that are used in Matthew 25:31 and 34. Second, the pope writes that Christ *questions* us, whereas Matthew writes that the king will "separate"—an activity of judgment. John Paul has thus, as it were, edited out Jesus' self-identification as the king who judicially separates the righteous from the cursed ones.[19]

John Paul averts his eyes from Christ's judgment when he quotes also from the parable of the talents, the pericope that falls in Matthew's gospel immediately before the judgment scene examined just above. The pope is addressing the duty people have to persist in "the *difficult yet noble task* of improving the lot of man in his totality" (*SRS* 30.6). The pope writes that "the Lord Jesus himself, in the parable of the talents, emphasizes the severe treatment given to the man who dared to hide the gift received" (*SRS* 30.7). But even after quoting "these harsh words" (*SRS* 30.8, referring to "the severe treatment" of the one who hid his talent), John Paul does not say that the slothful one was *judged* by Christ, nor does he say that Christ will judge us if we shirk our duty. John Paul emphasizes the duty, but is silent about Christ's possible judgment of those who shirk it.

Throughout his social teaching John Paul places radical emphasis on a passage from *GS* 22 that "by His incarnation the Son of God has united Himself in some fashion with every man." In his inaugural encyclical, *Redemptor Hominis*, John Paul makes it clear that he understands the union of Christ with each human being not as an ideal but as an accomplished reality. "We are not dealing with the 'abstract' man, but the real, 'concrete,' 'historical' man. We are dealing with 'each' man, for each one is included in the mystery of the Redemption and *with each one Christ has united himself forever through this mystery*" (*RH* 13.3; emphasis added).

The social encyclicals expand upon the meaning and implications of Christ's anthropological solidarity in several ways. Christ's union with every human being excludes no one, and hence the poor are particularly identified with Christ because, in society's eyes, they tend to be undervalued and overlooked—treated as objects rather than as persons. Thus the church proves its fidelity to Christ by being in solidarity with the poor (*LE* 8.6) and sees Christ himself in the poor (*CA* 57.1, 58), and what the church sees is what would be true even if not seen: that is, Christ is in the poor, having united himself with every human being. In a different context, the pope also speaks of how a Christian sees the neighbor (which means any human being, whether poor or not) as "the *living image* of God the Father" (*SRS* 40.2), which is to say, as Christ, the true *imago Dei*.

Christ's anthropological solidarity is not dependent upon a

human being having Christian faith. What Christ reveals is true for all people, regardless of their awareness of Christ ("Christ . . . guides him, even when he is unaware of it" [*CA* 62.3]). In the service of propounding Christ's anthropological solidarity, John Paul performs a slight but significant modification upon the teaching of Vatican II. *Lumen Gentium* 36 speaks of the grace of Christ that elevates from within, so that, through the activity of the faithful in the world, the spirit of Christ comes to permeate the world. John Paul quotes *Lumen Gentium* 36 in *LE* 25.6, but where *LG* speaks of the activity of the faithful, John Paul says that by means of work "man"—all people, not merely the faithful—"shares in the work of creation." Both passages bespeak the possibility of human action being the vehicle of divine influence upon the world. John Paul, however, goes beyond *LG*, and his theological advance is predicated precisely upon the union of Christ with all people—in this case, with all people in their work.

In John Paul's thought, human dignity is christologically bestowed. The human person is never isolated from Christ. Thus *CA* 26.4: what the church has to offer those who are searching for a new, authentic theory and praxis of liberation (along with its own commitment to the struggle) is "her teaching about the human person redeemed in Christ," which is not a teaching about what a Christian is, but what a person is, every person, as a result of Christ's redemption.

Comparison and Significance

With regard to explicit and implicit teaching about Christ and the state, John Paul II at once deepens, clarifies, and simplifies the teaching of Vatican II. The central claims of traditional political theology that were identified at the beginning of this essay—the providential institution of the state, and Christ's superior political rule and judgment—were found to be present in the examined documents of Vatican II but absent in the thought of John Paul II. In Vatican II, those traditional politico-theological claims were already somewhat attenuated; for instance, the state, although an institution of providence, is not described as a mediating institution of God's rule. Christ also was not found in a position of direct judgment over the state, although the church was—when necessary for either the freedom of the church or the general welfare. In Vatican II the traditional claims were also found admixed with other elements, particularly an emphasis upon rights inherent in the human subject.

John Paul simplifies Vatican II by omitting the traditional claims. To take one example, in his social encyclicals there is nothing corresponding to the pronouncement in *GS* 74 that secular political authority is divinely foreordained. Rather, John Paul takes the anthropological and christological claims of Vatican II and firmly grounds them in a vision of human dignity bestowed upon every person by the incarnation of Christ. He thus deepens and clarifies Vatican II. And in doing so he, as it were, moves Christ from a position above civil authorities to a place underneath them: Christ is now in solidarity with each person. The consequence is that the state is urged to protect and promote human rights and dignity, not because the state is ultimately accountable to a higher authority, but because each person under the authority of the state has been decisively united with Christ.

An aspect of the clarification that John Paul brings to this subject is the internal consistency of his thought about Christ and the state. His refusal to ascribe political functions and titles to Christ coheres with his emphatic affirmation of Christ's union with each person. For if Christ were to exercise judgment over humanity, he would have to have a certain distance from that very humanity, since judgment requires separation. So in pursuit of the strongest possible affirmation of *GS* 22, John Paul averts our eyes from Christ in the political functions of exercising power or judgment. His thought is thus more consistent than—and in this regard lacking the internal tensions of—the politico-theological claims of Vatican II.

Despite the significant achievement of giving clarity, christological coherence, and depth to Vatican II's theological anthropology, John Paul's thought bears a weakness that arises from the very element that gives his thought its strength, namely, his strong affirmation of the union of Christ with each person. This union seems to turn the judgment of Christ into something like an unthinkable thought. Indeed, when John Paul preaches on the eschatological parable of the sheep and the goats in Matthew 25, he does not dwell upon the punishment of the "goats," nor on Christ's identity as the "Son of Man" who actively judges between the righteous and the wicked; rather, he emphasizes Christ's solidarity with the poor, and also the commendable solidarity of the "sheep" with the poor.[20] But if Christ can never be seen exercising his judicial function—if he at most questions us and never passes judgment (see *SRS* 13.2, noted earlier)—then what interpretation can be given to the final affirmations of the christological paragraph of the creed: Christ's session in heaven and final judgment?

The author of this paper is a theologian, not a historian and not a psychologist. It may be that John Paul's views on the state arise from his experience, in crucial respects, as a representative twentieth-century man. He matured under Nazism and ministered as priest and bishop to people under the weight of communism. He knew personally the totalitarian state. It might be possible thus to identify a historical and/or psychological genesis for his reduction of the state to merely an instrument of the people and his avoidance of traditional political claims for Christ. Indeed, one might go further and say that John Paul's quite positive, christocentric anthropology may be rooted in the experience of the discovery, under totalitarian regimes, of an inalienable dignity and strength in the human person that the state could not take away, even by torture and death. Should all this be true, nonetheless a theological question would still remain. Is there not a theological necessity—based on the creedal tradition and the logic of the scriptures, if nothing else—that Christ exercise political functions such as judgment and rule? And if that question is answered affirmatively, then the theological problem presents itself: how shall John Paul's anthropology of christological solidarity be synthesized with traditional political theology?

To attempt such a synthesis is important and urgent. For the church to speak with plausibility in our time, it cannot speak in the mode of *Quas primas*. Yet for the church to speak as a voice of integrity across the ages, it cannot simply relegate to silence a large portion of its traditional speech. It is impossible as yet to see the full significance of John Paul's thought on Christ and the state, but if it should turn out that his thought can be brought into intelligible synthesis with the tradition of divine rule, then this pope will be reckoned as a signally important contributor to a revisioned Christian political theology. That revisioned theology must give an account of the perennial themes of authority, the human good of governed life together, the use of power, and the place of judgment. It would need to find a way to encompass in one coherent vision both what John Paul has affirmed and what he has passed over silently: the king of glory ruling at the right hand of Power, the powers of this world who both mediate and alienate his judgments, and every human being a subject with dignity, some of whom know the king's voice, with all of whom he is one.

Conclusion

Claims of traditional political theology are absent from the thought of John Paul II, who makes the state serve the christologically bestowed rights of persons. He thus gives a measure of theological coherence and depth to the modern perspectives of Vatican II documents as regards human dignity, the state, and Christ. At the same time he passes over such traditional politico-theological claims as are present in the Vatican II documents—not to mention the broader tradition generally. The task for theologians in the post-John Paul era is to see if and how his christological humanism can be synthetically comprehended with the traditional claims of the providential character of the state and the political authority of Christ.

Notes

[1]The subject of political theology is, of course, much vaster than any short list of propositions. For a masterful treatment of traditional Christian political theology, see Oliver O'Donovan, *The Desire of the Nations: Rediscovering the Roots of Political Theology* (Cambridge: Cambridge University Press, 1996). Claim A, above, is made famously in Romans 13, and Claim B most emphatically in Pius XI's encyclical *Quas primas* (1925), among countless other instances.

[2]All translations of Vatican II documents are taken from Walter M. Abbott and Joseph Gallagher, eds., *The Documents of Vatican II* (New York: America Press, 1966). Citations will be made parenthetically and refer to section numbers in the documents.

[3]Pius XI had made the same point, but in *Quas primas* (1925) the emphases are different. See, for example, section 17: Although Christ did not exercise his civil authority while on earth, nonetheless his authority embraces earthly politics "by virtue of the absolute empire over all creatures committed to him by the Father" (translation from Claudia Carlen, *The Papal Encyclicals 1903–1939* [Wilmington, N.C.: McGrath, 1981]).

[4]One should note, however, that the Council bestows praise on those who

have political office and work for the common good. See, for example, the reference in *Gaudium et Spes* 75 to "the difficult but most honorable art of politics."

[5]Hereinafter, *GS* refers to *Gaudium et Spes*. This essay agrees with Oswald von Nell-Greuning's argument, if not with his regret, that *GS*'s "political community" is equivalent to "the state." Nell-Greuning is the author of the commentary on this section of *GS* in *Commentary on the Documents of Vatican II*, vol. 5, ed. Herbert Vorgrimler (New York: Herder & Herder, 1969); here, 315-16. See 207-11 where, in the same volume of the *Commentary*, Yves Congar argues that the Council avoids the term "the state" because it wishes to broaden the perspective of the traditional church and state problem, focusing not on the relation of authority to authority but of church community and civil community. Still, to say "political community" is to refer to civil society from the perspective of its governing structure, the state.

[6]Earlier in *GS* praise was given to "those national procedures which allow the largest possible number of citizens to participate in public affairs with genuine freedom" (31).

[7]Nell-Greuning agrees with others who find here "Aristotle's definition of the State" (*Commentary*, vol. 5, 318).

[8]"There are forms of society which are prior to the life of the individual and which are absolutely required if the existence of the individual is to be possible, and which then permanently affect his individual life . . . the family and political society for example. . . . What is meant is the fact that no human person can exist except in an actual community organized as a State" (Otto Semmelroth, in *Commentary*, vol. 5, 168).

[9]It is an account "[i]n complete accordance with the traditional line," according to Nell-Greuning (*Commentary*, vol. 5, 319).

[10]Francisco de Vitoria, the leading figure of what is often considered the "high tradition" of Christian political theology, puts the matter thus: the final cause of political authority ("civil power") is natural necessity; the efficient cause is God; and the material cause is the commonwealth itself, which "takes upon itself the task of governing and administering itself and directing all its powers to the common good" (Vitoria, *On Civil Power*, 1.2-4, in Francisco de Vitoria, *Political Writings*, ed. Anthony Pagden and Jeremy Lawrance [Cambridge: Cambridge University Press, 1991], 6–12).

[11]Traditional political authority holds a place for the response of a governed people to the fact of experienced political community. Its foundational structure is seen when Israel recognizes the Lord as its king and offers him praise. By doing so, Israel proves its political identity. Praise, however, remains but the recognition of political authority, and is not constitutive of it. Praise is the proper response of a governed people to their recognition of the human good of government. See O'Donovan, *The Desire of the Nations*, 46-49.

[12]Some of the following argument draws upon Victor Lee Austin, "John Paul II's Ironic Legacy in Political Theology," *Pro Ecclesia* (forthcoming). For a broader treatment that tests these conclusions against other relevant encyclicals, John Paul's catecheses, his U.N. addresses, and his homilies on Christ the King, see Victor Lee Austin, "A Christological Social Vision: The Uses of Christ in the Social Encyclicals of John Paul II" (Ph.D. dissertation, Fordham University, 2002).

[13]These are the three encyclicals that John Paul II explicitly places in the line of the social tradition of his predecessors: *Laborem Exercens* (1981), *Sollicitudo Rei Socialis* (1987), and *Centesimus Annus* (1991). English translations quoted in the present paper are from J. Michael Miller, ed. and intro., *The Encyclicals of John Paul II* (Huntington, Ind.: Our Sunday Visitor, 1996). Parenthetical citations are to section and paragraph number as given in Miller, which occasionally diverge from the Latin published in *Acta apostolicae sedis.*

[14]The list includes, from the Old Testament: doctor, pharmacist, craftsman or artist, blacksmith (identified with today's foundry workers), potter, farmer, scholar, sailor, builder, musician, shepherd, fisherman, and the work of women; from Jesus' kingdom parables: shepherd, farmer, doctor, sower, householder, servant, steward, fisherman, merchant, laborer, women's work, the apostolate (compared with the manual work of harvesting or fishing), and scholars' work; from St. Paul: tentmaker.

[15]A partial list would include judges and kings from the Old Testament, rulers and judges as characters in Jesus' parables, and Paul's admonitions to pray for those in authority.

[16]The pope's expansive list of types of work includes, at the end, the work of scholars (*LE* 26.2), although, as noted above, he seems blind to political work. In *LE* and elsewhere he seems to include even contemplation and play as types of "work," in that they also are means by which a subject becomes who he or she is. See Karol Wojtyla, "The Problem of the Constitution of Culture Through Human Praxis," in *Person and Community: Selected Essays* (New York: Peter Lang, 1993), 271.

[17]Regarding the link of the incarnation with human rights and the relationship of Vatican II to John Paul II, Édouard Hamel writes: "The statements are there [*GS* 22, etc.], but the theological development remains minimal. It would be left to John Paul II to expand on them and provide them with greater depth by showing more clearly the meaning of the incarnation for teaching on human rights" (Édouard Hamel, "The Foundations of Human Rights in Biblical Theology Following the Orientations of *Gaudium et Spes*," in *Vatican II: Assessment and Perspectives*, ed. René Latourelle [New York and Mahwah: Paulist Press, 1989], 2:467).

[18]Here is the passage from *GS* 39 as quoted in *SRS* 48.2: "When we have spread on earth the fruits of our nature and our enterprise—human dignity, fraternal communion, and freedom—according to the command of the Lord

and in his Spirit, we will find them once again, cleansed this time from the stain of sin, illumined and transfigured, when Christ presents to his Father an eternal and universal Kingdom. . . . Here on earth that kingdom is already present in mystery" [ellipsis in original Latin; see *AAS* 80 (1988):583]. In *GS* 39, the immediate context speaks of "the growth of Christ's kingdom"; the words omitted by John Paul's ellipsis are a quotation from the preface of Christ the King.

A further instance in which John Paul avoids stating that Christ has a kingdom involves an alteration of a direct quotation from Vatican II. In what is set forth as a direct quotation of *Lumen Gentium* 3, the pope says in a catechetical talk, "The Church, or in other words, the kingdom of God now present in mystery, grows visibly through the power of God in the world." *LG* 3, however, reads, *Ecclesia, seu regnum Christi iam praesens in mysterio, ex virtute Dei in mundo visibiliter crescit*. See John Paul II, *Jesus, Son and Savior: A Catechesis on the Creed* (Boston: Pauline Books & Media, 1996), 369, and *Acta apostolicae sedis* 57 (1965): 6.

[19]Avery Cardinal Dulles uses this instance to buttress his judgment that, in political theology as on some other points, John Paul's "personalist perspective," which Dulles sees as important, nonetheless "stands in tension with previous Catholic tradition" (Avery Cardinal Dulles, *John Paul II and the Mystery of the Human Person*, Laurence J. McGinley Lecture, October 21, 2003 [New York: Fordham University Press, 2003], 13, and see 19.

[20]John Paul II's homilies on the solemnity of Christ the King are published in the English weekly edition of *L'Osservatore Romano*. For further analysis see Austin, "A Christological Social Vision," 185-93.

Catholic Teaching on War, Peace, and Nonviolence since Vatican II

John Sniegocki

Several fundamental transformations have taken place in the history of the Catholic Church's teaching on issues of war and peace. One of these was the so-called Constantinian transformation, which involved a shift from the predominantly nonviolent ethos of the church of the first three centuries to the development of a Christian just-war theory in the fourth century. A second transformation was the development of the crusade in the Middle Ages, an approach to war that would later be repudiated. A third transformation, still in process, began at the time of the Second Vatican Council. Features of this post-Vatican II transformation have included an increasingly stringent application of just-war criteria, a renewed appreciation for pacifism as a Catholic option, increased emphasis on the need for structural reforms to establish the conditions necessary for peace, and a strong emphasis on the efficacy of active nonviolence as a method to combat injustice. These new emphases have contributed to a nearly complete rejection of modern warfare in official Catholic teaching, particularly in the thought of Pope John Paul II. After some preliminary comments on earlier church teaching, I will focus on this post-Vatican II transformation of magisterial thought on war, peace, and nonviolence.

Early Church Pacifism and the Development of Just-War Theory

Leaders of the early Christian community strongly emphasized the nonviolent nature of the teachings of Jesus. According to church historians, there exists no evidence of Christian participation in the Roman military until approximately the year 170 C.E.[1] After this time sporadic accounts of Christian soldiers appear in the historical record. Many of these earliest Christian soldiers seem to have been men who converted to Christianity while already serving in the military. According to the *Apostolic Tradition*, an early church law code, any person who was already Christian or who was a catechumen and who sought to join the military was to "be dismissed [from the church], for they have despised God."[2] Those who converted while already serving in the military were to refuse to obey any orders to kill. Verse 17 of the *Apostolic Tradition* states: "A soldier . . . shall not kill anyone. If ordered to, he shall not carry out the order, nor shall he take the oath. If he does not accept this, let him be dismissed [from the church]."[3]

Prior to the time of Constantine in the fourth century, we have no record of any church leader explicitly approving of Christians joining the military, while there exist numerous accounts of church leaders opposing military service.[4] The reasons for this opposition were multiple, including concerns about idolatrous worship of the emperor and the sexual immorality that often characterized military life. The primary reason for opposition to military service, however, seems to have been the conviction that the act of killing (in war or any other context) constituted a direct and fundamental violation of the teachings of Jesus. "We [Christians]," the early church theologian Origen states, "no longer take up sword against nation, nor do we learn war any more, having become children of peace for the sake of Jesus, who is our leader."[5] "The Christian Lawgiver," Origen explains, "did not deem it in keeping with laws such as this, which were derived from a divine source, to allow the killing of any individual whatever."[6] This pacifist rationale for opposing military service is further explained in another early Christian text, Lactantius' *Divine Institutions*:

> When God prohibits killing, he not only forbids us to commit brigandage, which is not allowed even by the public laws, but he warns us not to do even those things which are regarded as legal among men. And so it will not be lawful for a just man to serve as a soldier—for justice itself is his military service—nor to accuse anyone of a capital offense, because it makes no difference whether you kill with a sword or with a word, since killing itself is forbidden. And so, in this commandment of

> God, no exception at all ought to be made to the rule that it is always wrong to kill a man, whom God has wished to be a sacrosanct creature.[7]

In the late fourth and early fifth centuries the Christian just-war theory was developed by Augustine, drawing upon the work of his teacher Ambrose and the Roman philosopher Cicero. These thinkers argued that war could be morally acceptable if certain strict conditions were met, such as just cause (for example, defense of the innocent), proper intention, and declaration of war by a legitimate authority. It was at this time that Christian participation in warfare first became officially accepted by church leaders. As the just-war theory took root, the nonviolent ethos of the early Christians largely receded from church teaching. In the Middle Ages the church's acceptance of violence would extend even to the crusades. Following the crusades the just-war tradition reasserted its dominant role in Christian thought and the criteria for a just war were further refined.[8] The dominance of just-war thinking and the marginalization of pacifism became so strong in Catholic thought that as recently as 1956 Pope Pius XII could declare that it was morally unacceptable for a Catholic to be a pacifist and to refuse to serve in a justified war.[9] Only after Vatican II would pacifism again be officially acknowledged as a legitimate Catholic option.

Pope John XXIII: *Pacem in Terris*

In the early 1960s, official Catholic teaching on war began to undergo a major transformation. In his encyclical *Pacem in Terris*, issued in 1963, Pope John XXIII asserted the inappropriateness of war in the modern world and highlighted the conditions needed for authentic and lasting peace. In light of the destructiveness of current weaponry, Pope John declared, "it is contrary to reason to hold that war is now a suitable way to restore rights which have been violated" (*PT* 127). Pope John continued to adhere to the just-war tradition, but expressed serious doubts as to whether any modern war could meet the just-war criteria. Focusing attention instead on the conditions needed for peace, Pope John emphasized the importance of respect for a broad range of human rights, including not only civil/political rights (such as freedom of speech and assembly, which were generally stressed in Western, capitalist countries) but also social/economic rights (such as the right to employment, food, housing, education, and health care, which tended to be more strongly stressed in socialist countries). Both types of rights, Pope John argued, were integrally related.

Pope John also highlighted the urgency of creating a "worldwide political authority" that would be democratically organized and would have sufficient power to effectively prevent war, including the authority to enact the social and economic reforms needed for greater equity in the global system (*PT* 137-41). Pope John's thought thus helped to consolidate an important shift of focus away from debates concerning justification of war to an emphasis on the responsibility for building structures of peace.

The "New Attitude" of Vatican II

The rethinking of official Catholic approaches to war that Pope John XXIII initiated was taken up and further developed by the Second Vatican Council in the document *Gaudium et Spes*. In this document the Council proclaimed the need to "undertake an evaluation of war with an entirely new attitude" (*GS* 80). Part of this "new attitude" included an affirmation of the legitimacy of pacifism as a Catholic option (in direct contrast to the teaching of Pius XII) and a call for governments to provide legal protection for conscientious objectors (*GS* 78-79). Another part of the new approach was an affirmation of the need to more rigorously apply just-war criteria. The Council issued, for example, a strong condemnation of attacks directed at civilian populations, such as the atomic bombing of Hiroshima and Nagasaki. "Any act of war aimed indiscriminately at the destruction of entire cities or of extensive areas along with their population," the Council declared, "is a crime against God and man himself. It merits unequivocal and unhesitating condemnation" (*GS* 80). The Council also critiqued the arms race between the superpowers, which it described in powerful terms as "an utterly treacherous trap for humanity, and one which injures the poor to an intolerable degree" (*GS* 81). Like Pope John XXIII, the Council viewed the ultimate solution to the problem of war to lie in the creation of a democratically established "universal public authority." This international authority, the Council argued, should be "endowed with effective power to safeguard, on the behalf of all, security, regard for justice, and respect for rights" (*GS* 82).

Pope Paul VI: "No More War, War Never Again!"

The critical views expressed by the Second Vatican Council concerning war and the need for alternatives to war were strongly influenced by the witness of both Pope John XXIII and Pope Paul VI. It was Pope Paul's famous speech at the United Nations, in which he passionately declared "No more war, war never again!," that provided the context for the Council's deliberations on war. Pope Paul's U.N. speech took place on October 4, 1965. The Council began formal discussion of the war and peace section of *Gaudium et Spes* on October 5, the very next day.[10]

One particularly important contribution that Paul VI made to Catholic reflection on war and peace was his proclamation each year of the first day of January as the "World Day of Peace," which he commemorated with an annual World Day of Peace message. These papal messages, continued by John Paul II, have become a rich resource for the church's moral reflection on war. Common themes in the World Day of Peace reflections of Paul VI included the immorality of the arms race, the dangers of nuclear war, the importance of international organizations such as the United Nations, the assertion that peace is a viable possibility and not an unrealistic dream, and the declaration that Catholics have a fundamental duty to work for the realization of peace. It is essential, Pope Paul emphasized, to proclaim "at the top of our voice the absurdity of modern war and the absolute necessity of Peace."[11]

Along with discouraging war between states (which was the main focus of his World Day of Peace messages), Pope Paul also sought to discourage revolutionary violence. In his encyclical letter *Evangelii Nuntiandi*, for example, Pope Paul stated: "The Church cannot accept violence . . . as the path to liberation, because she knows that violence always provokes violence and irresistibly engenders new forms of oppression and enslavement. . . . We must say and reaffirm that violence is not in accord with the Gospel, that it is not Christian" (*EN* 37). Such bold statements in opposition to "violence" in general (rather than focusing on distinctions between justified and unjustified violence) were reiterated many times in the social teaching of Pope John Paul II.

Pope John Paul II: Deepening the Rejection of War

The tradition of Catholic teaching on war and peace has been further developed in a variety of important ways during the papacy of Pope John Paul II. These developments include deepened attention to the negative consequences of *all* wars (even those that may have a just cause), a further move away from the use of just-war language, an increased emphasis on the efficacy of nonviolence, and an increased emphasis on forgiveness as the basis for authentic and lasting peace.

Throughout his papacy, John Paul II was a prominent critic of war. His opposition to the Persian Gulf War of 1991 and his opposition to the ongoing war in Iraq are perhaps the most well-known examples of his opposition to war, though his rejection of war was expressed in many other contexts as well. One of the most striking features of John Paul's statements on war is that he rarely made use of the language of the just-war tradition. Rather, his comments almost always consisted of broad critiques of the very notion of war itself, and even of all forms of violence:

> Today, the scale and horror of modern warfare—whether nuclear or not—makes it totally unacceptable as a means of settling differences between nations. War should belong to the tragic past, to history; it should find no place on humanity's agenda for the future. (Homily at Bagington Airport, England, 1982)[12]

> Is it not necessary *to give everything in order to avoid war*, even the "limited war" thus euphemistically called by those who are not directly concerned in it, given the evil that every war represents, its price that has to be paid in human lives, in suffering, in the devastation of what would be necessary for human life and development, without counting the upset of necessary tranquility, the deterioration of the social fabric, the hardening of mistrust and hatred which wars maintain towards one's neighbor? (Message for 1983 World Day of Peace—emphasis in original)[13]

Recent history clearly shows the failure of recourse to violence as a means for resolving political and social problems. War destroys, it does not build up; it weakens the moral foundations of society and creates further divisions and long-lasting tensions. . . . How often have my Predecessors and I myself called for an end to these horrors! I shall continue to do so until it is understood that war is the failure of all true humanism. (Message for 1999 World Day of Peace)[14]

It is essential, therefore, that religious people and communities should in the clearest and most radical way repudiate violence, all violence. (Address to representatives of the world's religions gathered at Assisi, Italy, to pray for peace on January 24, 2002)[15]

When, as in Iraq in these days, war threatens the fate of humanity, it is even more urgent to proclaim with a strong and decisive voice that peace is the only path for building a society which is more just and marked by solidarity. Violence and weapons can never resolve the problems of man. (March 22, 2003)[16]

[I]t is crucial for humanity to resolutely make a true commitment to peace. Peace never requires violence. . . . Especially those who come from countries whose soil is stained with blood know well that violence constantly generates violence. War throws open the doors to the abyss of evil. . . . This is why war should always be considered a defeat: the defeat of reason and of humanity. . . . War never again! I was convinced of this in October 1986 in Assisi, when I asked people belonging to all religions to gather side by side to invoke God for peace. I am even more convinced of it today. (September 3, 2004)[17]

To attain the good of peace there must be a clear and conscious acknowledgement that violence is an unacceptable evil and that it never solves problems. Violence is a lie, for it goes against the truth of our faith, the truth of our humanity. Violence destroys what it claims to defend: the dignity, the life, the freedom of other human beings. (Message for World Day of Peace 2005)[18]

In these passages Pope John Paul II frequently sounds like a pacifist, expressing his moral opposition to *all* war and violence. Nonetheless, he did not think of himself as a pacifist.[19] Although he chose only infrequently to speak in the specific language of just-war theory, his strong opposition to war appears to have been rooted in a very strict interpretation of just-war criteria as applied to our present context. John Paul acknowledges, for example, that "peoples have a right and even a duty to protect their existence and freedom by proportionate means against an unjust aggressor." In theory these "proportionate" means could include the use of violence. John Paul immediately qualifies this statement, however, by highlighting differences between our current context and past contexts, differences that undercut the legitimacy of recourse to war. "[I]n view of the difference between classical warfare and nuclear or bacteriological war, a difference so to speak of nature, and in view of the scandal of the arms race seen against the backdrop of the needs of the Third World, this right [of armed self-defense], which is very real in principle, only underlines the urgency" of finding alternatives to war. "War," John Paul concludes, "is the most barbarous and least effective way of resolving conflicts."[20]

While John Paul affirms the right of national defense by proportionate means, he seems to question whether modern war can any longer meet this criterion of proportionality. One factor in this assessment, of course, is the high percentage of civilian deaths and injuries that have characterized modern wars. It is commonly estimated, for example, that civilians have constituted about 90 percent of the casualties of war in the past couple of decades.[21] In addition, the pope highlights a range of other negative consequences of war, including the destruction of infrastructure, the waste of funds that could be used to meet the needs of the poor, the destruction of the environment, the psychological and spiritual impact of killing on those who kill, and the cycles of animosity and desire for vengeance that wars fuel. Reflecting upon the Persian Gulf War of 1991, for example, John Paul stated:

> I myself, on the occasion of the recent tragic war in the Persian Gulf, repeated the cry: "Never again war!" No, never again war, which destroys the lives of innocent people, teaches how to kill, throws into upheaval even the lives of those who do

> the killing and leaves behind a trail of resentment and hatred, thus making it all the more difficult to find a just solution of the very problems which provoked the war.[22]

John Paul made similar comments on the negative impacts of war and on the failure of war to solve problems in his 1993 World Day of Peace message:

> Recourse to violence, in fact, aggravates existing tensions and creates new ones. *Nothing is resolved by war; on the contrary, everything is placed in jeopardy by war.* The results of this scourge are the suffering and death of innumerable individuals, the disintegration of human relations and the irreparable loss of an immense artistic and environmental patrimony. War worsens the sufferings of the poor; indeed, it creates new poor by destroying means of subsistence, homes and property, and by eating away at the very fabric of the social environment. . . . After so many unnecessary massacres, it is in the final analysis of fundamental importance to recognize, once and for all, that *war never helps the human community*, that violence destroys and never builds up, that the wounds it causes remain long unhealed, and that as a result of conflicts the already grim condition of the poor deteriorates still further, and new forms of poverty appear. (emphasis in original)[23]

Pope John Paul II, the U.S. Catholic Bishops, and Nonviolence

In addition to a very strict interpretation of the just-war criterion of proportionality, Pope John Paul II also highlighted important issues related to the just-war criterion of last resort. In particular, the pope argued that the efficacy of nonviolence in defending violated rights shows that recourse to violence is often not truly the only remaining option. This emphasis on nonviolence comes to the fore in John Paul's thought, especially after the successful nonviolent overthrow of the communist regimes of Eastern Europe, in which his own support for the Solidarity movement in Poland played an important role. The end of communism, the pope states, was brought about by

> the nonviolent commitment of people who, while always refusing to yield to the force of power, succeeded time after time in finding effective ways of bearing witness to the truth. This disarmed the adversary, since violence always needs to justify itself through deceit, and to appear, however falsely, to be defending a right or responding to a threat posed by others. . . . I pray that this example will prevail in other places and other circumstances. May people learn to fight for justice without violence, renouncing class struggle in their internal disputes and war in international ones.[24]

"Those who have built their lives on the value of non-violence," John Paul states, "have given us a luminous and prophetic example."[25] In addition to the success of nonviolence in Eastern Europe, the pope could also have cited numerous other cases from recent decades, in which mass nonviolent action has brought about the end of repressive, dictatorial regimes. Utilizing methods such as strikes, boycotts, refusal to carry out orders, and mass nonviolent intervention, oppressive regimes have been removed from power in countries such as the Philippines, South Africa, Chile, Serbia, Uruguay, Bolivia, and numerous others. Indeed, never has the historical evidence for the power of nonviolent action been stronger.[26]

This emphasis on nonviolence seen in the thought of John Paul II has also played an increasingly important role in the reflections of the U.S. Catholic bishops. The U.S. bishops' discussion of nonviolent action in *The Challenge of Peace* (nos. 221-230) represents the most extensive discussion of nonviolence in the Catholic social teaching documents. "Nonviolent means of resistance to evil," the bishops assert, "deserve much more study and consideration than they have thus far received."[27] The bishops (writing prior to the nonviolent revolutions in Eastern Europe and elsewhere) cite several historical examples of successful nonviolent action, including effective nonviolent resistance to the Nazis in Norway and Denmark.[28] In their pastoral letter *The Harvest of Justice Is Sown in Peace*, which was published in 1993 to commemorate the tenth anniversary of *The Challenge of Peace*, the bishops return to this theme of nonviolence and incorporate new examples from the preceding decade. They stress that nonviolence, properly understood, is a powerful way of actively challenging injustice:

> The vision of Christian nonviolence is not passive about injustice. . . . For it consists of a commitment to resist manifest injustice and public evil with means other than force. . . . Dramatic political transitions in places as diverse as the Philippines and Eastern Europe demonstrate the power of nonviolent action, even against dictatorial and totalitarian regimes. . . . National leaders bear a moral obligation to see that nonviolent alternatives are seriously considered for dealing with conflicts.[29]

The assertion that governments have a moral obligation to actively consider nonviolence represented a new insight in Catholic social thought. The U.S. bishops in fact recognized it as constituting "development of doctrine" and requested Vatican approval of this material prior to publication. Such approval was received.[30] With this increased recognition of the power of nonviolence, assert the U.S. bishops, the "presumption against the use of force" is strengthened. The "threshold for the use of force," they argue, is raised.[31] In other words, according to the bishops, recognition of the power of nonviolent action has made it even more difficult to meet the criteria for a just war.

Humanitarian Interventions

We have seen that Pope John Paul II issued many broad statements critical of modern war and supportive of nonviolent alternatives. At the same time, John Paul's opposition to the use of force was not absolute. In cases of severe danger to human rights, such as attempts at genocide, he continued to affirm the moral obligation to "disarm the aggressor," including by the use of force if necessary. This use of force, however, would need to adhere to very strict guidelines (especially concerning noncombatant immunity), would need to be limited in scope, and would need to be conducted "in full respect for international law, guaranteed by an authority that is internationally recognized."[32] In other words, the pope seemed to be envisioning some type of U.N.-authorized peacekeeping mission. Significantly, such an envisioned use of force never seems to be described by John Paul as "war," but appears rather to be viewed as constituting a separate category, perhaps better thought of in terms of "international policing." There is therefore no contradiction, in John Paul's mind, between his general critique of "war" and his support for limited, U.N.-authorized uses of force to prevent genocide or other massive violations of human rights.

Expanding the Discussion to Focus on the Conditions for Peace

The reflections of Catholic social teaching on the legitimacy or illegitimacy of recourse to violence make an important contribution to moral reflection on war. Equally important, however, is the attention that Catholic social teaching places upon building the conditions for peace. Questions of just war and pacifism are in a very real sense subordinate in recent Catholic teaching to this broader issue of constructing peace. We have seen above the emphasis placed by Pope John XXIII and the Second Vatican Council on the need to develop a "worldwide public authority" with the power and mandate to act effectively on behalf of peace. John Paul II continued this emphasis. In practice this has primarily meant a call for a strengthening of the United Nations, with an expansion of capacities in areas such as peacemaking/peacekeeping, economic justice, and ecological regulation, along with a general call for increased respect for international law.[33]

Catholic social teaching also strongly emphasizes the need for greater economic and political democracy as essential preconditions for peace. Economic democracy would include a more equitable distribution of the world's resources and more widespread participation in economic decision-making. Guaranteeing the basic rights of all to employment, food, housing, health care, education, and other basic goods and services is an integral part of the comprehensive understanding of human rights that is at the heart of the vision of peace of Catholic social teaching. Measures such as relief of third-world debt, more fair terms of trade (as opposed to "free trade"), and increased levels of aid (without harmful conditions attached) are some of the reform suggestions that Catholic social teaching makes with regard to the international arena. Significantly, Pope John Paul II repeatedly stressed that the overcoming of injustice through respect for a broad range of human rights was the key to combating terrorism. In his 2002 World Day of Peace message, for example, John Paul highlighted the need for "a courageous and resolute political, diplomatic, and economic commitment to relieving situations of oppression and marginalization which facilitate the designs of terrorists."[34]

Another important condition for authentic and lasting peace that Pope John Paul II has repeatedly stressed is forgiveness. In light of the many historical animosities and cycles of violence and vengeance that exist, John Paul strongly emphasized the need for "healing of memory" and for the reconciliation that only forgiveness can bring. Forgiveness, John Paul argues, is not in tension with justice, but is rather the fullest expression of justice, which is concerned with repairing relationships that are broken. Forgiveness and reconciliation are part of truly divine justice, modeled by Jesus.[35]

These reflections on forgiveness point to the underlying Christological foundation of John Paul's understanding of peace. The motivation for Christians to eschew violence, embrace nonviolent action, and seek reconciliation is ultimately rooted in their relationship with Jesus Christ. "It is by uniting his own sufferings for the sake of truth and freedom to the sufferings of Christ on the Cross," says John Paul, "that man is able to accomplish the miracle of peace and is in a position to discern the often narrow path between the cowardice which gives in to evil and the violence which, under the illusion of fighting evil, only makes it worse."[36] The life and teachings of Jesus, the pope argues, stand as a powerful witness against violence. "Violence is a lie," John Paul states,

> for it goes against the truth of our faith, the truth of our humanity . . . ; do not believe in violence; do not support violence. It is not the Christian way. It is not the way of the Catholic Church. Believe in peace and forgiveness and love, for they are of Christ. Yes, the Gospel of Christ is a Gospel of peace: "Blessed are the peacemakers; for they shall be called children of God."[37]

Increased Emphasis on Peacemaking and the End of Just Wars?

In this overview of magisterial reflections on war and peace, we have seen that some very significant developments have taken place in Catholic teaching since the time of the Second Vatican Council. There has been, for example, a renewed emphasis on pacifism as a legitimate option for Catholics.[38] Increased emphasis has also been placed on the imperative of building peace—through the overcoming of economic injustice, respect for human rights and international law, and the strengthening of international organizations such as the United Nations. The power of active nonviolence as a response to injustice and the importance of forgiveness in the process of building peace have been stressed. While the just-war theory has not been disavowed, serious doubts have been expressed as to whether any modern war could meet the criteria. Some have suggested that a development similar to that which took place concerning Catholic teaching on capital punishment may be taking place on the issue of war, namely, that while the legitimacy of these practices is not inherently denied, their appropriateness in our contemporary context is rejected. Very significantly, one person who has put forth such an argument is Cardinal Joseph Ratzinger, now Pope Benedict XVI. In the context of expressing his opposition to the war in Iraq in May of 2003, Cardinal Ratzinger stated: "There were not sufficient reasons to unleash a war against Iraq. To say nothing of the fact that, given the new weapons that make possible destructions that go beyond the combatant groups, today we should be asking ourselves if it is still licit to admit the very existence of a 'just war.' "[39]

Toward the Future: Concluding Reflections

The recent tradition of Catholic reflection on war, peace, and nonviolence is a rich one and has much to contribute to the discernment of a Christian moral response to the problems that our world currently faces. The challenge for church leaders, educators, and all Catholics is to take these teachings seriously and to find ways to make them come alive. Currently, many Catholics are sadly unaware of the magisterium's teachings on war, nonviolence, and the building of peace. With regard to the increasingly central role of nonviolence in magisterial thought, for example, Drew Christiansen has stated: "The Church's gradual embrace of nonviolence is a well-kept secret in need of much catechizing among ordinary Christians and institutionalizing in the life of parishes and dioceses as well."[40]

Part of the responsibility for this lack of knowledge among Catholics of church teaching on war and peace issues has been the widespread failure of Catholic bishops, priests, and other church leaders to publicly proclaim the teachings due to their controversial nature. The current war in Iraq provides a telling example. Despite the Vatican's position that the war did not meet the criteria for a just war, there were very few bishops or priests in the United States who expressed public encouragement to Catholics to conscientiously object to participation in the war. Such support for refusal to participate, however, should be an integral part of a serious application of the church's just-war principles, which include the moral obligation not to serve in unjustified wars.[41]

A major campaign of education concerning church teaching on war, peace, and nonviolence is direly needed. This could take a variety of forms in parishes, in diocesan media, in elementary and high schools, and in Catholic universities. Education on the Christian call to peacemaking, rather than being relegated to an occasional program sponsored by a "peace and justice" committee, must become an integral part of all Catholic catechesis and education. One important part of these efforts to deepen the formation of Catholic conscience on war and peace issues would be to acquaint Catholics with the reflections on war of the pre-Constantinian church, thereby helping Catholics to see the deep roots of principled nonviolence in the Christian tradition, an approach grounded ultimately in the life and teachings of Jesus himself. Education on the history of nonviolent action and its proven success in overcoming repressive regimes and bringing about needed social reforms throughout the world is also crucial, enabling a recognition that commitment to nonviolence does not mean succumbing to injustice. Needed as well are efforts to more fully operationalize the principles of the just-war tradition, including sustained emphasis on the moral obligation to refuse to serve in unjustified wars (which must take precedence over uncritical nationalism or appeals to patriotic "duty") and the creation of structures within the church to actively encourage and support those who make such a choice.

Too often the just-war tradition has simply functioned to provide a rationalization for war and to justify whatever war one's government was currently engaged in. As John Yoder has rightly pointed out, unless there is a willingness to prepare for and follow through on a judgment that a war does not meet just-war criteria (which requires the advance education and preparations necessary to make such a course of action realistically possible), then the just-war tradition is not in fact being sincerely adhered to.[42] Given the strong movement in Catholic magisterial thought toward a judgment that no modern war could meet the just-war criteria, preparation for such non-participation in war is especially critical at the present time.

In addition to the widespread effort that is needed to more fully inform Catholics about church teaching and to put this teaching into practice, I would suggest that there are also several ways in which magisterial thought on war, peace, and nonviolence could be enhanced through further clarification and development.

There is the need for greater clarity concerning the conditions that must be met to justify armed humanitarian intervention. Several of the criteria given by Pope John Paul II were highlighted above, including, for example, that intervention must be in response to grave violations of human rights, must respect noncombatant immunity, must be in accord with international law, and must be "guaranteed by an authority that is internationally recognized." These criteria are a helpful start, but could profitably be explored in more detail. What constitute the essential differences, for example, between a justified "humanitarian intervention" or "police action" and an unjustified "war"? Unless the criteria are sufficiently clear, there seems to be the danger that these criteria for "just intervention" can be abused just as the criteria for "just war" have often been.

Christian theologian Walter Wink has argued that when the church allows for any use of violence, this limited acceptance of the use of violence opens the door in practice to widespread acceptance of violence, far exceeding what the church intends. Therefore, Wink claims that it is essential that the church reject all violence.[43] If the Catholic Church is to continue to accept some forms of violence (namely, "just interventions"), then it seems crucial to try to explain why and how these implications that Wink warns against can be avoided.

If the church takes seriously the broad condemnation of modern warfare and the increased emphasis on the imperative of nonviolent responses to evil that have been articulated in church teaching by Pope John Paul II and others, it is inevitable that fundamental tensions will arise between the church and any nation-state that relies on the use of force and that continues to devote enormous sums of money to preparations for warfare. In these circumstances, how are Catholics to respond? If no modern war can meet the criteria for a just war, is traditional military service (as opposed to service in some type of U.N.-organized peacekeeping force) morally licit? Also, what are the implications for the payment of taxes that support war or that support the continued possession of nuclear weapons? In a recent statement to a Review Conference of the Nuclear Non-Proliferation Treaty, the Vatican declared that strategies of nuclear deterrence are no longer morally acceptable.[44] What concrete actions should follow for Catholics from this and similar judgments? These are questions that need to be explored.

Catholic teaching concerning just war has traditionally been based on an understanding of natural law derived from the thought of Thomas Aquinas, which includes the right to violent self-defense as one of its principles. If increased emphasis continues to be placed in church teaching on a christologically grounded embrace of nonviolence (as seen in the thought of Pope John Paul II), what implications would this have for Catholic understanding of natural law? Perhaps Catholic thought on natural law could be enhanced here through dialogue with the thought of Gandhi, who conceptualized nonviolence as being most in accord with human nature properly understood. "Nonviolence is the law of our species," Gandhi stated, "as violence is the law of the brute."[45] Particularly since Catholics understand Jesus to be the fullest embodiment of true human nature, it seems only fitting that Jesus' example of nonviolence be incorporated more deeply into Catholic natural law perspectives.

Lastly, it is crucial for the church to continue to seek to foster a spirituality of nonviolence and reconciliation. This spirituality of nonviolence must be an integral part of the efforts to create a "culture of life." Without a foundation in prayer and without moral formation deeply grounded in the life and teachings of Jesus, it seems unlikely that the church's increasingly strong rejection of war and embrace of nonviolence will ever take root. Too often in church life there has been a divorce between those concerned with the practice of spiritual disciplines and those concerned for peace and justice issues. Efforts to integrate these emphases more consistently in church education and activities are essential.

The challenges raised by magisterial teaching on issues of war, peace, and nonviolence since the Second Vatican Council are profound. By attending to them seriously, may we all grow into greater faithfulness to Jesus Christ, the prince of peace.

Notes

[1]C. John Cadoux, *The Early Christian Attitude Toward War* (New York: Seabury, 1982), 97; John Driver, *How Christians Made Peace with War* (Scottdale, Penn.: Herald Press, 1988), 14.

[2]*Apostolic Tradition*, v. 17. Quoted in Driver, *How Christians Made Peace*, 49.

[3]*Apostolic Tradition*, v. 19. Quoted in ibid.

[4]In addition to the works cited above, see Jean Michel Hornus, *It Is Not Lawful for Me to Fight: Early Christian Attitudes Towards War, Violence, and the State*, rev. ed. (Scottdale, Penn.: Herald Press, 1980).

[5]Origen, *Contra Celsus*. Quoted in Eileen Egan, *Peace Be with You: Justified Warfare or the Way of Nonviolence* (Maryknoll, N.Y.: Orbis Books, 1999), 27.

[6]Origen, *Contra Celsus*. Quoted in Driver, *How Christians Made Peace*, 67.

[7]Lactantius, *Divine Institutions*. Quoted in John Ferguson, *The Politics of Love: The New Testament and Nonviolent Revolution* (Nyack, N.Y.: Fellowship Publications, 1979), 59-60.

[8]For a classic overview of the Christian tradition on war and peace, see Roland Bainton, *Christian Attitudes Toward War and Peace: A Historical Survey and Critical Re-evaluation* (New York: Abingdon Press, 1960). Also see Lisa Sowle Cahill, *Love Your Enemies: Discipleship, Pacifism, and Just War Theory* (Minneapolis: Fortress Press, 1994).

[9]Pope Pius XII declared in his 1956 Christmas Message that, in the case of a defensive war embarked upon by a legitimately elected government, "a Catholic citizen cannot invoke his own conscience in order to refuse to serve and fulfill those duties the law imposes." It should be noted that this statement refers to lay Catholics, as Catholic clergy are forbidden by canon law to directly participate in warfare. This rule that clergy should not participate in warfare is one area where the nonviolent ethos of the early church endured throughout Roman Catholic history, even if the explicit underlying rationale has more to do with the proper role of priests than with principled pacifism as such.

[10]The Council's deliberations were also influenced by the moral witness of a group of pacifist women, including Dorothy Day, who undertook ten days of fasting and prayer in Rome and who met with numerous bishops as the section of *Gaudium et Spes* on war and peace was being drafted. For a good discussion of the events surrounding the drafting of this text, see Egan, *Peace*

Be with You, 166-80. For a good discussion of Catholic pacifism in the United States in the last century, including the witness of Dorothy Day and the Catholic Worker movement, see Patricia McNeal, *Harder than War: Catholic Peacemaking in 20th Century America* (New Brunswick: Rutgers University Press, 1992).

[11]Pope Paul VI, "Message for World Day of Peace 1978." All of the World Day of Peace messages of Pope Paul VI and Pope John Paul II can be found online at http://www.vatican.va

[12]Pope John Paul II, "Homily at Bagington Airport," *Origins* 12 (1982): 55.

[13]Pope John Paul II, "Dialogue for Peace, a Challenge for Our Time" (Message for World Day of Peace 1983), 4.

[14]Pope John Paul II, "Respect for Human Rights: The Secret of True Peace" (Message for World Day of Peace 1999), 11.

[15]"Pope Asks for Believers' Commitment against Violence." Available online at http://www.zenit.org/english/war/visualizza.phtml?sid=15609

[16]"Pope Says Iraq War Threatens Humanity." Available online at http://www.cathnews.com/news/303/124.php

[17]Pope John Paul II, "Message for 'Religions and Cultures' Meeting" in Milan, Italy (September 3, 2004). Available online at http://www.mercyoma.org/documents/Justice/kaspar.pdf

[18]Pope John Paul II, "Do Not Be Overcome by Evil But Overcome Evil with Good" (Message for World Day of Peace 2005), 4.

[19]For example, during an interview with an Italian journalist concerning his opposition to the Persian Gulf War of 1991, Pope John Paul II is reported to have said, "I am not a pacifist." See Drew Christiansen, "Peacemaking and the Use of Force: Behind the Pope's Stringent Just-War Teaching," *America* (May 15, 1999), 14.

[20]Pope John Paul II, "Peace: A Gift of God Entrusted to Us" (Message for World Day of Peace 1982), 12.

[21]Walter Wink, *The Powers That Be: Theology for a New Millennium* (New York: Doubleday, 1998), 137. For further discussion of the effects of war on civilians, especially children, see UNICEF, *State of the World's Children 1996* (New York: Oxford University Press, 1995).

[22]Pope John Paul II, *Centesimus Annus*, 52.

[23]Pope John Paul II, "If You Want Peace, Reach Out to the Poor" (Message for World Day of Peace 1993), 4.

[24]Ibid., 23.

[25]Pope John Paul II, "Peace on Earth to Those Whom God Loves" (Message for World Day of Peace 2000), 4.

[26]For several excellent books exploring the theory and history of nonviolent action, especially the history of nonviolence in the twentieth century, see Peter Ackerman and Jack Duvall, *A Force More Powerful: A Century of Nonviolent Conflict* (New York: St. Martin's Press, 2000); Gene Sharp,

Waging Nonviolent Struggle: 20th Century Practice and 21st Century Potential (Boston: Porter-Sargent, 2005); Stephen Zunes, Lester Kurtz, and Sarah Beth Asher, eds., *Nonviolent Social Movements* (Malden, Mass.: Blackwell, 1999); Peter Ackerman and Christopher Kruegler, *Strategic Nonviolent Conflict: The Dynamics of People Power in the 20th Century* (Westport, Conn.: Praeger, 1994); Jonathan Schell, *The Unconquerable World: Power, Nonviolence, and the Will of the People* (New York: Metropolitan Books, 2003).

[27]National Conference of Catholic Bishops, *The Challenge of Peace: God's Promise and Our Response* (Washington, D.C.: United States Catholic Conference, 1983), 222.

[28]Ibid. For additional discussion of nonviolent resistance to the Nazis, see Jacques Sémelin, *Unarmed Against Hitler: Civilian Resistance in Europe, 1939-1943* (Westport, Conn.: Praeger, 1993). Also see discussion of these cases of resistance to the Nazis in the works on nonviolent action cited above.

[29]National Conference of Catholic Bishops, *The Harvest of Justice Is Sown in Peace* (Washington, D.C.: U.S. Catholic Conference, 1993). The document is also included in Gerard Powers, Drew Christiansen, and Robert Hennemeyer, eds. *Peacemaking: Moral and Policy Challenges for a New World* (Washington, D.C.: U.S. Catholic Conference, 1994), 311-46. The passage quoted can be found on page 319.

[30]This information concerning "development of doctrine" is recounted by Drew Christiansen, former director of the United States Catholic Conference Office of International Justice and Peace, in a lecture entitled " 'No, Never Again War': The Evolution of Catholic Teaching on Peace and War," available online at http://www.scu.edu/bannancenter/eventsandconferences/visitors/christiansen.cfm

[31]NCCB, *The Harvest of Justice Is Sown in Peace.*

[32]Pope John Paul II, "Peace on Earth to Those Whom God Loves" (Message for World Day of Peace 2000), 11.

[33]See Pope John Paul II's World Day of Peace messages for 2003 and 2004.

[34]Pope John Paul II, "No Peace Without Justice, No Justice Without Forgiveness" (Message for World Day of Peace 2002), 5. See Pope John Paul II's World Day of Peace messages from 2002 to 2005 for his reflections on proper ways to respond to the danger of terrorism.

[35]See Pope John Paul II, "No Peace Without Justice, No Justice Without Forgiveness" (Message for World Day of Peace 2002).

[36]Pope John Paul II, *Centesimus Annus*, 25.

[37]Pope John Paul II, "Truth, the Power of Peace" (Message for World Day of Peace 1980), 10. The pope is citing here some lines from a very powerful homily that he gave in Ireland in 1979. These lines are repeated in his World Day of Peace 2005 message. For the full text of his homily in Ireland, see http://www.ireland.com/focus/papaldeath/drogheda.htm

[38]The legitimacy of pacifism along with the just war tradition as options

for Catholics is a central assertion of the U.S. Catholic bishops' document *The Challenge of Peace*. See especially nos. 111-21.

[39]For a transcript of the interview in which Cardinal Ratzinger made these comments, see http://www.zenit.org/english/visualizza.phtml?sid=34882

[40]Christiansen, "No, Never Again War."

[41]One prominent exception to this lack of outspokenness concerning the implications of church teaching was Bishop John Michael Botean. Botean is bishop of all of the Byzantine-rite Romanian Catholics in the United States. Botean issued a pastoral letter declaring that direct participation in the war in Iraq would constitute mortal sin. For Bishop Botean's letter to the people of his eparchy (diocese), see http://www.jonahhouse.org/boteanRCbishop.htm. Some additional commentary on the letter can be found at http://www.al-bushra.org/hedchrch/bishop1.html. Even if one allows a greater role for individual conscience in this matter than does Botean (who asserts that his views are morally binding), it would seem that there should at least be a strong presumption against the war on the part of Catholic church leaders, particularly in light of the Vatican's critical comments on the war. Thus, public encouragement and support for those who choose for reasons of conscience not to fight in the war (even if this is not seen by a particular bishop as the only morally legitimate option) should be expected from all bishops. Sadly, however, this has not been the case.

[42]See John Howard Yoder, *When War Is Unjust: Being Honest in Just-War Thinking*, 2nd ed. (Maryknoll, N.Y.: Orbis Books, 1996). For a book that explores the need to move beyond pacifist-just war debates and to embrace a "just peacemaking" paradigm, see Glen Stassen, ed., *Just Peacemaking: Ten Practices for Abolishing War*, 2nd ed. (Cleveland: Pilgrim Press, 2004).

[43]Wink, *The Powers That Be*, 144.

[44]"The time has gone for finding ways to a 'balance of terror'; the time has come to reexamine the whole strategy of nuclear deterrence. When the Holy See expressed its limited acceptance of nuclear deterrence during the Cold War, it was with the clearly stated condition that deterrence was only a step on the way towards progressive nuclear disarmament. The Holy See has never countenanced nuclear deterrence as a permanent measure, nor does it today when it is evident that nuclear deterrence drives the development of ever new nuclear arms, thus preventing genuine nuclear disarmament" (Address to the Review Conference of the Nuclear Non-Proliferation Treaty by Archbishop Celestino Migliore, permanent observer of the Holy See to the United Nations [May 4, 2005]). This address by Archbishop Migliore can be found online at http://www.holyseemission.org/4may2005.html

[45]Mohandas Gandhi, *Young India* (August 11, 1920). The quote can also be found online at http://www.mkgandhi.org/nonviolence/phil1.htm

Part III

THE ENCOUNTER WITH OTHER CHRISTIANS AND OTHER RELIGIONS

Vatican II and the Twentieth Century's "Conciliar Renaissance"

Elaine Catherine MacMillan

Forty years after the Council many Roman Catholics would claim that Vatican II was *the* most important conciliar event of the twentieth century. Using an ecumenical lens, however, we can see that Vatican II was convoked at the tail end of about one hundred years of intense conciliar activity in all the mainline churches. Since the middle of the nineteenth century Christians throughout the world had been developing international conciliar structures, and by the time Vatican II was convoked these conciliar structures were well established in the Anglican Communion, the Reformed churches, the Lutheran churches and the Orthodox Church. From this optic, Vatican II was one of many conciliar initiatives that occurred during the twentieth century and it is this perspective that I will explore.

I will first survey the history of councils in the life of the church and explain how the surge in conciliar activity during the nineteenth and twentieth centuries prompted the Faith and Order Commission of the World Council of Churches to conduct research into this history. Second, I will situate Vatican II within this history. Third, I will examine how successfully the Roman Catholic Church has recovered the conciliar dimensions of its ecclesial life in the forty years since the Council.

Councils in the History of the Church

Given the surge in conciliar activity in the mainline churches during the nineteenth and twentieth centuries, the New Delhi Assembly of the World Council of Churches in 1961 mandated the Faith and Order Commission to study the ecclesiological significance of councils, conciliarity, and the role of councils in the life and structure of the church. This ecumenical research and reflection continued until 1975 under the able direction of the director of the Secretariat of the Commission, Lukas Vischer (1965-1979).

Conciliarity first entered the ecumenical lexicon at the Uppsala General Assembly of the World Council of Churches in 1968 thanks to the work of the Faith and Order Commission. The Faith and Order Commission defined conciliarity in the following way:

> By conciliarity we mean the fact that the Church in all times needs assemblies to represent it and has in fact felt this need. These assemblies may differ greatly from one another; however, conciliarity, the necessity *that* they take place, is a constant structure of the Church, a dimension which belongs to its nature. As the Church itself is an "assembly" and appears as assembly both in worship and many other expressions of its life, so it needs both at the local and on all other possible levels representative assemblies in order to answer the questions which it faces.
>
> Synods and councils are the historical expression of this basic necessity. They are to be found in one form or another in all churches. Everywhere and at all times there are assemblies which not only serve for joint counsel, but also confront the local church, larger groups of congregations, or even the totality of the churches with an authoritative claim.[1]

The most important point that this definition of conciliarity makes is that "the necessity that these assemblies take place is a constant structure of the Church, a dimension which belongs to its nature."[2] When the conciliar dimensions of ecclesial life lie dormant in a church, then the church is, in effect, ignoring a fundamental dimension of its ecclesial nature. Yves Congar argues this point in an article entitled "Remarks on the Council as an Assembly and on the *Church's Fundamentally Conciliar Nature*."[3]

Conciliarity is so important to the life of the church that from the church's inception it has felt the need for representative assemblies and has developed assemblies to meet this need. This conciliar tradition began in the nascent church with the Council of Jerusalem (Acts 15), which became the prototype for all subsequent synods and councils. The first records of regular synods occur around 160 C.E., and so many synods were held after the peace of Constantine that bishops were accused of tying up the transportation systems of the empire and draining the imperial coffers by meeting so frequently.[4] Nicea I, the first ecumenical council, declared in Canon 5 that synods should be held twice a year, once before Lent and once again later in the year. By the end of the fourth century, provincial synods were well established in the church and two ecumenical councils had taken place.

Diocesan synods were a regular occurrence in the West from the sixth century on. The period from 523-787 C.E. was marked by numerous ecumenical and imperial councils convoked, and often presided over, by the emperor, who was a layperson.[5] From the thirteenth to the fifteenth century many reform and reunion councils were convoked in the West. Even after the Great Schism (1054), the Fourth Lateran Council (1215) decreed that diocesan synods should be held annually, and the Council of Trent reaffirmed this position in 1563, adding that provincial synods should be held every four years. Diocesan synods were held regularly until the end of the seventeenth century, but during the turbulent years of the eighteenth century European government leaders banned their convocation. As a result, diocesan synods disappeared from regular Roman Catholic practice after the late seventeenth century.[6] Conciliar activity waned dramatically in the Roman Catholic Church after the Reformation but remained strong in Protestantism and Anglicanism, which developed other conciliar structures to meet the needs of their respective churches.

Because the churches of the East have preserved the conciliar tradition for over two millennia, it is helpful to examine their understanding of conciliarity. "Orthodox theologians trace the Church's synodical institution back to the election of Matthias and of the seven deacons, and to the Council of Jerusalem, underlining the fact that the latter's decisions were taken 'in agreement with the whole Church.' "[7] Although the churches of the East trace their synodical structures to the apostolic era, this does not mean that these structures have remained static. Throughout the millennia the churches of the East have developed and adapted their conciliar structures to meet their different ecclesial needs. These conciliar structures include provincial synods, permanent synods, *synodon endemousa*, and ecumenical councils.[8] Individual patriarchates and autocephalous churches also developed synods.[9]

In the last one hundred and fifty years, Orthodox theologians have made substantial contributions to a theological understanding of conciliarity and how it functions within the church. Todor Sabev, a Bulgarian Orthodox professor, argues that "much of what has been written about conciliarity in fact draws from or is inspired by *sobornost*."[10] Sergei Bulgakov, a Russian Orthodox theologian, popularized the term *sobornost* in the twentieth century and he is the theologian most often associated with the term, even though Alexei Khomiakov had used *sobornost* in his work a century earlier. *Sobornost*, within the Orthodox understanding, includes conciliarity and is often translated as conciliarity, but it is not limited to this. *Sobornost* is a richly multivalent term, one deserving more attention and study by Roman Catholic theologians.

The importance given to synods in Eastern theology is rooted in the conviction that synods are the most appropriate way for the church to deal with "grave problems."[11] "[I]t is only by meeting in synod and listening to what the Spirit is saying to the Church that it will be able to find *the* solution."[12] Like the theologians of the Eastern churches, Congar emphasizes the importance of the pneumatological dimension in councils and synods. "It is Christ and the Holy Spirit who act in councils and are the real authors of their decrees so that the final judgment, the sole act which is properly the conciliar act, is the common act of the assembled college *and* of the Holy Spirit."[13]

Over time a juridical and legalistic understanding of councils in the West supplanted this pneumatological dimension. So, too, the balance between conciliarity and primacy, which is so important in the Eastern understanding of councils, became skewed in the direction of papal primacy at the expense of conciliarity, especially in the wake of the Council of Constance (1414-1418). Eastern theologians are very critical of this development in Roman Catholicism. Kallistos Ware argues that the pope should always be seen "as the first within [the college of bishops] and as the first *among equals*."[14] The pope should never be above the college or an ecumenical council. Dumitry Stãniloae, a Romanian Orthodox theologian, criticizes the Roman Catholic Church's neglect of conciliarity and its emphasis upon primacy because "the doctrine of papal primacy and the ecclesiastical magisterium make impossible the communion of all the members of the Church in all things."[15]

Since Vatican II, many bilateral and multilateral ecumenical dialogues have studied the relationship between primacy and conciliarity.[16] Drawing upon the Orthodox understanding of the relationship between conciliarity and primacy, the first Anglican-Roman Catholic International Commission (ARCIC-I), for example, wrote that conciliarity and primacy are complementary aspects of oversight (*episcope*) and both need to be kept in balance.[17] According to ARCIC-I an ecclesiology becomes skewed when either conciliarity or primacy is emphasized at the expense of, or to the exclusion of, the other.

Vatican II and the Twentieth Century's "Conciliar Renaissance"

Vatican II was convoked during a period of intense conciliar activity. The Third General Assembly of the World Council of Churches in New Delhi (1961) and the first of the Pan-Orthodox Conferences in Rhodes, Greece (1961), had just been completed. The third assembly of the Lutheran World Federation was scheduled for Helsinki, Finland, in the summer of 1963. The second Pan-Orthodox Conference in Rhodes was also scheduled for the summer of 1963. Vatican II was thus one conciliar event among many that occurred during the "conciliar renaissance" of the twentieth century.

The term "conciliar renaissance" was used in a 1974 booklet prepared by the West German Ecumenical Study Committee (WGESC) at the request of the Faith and Order Commission of the World Council of Churches.[18] This inter-confessional study group used the term to describe the modern ecumenical movement. Given the growth of so many conciliar initiatives in different parts of the universal church during the twentieth century, the term aptly describes the growth in conciliar activity that occurred in the mainline churches prior to, and concurrent with, Vatican II.[19]

The WGESC credits the Second Vatican Council with "the creation of a new conciliar awareness in more or less all the churches."[20] Vatican II may have raised the conciliar awareness in many churches, but, as noted above, intense conciliar activity had already been taking place throughout Christianity since the middle of the nineteenth century and throughout the twentieth century. In many ways the Roman Catholic Church was a latecomer onto the conciliar scene, for the Second Vatican Council was one of the last in a series of international conciliar initiatives that were well established by the time the Council was finally convoked.

Though there was a surge of conciliar activity in the twentieth century, three nineteenth-century conciliar initiatives are worth mentioning. The first took place within the Anglican Communion and the other two in the Reformed churches. In the Anglican Communion, at the request of the Synod of Bishops of the Anglican Church in Canada, the first Lambeth Conference of the Anglican Communion was convened in 1867. Approximately once every ten years since 1867 the bishops of the Anglican Communion have assembled as the Lambeth Conference. From its inception, the Lambeth Conference has met a need within the Anglican episcopate for a universal gathering of bishops to discuss doctrinal, disciplinary, and pastoral matters of the day. "[T]he resolutions [of the Lambeth Conference], though not binding, are significant expressions of the opinions of the Anglican episcopate."[21]

The second and third examples come from the Reformed tradition. The Alliance of the Reformed Churches throughout the world was first formed in 1875.[22] Sixteen years later, the International Congregational Council (1891) was created. These two bodies joined in 1970 to form the World Alliance of Reformed Churches. The World Alliance of Reformed Churches (WARC) has grown to include over 218 churches in 107 different countries and has seventy-five million members. [23] Every seven years the WARC meets in a General Council, which is "the Alliance's highest governing body."[24] The twenty-fourth General Council was held in Accra, Ghana, in 2004.

These nineteenth-century initiatives were followed by others in the early years of the twentieth century. In 1920 the Patriarchate of Constantinople sent an encyclical entitled "Unto the Churches of Christ Everywhere" to the heads of all the churches, inviting them to form a league or fellowship of churches.[25] The Lambeth Conference, independent of the Patriarchate of Constantinople, also sent out a letter in 1920 entitled "An Appeal to All Christian People," which invited Christians to work for reunion.[26] These letters, combined with other ecumenical initiatives in the first half of the twentieth century, bore fruit in 1948 with the formation of the World Council of Churches. The World Council of Churches (WCC) is by definition a "fellowship of churches," though Roman Catholics, by mutual agreement, are not part of this fellowship. The WCC describes itself as "the broadest and most inclusive among the many organized expressions of the modern ecumenical movement, a movement whose goal is Christian unity."[27] The 340 member churches, representing over 550 million Christians, support the WCC's claim to inclusivity.[28] Most of the WCC's member churches are found outside Europe and North America and this attests to its diversity as a conciliar body. Its general assemblies are held approximately every six or seven years. The ninth general assembly was held in Porto Alegre, Brazil, in February 2006.

Many other international conciliar initiatives, such as the creation of the Lutheran World Federation, occurred around the world during the twentieth century. The Lutheran World Federation (LWF), which was founded in 1947 in Lund, Sweden, one year prior to the founding of the World Council of Churches, has 138 member churches. These can be found in seventy-seven countries and about sixty-six million Christians are members of the Lutheran World Federation. The assemblies of the LWF are held at six-year intervals and in the intervening years a council, which is convoked annually, governs the body.[29]

Though the churches of the East have faithfully maintained the synodical and conciliar traditions since the inception of Christianity, one can also include them in this twentieth-century conciliar renaissance. Within Orthodoxy examples of this conciliar renaissance are the Pan-Orthodox Conferences held in Rhodes, Greece, in 1961, 1963, and 1964. These Pan-Orthodox Conferences resulted in the first "Pre-Synodal Pan-Orthodox Conference" held in Geneva in 1976, during which the agenda for a Great and Holy Synod of the Orthodox Church was determined.[30] The preparatory committee hoped that this synod would be received as the eighth ecumenical council. Eight volumes of preparatory texts dealing with a wide range of topics have been collected. Though the preparatory materials are complete, as of 2005 the Great and Holy Synod has not yet been convoked.[31]

This growth of conciliar activity in the churches of the East, Protestantism, and Anglicanism since the nineteenth century coincided with an ongoing decline of conciliar activity in the Roman

Catholic Church that continued until Vatican II. A sentiment was growing in some Roman Catholic theological circles at the time that even ecumenical councils were unnecessary. As early as 1819 Joseph le Maistre had asked "Why is an ecumenical council necessary, when it is enough to have a pillory?"[32] Le Maistre was not alone in his thinking. "Even before Vatican I was convoked, some Catholics said, for example: 'Have we not the Pope? Does the Pope not have the power to decide every question?' "[33] Vatican I's teaching on infallibility served to reinforce this idea among many Roman Catholics as well as Protestants, Anglicans, and members of the churches of the East. The teaching on infallibility seemed to make councils obsolete in the Roman Catholic Church.[34] On the eve of Vatican II, John Meyendorff, Stephen Neill, and Henri Daniel-Rops argued that Vatican I's teaching had made councils superfluous.[35] Meyendorff, an Orthodox theologian, observed, "Many of those who belong to the Roman Church and many outside it believe that the decisions taken in 1870 could not be reconciled with the conciliar institution. . . ."[36] From the beginning of the nineteenth century it seemed that the Roman Catholic Church would have difficulty recovering the conciliar dimensions of its ecclesial life.

The Roman Catholic Church Reopens the Book on Its Conciliar Life

Pope John XXIII made a bold decision when he convoked Vatican II. History tells us that his predecessors, Pius XI and Pius XII, had both considered reconvening Vatican I, which had been suspended *sine die*. This option was open to Pope John as well. He chose, rather, to convoke a Second Vatican Council and by doing so began a recovery of the conciliar tradition for the Roman Catholic Church. The Second Vatican Council helped the Roman Catholic Church to begin to recover some of its synodical and conciliar aspects, which had lain dormant for so many years. Edward Schillebeeckx observed that at the Council, "The contact that the bishops had with each other . . . released something which had for a long time clearly been calling for official expression."[37] The collegiality the bishops experienced at the Council and the conciliar authority they exercised during the Council had a profound impact upon them.

Based on their positive conciliar experiences during Vatican II, the Council fathers argued strongly for the continuation of this conciliar experience after the Council. Pope John XXIII had set a precedent for this ongoing conciliar recovery by convoking a diocesan synod in Rome at the same time that he convoked Vatican II.[38] Diocesan synods had been suppressed in Western Europe since the eighteenth century so this was an important first step. The Council fathers supported Pope John in both initiatives. "This sacred Ecumenical Synod earnestly desires that the venerable institution of synods and councils flourish with new vigor," declared the bishops in *Christus Dominus* 36.[39] This flourishing took many forms, two of which are the Synod of Bishops, created during the last session of the Council and the recovery of diocesan synods.

Despite its promising origins, the Synod of Bishops in the last forty years remains an act of papal primacy rather than a genuine expression of conciliarity. When creating the Synod of Bishops, Pope Paul VI added the following restrictions: "By its very nature it is the task of the Synod of Bishops to inform and give advice. It may also have deliberative power, when such power is conferred on it by the Supreme Pontiff, who will in such cases confirm the decisions of the synod."[40] Despite all the synods that have taken place in the last forty years, to date no pope has conferred this deliberative power upon the Synod of Bishops. This is contrary to the Orthodox understanding of synods, for the pope should be the first among equals in the synod and the synods exercise authority by virtue of being synods. Despite the positive experiences of collegiality and conciliarity at the Council, Pope Paul VI created the Synod of Bishops so that it is "directly and immediately subject to the authority of the Roman Pontiff."[41]

None of the Synods of Bishops convoked since Vatican II, whether general, ordinary, or extraordinary, has exercised any deliberative authority over the regions they represent. This too is contrary to the ancient understanding of synods. Within the ancient church, synods exercised, at a minimum, authority over the regions of the church represented by the synod. In fact, in the early church, the decisions of a particular synod were also authoritative in those churches which, due to extenuating circumstances, wanted to but could not send representatives. In other circumstances the authority of a synod even extended beyond its region when its canons were received by other churches.

The authority of the Synod of Bishops is seriously undermined also by the fact that the final document that results from the Synod of Bishops is the work of an editorial team. The bishops have usually returned to their dioceses when the final document is published. They are not consulted once the final draft is written nor do they vote on the final text. From Congar's perspective, the final judgment of a synod or council is, in fact, the conciliar act *par excellence*. In light of this, when the final decision about the synod is made by the pope independent of the bishops, the synods become acts of papal primacy rather than conciliarity.

As they are currently constituted, the Synods of Bishops are also problematic for Eastern Catholics in communion with Rome. Archbishop Elias Zoghby, a Melkite-Greek Catholic, critiques the Synod of Bishops from the perspective of the Byzantine East:

> Episcopal synods or conferences in the Catholic Churches of the East have been deprived of all real power, which has been transferred to the hands of the Roman Curia, especially the Congregation for the Eastern Churches. . . . What this congregation actually does is to assume the role of a pseudo-patriarchate.
>
> To take Eastern Catholic patriarchs, who by right are the presiding officers of the Synods, and make them secondary and minority members of a congregation with authority to deal with the affairs of their own patriarchates . . . is actually a condemnation of collegiality in the Eastern form, namely the synodal form of government under the chairmanship of the patriarch.[42]

Diocesan synods have not fared much better in the forty years since Vatican II. Parallels can be made with the Synod of Bishops, for only the local ordinary has a deliberative vote in them. The other members of the synod simply have a consultative role. The bishop alone chooses the topics for discussion and only the bishop can convoke a diocesan synod. The 1983 Code of Canon Law, in its description of diocesan synods, ostensibly draws upon ecclesiological principles from Vatican II that, unfortunately, are not realized in the actual synodical process at the diocesan level.

These are just two examples that illustrate that it has been difficult for the Roman Catholic Church to recover the conciliar dimensions of its ecclesial life, even after the positive conciliar experience of Vatican II. It is clearly going to take more than forty years for the Roman Catholic Church to recover this conciliar tradition. Until it does, it is compromising its fundamentally conciliar nature and living out of a skewed ecclesiology.

The Importance of Ecumenical Dialogues

The Roman Catholic Church has much to learn from the synodical and conciliar traditions of other churches. Shortly after Vatican II the Roman Catholic Church entered into formal dialogues with the Anglican Communion, the Orthodox, and many Protestant communions. The bilateral and multilateral dialogues in which Roman Catholics now participate provide the Roman Catholic Church with a privileged opportunity to learn about the creative ways in which Anglican, Orthodox, and Protestant Christians have developed effective conciliar and synodical structures in their respective communions, structures that are faithful to the fundamentally conciliar nature of the church. Especially important among these are the dialogues with the Orthodox, who have preserved the conciliar life of the church for over two millennia. One can hope that through these ongoing dialogues the Roman Catholic Church will continue to seek ways in which to recover its fundamentally conciliar nature, just as Vatican II desired.

Notes

[1]Faith and Order Commission, ed., *Councils and the Ecumenical Movement. World Council of Churches Studies No. 5* (Geneva: World Council of Churches, 1968), 10.

[2]Ibid.

[3]Yves Congar, "Remarks on the Council as an Assembly and on the Church's Fundamentally Conciliar Nature," in *Report from Rome II: The Second Session of the Vatican Council*, trans. Lancelot Sheppard (Montreal: Palm Publishers, 1964), 173. My emphasis.

[4]Charles U. Clark, ed., *Ammiani Marcellini Rerum Gestarum Liber*, vol.

1 (Berlin: Weidmann, 1910), 250; referred to in Brian Daley, "Structures of Charity: Bishops' Gatherings and the See of Rome in the Early Church," in *Episcopal Conferences: Historical, Canonical and Theological Studies*, ed. Thomas Reese, S.J. (Washington, D.C.: Georgetown University Press, 1989), 28-29.

[5]Faith and Order Commisssion, ed., *Councils and the Ecumenical Movement*, 10.

[6]Lawrence J. Jennings, "A Renewed Understanding of the Diocesan Synod," *Studia Canonica* 20 (1986): 323-24.

[7]Pierre Duprey, "The Synodical Structure of the Church in Eastern Theology," *One in Christ* 7 (1971): 152-82. The cited pages are 152-53.

[8]The *synodon endemousa* are permanent synods that assist a patriarch, like the patriarch of Constantinople, in the administration of the patriarchate.

[9]Duprey, "The Synodical Structure of the Church in Eastern Theology," 169.

[10]Todor Sabev, "The Nature and Mission of Councils in the Light of the Theology of Sobornost," *Ecumenical Review* 45 (July 1993): 261.

[11]Duprey, "The Synodical Structure of the Church in Eastern Theology," 162.

[12]Ibid., 163. His emphasis.

[13]Congar, "Remarks on the Council [not Church] as an Assembly," 190. His emphasis.

[14]Kallistos Ware, "Primacy, Collegiality, and the People of God," in *Orthodoxy: Life and Freedom*, ed. A. J. Philippou (Oxford: Studion Publications, 1973), 125.

[15]Dumitry Stãniloae, "Theology and the Church," trans. Robert Barringer (Crestwood, N.Y.: St.Vladimir's Press, 1980), 56-57, quoted in Michael A. Fahey, S.J., "Eastern Synodal Traditions: Pertinence for Western Collegial Institutions," in *Episcopal Conferences: Historical, Canonical and Theological Studies*, 253.

[16]These include the Anglican Roman Catholic International Commission (ARCIC), the Faith and Order Commission (World Council of Churches) and the Orthodox-Roman Catholic (U.S.A) dialogue, to mention a few.

[17]Anglican-Roman Catholic International Commission, *The Final Report* (London: SPCK, 1982), 63-64.

[18]West German Ecumenical Study Committee, "*Councils, Conciliarity and a Genuinely Universal Council,*" *Faith and Order Paper No. 70, Study Encounter*, X/2 (1974): 1.

[19]Ibid.

[20]Ibid.

[21]*The Oxford Dictionary of the Christian Church*, 2d ed., s.v. "Lambeth Conferences."

[22]Ibid., s.v. "World Alliance of Reformed Churches," *The Dictionary of*

the Ecumenical Movement, 2d ed., s.v. "World Alliance of Reformed Churches."

[23]"More About WARC," http://warc.jalb.de/warcajsp/side.jsp?news_id=3&navi=9, 1. Accessed: June 20, 2005.

[24]"That All May Have Life in Fullness," http://www.warc.ch/24gc/index.html, 1. Accessed: June 20, 2005.

[25]Patriarchate of Constantinople, "Encyclical of the Ecumenical Patriarchate, 1920: Unto the Churches of Christ Everywhere," in *Orthodox Visions of Ecumenism: Statements, Messages and Reports on the Ecumenical Movement 1902-1992* (Geneva: WCC Publications, 1994), 9-11.

[26]*The Oxford Dictionary of the Christian Churches*, 2d ed., s.v. "Lambeth Conferences."

[27]"Who are we? What is the World Council of Churches?" http://www.wcc-coe.org/wcc/who/index-e.html, 1. Accessed: June 21, 2005.

[28]"WCC 9th Assembly: God, in your grace, transform the world," http://www.wcc-assembly.info/, 1. Accessed: June 21, 2005.

[29]"The Lutheran World Federation: Who we are," http://www.lutheranworld.org/Who_We_Are/LWF-Welcome.html, 1. Accessed: June 20, 2005.

[30]*The Dictionary of the Ecumenical Movement*, s.v. "Pan-Orthodox Conferences."

[31]Father George Dragas, Holy Cross Greek Orthodox School of Theology, interview by author, June 2005.

[32]Quoted in Yves Congar, "A Last Look at the Council," in *Vatican II Revisited by Those Who Were There*, ed. Alberic Stacpoole (Minneapolis, Minn.: Winston Press, 1986), 338.

[33]Ibid., note 7, 353.

[34]Ibid., note 7, 354. Here Congar cites a wide range of theologians who share this position.

[35]Ibid., note 7, 354.

[36]John Meyendorff, "Voeux pour le Concile," *Esprit* (December 1961): 793; quoted in Congar, "A Last Look at the Council," note 7, 354.

[37]Edward Schillebeeckx, *L'Eglise du Christ et l'homme d'aujourd'hui selon Vatican II* (Lyons and Paris: Le Puy, 1965), 37; quoted in Congar, "A Last Look at the Council," note 13, 354.

[38]Congar, "A Last Look at the Council," 337.

[39]*Christus Dominus* 36 in *The Documents of Vatican II*, ed. Walter J. Abbott, S.J. (Piscataway, N.J.: New Century Publishers, 1966). The English title of this document is the Decree Concerning the Pastoral Office of Bishops in the Church.

[40]Pope Paul VI, *Apostolica Sollicitudo* in *The Documents of Vatican II*, ed. Walter J. Abbott, S.J., §II, 721. Unlike the Council documents such as *Lumen Gentium* that were signed by the pope and all the bishops and were thus conciliar acts, this apostolic constitution was issued *motu proprio*. This means that it was written at Pope Paul's instigation and he alone signed it.

This reinforces the primatial rather than conciliar dimensions of the Synod of Bishops.

[41]Ibid., §III, 722.

[42]Archbishop Elias Zoghby, quoted by Archbishop Vsevolod of Scopelos in "The Synod of Bishops—Catholic and Orthodox" (unpublished paper presented at *Orientale Lumen* IX, San Diego, California, June 14-16, 2005), 19.

Bridge or Boundary?

Vatican II and Other Religions

Paul F. Knitter

This essay explores a question that has been disturbing the Christian faithful over the past couple of decades—something like an itch that, for one reason or another, people are afraid to scratch. The question is: Does the Second Vatican Council stand as a boundary or as a bridge for the way Christians are to understand and relate to persons of other religions?

Vatican II: A Boundary

When I ask if the teachings of Vatican II are a boundary, I'm recognizing all the wonderful, even revolutionary, things the Council said about followers of other religious paths, but I'm also asking whether this is as far as we can go. Is Vatican II a limit beyond which Christians cannot step without losing their own identity? What I'm asking, stated more forthrightly, is whether the Catholic/Christian community can move beyond the perspective of "inclusivism"—or what I prefer to call "fulfillment"[1]—that characterizes Vatican II's theology of religions. We must first recognize that this is a theology that does something never before done in the official statements of any Christian church: it recognizes and affirms in other religions "elements that are true and good" (*LG* 16), "precious things, both religious and human" (*GS* 92), "elements of truth and grace" (*AG* 9), "spiritual and moral goods" (*NA* 2), "seeds of the Word" (*AG* 11, 15), "rays of that Truth which illumines all humankind" (*NA* 2)—and then calls upon all Catholics "prudently and lovingly" to engage in dialogue with other believers (*NA* 2). What a liberating, positive vision. What a bold step forward in Christian relations with other faiths.

But the Council said more. It went on to affirm that since Jesus Christ is the one and only savior of all humanity, all these "precious things," all this "truth and grace," are there as a "preparation for the Gospel" (*LG* 16). They are meant to be "included" or "fulfilled" in the one church of Jesus, the one religion that God intends, ideally, for all peoples of all times.

So the question is: Might the Catholic community move beyond this "fulfillment model"? In some aspects, it has. The magisterium itself has moved forward: what was left open in the Council has been affirmed by John Paul II and by the Council for Interreligious Dialogue—that is, that the religions themselves can serve as "ways of salvation"[2]; also, the magisterium has proclaimed dialogue—authentic, mutually enriching and challenging dialogue—to be an essential piece of the church's mission to the world.[3] But there has been no movement beyond the basics of the fulfillment model. Official magisterial statements—*Redemptoris Missio, Dialogue and Proclamation,* and especially *Dominus Iesus*, together with restraining actions toward theologians such as Jacques Dupuis, Tissa Balassuriya, and Roger Haight, have clearly and aggressively mounted "no trespassing" signs on territory beyond the fulfillment model.[4]

But my question is whether these borders represent where many Catholics in multiple cultural settings really are. Are Catholics "itching" to explore beyond the borders? Can theologians help them "scratch" that itch? In other words, can we consider Vatican II a bridge?

Vatican II: A Bridge

John Hick observed many years ago that what Vatican II had to say about other religions was a milestone in the history of the church—but a milestone mounted on a bridge, not on a border. It was not just something new; it was the *beginning* of something new. And as Hick put it teasingly: eventually, the Catholic Church would have to move off the bridge.[5]

Move off the bridge to what? As much as categories or models are dangerous and controversial because they are too neat, let me put it in the language of models: move toward what has been called the perspective of *pluralism* or, as I prefer, *mutuality*. Whatever you want to call this perspective, it would be one in which Christians (as well as members of all religions) move beyond what is called "the myth of religious superiority."[6] In a mutualist perspective, religious people no longer "regard their own religion as the one and only 'true' faith and way of 'salvation,' uniquely superior to all others."[7] While holding firm to their own distinct identity, they recognize the distinct, valued identity of others without asserting that their religion—or any religion—is the one superior, normative, fulfilling, end-point religion for all others. Now my question becomes more pointed: Can Catholics cross the bridge of Vatican II toward such a mutualist theology of religions?

Such a crossing would be understood as an example of what Catholics call "the development of dogma." There has been—or *I think* there has been—a certain development or evolution within the Catholic Church's understanding of other religions, which also means her understanding of herself. Briefly, in terms of Christology, during much of the history of the church, the approach to other religions has been one of "Christ *against* the religions." Other religious paths were viewed as either diabolical or useless and would have to be *replaced* by Christianity. Given the belief that outside the church there was no salvation, the goal was to get everyone inside. But that was to change. Already with the Council of Trent, but especially in Vatican II, doctrine developed and shifted to view other traditions from the perspective of "Christ *within* the religions." Universally, cosmically, anonymously Christ and his Spirit are recognized as working salvifically within other religions, providing them with grace and truth, preparing them for fulfillment in the church. That's where we are now, officially.

I'm asking if a further step is possible, or even necessary. This would be a perspective of "Christ *together with* the religions," one in which Christianity and all religions mutually interact to affirm each other, challenge each other, and collaborate to further the well-being of humanity and the earth. No one religion would be in a universal or final sense *superior* to all the others, although in particular issues or contexts, one religious belief or practice can show itself, in the dialogue, to be more "life-giving" and therefore preferable to another.

The suggestion that the church should move off the bridge of

Vatican II toward something like this mutualist model has met with multiple criticisms and caveats. Some of these are very valid concerns.

First, I trust that His Holiness Benedict will see what His Eminence Joseph did not—that *to affirm pluralism is not to affirm relativism.* The mutualist model in no way denies the possibility and necessity of truth claims for which one can live and die; it just denies the possibility and necessity of *absolute* truth claims. There is a middle path between absolutism and relativism that is called dialogue, that is, a conversation in which all participants are as committed to witnessing to their own truth as they are open to learning from the truth of others.

Second, I would want to assure my neo-liberal colleagues (such as Gavin D'Costa, S. Mark Heim, and Joseph DiNoia) and my friends in comparative theology (including Jim Fredericks, Frank Clooney, and perhaps Peter Phan) that the mutualist (pluralist) perspective is not presupposing or trying to identify a "common essence" or "common mystical experience" within all the religions that would minimize the real differences between them. The differences between the religions are deep, incorrigible, often oppositional. Mutualists trust, however, that these differences are *not* incommensurable—that is, they don't shut down conversation; we can still talk to each other about our differences to teach and learn and to challenge and correct each other.

Finally, to those fellow-Christians who take it for granted that to question the unicity of Jesus Christ as the world's only savior and as God's universal final revelation is to place oneself outside the Christian camp, I respectfully and (I hope) carefully respond: But that's precisely the question that our church has to take up again. "Who do you say I am?" To be *truly* savior, does Jesus have to be the *only* savior?

Reasons for Crossing the Bridge

So let me now summarize what I think are three forces or reasons that are pushing us to make the crossing. Then I'd like to suggest some theological and pastoral maps with which we can explore what I'm calling the pluralistic-mutualist territory on the other side of the bridge.

The Sensus Fidelium

As I've already suggested, we theologians (working always with the bishops and they with us) must come up with better answers for how Christians are to understand the uniqueness or distinctiveness of Christianity and of Christ in a world of many religions. Why? Mainly because Christian believers keep asking the question. Many such believers don't seem to be happy with the answers they have received or are receiving.[8] And judging from what I hear from my fellow parishioners at St. Robert Bellarmine Parish in Cincinnati and from my students at Xavier University, the primary cause of their uneasiness (or their doctrinal "itchiness") is all the "one and only," "King of kings," "one true church" language that they hear in the liturgy and the catechism. Just as there are many Catholics (perhaps some 70 percent in the United States) who just can't believe or practice the church's official teaching on artificial contraception, so there are many Catholics who have difficulties believing that theirs is the only savior and the one true church meant for all. Marcus Borg may overstate it, but not by much, when he observes: "We are living in a time when many Christians are beginning to let go of exclusivist and absolutist claims. . . . I am convinced that there are millions of mainline Christians in North America for whom the statement that Christianity is *not* the only true religion is 'good news.' "[9]

I'm talking mainly about North America and Europe, realizing that things might be different in the South, where Christians/Catholics now outnumber their "godparents" in the North. Perhaps also in Africa. But I'm not so sure about Asia. One of the strong messages that the Asian bishops delivered to Rome before and during their synod of 1998 was that the traditional ways of understanding the uniqueness of Jesus and Rome's insistence that Jesus be proclaimed as the one and only savior just weren't working pastorally, and therefore theologically, in Asia. It didn't fit their understanding of a dialogical church, which, as the bishops insisted, is the only way to authentically be church in Asia.[10] In the opinion of many, John Paul II's report on the synod in his apostolic exhortation *Ecclesia in Asia* did not really hear or respond to these concerns.[11] It seems safe to say that in Asia as well the *sensus fidelium* is itching for new answers.

Tensions between Practice and Theory

Some years back, I tried to describe a tension within the Catholic Church that, in our present context, has become only more evident.[12] This is the same tension between theory and praxis that has appeared throughout the history of the church in the form of the *lex orandi* and the *lex credendi*—between the practical norms for prayer and spirituality and the theoretical norms for belief. Today in the Catholic Church I think we seem to be experiencing a tension between the *lex dialogandi* and the *lex credendi*—between the practice of dialogue with other religions and the theory or theology of other religions.

Ever since *Nostra Aetate* gave orders to pursue dialogue "prudently and lovingly" with persons of other faiths, Catholics, obedient as they generally are, have been doing just that. In many ways, the Catholic Church has become—especially in Asia but not only in Asia—a church in dialogue with other religious traditions, both on the official level in the activities of the previous pope and of the Pontifical Council for Inter-religious Dialogue, but also, and more significantly, on the grassroots level in dioceses and parishes around the world. And here we have the source of the tension. Catholic Christians are discovering that their beliefs about other religions don't fit or don't support their experience in actual dialogue. This discovery comes both intellectually and interpersonally, that is, in the form of both questions and feelings.

The questions have to do with the nature and process of dialogue. John Paul II in his encyclical *Redemptoris Missio* (*RM*) and the Pontifical Council for Inter-religious Dialogue with the Congregation for the Evangelization of Peoples in the statement *Dialogue and Proclamation* (*DP*) are astoundingly clear about the requirements for authentic dialogue: 1) dialogue is "a method and means of *mutual* knowledge and enrichment" in which "a witness [is] *given and received* for mutual advancement" (*RM* 55, 56); 2) in dialogue "Christians too must allow themselves to be questioned" and corrected (*DP* 32) since "other religions constitute a positive challenge to the church" (*RM* 56); and 3) in the dialogue, all sides must be ready to change their minds and even their religious identities, for "the decision may be made to leave one's previous spiritual or religious situation in order to direct oneself toward another" (*DP* 41).[13]

Many Catholics are asking themselves, explicitly or implicitly, how is such openness, such mutual enrichment, such readiness to learn and even to change possible if Catholics are supposed to enter the circle of dialogue with the theological conviction that God has given them the full and the final truth and the only source of God's saving grace? How can one learn anything or be ready to change if one thinks he/she already has the God-given final word on all truth? At the most, one could only understand more clearly what one already has.

But these are the theoretical or intellectual problems. The personal issues are more pressing and telling. Catholics in America and Europe have come to experience what Catholics in Asia have long known: they have made interreligious friends. Other believers are not just strangers who follow different ways. Rather, they have become friends whom we like, esteem, value. Through these Muslim, Buddhist, Hindu, and Native American friends, Catholics have come to see and understand things about the world, themselves, and the Divine that they never would have known in and through Jesus alone. They have discovered what Edward Schillebeeckx has so succinctly described: There is more truth in many religions than there can be in any one, Christianity included.[14] In the light of such experiences, how can Catholics continue to affirm what they have been taught, that in Christ they have the full and final revelation, that theirs is the superior path meant for all? Such talk and attitudes, it seems, are foreign to friends. Friends don't claim that one is superior to the other. Yes, they do want to learn from each other, but no one friend claims or thinks she or he always has the final word.

Our theology of religions, I believe, has to catch up with our dialogue with religions. In one particular instance it already has. In one form of interreligious dialogue and relationship, the Catholic Church has already crossed the bridge. I'm referring to the new relationship of the Roman Catholic Church with the Jews, as that relationship has been revised and developed since *Nostra Aetate*. In *NA*'s section on Judaism, especially in its explicit statement (based on Romans 11) that "the gifts and calling of God are irrevocable" and that therefore the covenant with the Jews retains its validity also after Christ, the Council did what John Pawlikowski terms "an about-face" on the supersessionist theology of Judaism that characterized most of the church's history.[15]

John Paul II carried this "mutualist" theology of Judaism even further in numerous talks in which he stated that the covenant with the Jews was "never revoked by God"[16] and that therefore Jews and Christians are "partners in a covenant of eternal love which was never revoked"[17] and are "to be a blessing to one another."[18] Gregory Baum holds that "Implicit in the conciliar Statement [and more so in John Paul's statements] is a totally new attitude towards the Jews: the Church has no intention of converting them to the Christian faith, it wants Jews to remain faithful to their own spiritual tradition. . . ."[19] What was implicit for Baum, Cardinal Kasper makes explicit: "[there] does not exist any Catholic missionary organization for Jews. There is dialogue with Jews; no mission in this proper sense of the word towards them."[20]

In this new dialogical "praxis" with the Jews in which Catholics have abandoned supersessionism and recognized the ongoing validity of Judaism (without having to convert to Christ), there is at least implicitly what we might call a "paradigm shift" in Christology and ecclesiology. In John Pawlikowski's measured words:

> The extent to which we create theological space for Jewish faith, against which Christianity had defined its identity, to that extent we moderate, albeit implicitly, the absolute claim of Christianity. . . . [T]he Vatican is well aware that formally to relinquish evangelical outreach to the Jews has profound Christological implications that it is unwilling to confront at this time.[21]

But, according to Pawlikowski, it is not just the Vatican who is afraid to draw the theological-Christological consequences from this new dialogical praxis with the Jews. His further words lose some of their measured reserve:

> The rethinking of the Christ-Event which this [i.e. the new view of Judaism in *NA*] demands has been avoided by most theologians, including the authors of radical theologies writing from a feminist or Third World perspective. Regrettably,

> the Church has undertaken little theological reflection exploring the meaning and power of *Nostra aetate* for the revision of Christology and ecclesiology in keeping with God's abiding covenant with the Jews.[22]

We might say that in its dialogical praxis with Jews, and in the theology implicit in that praxis, the church has made a first, rather timid, foray across the bridge of Vatican II—but at the moment it does not have the clarity or the gumption to send further explorers.

Religion and Violence

A third reason why Catholics should move across the bridge of Vatican II is political, and I believe it is less of an imperative than an incentive that might be more impelling than any air-tight theological argument. It has to do with a reality of which we are all disconcertingly aware, especially since 9/11, the link between religion and violence.

There is no doubt that religion can be a key reason why people fly planes into buildings or drop bombs on cities and villages. To say that such people who justify their violence in the name of Allah/God—be they terrorists or imperialists—are *misusing* religion may be true. But to leave it there is also much too facile. It lets religious people, and especially religious leaders and theologians, off the hook much too easily. We must ask *why* has it been and *why* is it today so easy for demagogues or ideologues or ayatollahs or presidents to call upon religious faith and feelings in order to justify and intensify violence. What is it in the teachings, the beliefs, the scriptures of religions that makes it so easy for people to beat the plowshares of religious faith into the swords of religious violence?

As a raft of recent studies are claiming, one of the reasons why religion today, as throughout history, is producing more swords than plowshares has to do with exclusive or superior truth claims.[23] I'm not saying that there is a neat, necessary causal link between superior truth claims and violence. But there *is* a link, call it facilitating, or conducive, or condoning. If I feel that God has given me the "only Savior" or the "final prophet" or the "supreme enlightenment," and if I also feel that other people, by the use of terrorist tactics or imperial might, are attacking or exploiting or suppressing this religion or culture that is the bearer of God's only or superior truth, I will feel obliged to defend by any means I have at my disposal God's highest truth. It is true that *abusus non tollit usum* (abuse does not prevent use), but when there has been and is so much abuse of superior truth claims, we must question their use.

I offer the observations of an interreligious friend of mine, Rita Gross, who tells us how a Buddhist regards claims to have the only or the highest truth.

> The result of exclusive truth claims is not religious agreement; it is suffering. The track record of religions that claim exclusive and universal truth for themselves is not praiseworthy or uplifting. How much empire building, how many crusades and religious wars, big and small, have gone on in the name of defending the "one true faith." There seems to be a cause and effect link between claims of exclusive truth and suffering; or to say it more strongly, the main result of exclusive truth claims has been suffering, not salvation.[24]

How to Make the Crossing

In the hope that these three considerations—the *sensus fidelium*, the need for theological theory to catch up with dialogical practice, and the problem of religion and violence—are valid reasons to begin crossing the Vatican II bridge, let me sketch—more than this is not possible—some theological triptychs that might help us explore the other side without losing our Christian way.

A Pneumatological Theology of Religions

In surveying the present *status quaestionis* of a Christian theology of religions, I see a growing number of theologians taking up the advice that Karl Rahner offered back in the 1980s: to make "pneumatology . . . the fundamental point of departure for its entire theology [of religions] and then attempt from this point . . . to gain a real and radical understanding of Christology."[25] Back then, Rahner already felt what today is being called "the Christological impasse" in working out a theology of religions. In the words of Pentecostal theologian Amos Yong, "The Christian dialogue with other religious traditions has stalled at the christological impasse on more than one occasion. . . ."[26] It is the uniqueness question—or what then Cardinal Ratzinger called "the unicity of Christ"—that keeps tripping up theologians or getting them into trouble. So pneumatology, which Rahner described in the passage just cited as "a teaching of the inmost, divinizing gift of grace for all human beings,"[27] might be a way around the impasse.

But as Yong and others point out, it will be a helpful route only if we take seriously an ingredient of our traditional Trinitarian theology that can be epitomized in the patristic image of "the two hands of the Father." Viewed *ad intra,* there are two really different processions within the Trinitarian life of God. *Ad extra,* there are two truly different, but always related, movements or missions by which the infinite parental Source of life reaches into the world to embrace and save it. The first Christians have found incarnated intimately in the person of Jesus the Christ. The other is the brooding Spirit of God who has hovered over and inspired creation from its very inception. So "while the person of Jesus Christ is a historical symbol of God's reality in the world, the Holy Spirit is par excellence the symbol of the divine presence and activity in the cosmic realm."[28]

The problem with many of the recent efforts to fashion a pneumatological or Trinitarian theology of religions is that they end up tinged with the heresy of subordinationism. After speaking eloquently and profusely of the revealing, saving presence of the Spirit in the religious world, theologians like Gavin D'Costa end up insisting that whatever is disclosed by the Spirit must be "measured and discerned by their conformity to and in their illumination of Christ. . . . Jesus is the normative criterion of God."[29] Jacques Dupuis was more explicit: "Christ, not the Spirit, is at the center as the way to God."[30] I believe the conclusion of Amos Yong is hard to refute: Such "failure to differentiate between the two economies inevitably risks the subordination of the mission of the Spirit to that of the Son, and ultimately to an ecclesiological definition of soteriology."[31] More forcefully, he speaks of a "denigration" or a "domination" of the Spirit by the Son.[32]

I do want to affirm a pneumatological route around the Christological impasse.[33] But it must be a pneumatology that is soundly and consistently Trinitarian, one that recognizes the difference between the Trinitarian persons, processions, and missions.

This means that what the Spirit is up to in other religions may be truly and perhaps surprisingly different from what has been revealed in the Incarnate Word. God's revelation through the Spirit in the religions cannot be reduced to what God has revealed in Jesus. Michael Amaladoss offers this advice: "The Spirit is the Spirit of Jesus. But she does not just repeat what Jesus has done in the Christian community. Otherwise, the other religions would not be different. Perhaps, together with the phrase, 'the Father is greater than I,' we must take another phrase, 'The Spirit is not I,' though we may not find it in this form in the Bible."[34]

But what is truly different in the Spirit's activity in other religions will always be intimately related to the Incarnate Word's revelation in Jesus. The Spirit may be saying something new, something beyond the good news of Jesus, but it will connect with the good news, so that between the two very different revelations, as between the two very different persons of the Trinity, there will be an exciting, life-giving *perichoresis*, a dancing together and a transformative acting together. I believe that a synonym for such *perichoresis* is dialogue.

A Dialogical Christology

But Rahner suggested, as we heard, that after the Spirit helps us around the impasse of Christology, she can also backtrack a bit and assist us "to gain a real and radical understanding of Christology." I believe that this is exactly what is happening within Christian theology today. In an effort to carry on the task of Christology in relation to religious pluralism or, more precisely, in an effort to link Christology to a pneumatological theology of religions, theologians are reinterpreting, renewing, and revising their understanding of Christ; they are coming to new ways of appreciating the uniqueness or unicity of Christ as savior and Son of God. Such efforts, I believe, can be summarized and described under one heading: we're moving toward a more *dialogical Christology*. Such a Christology provides another roadmap for exploring the other side of the Vatican II bridge.

For me, the most incisive and inspiring way to get at the content and intent of a dialogical Christology is John B. Cobb, Jr.'s simple witness of faith: "Christ is the Way that is open to other ways."[35] We cannot follow Christ as the Way, the Truth, and the

Life unless we are also learning about other ways, exploring other truths, entering other lives. Christian discipleship is essentially, imperatively, *dialogical*. Relationships with others, with those who have other views and follow other paths, are essential not just to faithfully follow Christ and his message but to *understand* Christ and his message. As Michael Barnes puts it, "It is impossible to be Christian 'without the others'. . . . Christian living . . . depends not on occupying a 'place' alongside others, but on practicing faith face to face with others, . . . by constantly departing for another place. . . . [T]o be Christian is to exist in relationship. . . ."[36]

Such a dialogical Christology is being developed and deepened from a variety of perspectives. Following a more Trinitarian approach, theologians like Amos Yong and Michael Ipgrave and, to a lesser extent, S. Mark Heim stress that just as there is a diversity of relationships within the very Godhead, so there is a diversity of relationships between the Divine and humans, and that implies a diversity of relationships *among* the religions. Or more particularly, just as the Word cannot be what it is and realize its identity without a constitutive relationship with the Spirit, so too must Christians who are trying to understand this Word in Christ be in a constitutive relationship with what the Spirit is revealing in other communities. As stated earlier, the *perichoresis* of Word and Spirit is danced out historically in the dialogue of Christians and other believers.[37]

One of the most coherent and engaging efforts to work out a dialogical Christology is through the symbol of *kenosis*. David H. Jensen does this in *In the Company of Others: A Dialogical Christology*. Unpacking the Pauline insistence that Jesus' divinity and his role as savior are tied tightly but mysteriously to the act of emptying and letting go of himself in his love for and reaching out to others, Jensen arrives at an image of Jesus and discipleship that is essentially dialogical. In Jensen's own words:

> Jesus Christ is the *One who embodies openness to* others. . . . He is the One who goes *ahead* of all who would enclose him, manifesting himself throughout time whenever openness to others is embodied in love.
>
> [Therefore] "Christomonism"—the proclamation of Jesus Christ at the expense of everything else—is a distortion of the life of discipleship and not its faithful execution. Indeed,

> conformity to Christ involves being claimed by others, and not claiming others as our own. . . . In order to become more faithful disciples, Christians need the insights of persons who profess distinctly different religious commitments.[38]

Another formulation of a Christology that calls for dialogue with others is via the non-dual dynamic of particularity and universality. If we Christians rightly affirm the scandal of particularity, we must also remind ourselves that it is a paradoxical scandal. The particular is a sacrament of the universal. In his particularity, Jesus calls us beyond his own identity to open ourselves to the universal divine reality that beckons us through diversity. Douglas John Hall puts it this way:

> [W]hat is so fascinating about the "necessary," if "scandalous," *particular* named Jesus is that, being person, he puts us in touch with a *universal* God, who as living Person transcends our ideas and images of the divine *in the very act of coming close to us*. . . . Contrary to later (and usually heretical) Christologies, Jesus as he is depicted in the Gospels and epistles of the newer Testament, does not wish to be considered (as it were) all the God of God there is.

On the basis of such theological analysis, Hall makes a personal confession of faith that epitomizes a dialogical Christology: "I can say without any doubt at all that I am far more open to Jews and Muslims and Sikhs and humanists and all kinds of other human beings, including self-declared atheists, *because* of Jesus than I should ever have been *apart* from him."[39]

Finally, I believe that one of the most solid—certainly one of the most discussed—foundations for a dialogical Christology is being laid by what is called *comparative theology*, as that theology is being formulated by people like Frank Clooney, James Fredericks, and Catherine Cornille. In their various ways, all of them insist that Christian theology not only can be but must be done *comparatively*. Only through the study of other traditions can we adequately study our own. The so-called sources of theology must be expanded; "scripture and tradition," which mean *primarily* the Bible and church history, must also include the sacred texts and beliefs of other traditions. As far as I know, none of these comparative theologians have explicitly laid out the implicit Christological foundations for such a comparative theology, although Frank Clooney recognizes such foundations: "A person who is, or by God's grace seeks to be, entirely committed to Christ, is also a person willing to take other religious traditions seriously, listening with a critical but deeply open mind to what people in that tradition have said."[40]

A Prophetic Dialogue

If a dialogical Christology truly guides our explorations of the pluralistic terrain on the other side of the Vatican II bridge, it will also be a means of preserving what many, including our new pope, fear can so easily be lost: the uniqueness of Jesus the Christ. What I'm getting at has to do with the nature of dialogue. If Jesus is the Way that is open to other Ways, if that openness is truly dialogical, then the relationship with others is not just a matter of listening and learning, it also must include speaking and challenging. And this brings us to the question of what it is that we Christians can and must bring to the conversation: what is our distinctive Christian contribution?

This is another version of the ever-recurring, never-finally-to-be-answered question: "Who do you say I am?" It must be formulated and answered according to the signs of the times. And with many Christians today, when I survey the signs of our times, I see incredible human and environmental suffering due to incredible human exploitation and injustice. In such a world, Christian witness must include what we know was distinctive of the identity and the message of Jesus: his particular (though certainly not exclusive) concern for the poor and the marginalized. Jesus did not just call for belief in God; he called for belief in the reign of God, a new way of organizing society based on compassion, mutuality, and justice, especially for those who had been pushed aside. For Aloysius Pieris, today the most appropriate and effective way of speaking about Jesus' uniqueness is to show how he "is the covenant between YHWH and the non-persons of the world . . . the irrevocable covenant between God and the poor."[41] Therefore "Our specifically Christian mission is to share the Crucified God's solidarity or friendship with the poor, a friendship which led him to lay down his life for them (Jn 15:13)."[42]

A dialogical Christology, in other words, calls for a prophetic dialogue. This, I believe, is one of the most effective ways, in our present world, to preserve and proclaim the uniqueness of Christ. As followers of this Christ we announce that to know God, or to experience Enlightenment, or to submit to Truth may include many things, but it must also include not just loving our neighbor but doing justice and seeking reconciliation for the marginalized of the world. Other religious traditions may contain a similar concern, something we may perhaps discover in the dialogue. But what we *do* know is what we have seen in and learned from Jesus: that this concern for victims is integral to the experience of God or Truth. As Asian theologians and bishops are trying to make clear, it is by emphasizing or starting with this image of Jesus the prophet for the poor that we can best announce the good news about our belief in Jesus as savior or Son of God.[43]

Pastoral Recommendations

Finally, I would like to offer a few pastoral recommendations. The territory on the other side of the Vatican II bridge might be strange and even menacing for many of the so-called ordinary faithful. So if a pneumatological theology, a dialogical Christology, and a prophetic dialogue are the community's roadmaps for exploring a new relationship of mutuality with persons of other religions, how can we assist the faithful to make use of those maps? Again, my suggestions can only be brief.

Commitment and Openness

One of the greatest fears that Christians, both lay and clerical, have about any effort to move beyond the fulfillment perspective toward a recognition of the possible equal validity of other religions is that it will threaten or diminish one's commitment to Christ. Here I believe we can make clear that just as commitment to Christ is thoroughly compatible with openness to others, so openness to others is thoroughly compatible with commitment to Christ. To open oneself to the surprises of what the Spirit may be doing in other religions need not threaten at all what we know God has done in Jesus. Or, more generally and more psychologically, we do not have to know or even believe that our way is God's only or best way in order to be fully committed to our way. There may be other aspects of divine truth or other ways in which God transforms human lives, and because they are from God, we can respect and learn from them. The recognition that there may be no "best way" need not threaten the love and devotion I have for my way.

Analogies with marriage, like all analogies, limp. But I do believe that at least a partial comparison between one's personal commitments to one's spouse and the Christian community's commitment to Christ can help. One's relationship to one's husband or wife bears a depth, a centrality, yes, an exclusivity that cannot be found in other relationships; this unique quality is felt especially but not only in its physical-sexual expression. But the uniqueness of this marital commitment does not prevent, indeed it generally increases, our ability to appreciate, enjoy, and learn from relationships with other men and women whose friendship can very much contribute to and enrich the relationship with one's spouse. Total commitment to Christ and full openness to others can indeed enrich each other.

A Confessional Openness

Another danger that many Christians see lurking on the pluralistic opposite shore of Vatican II is a loss or lessening of missionary outreach. If other people can not only be saved but be saved just as easily through other religions, what's the purpose of preaching the gospel to them? A perhaps somewhat glib response might be that we're calling for dialogue and that you can't have dialogue without preaching. Generally, in promoting dialogue, we call for the readiness to listen and learn, but there can't be any listening and learning unless someone is speaking and teaching, in other words, witnessing and preaching. Participants in dialogue must, in some real sense, be missionaries to each other; but missionaries who not only preach but also are ready to be preached to.

In a truly mutual dialogue, religious people still feel, and feel deeply, that they have something they want to and need to share with others. Christians may feel that their partners already know God or Truth, but that doesn't exclude the belief that they can learn more of God and Truth through the dialogue. Philosophically, to question or deny that any religion has the *exclusive* or the *final* truth is not to question that religions can still have *universal* truth. Just because I do not believe that my religion is superior to yours doesn't mean that I don't still believe that my religion has something important to say to yours. Therefore, Christians on the other side of the bridge will continue to witness to Christ and they will continue to feel that such witness can bring other religious people to a deeper, more engaging understanding of God's truth and vision for the world.

Thus, the Christian openness to other religions will always be a confessional openness. One of the most simple yet eloquent descriptions of what such a confessional openness implies was given by H. Richard Niebuhr way back in 1941. In relation to outsiders, he urged Christians to confess and state clearly what has been their experience of Jesus and the church and what they believe, without trying to "justify it as superior to all other faiths." Niebuhr felt that such claims of superiority "become more destructive of religion, Christianity, and the soul than any foe's attack can possibly be." So he counseled his fellow Christians to enter the conversation with others "by stating in simple, confessional form what has happened to us in our community, how we came to believe, how we reason about things, and what we see from our point of view."[44] Without any further talk of "only" or "superior," let the dialogue move forward.

"One and Only" Language for Inner Consumption Only

But what about all the "one and only language" that is woven into the fabric of our scriptures and liturgy? ("no other name" [Acts 4:12]; "only begotten Son" [Jn 1:18]; "one Mediator" [1 Tm 2:5]). Are we to erase it or put it all in brackets? Not at all. But we can use it for the kind of language we just said it is: confessional language, affective language, meant primarily to express the community's excitement about, commitment to and love for Jesus, and our conviction that he and his message could arouse the same feelings in other peoples. Its purpose is to stir love for and commitment to Jesus, not to put down Buddha or Muhammad.

So my pastoral suggestion is that we follow Niebuhr's advice and, as it were, keep such language to ourselves. It is, one might say, meant for internal consumption only, to be used in our liturgies and prayers to express the knowledge and hope of our hearts and not to be flaunted in the face of those who find their hopes rooted in other stories.[45] We continue to use this language, aware that most religious communities have similar confessional, superlative, "no other name" language. Such language is meant to feed the energies of the *full commitment* that religious experience always demands, but it must be used carefully, if at all, when full commitment to one's own way leads to *full openness* to other ways. Somehow, paradoxically but promisingly, my "only" must recognize and learn from your "only."

So, Vatican II and the religions, bridge or boundary? To end on a very personal note, I've spent a large part of these past forty years hoping and trying to urge that Vatican II is a bridge. I trust these reflections have shown why I continue to hope.

Notes

[1]Paul Knitter, *Introducing Theologies of Religions* (Maryknoll, N.Y.: Orbis Books, 2002), Part II.

[2]Ibid., 81-82.

[3]See my *Jesus and the Other Names: Christian Mission and Global Responsibility* (Maryknoll, N.Y.: Orbis Books, 1996), 136-40.

[4]And, we might add, the borders are clearly marked in the latest book of then Cardinal Ratzinger, now Pope Benedict XVI: Joseph Cardinal Ratzinger, *Truth and Tolerance: Christian Belief and World Religions* (San Francisco: Ignatius Press, 2004).

[5]John Hick, "Whatever Path Men Choose Is Mine," in *Christianity and Other Religions*, ed. John Hick and Brian Hebblethwaite (Philadelphia: Fortress, 1980), 180-81.

[6]*The Myth of Religious Superiority: A Multifaith Exploration*, ed. Paul F. Knitter (Maryknoll, N.Y.: Orbis Books, 2005).

[7]Ibid., Foreword.

[8]So Peter Phan is right when he recently wrote in *Theological Studies*, "essential theological issues such as the locus of divine revelation, the role of Christ as the universal and unique savior, the function of the Church as the necessary means of salvation, the role of non-Christian religions as possible ways of salvation, and the nature and purpose of Christian mission, are far from being settled" ("Cultures, Religions, and Power: Proclaiming Christ in the United States Today," *Theological Studies* 65 [2004]: 728-29).

[9]Marcus Borg, "Jesus and Buddhism: A Christian View," *Buddhist-Christian Studies* 19 (1999): 96.

[10]Knitter, *Introducing Theologies of Religions*, 96-98.

[11]See Edmund Chia, "FABC, Interreligious Dialogue and the Asian Synod," in *Manila Forum on the Asian Synod* (Geneva: Pax Romana ICMICA Asia, 1998), 173-81; John Mansford Prior, "A Tale of Two Synods," *Vidyajyoti* 62 (1998): 654-65; Tom C. Fox, *Pentecost in Asia: A New Way of Being Church* (Maryknoll, N.Y.: Orbis Books, 2002), 185-97.

[12]"Catholics and Other Religions: Bridging the Gap between Dialogue and Theology," *Louvain Studies* 24 (1999): 319-54.

[13]For texts and commentary on the Vatican's new understanding of dialogue, see Paul Knitter, *Jesus and the Other Names*, 136-40.

[14]Edward Schillebeeckx, *The Church: The Human Story of God* (New York: Crossroad, 1990), 166-67.

[15]John Pawlikowski, "Vatican II's Theological About-face on the Jews: Not Yet Fully Recognized," *The Ecumenist* 37 (2000): 4-6.

[16]Address to the Jewish community of Mainz, Germany, November 17, 1980. This statement is found in the document of the Vatican Commission for Religious Relations with Jews, *Notes on the Correct Way to Present Jews and Judaism in Preaching and Catechesis in the Roman Catholic Church* (June 24, 1985), no. 3.

[17]Address to Jewish leaders in Miami, September 11, 1987.

[18]Address on the Fiftieth Anniversary of the Warsaw Ghetto Uprising, April 6, 1993.

[19]Gregory Baum, *Amazing Church: A Catholic Theologian Remembers a Half-Century of Change* (Maryknoll, N.Y.: Orbis Books, 2005), 111.

[20]Cardinal Walter Kasper in his commentary on *Dominus Iesus,* section 3, quoted in Philip A. Cunningham, "Implications for Catholic Magisterial Teaching on Jews and Judaism," in *Sic et Non: Encountering* Dominus Iesus, ed. Stephen J. Pope and Charles Hefling (Maryknoll, N.Y.: Orbis Books, 2002), 148.

[21]Pawlikowski, "Vatican II's Theological About-face on the Jews," 5.

[22]Ibid., 6. Cunningham fully agrees: "the Catholic community has not yet integrated its recent recognition of God's perpetual covenant with Israel into its theologies of Christ, church, and salvation" ("Implications for Catholic Magisterial Teaching on Jews and Judaism," 140).

[23]Previous to 9/11: Mark Jergensmeyer, *Terror in the Mind of God: The Global Rise of Religious Violence* (Berkeley: University of California Press, 2000); and R. Scott Appleby, *The Ambivalence of the Sacred: Religion, Violence, and Reconciliation* (New York: Rowman & Littlefield, 2000). Post 9/11: Charles Kimball, *When Religion Becomes Evil* (San Francisco: HarperSan Francisco, 2002); Lloyd Steffen, *The Demonic Turn: The Power of Religion to Inspire or Restrain Violence* (Cleveland: Pilgrim Press, 2003); Lee Griffith, *The War on Terrorism and the Terror of God* (Grand Rapids, Mich.: Eerdmans, 2002); Jessica Stern, *Terror in the Name of God: Why Religious Militants Kill* (New York: HarperCollins, 2003); Charles Selengut, *Sacred Fury: Understanding Religious Violence* (New York: Alta Mira Press, 2003);

Bruce Lincoln, *Holy Terrors: Thinking about Religion after September 11* (Chicago: University of Chicago Press, 2003); and Oliver McTernan, *Violence in God's Name: Religion in an Age of Conflict* (Maryknoll, N.Y.: Orbis Books, 2003).

[24]Rita Gross, "Excuse Me, But What's the Question? Isn't Religious Diversity Normal?" in Paul F. Knitter, ed., *The Myth of Religious Superiority*, 75-87. According to Gregory Baum, it was precisely this danger of violence between Islam and Christianity, the specter of a "clash of civilizations," that moved John Paul II "to give full support to the United Nations project promoting 'the dialogue of civilizations.' " The pope, according to Baum, implicitly endorsed promoting dialogue rather than seeking conversion as the ideal of Muslim-Christian relations. In doing so, he "transcended the theology of Vatican II." The specter of religious violence, in other words, pushed the pope to the other side of the bridge in practice though not in theology (Baum, *Amazing Church*, 122-23).

[25]"Aspects of European Theology," in *Theological Investigations* Vol. XXI (New York: Crossroad, 1988), 97-98 [78-98]. Among those who are following Rahner's advice: Amos Yong, *Discerning the Spirit(s): A Pentecostal-Charismatic Contribution to Christian Theology of Religions* (Sheffield: Sheffield Academic Press, 2000); Gavin D'Costa, *The Meeting of Religions and the Trinity* (Maryknoll, N.Y.: Orbis Books, 2000); Michael Amaladoss, "Listen to the Spirit: 'The Father is Greater than I' (John 14.28)," *Vidyajyoti* 63 (1999): 687-89; Michael Ipgrave, *Trinity and Inter-Faith Dialogue: Plenitude and Plurality*, Religions and Discourse Series, vol. 14, ed. James M. M. Francis (New York: Peter Lang, 2003); Peter Hodgson, "The Spirit and Religious Pluralism," in Paul F. Knitter, ed., *The Myth of Religious Superiority*, 135-49; Paul F. Knitter, "A New Pentecost? A Pneumatological Theology of Religions," *Current Dialogue*, January 1991: 32-41.

[26]Yong, *Discerning the Spirit(s)*, 60, see also 25, 226, 288.

[27]Rahner, "Aspects of European Theology," 97-98.

[28]Yong, *Discerning the Spirit(s)*, 29.

[29]Gavin D'Costa, "Christ, the Trinity, and Religious Pluralism," in *Christian Uniqueness Reconsidered: The Myth of a Pluralistic Theology of Religions*, ed. Gavin D'Costa (Maryknoll, N.Y.: Orbis Books, 1990), 23. See also D'Costa, *The Meeting of Religions and the Trinity*, 114.

[30]Jacques Dupuis, *Toward a Christian Theology of Religious Pluralism* (Maryknoll, N.Y.: Orbis Books, 1997), 197.

[31]*Discerning the Spirit(s)*, 64.

[32]Ibid., 319, 320.

[33]And here we are following the lead of John Paul II, whose "singular contribution . . . to a theology of religions," according to Jacques Dupuis, was his insistence on taking seriously "the operative presence of the Spirit of God in the religious life of non-Christians. . . ," *Toward a Christian Theology of Religious Pluralism*, 171.

[34]Amaladoss, "Listen to the Spirit," 687-89.

[35]John B. Cobb, Jr., "Beyond Pluralism," in *Christian Uniqueness Reconsidered*, 91.

[36]Michael Barnes, *Theology and the Dialogue of Religions* (Cambridge: Cambridge University Press, 2002), 221-22, 230.

[37]Yong, *Discerning the Spirit(s)*; Ipgrave, *Trinity and Inter-Faith Dialogue*; S. Mark Heim, *The Depth of Riches: A Trinitarian Theology of Religious Ends* (Grand Rapids, Mich.: Eerdmans, 2001).

[38]David H. Jensen, *In the Company of Others: A Dialogical Christology* (Cleveland: Pilgrim Press, 2001), xi-xv, passim.

[39]Douglas John Hall, *Why Christian? For Those on the Edge of Faith* (Minneapolis: Fortress Press, 1998), 33-34.

[40]Francis X. Clooney, "Implications for the Practice of Inter-Religious Learning," in *Sic et Non*, 168.

[41]Aloysius Pieris, *Fire and Water: Basic Issues in Asian Buddhism and Christianity* (Maryknoll, N.Y.: Orbis Books, 1996), 150-51.

[42]Aloysius Pieris, *God's Reign for God's Poor: A Return to the Jesus Formula* (Gonawala-Kelaniya, Sri Lanka: Tulana Research Centre, 1998), chap. 4.

[43]Aloysius Pieris, "Christ beyond Dogma: Doing Christology in the Context of the Religions and the Poor," *Louvain Studies* 25 (2000): 187-231; Felix Wilfred, "Images of Jesus Christ in the Asian Pastoral Context: An Interpretation of the Documents of the Federation of Asian Bishops' Conferences," *Concilium* (1993/2): 51-62.

[44]H. Richard Niebuhr, *The Meaning of Revelation* (New York: Macmillan, 1962), 39, 41.

[45]For more on re-interpreting New Testament exclusive language as confessional language, see Krister Stendahl, "Notes on Three Bible Studies," in *Christ's Lordship and Religious Pluralism*, ed. Gerald H. Anderson and Thomas F. Stransky (Maryknoll, N.Y.: Orbis Books, 1981), 7-18; Paul F. Knitter, *No Other Name? A Critical Survey of Christian Attitudes toward World Religions* (Maryknoll, N.Y.: Orbis Books, 1985), 182-86; Knitter, *Jesus and the Other Names*, 67-71.

Interreligious *Prudentia*

Wisdom from Peter Lombard for the Post-Conciliar Church

Reid B. Locklin

In October 1965 the assembled bishops of the Second Vatican Council approved *Nostra Aetate*, their Declaration on the Church's Relation to Non-Christian Religions.[1] Interpretations of this document vary widely, and it has been the source of some controversy. Nevertheless, it has become customary to describe the teaching of *Nostra Aetate*—supported by that of other conciliar documents—as a "breakthrough" or even a "complete innovation" in the life of the church.[2] Through its recognition of a "ray of truth" reflected in the teachings of other religions (no. 2), its call for sincere "dialogues and cooperation" between Christians and the followers of other religions, and its repudiation of anti-Semitism and religious discrimination (nos. 4-5), the declaration seemed to open an entirely new chapter of church history. Robert A. Graham, writing shortly after the Council, could announce: "it is the first time an Ecumenical Council has expressed such an open approach to the other great faiths of the world."[3]

Forty years after the event, a straightforward assessment of *Nostra Aetate* and its impact on the Catholic Church would be a bit more difficult to formulate. First of all, one might observe the explosion of mutually critical, and sometimes mutually contradictory, proposals in the areas of missiology, inculturation, interreligious dialogue, the theology of religions, the theology of religious pluralism, and comparative theology.[4] What may have started as a polite dinner conversation, it seems, has been raised to a dull roar. In addition, a number of documents from Rome have tempered at least the most extravagant hopes raised by *Nostra Aetate*. The Congregation for the Doctrine of the Faith's 2000 declaration *Dominus Iesus*, in particular, has been sharply criticized by some as a turn toward a new Catholic "fundamentalism" or indeed as "nothing less than a conspiracy to overturn the Second Vatican Council" itself.[5] Mark Plaiss offers a more nuanced, but no less definite judgment: "For now, it seems, the upward trajectory begun in '*Nostra Aetate*' and climaxing in 'Dialogue and Proclamation' has leveled to a plateau."[6] Such claims may reveal more about their authors than about the actual state of the church. Be this as it may, these developments necessarily raise serious questions for any Catholic contemplating the "dialogues and cooperation" recommended by *Nostra Aetate*. Whither the promise of the church's relations with other religions? Has the Catholic Church really arrived at a kind of "plateau," to go no further?

I do not presume to be able to answer these questions in one short essay. Instead, I would like to suggest, tentatively, that some clarity might be gained by turning our attention from 1965 . . . *to 1165*. In that year, or shortly thereafter, the Parisian master Peter Comester wrote a prologue for the sentence collection of his own teacher, Peter Lombard (d. 1160).[7] In doing so, I suggest, Comester did not merely introduce a theology textbook to a new generation of students; he also highlighted a distinctive set of pedagogical tools and insights that charted an important "middle way" for his own period and perhaps, by extension, also for ours.

The key element of this middle way, at least for our purposes, will be the Lombard's apparent concern to educate for "prudence" or *prudentia*. One of the cardinal virtues, *prudentia* comprehends more than mere caution or restraint; instead, it might be aptly characterized as "practical intelligence," a cultivated capacity for discernment, sound judgment, and appropriate action in particular situations.[8] And, as we shall see, such practical intelligence emerges as a primary goal of the theological pedagogy of the *Sentences*. By selecting authorities from prior Christian tradition and juxtaposing them in problematic ways, the Lombard aimed to inculcate a specific set of skills—skill in the negotiation of apparent conflicts and skill in the resolution of ambiguities—as well as to encourage the moral disposition to use these skills to good effect. This combination of expertise and character, I claim, constitutes a distinctive form of *prudentia*. Precisely as *practical* intelligence, intended to be *applied* in a particular context, the *prudentia* of the *Sentences* addressed concerns specific to the twelfth century. Nevertheless, I hope to show that the Lombard's project can also offer a fresh perspective on interreligious dialogue and exchange in the contemporary era, one that subtly shifts our focus from the problematic, conflicting claims of different religious traditions, as such, to the persons Christians may become by engaging such claims with seriousness, creativity, and piety. It encourages us, in other words, to re-imagine the "dialogues and cooperation" of *Nostra Aetate* precisely in terms of *prudentia*.

My argument proceeds in three major steps. First, I offer an account of the religious pedagogy enacted in Peter Lombard's *Sentences*, attentive to the way this pedagogy aims to cultivate a distinctive *prudentia*, as already briefly outlined. Then, in the second section, I draw a rough correlation from the pedagogy of the *Sentences* to the comparative theological project of Francis X. Clooney, which may also be viewed as a kind of pedagogy for *prudentia*—albeit one that extends its scope well beyond the Christian fold. Finally, I attempt to generalize the test case and to suggest a few consequences for the post-conciliar church.

The *Sentences*: A Pedagogy for *Prudentia*

We can begin our treatment of Peter Lombard with a fairly straightforward observation: on one level, the *Sentences* is a thoroughly unoriginal work, by design. First of all, its evident focus lies, not on any positions or arguments of the Lombard's own, but on a string of *sententiae*, authoritative statements drawn from prior tradition. Moreover, in gathering these sentences together, the Lombard did what had already been done by others, including such great lights as Peter Abelard and Hugh of St. Victor in theology, and Ivo of Chartres and Gratian in canon law. Located firmly between the mercurial personalities of Abelard and Bernard of Clairvaux earlier in the twelfth century and the grand syntheses of Aquinas and Bonaventure in the thirteenth, the Lombard tends to emerge as a mere intermediary in an ultimately more significant historical development, an "unadventurous bore" who produced a kind of "defective" *summa* on the way to the real thing.[9]

Yet Peter Comester saw something distinctive in this work, something that recommended it as an ideal text for his Paris classroom.

And he was not alone. Marcia Colish has argued that the influence of the *Sentences* was so widespread between 1160 and 1215 that even those who disagreed with the Lombard did so largely on terms he had set for them.[10] This stature may have diminished since that time, but it is beginning to re-emerge. One might even say that there is a modest "Peter Lombard revival" underway in the English-speaking world. Significant recent works include Colish's own magisterial two-volume study in 1994, a shorter work for a general audience by Philipp Rosemann ten years later, and the first English translation of the *Sentences* by Giulio Silano, forthcoming.[11] In the hands of these scholars, contemporary readers can see in the Lombard what his peers, students, and successors saw: an innovative scholar and teacher who also exemplified the dramatic transformations of Catholic intellectual life taking place in the twelfth century. Drawing on such secondary sources, as well as selected examples from Book I of the *Sentences*, we can discern the rough texture of the Lombard's distinctive methodology and hypothesize the educational experience for which it was designed.

For simplicity's sake, we can start by focusing on a few central tasks that give the Lombard's project its distinctive shape. The first is also the most obvious: *selecting and organizing relevant authorities*. In his own prologue to the work, the Lombard introduces this as one of his main objectives: "In this brief volume, we have brought together the sentences of the Fathers and have adduced their testimonies so that one who seeks them shall find it unnecessary to rifle through numerous books. . . ."[12] The result? A kind of "convenient book of reference" for busy students, nicely arranged by topic and structured into a complete theological curriculum.[13] With the exception of John of Damascus, newly available in Latin translation, none of the selected *sententiae* and *testimonia* would have been unfamiliar to other twelfth-century theologians; most are drawn from the writings of Augustine. Indeed, the Lombard seems to have made ample use of other sentence collections and Bible glosses, drawing on what might be considered a common fund of well-recognized authorities.[14] But Lombard did so quite freely, selecting only those that most effectively advanced his theological positions or offered what he considered good "models of theological reasoning."[15] His contribution thus lay less in the generation of new insights than in the deft orchestration of old ones.

To illustrate the significance of this task, Silano offers the analogy of a legal casebook.[16] The author of such a casebook is largely invisible to the readers, who wrestle directly with the cases and rulings therein. Yet the judges who produced these rulings—the *sole* true authorities, in a strict sense—do not themselves have the right to determine whether and how their rulings are included in the casebook. This is the sole prerogative of the casebook author, who thus emerges as much more than a mere compiler. By analogy, although the Lombard may seem to "disappear" in the midst of the authoritative sources he has selected, the *Sentences* nevertheless reveals considerable creativity and authorial intent.

Authorities were not merely selected and placed in order in the medieval sentence collections; they were also juxtaposed in ways that forced students to think through the issues presented therein. This leads us to another central task at the heart of the Lombard's educational enterprise: namely, the deliberate *problematizing of the selected authorities*. Perhaps the most dramatic example of this strategy was Peter Abelard's *Sic et Non*, in which the master brought together conflicting opinions on 158 questions and provided a kind of "methodological toolbox" for students to use in resolving such conflicts.[17]

The Lombard, on the other hand, teaches primarily by example, adducing apparent contradictions and then demonstrating possible solutions. In places, he illustrates how authorities can be reconciled by placing their arguments in context or by employing better technical vocabulary.[18] Elsewhere, he corrects the improper use of such authorities by "some" others—presumably other masters—and thereby, to an extent, problematizes the very use of authorities itself.[19] When addressing internal conflicts in Augustine's thought, moreover, the Lombard sometimes offers more than one attempt at reconciliation, without feeling obligated to settle definitively on one or the other.[20] Throughout, prospective readers are being shaped to negotiate tensions in the tradition for themselves. Resolutions are certainly sought and, once formulated, defended with vigor. But these resolutions, as such, do not appear to represent the primary goal of the curriculum. The focus remains on the authorities themselves, deliberately problematized by their mutual juxtaposition.

Selecting, organizing, problematizing. In fulfilling these tasks, the Lombard offered a convenient reference that not only gathered the most important authorities in one place, but also put students through the paces in the practice of theological reasoning. This made the *Sentences* a good textbook in a purely technical sense. It also, as we shall see in the next section, establishes a basic parallel to at least one vision of interreligious dialogue and exchange. Yet these tasks do not seem to exhaust the distinctive methodology and aims of the *Sentences*. Two typical characteristics of the work add further depth to the Lombard's project and also point us in the direction of our contemporary application.

First, we can note that, in constructing the *Sentences*, the Lombard was evidently *less interested in origins than in applications*. By drawing together selected quotations from someone like Augustine, for example, the Lombard does not primarily intend to reconstruct Augustine's own thought. Silano writes:

> . . . Augustine wrote many things, only some of which end up being treated as sentences by Peter and his colleagues. In effect, for all the veneration which the masters show to Augustine, they end up claiming that they have a better sense of the theological system than he did, and so they can sift through his voluminous writings to choose the bits which they regard as truly interesting. They may be dwarves and Augustine may be a giant, but they see further for sitting on his shoulders, and so they get to decide what parts of Augustine's writings are of enduring and normative relevance.[21]

In one sense, Silano's remarks simply reaffirm the sentence collectors' authorial intent in selecting *sententiae*. But it also reveals their strong commitment to the tradition as a complex whole, in immediate contact with and relevant to the present—what one scholar calls the "enduring presence of the past."[22] Accordingly, in the *Sentences*, the Lombard rarely differentiates the concerns of his sources from his own. This cannot be too easily ascribed to historical naïveté or a narrowly "classicist" mindset, for the sentence collectors showed considerable historical acumen in their use of authorities when it suited them, appealing to changes in historical context, recognizing different phases of Augustine's development, and even doing a kind of "source criticism" when circumstances required it.[23] If the Lombard indeed claimed to "have a better sense of the theological system" than Augustine, he presumably did so with at least some degree of self-awareness. Unearthing original meanings from the past is not unimportant, but it is strictly subordinated to making the past tradition speak creatively to the present moment.

A second typical characteristic of the Lombard is a bit less obvious, but no less important. That is, despite all its order and inclusiveness, the *Sentences* tends to *resist complete explanation* and does so quite explicitly, particularly in relation to the mystery of God. Thus, the Lombard offers frequent reminders that God "exceeds all human understanding and worldly intelligence" as well as the "poverty of language," and he openly mocks those who presume "to bound immensity by their intellect."[24] To underscore this emphasis on mystery, he employs an important sentence from Hilary of Poitiers: "begin, advance, persist; and although I know that you will not reach the goal, yet I will rejoice in your progress. For one who pursues infinite things with piety, even though he never reaches his end, yet makes progress by the attempt."[25]

These words of Hilary find a strong echo in Peter Comester's prologue to the *Sentences*, briefly mentioned above. In this prologue, Comester characterizes his teacher's purpose as follows: "His [i.e., Peter Lombard's] intention is to confute blasphemers, encourage the learned and stir up the lazy. He does this, teaching three things about the faith: namely, what ought to be asserted, what ought to be said to the contrary [i.e., denied], and what ought to be piously doubted rather than rashly asserted."[26]

Both quotations—one from the Lombard's forebear and the other from his student—draw readers' attention squarely to the importance of a pious disposition, which both drives and circumscribes the inquiry. Because earnest seeking is entirely in the service of such piety, the confession of inadequacy or of "pious doubt" is not a polite add-on. It is essential to the whole enterprise. In searching after mystery, one can expect to make progress, but one cannot expect to reach the goal. Thus, again quoting Hilary, the Lombard privileges "the profession of prudent faith" above mere "reason of human intelligence" in ascertaining truths about God.[27]

This notion of "prudent faith"—or, more literally, "faithful prudence" (*prudentia fidelis*)—nudges us toward a preliminary assessment of Peter Lombard's pedagogy in the *Sentences*. In this work, as we have seen, the Lombard gathers sentences and authoritative testimonies from the tradition and problematizes them for his students. He is not primarily interested in coming to a greater understanding of these authorities on their own terms, but in applying their insights to the present situation.

At the same time, despite his decisive importance in the eventual development of systematic theology, he does not reveal much interest in constructing a "theological system" in a strict sense; that is, he resists complete explanation and leaves ample room for pious doubt. He takes up individual points, reconciles conflicts, and defends his own positions. But his project—not unlike, we might add, interreligious dialogue itself—appears intrinsically open-ended, permissive of further inquiry and development: future commentators would use it precisely as a tool to develop their own ideas.[28] Searching for language to characterize the intent of such a project, Silano takes a cue from the historian William of Tyre, another of the Lombard's students. In extolling his former teacher, William offers a distinctive phrase to describe those who applied themselves to his writings with reverence: *prudentium chorus*, the "company of *prudentes*."[29]

This phrase from William of Tyre suggests that at least some part of the *Sentences*' success may have stemmed from very concrete, practical, and personal results: the actual fostering of *prudentes*, the effective formation of those "experts" whose attentive and reverent study opened into a distinctive kind of *prudentia*. That is, it aimed to generate practical intelligence for a practical purpose. Peter Lombard's students would have included many destined for "higher office in church and state," not just priests or academics. And so, in the midst of a new educational context and an era of social transformation, the Lombard offered such students thorough training "in the *art of resolving ambiguities* in the text of Scripture and in theological questions."[30] An "art" is clearly not the same as a "system," and the Lombard's repeated injunctions against expecting final or complete results strongly suggest that it was the more practical *art* that claimed pride of place. Those students who proved themselves able to apply past insights to the present situation, to resolve conflicts and ambiguities, and also, we should add, to do so with pious restraint—precisely these students could be considered *prudentes*. Stated another way, using the analogy of legal training, the *Sen-*

tences of Peter Lombard aimed to produce a chorus or company of persons with both the personal character and the technical expertise to issue *sententiae* of their own. It was composed, not primarily to advocate a system of thought, but to foster a much-needed *prudentia*.[31]

A Test Case: The Interreligious Pedagogy of Francis X. Clooney

At this point, we may seem to have wandered a great distance from 1965 and the era of dialogue and cooperation initiated by *Nostra Aetate*. And wander we have: some eight hundred years, give or take. Further, it might seem a bit dubious to equate what is essentially an intra-Christian exercise in the twelfth century with the demands of interreligious relations in the twenty-first. Without doubt, one could not reasonably expect a complete correlation between the two endeavors, embedded as they are in different cultural and historical contexts. Yet the twelfth century was, no less than the twentieth, a tumultuous period, with the certainties of previous generations called into question and institutions, old and new, developing against the background of a changing social landscape.[32] In this time of transition, Peter Lombard's *Sentences* emerged as *the* key text of the theological curriculum and thus assumed a central place in one of the era's powerful new institutions: the university. It thus seems perfectly natural to ask whether the collective project of the twelfth-century sentence collectors and that of the twenty-first-century dialogist may, on reflection, bear some resemblance. The particular challenges, conflicts and ambiguities posed in each situation will certainly diverge sharply in content and even in type; the *prudentia* required to meet them effectively, however, may be essentially the same.

Rather than attempting to argue this point in a general way, it seems appropriately prudent to focus on the contribution of just one contemporary "master": Francis X. Clooney, S.J., an influential Indologist, theologian, and former director of interreligious dialogue for the Jesuits of the United States. Other voices could have been selected, of course—Jacques Dupuis, Diana Eck, Leo Lefebure, Raimon Panikkar, and Keith Ward spring to mind—but Clooney stands out as a particularly good partner for the Lombard, not least because both share a strong commitment to grounding their projects in *particular texts*. And Clooney, no less than the

Lombard, offers an innovative pedagogy in his works, one that aims to stand firmly in the Catholic tradition while also "transgressing" the boundaries of this same tradition.[33] He calls his project "comparative theology," a "truly constructive *theology*, distinguished by its sources and ways of proceeding, [and] by its foundation in more than one tradition. . . ."[34] With regard to the explicit inclusion of non-Christian sources, Clooney's project may seem to resemble the gradual incorporation of "Greco-Jewish" and "Greco-Arabic" materials into Christian theology in the late twelfth and early thirteenth centuries. But Clooney also—and, for my purposes, more intriguingly—describes this project as involving new "ways of proceeding" and thus invites comparison to the no less innovative "educational experience and methodology" of the sentence collectors.[35]

We can adduce some initial parallels by recalling the central tasks of the *Sentences*: namely, the gathering, organizing, and problematizing of relevant authorities from Christian tradition. A comparable set of objectives can be seen at work in Clooney's four major comparative studies.[36] In *Theology after Vedanta* (1993) and *Seeing through Texts* (1996), for example, Clooney gives primary attention to expositing texts, themes, and arguments from two major streams of Hinduism: the non-dualist commentarial tradition of Advaita Vedanta and the Srivaisnava devotionalism of the Tamil hymn *Tiruvaymoli*, respectively. *Hindu God, Christian God* (2001) and *Divine Mother, Blessed Mother* (2005) go a bit further, drawing a variety of Hindu theological traditions together with specific examples of Christian reasoning about God and, in the latter work, of Christian hymns to the Virgin Mary. In each of these cases, Clooney endeavors to identify significant texts from the Hindu tradition, to structure them in an intelligible way, and to pair them with comparable texts from within the Christian tradition.

Such a strategy reflects what Clooney calls "theologizing by way of particular examples," a systematic setting-aside of any "general theory about religion" in favor of careful, patient attention to specific texts and arguments.[37] As we saw above with reference to the *Sentences*, the mere selection of such texts already implies significant authorial intent. Given the breadth and depth of these traditions, why choose some texts and not others? Why focus on *texts*?[38] In a programmatic essay, Clooney alludes to two possible criteria. The first invokes David Tracy's notion of a "classic" to argue that some texts, such as the Christian Bible or the Srivaisnava *Tiruvaymoli*, possess intrinsic authority in their respective traditions and, thus, make decisive claims in and through the mere act of reading them. The second involves a more practical appeal: certain texts invite comparative inquiry simply because "they talk about a whole range of theologically important topics such as God, gods and goddesses, the ultimate reality, the creation of the world, death, sin and salvation, and so on."[39] The comparative theologian draws support, then, from both intrinsic and extrinsic warrants, from the claims of prior tradition(s) and from the concrete exigency of relevant questions. But it is ultimately the comparativist alone who decides whether and how particular texts are included.

Despite considerable fluidity in topic and organization from one work to the next, one key element of Clooney's project recurs in all these works: namely, the deliberate pairing of comparable arguments and texts; not infrequently, this takes the form of a very literal "juxtaposition" in two or more columns printed side-by-side.[40] In places, Clooney offers practical strategies for reconciling the apparent conflicts brought to light by such juxtapositions; elsewhere, he sides with some positions against others.[41] Finally, on occasion, he draws attention to truly "incomparable" texts, which seem to have no parallel outside their own tradition or theological context.[42] Determinations and strategies may vary, but the problematic character of the exercise remains. Indeed, Clooney identifies the tension between juxtaposed texts as an integral aspect of the whole project: comparative theology is, at its heart, "a novel, designedly arbitrary endeavor that is nevertheless truly creative of enduring theological results."[43] No less than the Lombard, then, does Clooney endeavor to render the selected texts and authorities "designedly" problematic.

Two further characteristics of Clooney's project support the parallels we have already made and, interestingly, also coincide with criticisms from his peers. Reviewers note that Clooney sometimes seems to introduce distortion when, for example, he calls Vedanta "theology" or when he treats Sanskrit grammatical arguments for the existence of God as though they are "basically the same" as Western philosophical ones.[44] It is worth asking, however, whether avoiding distortion represents a primary concern.

Certainly, when it suits his purposes, Clooney is perfectly capable of articulating sophisticated historical arguments to understand Hindu texts and traditions. At the same time, he sharply relativizes such historical understanding to comparative reading itself:

> To contextualize, to read one's Text along with other texts, is to create new meanings. Established meanings, simple or complex, are extended through previously unintended juxtapositions. Something of the independent, first meaning of one's Text may be changed, even distorted or lost, while new meanings, not intended by the author, occur to the reader.[45]

It would be considerably overstating the case to suggest that Clooney's project is indifferent to the "independent, first meanings" of the texts he selects. But Clooney does seem to claim that if one theologizes in this way, unearthing and preserving original meanings will not emerge as absolute values. Here, as for the Lombard, the primary focus remains squarely on the concrete application of these traditions to the present moment of learning and inquiry.

A second typical characteristic that pervades Clooney's work is what he refers to as the "patient deferral of issues of truth."[46] As just one example, Clooney explicitly distances himself from the theology of religions project, which aspires to offer a single "coherent and complete narrative" for all religious traditions. Careful comparative practice, he suggests, does not support such a grand meta-narrative; instead, ideally, it tends toward surrender when the comparativist runs out of "strategies and plans" and eventually, "somewhat desperately" gives herself completely to God.[47] Such reticence to theorize either fascinates or frustrates Clooney's critics. One reviewer complains: "can the believer, Christian or otherwise, wait for his or her faith to be theologically confirmed only at the end of protracted theological dialogue?"[48]

This reviewer's critique, of course, presumes that "confirmation," as such, lies within the purview of the comparative theological project. On the contrary, Clooney challenges such presumptions at their root. He is committed to the search for truth, to be sure, but such commitment need not, and in fact cannot, support comprehensive theological systems or claims; at least, he will sometimes add, "not yet."[49] To understand his position, we might recall one of the important *sententiae* from the previous section: "begin, advance, persist; and although I know that you will not reach the goal, yet I will rejoice in your progress. For one who pursues infinite things with piety, even though he never reaches his end, yet makes progress by the attempt."

These words of Hilary describe inquiry into the Trinity, but they also nicely capture one of Clooney's essential insights. It would be naïve in the extreme to expect some grand reconciliation between Hindu non-dualism and Christian monotheism or between hymns to the goddess Lakshmi and praises of the Virgin Mary. Nevertheless, Clooney's scholarship suggests that it is worthwhile and even necessary to make the attempt. One may not expect to reach a definitive "end," but that does not mean no progress has been made.[50]

We can still, however, press the question. What does it mean to make "progress" in this case? What, precisely, can we expect to gain if there is no final resolution in sight? With Peter Lombard in mind, we can again borrow from Hilary for an answer: *prudentia fidelis*, "faithful prudence." Certainly, as we have already noted in passing, Clooney's project differs from the *Sentences* in many ways. "Classics" are not the same as "sentences," and the gulf between such classics as the *Tiruvaymoli* and the Song of Songs is likely to be much wider than any theological distinction that might separate Augustine from Hilary. But Clooney, like Peter Lombard, teaches precisely by selecting, organizing, and problematizing texts. Both share a practical focus on allowing past tradition or traditions to speak directly to the present, and both do so in ways that explicitly resist complete explanation.

Given these methodological parallels, it seems a short jump to suggest a parallel intention. That is, in light of the *Sentences*, Clooney's pedagogy may be read as intending to foster a *prudentium chorus*, a company or cohort of persons able to navigate the newly complex terrain of interreligious dialogue and cooperation. What is needed in the present time, Clooney seems to claim, are not clever theories, but able *prudentes*: those individuals with the personal disposition and expertise—or, we might say, the practical intelligence—to cross religious boundaries, to assess competing claims, to enter into genuine conversation, and nevertheless to offer a robust confession of Christian faith.[51] And, just perhaps, shaping such *prudentes* and fostering such *prudentia* is precisely what his interreligious pedagogy sets out to do.

Interreligious *Prudentia*: Seeking a Middle Way

We may now be ready to generalize a bit, to ask what wisdom Peter Lombard has to offer to the post-conciliar church beyond this individual test case. We can begin such an assessment with the Lombard's own judgment on his textbook, offered in the prologue:

> Here you will find the precedents and teaching of our ancestors. Here, by the open-hearted profession of the Lord's faith, we have denounced the falsehood of viperine doctrine. Seeking access to the truth to be shown without incurring the danger of professing impiety, we have pursued a moderate middle course between the two. And if in some places our voice has rung out a little, it has not transgressed the bounds set by our forefathers.[52]

In part, this passage is purely descriptive: the *Sentences* is indeed a collection of "precedents and teaching," accompanied by vigorous argument. It is telling, however, that the Lombard further describes it as a kind of intermediate path between "seeking access to the truth" and avoiding impiety, between letting one's voice ring out and staying within the bounds of tradition. Such bounds are the sentences themselves, selected, organized, and problematized for those who, like the Lombard, would seek to tread a "moderate middle course." Systems and syntheses do not claim primary interest—these would come later. But neither does the Lombard restrict himself to mere exegesis. His aims, as we have seen, lie somewhere between these extremes, in a pedagogy that shapes students into *prudentes* on an anvil of tensions, complexities, and a pious striving to address them, one by one.

Having gained some familiarity with the rough texture of this middle way and having seen some parallels in the work of Francis X. Clooney, we may now be ready to ask: what insight can be drawn from this project for the post-Vatican II Catholic Church? What wisdom does Peter Lombard offer, forty years after *Nostra Aetate*?

A first appropriation simply draws our attention to the central importance of cultivating practical skills in thinking and acting interreligiously. If Clooney's comparative theological project may be read as a pedagogy for interreligious *prudentia*, comparable to that of the *Sentences*, this does not appear to be the result of self-conscious imitation; rather, it arises directly from the exigency of a changed social context. If so, then it would make good sense to look for signs of it elsewhere. Stepping back from the "theology of religions vs. comparative theology" debate, for example, we might more clearly identify a consistent set of practical concerns and a shared commitment to fostering authentic dialogue and co-operation, as recommended by *Nostra Aetate*.[53] And the work of someone like Clooney can be seen not only as critiquing other strategies, but also as exemplifying broader trends. When he says "not yet" to the theology of religions and the construction of systems, his positions are intelligible—even refutable—precisely because he shares a common agenda and significant common ground with others who disagree: namely, the cultivation of Christians who are piously disposed and technically capable of relating to religious others *cum prudentia et caritate* (*NA* 2). The primary question is not "Does this system or theory account for all the relevant data?" It is, instead, "Who are we—ourselves, our readers, our students—likely *to become* when we argue or reason this way?" The middle way of Peter Lombard thus highlights an important *middle ground* from which intra-Christian debates about religious pluralism might well profit.

Beyond this practical orientation, the pedagogy of the *Sentences* also offers a refreshing approach to authority, especially authoritative texts. When confronted with the claims of a document like *Dominus Iesus*, for example, we might look to the Lombard for another middle way, mediating this time between uncritical assent and impious dissent: that is, deliberate problematizating through juxtaposition. Thus Vincent P. Branick interprets *Dominus Iesus* as advancing a series of paradoxical claims to both universality and particularity—of God's love and salvation, of the presence of Christ, of the mediation of the church—which can be reconciled only on the order of metaphor and intuition, and he further suggests that the declaration can and should be brought into a constructive "dialectic" with other voices from the tradition.[54] We also find, close at hand, the International Theological Commission's

1997 document entitled "Christianity and the World Religions," explicitly recommended by the Congregation for the Doctrine of the Faith in the synthesis that accompanied *Dominus Iesus*.[55] These documents differ in levels of teaching authority, to be sure, but they deal with similar topics and share the decisive influence of at least one mind: Joseph Ratzinger, now Pope Benedict XVI, then prefect of the Congregation for the Doctrine of the Faith and president of the International Theological Commission.

Faced with a bald juxtaposition in *Dominus Iesus* of claims about the "fullness of Christ's salvific mystery" in the church and the "gravely deficient situation" of the members of other religions, on the one hand, with equally strong claims by the ITC about the theological certainty of salvific grace outside this same church and calls for self-giving renunciation of any "false" claim to superiority, on the other (*DI* 16, 22; "Christianity and the World Religions," 63, 104), readers might be tempted to choose one set of assertions over the other. The pedagogy of the *Sentences* does not exclude this entirely, of course, but it recommends an alternate, more dialectic route: thorough engagement of all apparently conflicting positions, wholehearted attempts to reconcile or resolve them, and, when such attempts inevitably fall short, a surrender to mystery. Such a strategy, performed repeatedly as a kind of spiritual and intellectual discipline, will not likely result in some kind of Archimedean perspective within which to comprehend all possible questions. It might, however, go some distance toward cultivating *prudentia* and shaping *prudentes*.[56]

Ultimately, of course, one would hope that the pedagogy promoted in the *Sentences* might offer wisdom beyond intra-Christian conversations *about* religious pluralism and interreligious dialogue to such dialogue itself. And this it does, at least indirectly. First of all, the Lombard's project might be interpreted to give a certain weight to those contemporary proposals, such as Clooney's comparative theological project, whose pedagogical strategies most closely resemble its own. More broadly, and more importantly, such correlations can also anchor what seems to be a new activity of the church in more well-traveled Christian traditions of education, inquiry, and virtue formation.

To explore this idea, we can turn briefly to a thoughtful study of interreligious dialogue and virtue theory by James Fredericks, another comparative theologian and specialist in Buddhist-Christian dialogue. In this study, Fredericks points out that the virtues are not simply static and immutable principles; they "have histories," including changes in interpretation and application from one era to the next.[57] For the cardinal virtue of *prudentia*, at least as I have treated it in this essay, such a "history" might include both the project of the Lombard and that of Francis X. Clooney, among others. Both "masters" ask serious, discerning questions about how to educate for the interpretive skills, moral character, and practical intelligence required for Christians living in a particular social context. Both wed what is intrinsically an open-ended process of inquiry to a healthy dose of pious restraint. If Clooney does in fact "transgress the bounds" set by prior tradition, he does so in a strictly provisional way: juxtaposing texts, taking up questions as they arise, and attempting to bring disparate traditions into constructive exchange in the very person of the comparativist. Such an approach appears to transpose an old educational strategy to the new context created by Vatican II, to heed—albeit in a way he could scarcely have imagined—the Lombard's call for a "middle course" that is, for all its moderation, also deeply challenging and creative.

Fredericks himself calls for recognition of "interreligious friendship" as a new theological virtue for the present moment of church history, a virtue that encourages Christians to seek out relationships with religious others from a sense of self-interested love (*philia*).[58] If we follow his suggestion, we might also come to see interreligious *prudentia* as a helpful complement and balance to such "interreligious friendship," shifting our attention from interpersonal relationships as such to the expertise and disposition that may be required to sustain such relationships in a religiously fruitful way.[59] Such *prudentia* would necessarily remain vigilant for "what ought to be piously doubted rather than rashly asserted," to be sure, but it could also embrace the problematic character of genuine interreligious encounter as a potentially fruitful spiritual discipline. In the new era of dialogue and cooperation inaugurated by *Nostra Aetate*, Christians need not shrink from religious others because their texts, traditions. and rituals set them so clearly apart from Christian faith. Instead, creative engagement of precisely such distinctively different texts and traditions can be understood as ongoing experiments in personal formation, aiming to cultivate a faithful *prudentia* that is simultaneously personal and communal, thoroughly interreligious and thoroughly Christian, and, above all, deeply pious. Given the social location of both Clooney and the Lombard, moreover, we might come to see the theological curricula and social settings of Catholic higher education as particularly important places in which such experiments can and should concretely occur.[60]

In speaking of "ongoing experiments," we arrive at the beginning of what could be a much broader and more ambitious study, one which attempts to show, beyond this single test case, how a pedagogy for *prudentia* might be concretely universalized and put into practice. But we also arrive at a place where the analogy I have attempted to build in this essay breaks down. For, if *Nostra Aetate* indeed opened a new chapter for the church, it should be evident that we are in the very early pages of this chapter, still in the midst of our first experiments. As a sentence collector, however, the Lombard did not stand at the beginning of a development; he stood at the end of one. R. W. Southern offers a comparison with Benedict of Nursia:

> The two legislators of religious life and scholastic thought were no doubt very different types of men, but they had some things in common. They both came at the end of a period of experiment. They both put in order the materials which had been assembled in the course of these experiments. They both cut out all extravagance and limited their personal contribution to a minimum. Yet in both cases, the personal contribution was all-important. It was the contribution of sound sense, sobriety and staying power.[61]

Forty years after *Nostra Aetate*, we are still in an experimental phase, assembling materials for those who may follow. On the model, perhaps, of those who assembled the first Bible glosses, so too the primary task in the contemporary period may involve merely identifying relevant *sententiae* from prior Christian tradition, seeking out true "classics" from other religious traditions, and struggling, insofar as possible, to hold them together as a kind of ascetic spiritual practice. A definitive collection of such materials, analogous to Peter Lombard's *Sentences*, may at some point become conceivable, or it may not.[62] In the meantime, those engaged in such study and dialogue can draw insight from its pedagogy and can attempt to emulate the "sound sense, sobriety and staying power" of its author. We can, in other words, seek a middle way.[63]

Notes

[1]Latin text and English translation in Norman P. Tanner, S.J., ed., *Decrees of the Ecumenical Councils, Volume II: Trent to Vatican II* (London: Sheed & Ward, and Washington, D.C.: Georgetown University Press, 1990), 968-71.

[2]See John D'Arcy May, "Catholic Fundamentalism? Some Implications of *Dominus Iesus* for Dialogue and Peacemaking," *Horizons* 28 (2001): 278, and Paul Knitter, *Introducing Theologies of Religions* (Maryknoll, N.Y.: Orbis Books, 2002), 63-79.

[3]From Graham's introductory preface to the declaration in Walter M. Abbott, S.J., ed., *The Documents of Vatican II* (New York: America Press, 1966), 659.

[4]Particularly illustrative are the ongoing conversations and debates about the "triple dialogue" and "new way of being church" envisioned by the bishops of Asia. See, for example, Edmund Chia, F.S.C., "Of Fork and Spoon or Fingers and Chopsticks: Interreligious Dialogue in *Ecclesia in Asia*," *Horizons* 28 (2001): 294-306, and Peter C. Phan, *In Our Own Tongues: Perspectives from Asia on Mission and Inculturation* (Maryknoll, N.Y.: Orbis Books, 2003), esp. 13-31, as well as Phan's contribution to this volume. For more general overviews, see Knitter, *Introducing Theologies of Religions*; Jacques Dupuis, S.J., *Toward a Christian Theology of Religious Pluralism* (Maryknoll, N.Y.: Orbis Books, 1997); and Jacques Dupuis, S.J., *Christianity and the Religions: From Confrontation to Dialogue* (Maryknoll, N.Y.: Orbis Books, 2001).

[5]May, "Catholic Fundamentalism?" 274-80, and Edward Kessler (himself characterizing others' positions), quoted in James Fredericks, "The Catholic Church and the Other Religious Paths: Rejecting Nothing That Is True and Holy," *Theological Studies* 64 (2003): 226.

[6]Mark Plaiss, " 'Dialogue and Proclamation' A Decade Later: A Retreat?" *Journal of Ecumenical Studies* 38 (2001): 195. For a broader range of responses to the document from North America and from Asia, respectively, see Stephen J. Pope and Charles Hefling, *Sic et Non: Encountering* Dominus Iesus (Maryknoll, N.Y.: Orbis Books, 2002), and Edmund Chia, F.S.C., "*Dominus Iesus* and Asian Theologies," *Horizons* 29 (2002): 277-89.

[7]See Nancy Spatz, "Approaches and Attitudes to a New Theology Textbook: The *Sentences* of Peter Lombard," in *The Intellectual Climate of the Early University: Essays in Honor of Otto Gründler*, ed. Nancy Van Deusen, Studies in Medieval Culture 39 (Kalamazoo: Western Michigan University, 1997), 29-30.

[8]See *The Catechism of the Catholic Church* (New York: Doubleday, 1994), 496 (#1806). Also see the very helpful discussions in Romanus Cessario, O.P., *Introduction to Moral Theology* (Washington, D.C.: Catholic University of America Press, 2001), 128-44, and Servais Pinckaers, O.P., "Conscience and the Virtue of Prudence," in *The Pinckaers Reader: Renewing Thomistic Moral Theology*, ed. John Berkman and Craig Steven Titus, trans. Sr. Mary Thomas Noble, O.P., Craig Steven Titus, Michael Sherwin, O.P., and Hugh Connelly (Washington, D.C.: Catholic University of America Press, 2005), 342-55. In describing *prudentia* in terms of "intelligence," I do not intend to reduce it to what Cessario—referring to Duns Scotus—calls "a kind of pure knowing" (130); indeed, for both the Lombard and for Clooney, *prudentia* does not arise in the abstract, but only through careful negotiation of particular texts, arguments, and apparent conflicts. That is, it arises only through sustained practice and application.

[9]Marcia Colish, "Systematic Theology and Theological Renewal in the Twelfth Century," *Journal of Medieval and Renaissance Studies* 18 (1988): 136; and Marcia Colish, "From the Sentence Collection to the *Sentence* Commentary and the *Summa*: Parisian Scholastic Theology, 1130-1215," in *Manuels, programmes de cours et techniques d'enseignement dans les universités médiévales: Actes du colloque international de Louvain-la-Neuve*, ed. Jacqueline Hamesse, Publications de l'Institut d'Études Médiévales 16 (Louvain-la-Neuve: Institut d'Études Médiévales de l'Université Catholique de Louvain, 1994), 11-12. For more extensive treatments of the emergence of systematic theology as a scientific discipline in the twelfth century, see M.-D. Chenu, O.P., *Nature, Man and Society in the Twelfth Century: Essays on New Theological Perspectives in the Latin West*, ed. and trans. Jerome Taylor and Lester K. Little (Chicago and London: University of Chicago Press, 1968), esp. 270-309; J. de Ghellinck, S.J., *Le mouvement théologique du XIIe siècle, sa préparation lointaine avant et autour de Pierre Lombard, ses rapports avec les initiatives des canonistes: études, recherches et documents*, 2d ed., Museum Lessianum, Section Historique 10 (Bruges: Éditions "De Tempel," 1948); and R. W. Southern, *Scholastic Humanism and the Unification of Europe, Volume 1: Foundations* (Oxford and Cambridge: Blackwell Publishers, 1995), and *Volume 2: The Heroic Age* (Oxford and Malden: Blackwell Publishers, 2001).

[10]See Marcia Colish, "The Development of Lombardian Theology, 1160-1215," in *Centres of Learning: Learning and Location in Pre-Modern Europe and the Near East*, ed. Jan Willem Drijvers and Alasdair MacDonald (Leiden: E. J. Brill, 1995), 207-16.

[11]Marcia Colish, *Peter Lombard*, 2 vols., Brill's Studies in Intellectual History 41 (Leiden: E. J. Brill, 1994); Philipp W. Rosemann, *Peter Lombard*, Great Medieval Thinkers (New York: Oxford University Press, 2004); Peter Lombard, *The Book of Sentences*, trans. Giulio Silano (forthcoming from the Pontifical Institute of Medieval Studies, Toronto). Citations in this essay from

the *Sentences* and from Silano's general introduction are taken from a manuscript of this translation, provided by the author. A critical edition of the Latin text is available in Magistri Petri Lombardi, *Sententiae in IV libris distinctae*, ed. Ignatius Brady, 2 vols., Spicilegium Bonaventurianum 4-5 (Grottaferrata: Editiones Collegii S. Bonaventurae Ad Claras Aquas, 1971-81).

[12]Peter Lombard, Bk. I, prol., no. 5.

[13]G. R. Evans, *Old Arts and New Theology: The Beginnings of Theology as an Academic Discipline* (Oxford and New York: Oxford University Press, 1980), 43.

[14]See Jacques-Guy Bougerol, "The Church Fathers and the *Sentences* of Peter Lombard," in *The Reception of the Church Fathers in the West: From the Carolingians to the Maurists*, ed. Irena Backus, vol. 1 (Boston and Leiden: Brill Academic Publishers, 2001), esp. 140-41. On the Lombard's contact with works of John of Damascus, see ibid., 133-37, and Ghellinck, 374-415.

[15]Marcia Colish, "The Sentence Collection and the Education of Professional Theologians in the Twelfth Century," in van Deusen, *The Intellectual Climate of the Early University*, 11. See Bougerol, "The Church Fathers and the *Sentences* of Peter Lombard," 160-61.

[16]See Silano (note 11), Vol. 1, xviii-xx, xxii-xxiii.

[17]See Marcia Colish, *Medieval Foundations of the Western Intellectual Tradition, 400-1400* (New Haven and London: Yale University Press, 1997), 280-81.

[18]For examples that involve the reconciliation of different authorities, see, for example, Peter Lombard, Bk. I, dist. XIII, ch. 4 (Augustine and "Jerome"/ Bishop Syagrius); dist. XIX, ch. 9-10 (Augustine and John of Damascus); and dist. XXVII, ch. 1 (Augustine and Hilary), as well as the discussion in Ghellinck, 233-44.

[19]See, for example, Peter Lombard, Bk. I, dist. XXXIV, ch. 1 (correcting the improper use of Hilary) and dist. XXXVII, ch. 7 (correcting the improper use of Augustine). The Lombard refuted theological positions on the Trinity—and other topics—of such masters as Abelard and Gilbert of Poitiers, but also felt comfortable incorporating their ideas or clarifying them with better technical language. See the discussions in Colish, *Peter Lombard*, 254-63, and Marcia L. Colish, "Gilbert, the Early Porretans, and Peter Lombard: Semantics and Theology," in *Gilbert de Poitiers et ses contemporains: Aux origines de la* logica modernorum, *Actes du septième symposium Européen d'histoire de la logique et de la sémantique médiévales*, ed. Jean Jolivet and Alain de Libera (Napoli: Bibliopolis, 1987), 229-50. See Chenu, *Nature, Man and Society in the Twelfth Century*, 274-76.

[20]See Peter Lombard, Bk. I, dist. I, ch. 3, no. 2, and dist. XLI, ch. 2.

[21]Silano (see note 11), Vol. 1, xxii-xxiii.

[22]Burcht Pranger, "*Sic et Non*: Patristic Authority Between Refusal and Acceptance: Anselm of Canterbury, Peter Abelard and Bernard of Clairvaux,"

in Backus, *Reception of the Church Fathers in the West*, 171. Pranger is referring to Abelard in this quotation, but the idea applies equally well to Peter Lombard.

[23]See especially Colish, "Parisian Scholastic Theology," 14-15 and Colish, "The *Sentences* of Peter Lombard," 14-17. See Colish, *Peter Lombard*, 44-47.

[24]Peter Lombard, Bk. I, dist. IX, ch. 5, no. 3 (quoting Hilary); dist. XXIII, chs. 1-2 (drawing together Augustine and John of Damascus); and dist. XXXVII, ch. 3, no. 5. See Bk. I, dist. XXXIV, ch. 5, no. 3.

[25]Hilary, *De Trinitate* II.9-10, quoted in Peter Lombard, Bk. I, dist. XXXIII, ch. 2, no. 1. See also Silano (note 11), Vol. 1, l-li.

[26]Quoted in Spatz, "Approaches and Attitudes to a New Theology Textbook," 32.

[27]Peter Lombard, Bk. I, dist. IX, ch. 5, no. 2.

[28]See especially Rosemann, *Peter Lombard*, 199-211.

[29]For this quotation and the following discussion, see Silano (note 11), Vol. 1, xx-xxi.

[30]William J. Courtenay, "The Institutionalization of Theology," in *Learning Institutionalized: Teaching in the Medieval University*, ed. John Van Engen (Notre Dame: University of Notre Dame Press, 2000), 254 (emphasis added). See Silano (note 11), Vol. 1, xi-xiii and xxv-xxvii.

[31]It is perhaps worth noting at this point, however, that the Lombard gives no special prominence to *prudentia* in his discussion of the virtues, but simply quotes Augustine: "prudence [consists] in guarding against treacheries" (*prudentia in praecavendis insidiis*). See Peter Lombard, Bk. III, dist. XXXIII, ch. 1 and ch. 3, nos. 3-4, as well as the discussion in Colish, *Peter Lombard*, 504-7. In using the terms *prudentes* and *prudentia* to characterize his project, I am following Silano (and William of Tyre) more closely than the Lombard himself.

[32]See, for example, Southern, *Scholastic Humanism, Vol. 1: Foundations*, 134-62.

[33]For an overview, see Matthew N. Schmaltz, "Tradition and Transgression in the Comparative Theology of Francis X. Clooney, S.J.," *Religious Studies Review* 29 (2003): 131-36.

[34]Francis X. Clooney, S.J., "The Emerging Field of Comparative Theology: A Bibliographical Review (1989-95)," *Theological Studies* 56 (1995): 522.

[35]Colish, *Medieval Foundations*, 274. See also 289-301, and Louis Roy, O.P., "Medieval Latin Scholasticism: Some Comparative Features," in *Scholasticism: Cross-Cultural and Comparative Perspectives*, ed. José Ignacio Cabezón, Toward a Comparative Philosophy of Religions series (Albany: State University of New York Press, 1998), 19-34.

[36]They are: Francis X. Clooney, S.J., *Theology after Vedanta: An Experiment in Comparative Theology* (Albany: State University of New York Press, 1993); Francis X. Clooney, S.J., *Seeing through Texts: Doing Theology*

among the Srivaisnavas of South India (Albany: State University of New York Press, 1996); Francis X. Clooney, S.J., *Hindu God, Christian God: How Reason Helps Break Down the Boundaries between Religions* (Oxford and New York: Oxford University Press, 2001); and Francis X. Clooney, S.J., *Divine Mother, Blessed Mother: Hindu Goddesses and the Virgin Mary* (Oxford and New York: Oxford University Press, 2005).

[37]Clooney, *Hindu God, Christian God*, 14-15.

[38]For a critique of this aspect of Clooney's work, see Phan, *In Our Own Tongues*, 171-72.

[39]Francis X. Clooney, S.J., "Reading the World in Christ: From Comparison to Inclusivism," in *Christian Uniqueness Reconsidered*, ed. Gavin D'Costa (Maryknoll, N.Y.: Orbis Books, 1990), 69.

[40]See especially the long strings of such juxtapositions in Clooney, *Seeing through Texts*, 259-95, and in Francis X. Clooney, S.J., "In Ten Thousand Places, in Every Blade of Grass: Uneventful But True Confessions about Finding God in India, and Here Too," *Studies in the Spirituality of Jesuits* 28/3 (1996): 1-42.

[41]For example, Clooney, *Theology after Vedanta*, 168-75; Clooney, *Divine Mother, Blessed Mother*, 227-37; and Clooney, *Hindu God, Christian God*, 29-61, 177-78.

[42]For example, Clooney, *Theology after Vedanta*, 175-79. See Clooney, *Hindu God, Christian God*, esp. 123-28.

[43]Clooney, "Reading the World in Christ," 70. See Clooney, *Theology after Vedanta*, 171-73.

[44]See Gavin D'Costa, "Review of *Theology after Vedanta*," *Modern Theology* 10 (1994): 432; William Cenkner, "Review of *Theology after Vedanta*," *Theological Studies* 54 (1993): 769; and Jonathan C. Gold, "Review of *Hindu God, Christian God*," *Journal of Religion* 84 (2004): 133.

[45]Clooney, "Reading the World in Christ," 70.

[46]See especially Clooney, *Theology after Vedanta*, 187-91, and Schmaltz, "Tradition and Transgression in the Comparative Theology of Francis X. Clooney, S.J.," 134.

[47]Clooney, *Seeing through Texts*, 298-304. See Clooney, *Theology after Vedanta*, 193-96, and Clooney, *Hindu God, Christian God*, 20-27. In "Reading the World in Christ," 72-75, Clooney identifies himself as an inclusivist only after significantly revising the meaning of the term away from theory and toward comparative practice.

[48]Jacques Dupuis, S.J., "Relating to Other Faiths: How Far Can You Go?" *The Tablet*, 8 June 2002, 17. See A. J. Nicholson, "Review of *Hindu God, Christian God*," *Philosophy East and West* 53 (2003): 599-601.

[49]For example, Clooney, *Seeing through Texts*, 298-99.

[50]On this point, see especially Francis X. Clooney, "Peering into the Mouth of God: Reflections on the Dangerous Possibility of Really Taking Religions Seriously," *The Santa Clara Lectures* 2/2 (22 January 1996), esp.

14-15: "As we begin to take our own religion and other religions seriously, it is not wise for us to speak glibly of progress; because pluralism is a religious issue, it is not simply a comforting or troubling fact of modern life. It is about finding God in new ways, seeing more of God, differently. . . . It can begin in words; but it cannot come just from words; it has to be a kind of vision that both appalls us and opens us to God. The vision that comes in the end may be overwhelming, shattering, no matter how well we understand it. And that is good for us."

[51]See Clooney, *Hindu God, Christian God*, 7-12, 163-77, and Clooney, *Theology after Vedanta*, 198-207, and especially the discussion in Schmaltz, "Tradition and Transgression in the Comparative Theology of Francis X. Clooney, S.J.," 134-35.

[52]Peter Lombard, Bk. I, prol., no. 4.

[53]See, for example, Stephen J. Duffy, "A Theology of Religions and/or A Comparative Theology?" *Horizons* 26 (1999): 105-15, and Paul Knitter, "The Vocation of an Interreligious Theologian," *Horizons* 31 (2004): 135-49.

[54]Vincent P. Branick, " '*Dominus Iesus*' and the Ecumenical Dialogue with Catholics," *Journal of Ecumenical Studies* 38 (2001): 412-31.

[55]See International Theological Commission, "Christianity and the World Religions," *Origins* 27 (1997): 151-66, and Vatican Congregation for the Doctrine of the Faith, "Synthesis of the Declaration 'Dominus Iesus,' " *Origins* 30 (2000): 221. Of course, this document has also been the object of some criticism. See Terrence W. Tilley, " 'Christianity and the World Religions,' A Recent Vatican Document," *Theological Studies* 60 (1999): 318-37.

[56]The recommended approach to reading *Dominus Iesus* also implicitly subordinates or relativizes the precise intentions of its authors, as well as their own *prudentia*—or lack thereof—in releasing the declaration the way that they did. This should not be read, however, to dismiss the importance of such critical inquiry in and of itself. See the discussion in May, "Catholic Fundamentalism?" 289-90, and especially in Chia, "*Dominus Iesus* and Asian Theologies," 283-88.

[57]James L. Fredericks, "Interreligious Friendship: A New Theological Virtue," *Journal of Ecumenical Studies* 35 (1998): 161-62.

[58]See ibid., 167-72, as well as James L. Fredericks, *Faith among Faiths: Christian Theology and Non-Christian Religions* (New York/Mahwah: Paulist Press, 1999), 173-77.

[59]See Fredericks, "Interreligious Friendship," 172-74.

[60]See, for example, Clooney's own applications of his comparative theological project to the mission of Jesuit universities in "In Ten Thousand Places, in Every Blade of Grass," 19-23 and especially in Francis X. Clooney, S.J., "Goddess in the Classroom: Is the Promotion of Religious Diversity a

Dangerous Idea?" *Conversations in Jesuit Higher Education* 16 (1999): 29-39.

[61]Southern, *Scholastic Humanism, Vol. 2: The Heroic Age*, 146.

[62]In addition to Clooney's work in this regard, see also the "sentence collection" in J. Neuner, S.J., and J. Dupuis, S.J., eds., *The Christian Faith: In the Doctrinal Documents of the Catholic Church*, 7th ed. (New York: Alba House, 2001), esp. ch. 10. Setting aside its theoretical agenda, the Comparative Religious Ideas Project at Boston University may be read as an intriguing and ambitious attempt simply to identify relevant *sententiae*—texts and arguments from a variety of religious traditions—on issues of common concern. See Robert Cummings Neville, ed., *The Human Condition: A Volume in the Comparative Religious Ideas Project* (Albany: State University of New York Press, 2001); Robert Cummings Neville, ed., *Ultimate Realities: A Volume in the Comparative Religious Ideas Project* (Albany: State University of New York Press, 2001); and Robert Cummings Neville, ed., *Religious Truth: A Volume in the Comparative Religious Ideas Project* (Albany: State University of New York Press, 2001).

[63]Warm thanks for assistance in the preparation and revision of this essay are due to: Jennifer Harris, Giulio Silano, Michael McLaughlin, Patricia Murphy, Jolie Chrisman, William Madges, and two anonymous referees. I am very grateful for their valuable insights and suggestions.

Heir or Orphan?

Theological Evolution and Devolution before and after *Nostra Aetate*[1]

Elena Procario-Foley

The fortieth anniversary commemorations of the October 28, 1965 promulgation of *Nostra Aetate,* the Declaration on the Church's Relationship to Non-Christian Religions, provide Christians and Jews the opportunity to consider the effects of *Nostra Aetate* on the Jewish-Christian relationship and on the religions individually. It is not too much to claim that we must do so for our very self-understanding; identities, and even survival, some would argue, are at stake.[2] The following essay will present some history about the document, review some of the related documentary history of the past forty years, consider the issues of progress and regress since *Nostra Aetate*, and consider ways of moving the discussion into the next forty years. The processes of evolution and devolution appear as helpful images because, while constructive progress in Jewish-Christian relations has been difficult and slowly gained (including achieving a majority vote from the Council on *Nostra Aetate*), real and perceived roadblocks in the journey have threatened to reverse the process of dialogue.

History of *Nostra Aetate*

That Pope John Paul II (1920-2005) was profoundly affected by witnessing the Nazi destruction of the Jewish community in his town is well known, especially after his millennial visits to Yad Vashem and the Western Wall and in the wake of the blanket news coverage of his final days and funeral.[3] What may not be so well known, however, is that his predecessor Pope John XXIII's (1881-1963) own personal experiences during World War II helped to motivate the production of a Council statement on the Jews (*Nostra Aetate* 4; hereafter: *NA*). John XXIII served as an apostolic delegate in Turkey from 1935 to 1944. During that time he saw not only the effects of the Nazis' genocidal policies, but also personally saved thousands of Jews by providing them with citizenship and ersatz baptismal papers. He also provided food to needy Jewish communities.[4] After he became pope in 1958, John XXIII gave evidence of his sensitivity to the situation of the Jewish people and his desire to improve relations between the Catholic Church and Judaism.[5]

Significantly, Pope John sent a message to inform the Israeli government of his election to the papacy. The exchange between John XXIII and the Grand Rabbi of Israel, Dr. Isaac Halevy Herzog, was significant because the Vatican did not recognize the State of Israel at the time of John's election. Rabbi Herzog responded to the pope's message with "sincere blessings." Further indication of Pope John's attentiveness to the church's posture toward Judaism came during Holy Week 1959 when he famously removed the infamous phrase "perfidious Jews" from the Good Friday liturgy; subsequently John removed similar phrases from the liturgy for adult baptism that referred to Jews, Muslims, unbelievers, and heretics.

Two direct encounters with the international and local Roman Jewish communities also highlight the sensitivity of John XXIII to the state of Jewish-Christian relations. At the Vatican, on October 17, 1960, the pope greeted 130 American Jews from the United Jewish Appeal with the words "I am Joseph Your Brother."[6] It must have been a poignant moment as his greeting utilized the double entendre of his middle name and the Genesis story. Additionally, on March 17, 1962, Pope John found himself driving by the synagogue in Rome just as the congregation was exiting. He had his car stopped and the roof removed; he then stood and blessed the group. In the words of eyewitness Rabbi Toaff, who would later receive John Paul II in the first papal visit at the Great Synagogue, "after a moment of understandable bewilderment, the Jews surrounded him and applauded him enthusiastically. It was in fact the first time in history that a pope had blessed Jews and it was perhaps the first real gesture of reconciliation."[7]

Finally, and most immediately relevant to the content of *NA*, was Pope John's invitation to the noted French historian Jules Isaac (1877-1963) to come to the Vatican during preparations for the Council. On June 3, 1960, Isaac, who had lost his wife and daughter[8] to the *Shoah*, presented the pope with a file of material and a memo including a list of eighteen points concerning Christianity and anti-Semitism.[9] Isaac coined the term "the teaching of contempt." The table of contents in Isaac's *The Teaching of Contempt: Christian Roots of Anti-Semitism*[10] identifies "three main themes of the teaching of contempt": 1) "the dispersion of the Jews: providential punishment for the crucifixion"; 2) "the degenerate state of Judaism at the time of Jesus"; and 3) "the crime of deicide." These three themes have fueled a history of Christian anti-Semitism[11] that has manifested itself in a variety of ways from sermons[12] to legislation[13] to spontaneous acts of persecution. Thus the phrase, "the teaching of contempt," can be usefully employed (especially with students) as a summary reference to the Christian history of attitudes, texts, and acts that oppressed and persecuted Jews through the centuries. After meeting with Isaac and reading his materials, John XXIII is reported to have said, "You can expect more than a little from us."[14] Thus, the one elected to be a transitional pope initiated the church's transformation of the teaching of contempt into the teaching of respect. It is safe to claim that producing a conciliar text on Jews and Judaism was a priority for Pope John XXIII.

A Summary of the Development of *Nostra Aetate*

The journey that culminated in the acceptance of *NA* as one of the three declarations of the Council is one that in and of itself exemplifies the heir/evolution—orphan/devolution question of my title. Two examples demonstrate the opposing views that characterized the rocky road to the final affirmative vote on *NA* and easily illustrate the polar images of evolution and devolution. First of all, it is critical to recognize that the original desire for a document that addressed Jews and Judaism confronted persistent opposition from a well-organized minority. This opposition, taking both political and theological forms, caused the document to be broadened to include religions other than Judaism. Whether or not we want to attribute this result to the Holy Spirit writing straight with crooked lines is a reflection for another paper. The difference, however, between original intention and final document exposes the friction that has marked the past forty years of development in Jewish-Christian relations.

Preparations for the Council provide the second example. Pope John's wide-ranging pre-Council preparatory consultations yielded only two references to Jews and Judaism.[15] One bishop requested that the Council condemn "international freemasonry controlled by the Jews." By contrast, the other response came from a group of professors at the Pontifical Biblical Commission who raised the necessity of combating anti-Semitism. These two views, one of ignorant fear, one of sensitive insight, continued to play themselves out throughout the Council's four sessions and three intersessions as *NA* emerged from the fourth chapter of the schema on ecumenism into its own declaration.

The pope entrusted Isaac's materials to Jesuit Cardinal Augustin Bea, who was president of the Secretariat for Christian Unity. Quietly, a draft, *De Judaeis*, was produced. On February 1, 1962, Pope John told Bea that the schema could go directly to the Central Commission (CPC) without passing through other preparatory bodies.[16] The Central Commission, headed by the pope himself, coordinated the other secretariats and commissions. In June of 1962, a premature announcement by the World Jewish Congress that a Jewish observer would be present at the Council caused a storm of protest from Arab governments and bishops in those countries. The political suspicions that the text would be the first step toward the diplomatic recognition of Israel caused the document to be removed from the work of the Central Commission. But, in December of 1962, a handwritten note from Pope John to Cardinal Bea gave permission to restart work on the document. The note said, "I have carefully read this report of Cardinal Bea and I agree fully that the matter is serious and that we have a responsibility to take it up."[17] Nonetheless, significant political and polemical theological disputes (sometimes cloaked in the former)[18] continued to plague the development of the text and threatened to scuttle it on a number of occasions.[19] According to Miccoli, "It took the will of John XXIII and the perseverance of Cardinal Bea to impose the declaration on the Council."[20]

On November 18, 1963, the Secretariat for Christian Unity presented the text on ecumenism in the hall. At this point, the schema on the Jews existed as chapter four in the document on ecumenism. The minority raised objections at this time, and throughout1964, that the time was not right for the schema on the Jews and, if there were to be such a text, that Muslims and other religions should be included. The latter suggestion was not as foresighted as it might sound. The suggestion was made, it seems, because "other religions" were believed to be more receptive to conversion.[21] Further, Eastern patriarchs feared persecution of Christians in Arab lands if the text were simply about Judaism.[22] By the third intersession the theological experts began to understand that their text had to take into account this political reality.[23] Finally, the appearance of Rudolph Hochhuth's *The Deputy*, a play accusing Pope Pius XII of knowledge of the Holocaust and not taking action on behalf of the Jews, provided a source for concern; the framers of the text needed to avoid inadvertently giving strength to the play's claims about as well as raising the issue of Pius's so-called "silence."[24] American Cardinal J. Ritter of St. Louis, however, representing the majority of American bishops, endorsed the schema on ecumenism presented on November 18, 1963, including the text on the Jews.[25]

During the second day of discussions about the proposed text on ecumenism, Bea, who for political reasons had not initially presented the text on ecumenism, explained chapter four, the text on Judaism. In doing so he gave a lesson on interpreting Pauline texts to make the point that Jews are not rejected by God; he urged the Council to reflect on the *Shoah*, and urged a repudiation of the Christ-killer charge.[26] Cleverly and persuasively, Bea let it be known that when speaking about the document, he was carrying out the expressed wishes of the late John XXIII *and* he cited the December 1962 handwritten note.[27]

During the intersession, the schema on the Jews endured a "troubled redactional history"[28] that included: four versions; moving it from chapter to appendix status; taking out references to the deicide charge and putting it in again through the backdoor via the phrase "that what occurred in the passion of Christ is not to be imputed to the Jews of our time"; advocacy from Arab states; more debates over whether to include other religions; direct requests for changes from the Coordinating Council (CC); debates about whether to keep the text at all;[29] interventions from Paul VI, including a suggestion that the text include a reference to the hope for the conversion of Israel;[30] and, finally, the decision to make it a separate declaration.[31] It is important to note that "the Spanish bishops were extremely alarmed by the schema and ordered their experts to make a thorough analysis of it."[32]

As a result of the intersession, the revised text Bea presented to the hall in September 1964 was significantly different, some argued weakened, from the 1963 text.[33] He requested that the question of deicide be carefully examined because the lengthy interventions by the Coordinating Council on this issue had prevented the text from being reviewed by the members of the Secretariat. Despite the well-organized minority opposition, there was strong support for the document among the Council fathers. Further, arguments to justify the document matured from horror in the face of the *Shoah* to the first affirmations of a new theology of Judaism in relation to Christianity.[34] Bea's secretariat quickly revised the text based on the interventions and reinserted explicit condemnations of the deicide charge and anti-Semitism. By the end of the third session, approximately 1,700 fathers voted for the text.[35]

The forces for evolution in the church's attitude toward the Jews continued to collide, however, with the various reactionary forces during the intersession between the third and fourth periods. One voice with particularly persuasive power was that of Damascus Patriarch Maximus IV Saigh, who vowed to walk out of the *aula* in the fourth session if the text remained as it was at the end of the third session. In April 1965 Pope Paul told Cardinal Bea that he would "discontinue the discussion and not approve the declaration based on the schema on the Jews" if Maximus left the hall.[36] Maximus's attitude represents the position of Roman and Orthodox Christians of the Middle East who did not share the experience of the Holocaust, who had a difficult time with the document, and who did not understand the Council's focus on a schema on the Jews. Cardinal Willebrands, after two trips to the region to promote the schema, was concerned about their reactions to a vote.[37]

Pope Paul's attitude and actions with regard to the schema remain difficult to assess.[38] On the one hand, there is his strong directive about Maximus and his 1965 Passion Sunday homily employing the Christ-killer charge.[39] On the other hand, Paul VI also gave Bea a note that requested the Council demonstrate a change in the church's attitude regarding deicide and anti-

Semitism.[40] By the end of May 1965, Bea's Secretariat for Christian Unity conceded the problems raised by Paul VI; the text was modified to elide the words "guilty of deicide," and the reference to condemning anti-Semitism was softened to "deplores."[41] This emended text was presented at the fourth session.

The difficult struggle to bring a substantive text on the Jews to the Council illustrates the presence of long-established anti-Jewish habits of thought in the face of a majority determined to address a shameful history. The minority opposition included fathers from Africa, the Middle East, and Europe. In part two ("Two Sensitive Issues: Religious Freedom and the Jews") of Alberigo and Komonchak's *History of Vatican II*, Giovanni Miccoli summarizes well the opposition viewpoint; it is worthwhile to cite it at length because of the stubborn intransigence of these attitudes:

> The traditional doctrinal arguments, which concluded from the Jewish rejection of Christ a divine "rejection" of the Jewish people, served once again as the basis for denying the Jews any religiously positive function and for imputing to them an inauspicious role in history and in the life of society. In this perspective any rethinking, any even implicitly critical reference to activities of the Church, past or present, that ought to be abandoned, became utterly impossible.[42]

Cardinal Bea ultimately successfully represented the emerging new theology of the majority who wished to confront "the foundations and motivations on which . . . anti-Judaism had been built and perpetuated"[43] as well as assume responsibility for the historically catastrophic results for the Jews of Christian anti-Judaism. The fact, however, that curial internecine political maneuvering did alter the final form of the document must raise questions for us about how the moral teaching of the church is determined.

In the end, *NA*'s part four raises core issues at stake for Catholic theological self-understanding: how does relinquishing the Christ-killer charges alter Christology, missiology, and soteriology? What is the Catholic relation to other religions and is that different from its relationship to Judaism?[44] As Gregory Baum writes, "Although the Christian faith is derived from the experience and history of Israel, a strong anti-Jewish bias was built into Christian preaching almost from the beginning. While we proclaimed the doctrine of love, we also—unconsciously, most of the time—spread the seed of contempt of an entire people."[45] Moving to examine the completed conciliar and post-conciliar texts will help to illumine some perspectives on these questions.

Progress in Jewish-Catholic Relations since *Nostra Aetate*[46]

Nostra Aetate *and Implementation Documents*

After *NA*, the Vatican's Commission for Religious Relations with the Jews issued three related post-conciliar documents: "Guidelines and Suggestions for Implementing the Conciliar Declaration *Nostra Aetate*" (1974); "Notes on the Correct Way to Present the Jews and Judaism in Preaching and Catechesis in the Roman Catholic Church" (1985); and "We Remember: Reflections on the Shoah" (1998). These documents, together with *NA*, comprise, according to Eugene Fisher, the sum total of Catholic doctrine concerning "universal Roman Catholic teaching on Jews and Judaism."[47] Fisher explains that previous statements throughout history were "disciplinary in character, not doctrinal." This is a truly noteworthy observation because it takes us out of the familiar realm of debating whether or not the Council developed or even changed doctrine. With *NA* the Council fathers seized the opportunity to begin to establish positive doctrine toward Jews and Judaism. This section offers a brief review of the four documents in order to highlight the major issues and themes involved in the slow process of articulating the contemporary stance toward Judaism that has evolved since Vatican II.

In its final form, *NA* includes five parts with the fourth part devoted to Judaism. The radical newness of the church talking officially and positively about Jews, Judaism, and other religions is evident from the fact that all but two of the footnotes in this document are biblical. At the time of the Council, there was no basis for the typical practice of quoting previous church documents as the basis for the new one since affirmative doctrinal speech about Jews and Judaism emerged only with *NA*.

NA raises five themes that reappear in the subsequent documents from the Commission for Religious Relations with the Jews.

In some way all four documents emphasize the reality that Jesus, Mary, the Apostles, and "most of the early disciples" were Jewish (*NA* 4.3).[48] *NA* expresses a concern to "foster and recommend" mutual understanding, respect, and dialogue (4.5). The document directs that such dialogue must include pursuit of biblical and theological studies. Further, *NA* and its successors repudiate the Christ-killer charge and the idea that Jews are cursed by God (4.6). The rejection of anti-Semitism, a hotly debated element throughout the drafting process, is included in a general statement "deploring" persecutions of any kind (4.7). In the later documents, the relatively weak verb "deplores" is dropped in favor of stronger language as the dialogue between Catholics and Jews begins.[49] Finally, *NA* emphasizes that "Christ out of infinite love freely underwent suffering and death because of the sins of all men" (4.8).

From today's perspective, it is doubtful that Catholic theologians engaged in Jewish-Catholic dialogue would make a statement such as "Jerusalem did not recognize God's moment when it came" (*NA* 4.4) or that they would preface the repudiation of a lethal charge against Jews with the claim that "the Jewish authorities and those who followed their lead pressed for the death of Christ" (4.6). Yet *NA* clearly shows progress beyond what constituted the usual attitude toward Jews and Judaism prior to Vatican II. For example, the document also states that "Jews should not be spoken of as rejected by God or accursed as if this followed from holy Scripture." Such a strong statement indicates the beginning of creating a level playing field for dialogue. The strength of this statement is buttressed by an earlier and equally strong statement that "the Jews remain very dear to God, for the sake of the patriarchs, since God does not take back the gifts he bestowed or the choice he made" (4. 4).

In eight brief paragraphs, *NA* raises two key theological issues by which we may attempt to assess evolution or devolution with regard to Catholic teaching about Judaism: covenant and Christology. The "gifts" of the quotation immediately above include covenant. *NA* further states, "On this account the Church cannot forget that she received the revelation of the Old Testament by way of that people with whom God in his inexpressible mercy established the ancient covenant" (4.2). Pope John Paul II received and extended *NA*'s teaching on covenant. The statement, early in his pontificate, that God's covenant with the Jewish people was never revoked became a *sine qua non* of John Paul's teaching about Judaism.[50]

Christological issues are raised through the rejection of the deicide and Christ-killer charges as well as through comments such as: "Indeed, the Church believes that by His cross Christ Our Peace reconciled Jews and Gentiles, making both one in Himself" (*NA* 4.2). While the topics of covenant and Christology are broached by *NA*, their significance requires development. If the Jews are neither Christ-killers nor cursed and their divine gift (read: covenant) is not revoked, then more Christians must contribute to the substantial theological rethinking that has begun in the areas of covenant, Christology, and the renewal of Jewish-Christian relations.[51]

The 1974 "Guidelines and Suggestions for Implementing the Conciliar Declaration *Nostra Aetate*" consists of four short sections with a preamble and a conclusion. Its notes consist of references to *NA* and to other conciliar documents and scripture: a new tradition is evidently emerging. "Guidelines" is notably different in tone from *NA*, taking a stronger stand on every issue. For example, with respect to dialogue, which merited only a sentence in *NA*, this document includes a six-paragraph section stating: "To tell the truth, such relations as there have been between Jew and Christian have scarcely ever risen above the level of monologue. From now on, real discourse must be established" (Guidelines I.1). The strength and courage of the document is also evident when the Preamble firmly locates one impetus of *NA* in the *Shoah* and introduces the language of "condemnation" with respect to "all forms of anti-Semitism and discrimination" (Preamble 5).

The nature of the Jewish origins of Christianity is made a focal point throughout the "Guidelines," particularly in section three on "Teaching and Education." In this section the relations between the testaments, the diversity of Second Temple Judaism, and Jesus' ministry as a Jew are all given bullet points. The Christ-killer charge is again repudiated by quoting *NA*. A significant advance is the recognition that Judaism did not end in 70 C.E. but developed in new ways as a living religious tradition.[52] Two other additions are of note: placing dialogue in the context of prayer (I.6) and recommending joint social action, even perhaps as a tenet for dialogue and generating mutual understanding (IV). This is a well-rounded document that furthers the themes of *NA* and advances the dialogue by clearly teaching that Second Temple Judaism and the nascent Rabbinic Judaism of the post-70 era were the complex and vibrant religious progenitors of contemporary Judaism. "Guidelines" helps to dispel Christian misperceptions that Judaism had died by the time of Jesus or that any current manifestations of Judaism are similarly moribund.

The third document, "Notes on the Correct Way to Present the Jews and Judaism in Preaching and Catechesis in the Roman Catholic Church" is, given its title, a very specific document.[53] Therefore, in the interest of space limitations, suffice it to note three aspects. First, basic themes highlighted above (such as the Jewishness of Jesus or Judaism as a living religion after 70 C.E.) still require, after twenty years of rapprochement, explicit articulation. The new relationship of dialogue is developing slowly and thus its basic foundations bear repetition. Second, notes referring to the many, many statements on Jewish-Christian relations from Pope John Paul II[54] are added to the notes based on the previous two documents. Three popes have now become part of the development of the teaching of the church on Jews and Judaism. The teaching may be evolving slowly but it is clearly a consistent and persistent aspect of the implementation of Vatican II.

The implementation, I am bound to note, is not, however, without its rough edges. Though "Notes" as a whole represents progress, there are some elements that can be assessed negatively. Surely the statement, "there is moreover the sad fact that the majority of the Jewish people and its authorities did not believe Jesus" (IV.21.c), is an instance of devolution. Progress must be evaluated with a sharp eye toward identifying any vestige of the teaching of contempt.

The final document constituting the body of doctrine on Jews and Judaism developed since the Council is probably the best known. "We Remember: Reflections on the Shoah" was widely anticipated and drew equally strong praise and criticism from both the Jewish and Catholic communities.[55] Its composition, like the creation of *NA*, suffered from competing forces. Those who wanted to issue a very clear and strong statement concerning the *Shoah* were opposed by those who remained concerned about the concept of "apology" and the image of Pius XII. Consequently, the document contains both strengths and weaknesses.

Common criticisms of "We Remember" include: its differentiation of anti-Semitism from anti-Judaism; the misleading phrase "many did, others did not" (IV.8) when considering whether Christians did all that they could to assist Jews; footnote 16 on Pius XII; the technical distinction between the church, which cannot err, and its members, who can; the odd insertion of an ambiguous statement on the Middle East (IV.12); and the glaring disparity between the much stronger statements from individual bishops' conferences across Europe and the arguably more mild statement from the Roman Commission.[56]

Positive aspects of the document include the following: the Catholic Church is on record against Holocaust revisionists; the intrinsic relationship between Jews and Christians is emphasized; and the relationship of the teaching of contempt to the *Shoah* is officially considered. Further, the document's use of the Hebrew words *Shoah* (literally translated as "catastrophe") and *teshuva* ("repentance") require comment. Use of the word *Shoah* helps to distinguish the slaughter of the Jews from 1933-1945 from other genocides (the question of uniqueness apart); such usage also eliminates the possibility for a theologically abhorrent interpretation of "Holocaust" as implying a necessary sacrifice of the Jewish people. By adopting the Jewish terms for Holocaust and repentance, the church signals its respect for the Jewish experience of the *Shoah* and recognizes its own failure during that period and its need to repent—positive new steps indeed!

Surely the repetition and extremely careful development of ideas over the four texts from *Nostra Aetate* to "We Remember" demonstrate an evolution and a care for nurturing the dialogue envisioned by John XXIII. Moreover, despite the controversies sparked by it, "We Remember" marked something of a milestone in the journey of reconciliation. Thus, those who participate in Jewish-Christian dialogue today are heir to forty years of slowly developed theological progress.

Non-Roman Documents

Three non-Roman documents also illustrate the progress achieved since (and perhaps prompted by) *NA*.[57] "Reflections on Covenant and Mission," issued August 2000 by members appointed from the National Council of Synagogues and the United

States Bishops' Committee for Ecumenical and Interreligious Affairs; *Dabru Emet: A Jewish Statement on Christians and Christianity*, issued in September 2000 by an ad-hoc group of Jewish scholars; and "A Sacred Obligation," issued September 2002 by the Christian Scholars Group on Christian-Jewish Relations all demonstrate the deep theological sensitivities that have developed in certain sectors of Judaism and Christianity.[58] None of these documents claims the official endorsement of any authoritative body within either Judaism or Christianity and all of them are either interreligious or interdenominational. Nonetheless, the appearance of these three statements represents a new stage in the dialogue for at least three reasons.

On the Christian side, "Covenant and Mission" and "Sacred Obligation" exhibit the full flowering of the explicit theological rethinking that *NA* envisioned when it recommended biblical and theological studies for the purposes of mutual understanding. For example, the efforts to discover new and renewed theological language for mission, scripture, and Christian soteriology in light of a theology that affirms the Jewish covenant go well beyond efforts in previous decades to uncover shared roots and acknowledge sinful histories. Historical research and examination of conscience were and remain indispensable elements of the dialogue. Christian attempts, however, to think through theologically the implications of *NA* and to do so at times with Jewish dialogue partners are positive elements of progress in recent years.

The second, and closely related, reason for claiming that this set of documents marks a new moment of progress in the dialogue is that the writers and signatories to *Dabru Emet* publicly depart from a widespread Jewish reluctance to engage theological issues in Jewish-Christian dialogue. Commentators frequently ascribe such reluctance to the influence of Rabbi Joseph Soloveitchik's 1964 article "Confrontation" and the subsequent 1966 statement by the Rabbinical Council of America that Jews and Christians should collaborate in areas of joint social and cultural concern but should refrain from discussions proper only to individual faith communities.[59] Those Jewish scholars and leaders who signed *Dabru Emet* determined that a Jewish response to the Christian efforts to honor Judaism was now necessary and possible. Crafting Jewish responses to the renewed post-*NA* self-understanding of Christians is different from the respectful listening to Christian denominations as they came to terms with their shameful pasts. Again this was a necessary stage as Jews carefully discerned the authenticity of various Christian denominations' new posture toward them. The appearance of *Dabru Emet* indicates that a new level of trust and engagement has been achieved.[60]

Finally, the third reason for claiming that this set of documents represents new progress in the relationship is because they take the discussion public, beyond the religious authorities and scholars, to the proverbial lay person. *Dabru Emet* is the most explicit case in point. It was published as a full-page advertisement in *The New York Times* and other newspapers. Disputes concerning issues in the documents were discussed in a variety of religiously oriented periodicals intended to reach the laity.[61]

Having reflected on the general significance of these recent documents in Jewish-Christian dialogue, a few words on the documents themselves are in order. *Dabru Emet* was overshadowed by the publication a month earlier of *Dominus Iesus*. Nonetheless, *Dabru Emet*, a brief text of eight points with a preface, is significant because it stimulates theological dialogue about Christianity within Jewish communities as well as with Christian interlocutors. Covenant emerges as a key issue (just as it did with *NA*). The text notes, "as Jewish theologians we rejoice that, through Christianity, hundreds of millions of people have entered into relationship with the God of Israel" (point one). More explicitly, "Sacred Obligation," a similarly brief text of ten points with an explanatory preface, states: "With their recent realization that God's covenant with the Jewish people is eternal, Christians can now recognize in the Jewish tradition the redemptive power of God at work. If Jews, who do not share our faith in Christ, are in a saving covenant with God, then Christians need new ways of understanding the universal significance of Christ" (point six). Covenant and Christology are linked in this statement.

Some recent popular and scholarly exchanges illustrate that the issue of covenant (and its implications for Christology and soteriology) remains a crucial and delicate piece of the dialogue. Both "Sacred Obligation" and the joint Jewish-Catholic text "Reflections on Covenant and Mission," basing themselves on a new assessment of covenantal relationships, agree that "Christians should not target Jews for conversion."[62] Such statements have caused no little controversy. In the September 9, 2002, issue of

America, a brief news note on "Reflections" stated that the coordinator for Jewish ministries of the Southern Baptist Convention claimed that there was no greater anti-Semitism than to stop proselytizing Jews. Avery Dulles and Mary Boys, along with her coauthors, presented opposite views on the idea of conversion in the October 21, 2002, issue of *America*. Similarly to the Dulles-Boys opposition, intra-Jewish controversy accompanied the publication of *Dabru Emet*—most notably in an acrimonious repartee between Jon Levenson and the *Dabru* authors across *Commentary* and *First Things*.[63] Surely the robust interest generated by this group of three statements indicates progress in the dialogue.

Regress since *NA*

As a relative newcomer to the dialogue, I was recently both unnerved and puzzled by a virulent piece of hate mail that I received. The unsigned letter (the writer claimed s/he was "scared to give [a] name") was received shortly after I had conducted two public programs in Jewish-Catholic dialogue—one on the new anti-Semitism and one on faith in the public square. The letter was rife with hatred for Jews and focused primarily on Jewish government leaders and their alleged legislative acts that purportedly persecuted Christians and promoted Judaism.[64] It also included accusations that both the media and government elections are controlled and manipulated by the Jews, that the government hands over "life-long pensions" to Jews who "never contribute to the economy," while, on the other hand, it also ranted that "thousands and thousands of Jews are running a supermarket of fraud in New York." Such mail serves as a reminder that what may count for progress on the scholarly and institutional levels (as in the two sub-sections immediately above) does not necessarily account for what is happening on the ground. Just as the "professionals" in the dialogue think they are making progress, such a letter indicates that among some people and populations, certain attitudes toward Judaism and the Jewish people have not changed from what they have been for many, many years.

The letter raises old social and political canards about Judaism. The fear that Jews persecute Christians ironically and obtusely recalls the many theologically based recriminations synthesized by what Jules Isaac called the teaching of contempt.[65] It is important not to underestimate the staying power of centuries-old libel. Some educators in Jewish-Christian relations explicate Isaac's specific content of the teaching of contempt through the use of the five Ds device. Jews are: dispersed from the land, dismissed from revelation, a deicide people, a degenerate religion, and demonic (as seen in Christian art).[66] Of course, contempt for Judaism and the Jewish people culminates in the attitude of supersessionism, which is illustrated when one designates Judaism a dead-letter religion of law and Christianity a living religion of love. Recognizing the tenacity of such erroneous perspectives after several decades of official repudiation, it is worthwhile to take a brief look at some examples of regress or at least lack of progress in Jewish-Christian relations.

Persistent anti-Semitism and anti-Judaism[67] threaten progress, and theologians must continue to plumb the connections between the two. There are many facts and reminders about how prevalent and deeply rooted anti-Semitism remains.[68] One simple example is the recent controversy at the U.S. Air Force Academy. The Academy is attempting to investigate attitudes of anti-Semitism as well as instances of religious intolerance toward other non-Christian cadets. The media has reported that the Christ-killer charge is used at the Academy,[69] while ironically a movie clip from *Schindler's List* showing Nazis shooting Jews was taken out of a new tolerance training video as "too extreme"![70]

Web sites provide fertile ground for all sorts of misinformation and the spread of anti-Semitic ideas. Fatimaperspectives.com states that the fact that nuns on Mount Carmel refuse to pray for the conversion of Jews is "more evidence of the diabolical disorientation of the Church."[71] Similarly, Robert Sungenis of Catholic Apologetics International maintains that Catholics must continue to work for the conversion of Jews and that "Jews can certainly be incorporated into the Abrahamic covenant if they accept the Christ of Calvary."[72] Also, any simple Internet search of the Protocols of the Elders of Zion will reveal the resurgence, in many forms, of this intransigent manifestation of anti-Semitism.[73]

A particularly good example of the gap between scholarly and institutional progress and everyday attitudes comes in the form of an essay contest conceived and funded by Elizabeth Goldhirsh, heir to the *INC.* magazine fortune and a Harvard Divinity School graduate.[74] Concerned by the intense reactions to Mel Gibson's

The Passion of the Christ, Goldhirsh sponsored an essay contest intended to promote Jewish-Christian understanding. To underscore its importance, she offered a first prize worth $25,000. There were four thousand entrants but, according to a member of the staff at the Institute for Christian-Jewish Studies (which conducted the contest), a huge number of the entries were wildly anti-Semitic.[75]

The 2005 Anti-Defamation League Survey of American Attitudes toward Jews in America reveals more about persistent anti-Semitism. The survey discovered that 30 percent of Americans believe it is "probably true" that Jews are responsible for the death of Christ. Apparently, the teaching of contempt remains strong in the general population. The Anti-Defamation League 2005 Audit[76] of anti-Semitic incidents shows that incidents are at their highest level in nine years. Further, the survey found that the Hispanic-American population holds anti-Semitic propensities at a far greater rate than the rest of the population (29 percent). Thirty-five percent of foreign-born Hispanic-Americans hold hard-core anti-Semitic beliefs while 19 percent of those born in America hold similarly hard-core beliefs. This is an intriguing statistic in light of the fact (noted earlier) that the Spanish bishops were so alarmed at the prospect of *NA* that they put together a specialist group to study the matter.

Another important area of regress is the disappointment and concern among both Jewish and Catholic scholars that the dialogue seems to be shifting from official leadership levels and academia to only academia. For instance, there was concern about a lack of official Catholic response to Mel Gibson's *The Passion of the Christ*, especially in the United States, since the bishops had issued national guidelines in 1988 about presenting the Passion.[77] Currently, leadership in various Protestant denominations calling for financial divestment from Israel (as a way to call attention to the Israeli-Palestinian conflict and to force a quick resolution) has caused considerable distress within the dialogue.

Dominus Iesus, promulgated August 6, 2000, by the Congregation for the Doctrine of the Faith, offers a further example of the distance between academic and official approaches to the dialogue. *Dominus Iesus* unexpectedly forced the evolution/devolution question for many people. The benefit of the document now, regardless of how it is judged in the final analysis, is that it forces theologians to continue to wrestle with and clarify the questions of covenant and Christology and the attendant theological questions flowing from them. Cardinal Walter Kasper, president of the Pontifical Commission for Religious Relations with the Jews, has declared that *Dominus Iesus* is an "intra-Catholic" document. As such, it does not address the unique relationship between Judaism and Christianity, nor does it advocate missionary activity toward Jews.[78] Not all Catholic scholars subscribe to Kasper's sanguine interpretation. John Pawlikowski, president of the International Council of Christians and Jews, criticized the document at the ICCJ conference in Chicago in July 2005. He noted that the "objective language" of the document failed to account adequately for any of the personal relationships developed since *NA*. Thus, regardless of Kasper's position that the document does not affect Jewish-Christian relations, the language used has caused consternation and distress within some quarters of the Jewish community. Further, Mary Boys states that the document's serious flaws include supersessionist implications and the conflation of relativism with religious pluralism.[79]

Cultural phenomena such as Gibson's film, political efforts such as divestment from companies that directly or indirectly support the Israeli military, and official documents that appear to contradict church teaching on Jews and Judaism (such as *Dominus Jesus*) are stumbling blocks that have the potential to arrest the progress of dialogue. Jews and Christians seriously engaged in dialogue must figure out how to maintain a robust and constructive dialogue on a number of levels from the academic specialist to the religious leader to the person in the pew.

How to Move Forward: Constructive Proposals

The oscillation between progress and regress is inevitable when one considers the revolutionary changes that have occurred in the past forty years after two millennia of strife. Consideration of ways to increase progress and decrease regress is therefore in order. The following will review some proposals that have been tendered and projects that are in place dedicated to promoting the progress begun forty years ago.

It is no surprise to readers of this volume that formal education must be utilized as a central vehicle for progress. Philip Cunningham has demonstrated that enormous progress has been accomplished in excising anti-Jewish themes from Catholic primary and secondary religious education text books. In *Education for Shalom* he notes, however, that disparities exist between the improved quality of the text books and the preparation of the teachers.[80] Consequently, he recommends further study into the preparation of volunteer catechists.

My classroom experience attests to the need for such research. College students (both Catholic and Protestant) in either the introductory course on the study of religion or in the upper level course "Jesus and Judaism" exhibit a paucity of preparation for the study of the relationship between Judaism and Christianity. Two small examples illustrate my experience. On the first day of "Jesus and Judaism" last semester, I conducted two exercises. I asked my students to write down, anonymously, the answers to three questions: Into what religion was Jesus born? What religion was he when he died? What religion was he when his followers claimed his resurrection? The range of their answers was quite diverse. Several did answer "Judaism" to all three questions (though what they understood by Judaism is another question).[81] Some answered "Catholic" to all three questions while others employed a bewildering "mix and match" approach. The second exercise was a group assignment attempting to elicit any knowledge students had about commonalities between Judaism and Christianity. The omissions were glaring. For example, the notion of shared scripture, even with prompting, did not arise. By the end of the semester, however, the students handle such questions easily because they have been guided through: a comparison of the Jewish and Christian canons; a brief timeline of biblical Israel with an introduction to covenant; a survey of Second Temple Judaism with a focus on Jesus as an observant Jew; and an analysis of the teaching of contempt and respect. Students respond in passionate ways to the course and frequently demand to know, "Why did no one ever tell me this before?"

I respectfully submit that the answers to both exercises demonstrate the need for education about the teaching of respect at all levels. When speaking about the process of getting the official teachings of the church to the grassroots level, Eugene Fisher writes, "Stalin may be right that the Church has no troops. But it has its classrooms and pulpits, and that is where the battle for future generations is fought."[82] Thus, professors of Christianity, such as those gathered by the College Theology Society, must make conscious choices to teach accurately the Jewish background to Christianity because we cannot assume either that students accurately and adequately know the fundamentals of Christianity or that their thinking is free from the teaching of contempt (consciously or unconsciously). As theologians, we have a sacred obligation to incorporate the teaching of respect into our undergraduate, graduate, and seminary curricula. Our various communities and constituencies must be educated about the historical effects of our former beliefs and practices and we must work to rethink our theologies if we truly take seriously the rapprochement begun with *NA*.

Toward this end, the International Catholic-Jewish Liaison Committee at its seventeenth meeting in April/May 2001 issued recommendations on education in Catholic and Jewish seminaries.[83] One recommendation was that "courses dealing with the biblical, historical, and theological aspects of relations between Jews and Christians should be an *integral* part of the seminary and theologate curriculum and not merely electives." It further noted that all seminary and theology school graduates should study everything between *NA* and the pope's visit to the Western Wall. Eugene Fisher of the U.S. Bishops Secretariat for Ecumenical and Interreligious Affairs, responding to my email inquiry, said that he was not aware of a systematic implementation of this recommendation in the American seminary system but that the Cardinal Bea Institute at the Gregorian University in Rome would fully implement the proposal.

Those committed to the dialogue on any level will find numerous possibilities for learning about current issues in Jewish-Christian relations in the many programs in dialogue attached to colleges and universities. The links page of the web site for the International Council of Christians and Jews[84] lists forty-five programs in Jewish-Christian relations, nine in the Holocaust, thirty-three in interreligious issues, and thirty-one "other" (other ranges from the Vatican to the Academic Jewish Studies Internet directory). On the Council of Centers on Jewish-Christian relations[85] letterhead, one finds twenty-five centers as full members and the web site lists three affiliate members and four liaison representatives. Moreover, this Council only includes academic programs with a public outreach component; thus the numbers given do not account for all the academic degree programs and chairs that do not have a public face.

Different types of efforts exist to bring the official statements of various denominations and the insights of scholars in the field to people engaged in the everyday living of their faith. The Institute for Christian-Jewish Understanding at Muhlenberg College,[86] for example, offers programs divided into three categories: college, community, and clergy. One of the Institute's most successful programs is its "Interfaith Circles," which conducts dialogue between Jews and Christians in the intimacy of their individual homes. The "Clergy Colloquy" regularly convenes priests, ministers, and rabbis for shared text study. Both programs recognize the necessity of forging individual esteem and personal regard for the other partner in the dialogue and both help to distill the positions of the official and academic dialogues into effective progress on the ground.

Three programs that have primary and secondary education as their focus are the "Healing Deadly Memories" program at Xavier University,[87] the "C/JEEP" program[88] of the American Jewish Committee in cooperation with a number of American archdioceses, and the Anti-Defamation League's "Bearing Witness"[89] Holocaust education program in association with the United States Holocaust Memorial Museum and the Archdiocese of Washington. Xavier's program provides instruction to teachers about the anti-Jewish themes that spring up from the New Testament, and it is preparing a text to distill scholarship about the Jewish-Christian relationship for use at these first levels of education. C/JEEP provides priests and rabbis to high schools so that students may learn accurate information about both religions. "Bearing Witness" is a Holocaust teacher-training program.

Video resources are often a very effective method by which to begin a dialogue. Two recent productions provide excellent points of entry into discussing the Jewish-Christian relationship for either adult continuing education programs or the college classroom. *I Am Joseph Your Brother*,[90] a sixty-minute documentary, was produced by the Interreligious Coordinating Council in Israel in cooperation with the United States Catholic Bishops. *Walking God's Paths: Christians and Jews in Candid Conversation*,[91] produced by the Center for Christian Jewish Learning at Boston College along with the National Council of Synagogues and the Catholic

Communication Campaign, is a series of six fifteen-minute discussion segments featuring the top scholars in the field. Both films come with study guides, which make them ideal for parish and synagogue interreligious gatherings.

There are many more examples of programs and institutions laboring to make the new relationship between Judaism and Christianity a lived experience for the everyday person of faith. From the Sisters of Sion SIDIC Documentation Center in Rome to the Shoah Visual History Foundation in Los Angeles, educational and pastoral resources abound for those interested in participating in the next forty years of development after *NA*.

Finally, as can be inferred from the small sampling of resources presented, theologians are central to the development of high quality resources for dialogue. It is imperative for moving forward, then, that theologians do not stop at the repudiation of the teaching of contempt. A renewed Christian self-understanding within a positive valuation of Judaism demands that a renunciation of the teaching of contempt be followed by a theological reassessment of all areas of traditional systematic theology. Specifically reflecting on moving the dialogue forward in the context of *NA*'s anniversary, Rabbi Dr. Ron Kronish argues in favor of the dialogue's turn to theology. He writes, "We need to study each other's central ideas, such as: creation, revelation, redemption, justice and peace, salvation and messianism, sacred place (e.g. the Land of Israel) and sacred time (the Shabbat and the holidays), universalism and particularism, and much more."[92]

Covenant theology has been and remains the crucial doorway to Kronish's "much more." Michael Signer eloquently articulates the situation when he writes,

> In the search for a new relationship between Christians and Jews the question of covenant is ever present. As our two communities engage in theological reflection together and separately, discussions about the covenant generate great ambivalence and anxiety about our enterprise. We might understand this anxiety better if we understand that the notion of covenant is at the foundation of religious identity because it constitutes the primary designation of relationship between humanity and God with concomitant privileges and obligations.[93]

Therefore, moving Jewish-Christian relations into the church of the future requires courageous confrontation with all the implications of rethinking covenant theology; this has begun but must continue.[94] It is impossible to review here all the models that currently collide with each other as we fumble for the theological language to express the new reality between Jews and Christians. Indeed, there is no consensus about whether to choose "one covenant," "two covenants," "parallel covenants," or "multiple covenants."[95] Many thinkers suggest that use of the word "covenant" may need to be relinquished in favor of "relationships" or other images such as "twins" or "siblings." Certainly a new future is being forged when language such as "synchronicity of covenants" is employed.[96] Bold writers such as Irving Greenberg urge theologians to probe the dynamics of particularism and universalism within religions without falling into the sin of absolutism, because "God's love is capable of singling out again and again."[97] Within all the dizzying array of creativity surrounding the central issue of covenant, some constants are discernable. Christian theologians must build the church of the future on the following foundation stones: 1) there is no place for any trace of the former supersessionist, replacement, or fulfillment theologies in the new Jewish-Christian relationship; 2) the Christ event cannot be used to devalue Judaism; 3) Jesus must be explained within Second Temple Judaism and not over and against it; and 4) covenant language that is exclusive stands in sinful opposition to God's creative and redeeming love.[98]

Conclusion

While significant scholarly progress has evolved since *Nostra Aetate*, in the end, I find myself unable to answer my title's question. Severe scholarly and cultural disputes as well as persistent, virulent manifestations of anti-Semitism cause me pause when I get too optimistic about the past forty years. I wonder if we are losing ground. The relationships birthed with *Nostra Aetate* may not be orphaned, but I am not sure they are yet heir to an enduring heritage that honors the salvific paths of each other's religion.

Yet, for people of faith there is reason to hope. Mary Boys concludes, "In our time, Ecclesia's dialogue with Synagoga is meant to draw us into the boundlessness of the Divine. It challenges us to move beyond the narrow limits in which we confine the Holy One, and to acknowledge in our heart of hearts that God, Mother and Father of us all, has many children—and more than one blessing."[99]

Notes

[1]My deep appreciation goes to Dr. Elizabeth Groppe, Dr. Amy Rosenbaum, and Dr. Eugene Fisher for time spent reading drafts of this paper and for their perceptive editorial, bibliographic, and content suggestions. The efforts of the anonymous reviewers have also strengthened this work.

[2]Compare, for example, the introduction to "A Sacred Obligation: Rethinking Christian Faith in Relation to Judaism and the Jewish People." "A Sacred Obligation" is a statement produced in 2002 by The Christian Scholars Group on Christian-Jewish Relations and is available at http://www.bc.edu/research/cjl/meta-elements/sites/partners/csg/Sacred_Obligation.htm.

[3]Those interested in a new way to teach about John Paul II and Judaism should plan to see "A Blessing to One Another: Pope John Paul II and the Jewish People," an original, international multi-media exhibit now touring cities throughout the United States. For information visit www.blessingexhibit.org or call 513/745-3026.

[4]See *I Am Joseph Your Brother: Learning Resource*: 16. This text is jointly authored by the staffs of the Interreligious Coordinating Council in Israel (ICCI) and the Institute for Christian and Jewish Studies (ICJS), Baltimore (2003). It accompanies a tape (2001) and a DVD (2005). These materials are available from the ICCI, ICJS, or the Catholic Communication Campaign of the United States Conference of Catholic Bishops. Hereafter it will be cited simply as "*Joseph*." See also *Desperate Hours*, a film directed by Victoria Barrett, about Turkey's rescue of Jews. In addition, the official Raoul Wallenberg website at http://www.raoul-wallenberg.org.ar/english/walldefauing.htm has an entire section titled Angelo Roncalli International Committee. Clicking on that sub-link raises a series of links about Roncalli as well as three reports detailing his humanitarian efforts toward Jews in Turkey, Bulgaria, and Greece.

[5]All facts and quotes throughout the rest of this section, unless otherwise noted, are drawn from Giuseppe Alberigo, ed., *History of Vatican II*, vol. 1 (Maryknoll, N.Y., Orbis Books; Leuven: Peeters, 1995), 393-96. English edition, ed. Joseph A. Komonchak. Alberigo and Komonchak have completed a five-volume series. The dates for the other volumes are: vol. 2: 1997; vol. 3: 2000; vol. 4: 2003; vol. 5: 2006. Following the convention established by the editors within their series, citations hereafter will be in the following form: Komonchak, *History*, vol #: page #.

[6]I do not think it is worthwhile for the current discussion to quibble over

whether Pope John should have said, "You are my brother Joseph whom I sold into slavery." I would remark, however, that it is a useful pedagogy to have students debate the benefits of the two possible salutations.

[7]Komonchak, *History* 1: 395.

[8]For a brief biography of Isaac, see Claire Huchet Bishop, "Jules Isaac: A Biographical Introduction" in Jules Isaac, *The Teaching of Contempt: Christian Roots of Anti-Semitism*, trans. Helen Weaver (New York: Holt, Rinehart, and Winston, 1964), 3-15. Hereafter I will cite this text simply as *Contempt*.

[9]For an abbreviated form of the list, see *Joseph*, 9. For further exploration see Jules Isaac, *Jesus and Israel*, ed. Claire Huchet Bishop and trans. Sally Gran (New York: Holt, Rinehart, and Winston, 1971), 401-405.

[10]See n. 8 above for complete reference.

[11]It is important to note that there can be confusion amidst the proliferation of terms such as anti-Semitism, Christian anti-Semitism, theological anti-Semitism, racial and/or biological anti-Semitism, and anti-Judaism. The term "anti-Semitism" gained common usage after it was employed in the late nineteenth century by the German journalist Wilhelm Marr who desired a term with less religious and more scientific connotation than the then current phrase *Judenhass*. (See Carol Rittner, Stephen D. Smith, and Irena Steinfeldt, *The Holocaust and the Christian World: Reflections on the Past, Challenges for the Future* [New York: Continuum, 2000], 34-37 and 232-33.) The number of terms stems in part from the desire to separate historically negative Christian assessments of Judaism from Hitler's genocidal quest. To my knowledge there is no firm consensus among those who work in the field of Jewish-Christian relations about the term, pair of terms, or set of terms that is preferable. In many cases, meaning must be drawn from the context of a term's use. In general, when used with no modifier, "anti-Semitism" tends to refer to a negative racial and biological view of the Jewish people as inferior human beings; on the other hand, "anti-Judaism" refers to a theological assessment of the Jewish religion that does not necessarily make claims about the humanity of the Jewish people. Jules Isaac, however, makes no such distinction. He insists that the term "anti-Semitism" refers "to anti-Jewish prejudice to feelings of suspicion, contempt, hostility and hatred toward Jews, both those who follow the religion of Israel and those who are merely of Jewish parentage" (*Contempt*, 21). However, Isaac does subsequently use the term "Christian anti-Semitism" in order to link it to "Nazi anti-Semitism" (*Contempt*, 23-26). One question that can be asked is, "To what degree did Christian attitudes toward Judaism and the Jewish people as summarized by the teaching of contempt contribute to the near success of the Final Solution?" It is this link that is being clarified when the terms "anti-Judaism" and "anti-Semitism" are juxtaposed in any study. It is fair to say that *Nostra Aetate* and the debates that preceded its promulgation represent the early responses to the need of confronting both the anti-Semitism of the *Shoah* and the anti-

Judaism of the teaching of contempt. It must be noted, however, that many people disavow any distinctions, especially if the distinction is at all utilized by Christians to escape responsibility for a shameful history; also the distinction is rejected on grounds that religion and race are not so easily separated when analyzing anti-Semitism. See Benzion Netanyahu, *The Origins of the Inquisition in Fifteenth Century Spain* (New York: The New York Review of Books, 2001; originally published by Random House in 1995) for an argument that purports that *marranos* were persecuted despite evidence of authentic Christian faith. See also John M. Oesterreicher, *The New Encounter Between Christians and Jews* (New York: Philosophical Library, 1986), 22, for his explanation for the term "anti-Semitism" and his refusal to employ the hyphen in its spelling.

[12]Among the most famous of such sermons would be John Chrysostom's *Eight Homilies against the Jews.*

[13]Simply one example would be the Fourth Lateran Council's decree that Jews must wear a distinctive badge on their clothing.

[14]*Joseph*, 10.

[15]Komonchak, *History* 1: 393.

[16]Komonchak, *History* 1: 271 and 298 n. 467.

[17]As quoted in Komonchak, *History* 3: 276 n. 66.

[18]See, for example, Komonchak, *History* 4: 151, 165-66.

[19]See for just two examples, though there are many others throughout, Komonchak, *History* 4: 12 n. 25 and 96.

[20]See Giovanni Miccoli, "Two Sensitive Issues: Religious Freedom and the Jews," in Komonchak, *History* 4: 137.

[21]Komonchak, *History* 3: 268-69; see also *History* 1: 271 for a similar but politically laced argument from Amleto Cicognani, then secretary of state and president of the Coordinating Council.

[22]Komonchak, *History* 4: 141.

[23]Ibid., 554.

[24]Ibid., 140.

[25]Komonchak, *History* 3: 270-71.

[26]Ibid., 283-84.

[27]Ibid. and see *Joseph* 17,which quotes Cardinal William H. Keeler's eye witness recollection of Bea's presentation.

[28]The phrase belongs to Alberigo and is attributed along with the summary that follows to Komonchak, *History* 3: 430-32. See also, *History* 4: 136-42.

[29]See Komonchak, *History* 3: 379 and 430-31 for two references to the fact that the text was ultimately retained because of its objective importance and the expectations that it had already inspired in many quarters.

[30]Komonchak, *History* 4: 146 and n. 190.

[31]Komonchak, *History* 3: 379.

[32]Ibid., 432.

[33]See, for example, the quote by Heenan in Komonchak, *History* 4: 160.

[34]See, for example, Komonchak, *History* 4: 135, 159-63.

[35]Ibid., 546, 547.

[36]Ibid., 552.

[37]Ibid., see 552, n. 234 and 554 including note 239 with Congar's reaction to Willebrand's report.

[38]Komonchak, *History* 4: 551. According to this text, Pope Paul was looking for ways to resolve controversies over the schema.

[39]Komonchak, *History* 4: 551 and n. 231; see also Ratzinger's comment to Congar regarding Pope Paul's position on Jewish responsibility for Christ's death.

[40]Komonchak, *History* 4: 553 n. 236.

[41]Ibid., 558; but see also Cardinal Suenens' objections to the changes. Further, the removal of the word "condemn" was due to Pope Paul's wish to reserve the word "condemnation" for heresies; see 553.

[42]Miccoli, "Two Sensitive Issues: Religious Freedom and the Jews," in Komonchak, *History*, 4: 165.

[43]Ibid., 136.

[44]It is useful to remember that the document began as a piece of the document on ecumenism. The issue of articulating the Jewish-Christian relationship is also part and parcel of some of the debates concerning *Dominus Iesus*.

[45]Gregory Baum, "Salvation Is from the Jews: A Story of Prejudice," in *Disputation and Dialogue: Readings in the Jewish-Christian Encounter*, ed., F. E. Talmage (Jersey City, N.J.: KTAV Publishing House, 1975), 313.

[46]In the following two sub-sections discussing Vatican and non-Roman documents important to advancing Jewish-Christian understanding, I make no pretensions to be comprehensive. Regarding the work that has developed since the church repudiated the teaching of contempt with *Nostra Aetate*, Philip Cunningham notes "a massive body of scholarly, theological literature on the subject has emerged" (*Education for Shalom: Religion Textbooks and the Enhancement of the Catholic and Jewish Relationship* [Philadelphia: The American Interfaith Institute, 1995], 63). Cunningham's text provides an extremely valuable analysis of the origins of the teaching of contempt in the New Testament and patristic periods, an overview of the church's repudiation of that teaching with summaries of more documents than this article presents, and an in-depth study of Jews and Judaism in religion textbooks. Those interested in pursuing further study can consult Michael Shermis, *Jewish-Christian Relations: An Annotated Bibliography and Guide* (Bloomington/Indianapolis: Indiana University Press, 1988) and Eugene J. Fisher, "A New Maturity in Christian-Jewish Dialogue: An Annotated Bibliography 1975-1989," in *In Our Time*, ed. Eugene F. Fisher and Leon Klenicki (Mahwah, N.J.: Paulist Press, 1990), 107-61.

[47]Eugene Fisher, ed., *Catholic Jewish Relations: Documents from the Holy See* (London: The Catholic Truth Society 1999), 4.

[48]Quotations from *Nostra Aetate* are from Austin Flannery, O.P., ed., *Vatican Council II: The Conciliar and Post Conciliar Documents* (Boston: St. Paul Editions, 1975).

[49]See note 41 above for the use of "to deplore" in place of "to condemn."

[50]See, for example, Eugene J. Fisher and Leon Klenicki, eds., *Pope John Paul II on Jews and Judaism 1979-1986* (Washington, D.C.: United States Catholic Conference, 1987), 35.

[51]In addition to the bibliographies listed in note 46 and other sources throughout the notes, see the following for a representation of recent and current work: Roger Brooks, ed., *Unanswered Questions: Theological Views of Jewish-Catholic Relations* (Notre Dame: University of Notre Dame Press, 1988); Eugene J. Fisher, *Visions of the Other: Jewish and Christian Theologians Assess the Dialogue* (Mahwah, N.J.: Paulist Press, 1994); Edward Kessler, John Pawlikowski, and Judith Banki, eds., *Jews and Christians in Conversation: Crossing Cultures and Generations* (Cambridge: Orchard Academic, 2002); Howard Clark Kee and Irvin J. Borowsky, eds., *Removing the Anti-Judaism from the New Testament* (Philadelphia: American Interfaith Institute, 1998); Eugene B. Korn and John T. Pawlikowski, eds., *Two Faiths, One Covenant?* (Lanham, Md.: Rowman and Littlefield Publishers, 2005); Norbert Lohfink, *The Covenant Never Revoked* (New York: Paulist Press, 1991); John Pawlikowski, *Christ in the Light of the Jewish-Christian Dialogue* (New York: Paulist Press, 1982); Marvin Perry and Frederick M. Schweitzer, *Jewish-Christian Encounters over the Centuries: Symbiosis, Prejudice, Holocaust, Dialogue* (New York: Peter Lang, 1994); Paul M. van Buren, *A Theology of the Jewish-Christian Reality*, vols. 1-3 (San Francisco: Harper and Row Publishers, 1980, 1983, 1988).

[52]Statement four of "A Sacred Obligation" makes the living reality of Judaism a key focus.

[53]See also *God's Mercy Endures Forever: Guidelines on the Presentation of Jews and Judaism in Catholic Preaching,* a 1988 document from the United States National Conference of Catholic Bishops' Committee on the Liturgy.

[54]See, for examples, the following collections: Eugene J. Fisher and Leon Klenicki, eds., *Pope John Paul II on Jews and Judaism 1979-1986* (Washington, D.C.: United States Catholic Conference, 1987) and Lawrence Boadt, C.S.P. and Kevin di Camillo, eds., *John Paul II in the Holy Land: In His Own Words* (Mahwah, N.J.: Paulist Press, 2005).

[55]Strengths and weaknesses of the document as well as collections of texts on the Holocaust are discussed in the following: *The Catholic Church and the Holocaust: Perspectives on the Vatican Statement: We Remember: A Reflection on the Shoah* (Hartford, Conn.: Center for the Study of Religion in Public Life, Trinity College, 1998); *The Holocaust Never to Be Forgotten: Reflections on the Holy See's Document, We Remember* (Mahwah, N.J.: Paulist Press, 2001); *Catholics Remember the Holocaust* (Washington, D.C.: Secre-

tariat for Ecumenical and Interreligious Affairs, National Conference of Catholic Bishops, 1998); *Catholic Teaching on the Shoah: Implementing the Holy See's We Remember* (Washington, D.C.: Secretariat for Ecumenical and Interreligious Affairs, National Conference of Catholic Bishops, 2001).

[56]For European bishop conferences' statements, see *Catholics Remember the Holocaust* in note 55 above.

[57]The focus with which the Roman Catholic Church moved forward from *Nostra Aetate* (as represented by the implementation documents addressed above) has led observers from other Christian denominations to credit the Catholic Church with leadership in developing new approaches to Judaism. See, for example, Richard Harries, *After the Evil: Christianity and Judaism in the Shadow of the Holocaust* (Oxford: Oxford University Press, 2003), 231 and Christopher Leighton's statement that "the Roman Catholic Church has taken the lead in terms of redefining itself vis-à-vis the Jewish People. That has very far-reaching implications for how Protestants should reconceptualize who they are and how they are to be in the world as well" (*Joseph*, 17).

[58]Readers should be aware that both *Dabru Emet* and "Sacred Obligation" are accompanied by full-length scholarly collections, respectively: Tikva Frymer-Kensky et al., eds., *Christianity in Jewish Terms* (Boulder, Co.: Westview Press, 2000); Mary C. Boys, ed., *Seeing Judaism Anew: Christianity's Sacred Obligation* (Lanham, Md.: Rowman & Littlefield Publishers, Inc., 2005). These collections provide serious in-depth study of the core theological issues raised in the documents and belie any criticism that these statements are trendy, flash-in-the-pan theologies.

[59]See Joseph Soloveitchik, "Confrontation," *Tradition: A Journal of Orthodox Thought* 6:2 (1964). The article along with papers from a fortieth anniversary symposium on Soloveitchik can be found at http://www.bc.edu/research/cjl/meta-elements/texts/center/conferences/soloveitchik/. For an interesting interpretation of Soloveitchik's position see Irving Greenberg, *For the Sake of Heaven and Earth: The New Encounter between Judaism and Christianity* (Philadelphia: The Jewish Publication Society, 2004), 13-16.

[60]John Pawlikowski agrees that *Dabru Emet* marks a new moment and notes, "this increasingly emerging phase will not totally abandon the social agenda, but it will increasingly recognize the need to anchor the social agenda in a deeply theological and spiritual foundation" ("Christianity in Jewish Terms: Re-Visioning Our Self-Understanding," *The Living Light* 38:1 [Fall 2001]: 66-72).

[61]See "Symposium: A New Christian Document on Christian-Jewish Relations," *Midstream: A Monthly Jewish Review* (January 2003): 2-13, for brief essays on "Sacred Obligation" and note 63 for sources on *Dabru Emet*.

[62]See the explicit statement of point seven of "Sacred Obligation."

[63]See Jon D. Levenson, "How Not to Conduct Jewish-Christian Dialogue," *Commentary* 112, no. 5 (December 2001): 31; Tikva Frymer Kensky et al., "Jewish-Christian Dialogue," *Commentary* 113, no. 4 (April 2002): 8;

David Novak, "Instinctive Repugnance," *First Things* 123 (Mary 2002): 12-14; Jon D. Levenson, "Speaking the Truth," *First Things* 125 (August/September 2002); see also letters to the editor, 2-18.

[64]Writing this reminded me of one archbishop's suggestion that *Nostra Aetate* include the phrase, "that neither the Jews nor others cultivate hatred of Catholics"! (Komonchak, *History* 4: 164).

[65]Sadly, the wild invective of this poorly written letter is not far from the well-written broadsides circulated during the Council by the minority opposition; see Komonchak, *History* 4: 157-59 including n. 235.

[66]Margaret Obrecht, formerly of the Committee on Church Relations and the Holocaust of the United States Holocaust Museum, first brought this teaching device to my attention.

[67]See note 11 above. Also, it bears repeating that for many, such a distinction is untenable.

[68]For a tour-de-force review of the state of the question see Ron Rosenbaum, ed., *Those Who Forget the Past: The Question of Anti-Semitism* (New York: Random House, 2004).

[69]See "Group Probing Intolerance Missed 2 Academy Critics," Associated Press, May 22, 2005 found on the *Washington Post* web site at http://www.washingtonpost.com/wp-dyn/content/article/2005/05/21/AR2005052100495_p; Mindy Sink's Religion Journal Column, "Cadets Embark on Basic Training in Religious Tolerance," *The New York Times* (February 5, 2005), 13, and David van Biema, "Whose God Is Their Co-Pilot?" *Time* (February 27, 2005), 61-62.

[70]Robert Weller and Jon Sarche, "Air Force Academy Chaplain 'Was Fired,' " Associated Press report of May 13, 2005 found on the *Chicago Tribune* website at http://www.chicagotribune.com/news/nationworld/chi-0505130271may13,1,4673701.story?coll=chi-newsnationworld-hed.

[71]www.fatimaperspctives.com/ef/perspective306.asp?printer; for related report, see also Julia Lieblich, "Cloistered Nuns on Mt. Carmel Pray for Jews to Be Jews" on http://www.beliefnet.com/story/16/story_1675.html.

[72]See http://www.catholicintl.com/epologetics/articles/pastoral/when-pope-errs-print.htm. I am indebted to Professor Elizabeth Groppe for bringing this reference to my attention.

[73]See Steven Jacobs and Mark Weitzman, *Dismantling the Big Lie: The Protocols of the Elders of Zion* (Los Angeles: Simon Wiesenthal Center in Association with KTAV Pub. House, Jersey City, N.J., 2003).

[74]Louise Chu, "Contest Stirs Interfaith Dialogue," *The Journal News*, December 24, 2004, 5B.

[75]Personal conversation with Rabbi Charles Arian, October 20, 2004.

[76]Both the ADL Survey and Audit are easily available at http://www.adl.org.

[77]"Criteria for the Evaluation of Dramatizations of the Passion," issued in 1988 by the Bishops' Committee for Ecumenical and Interreligious Affairs of the National Conference of Catholic Bishops, is accessible at http://

www.bc.edu/research/cjl/meta-elements/texts/cjrelations/resources/documents/catholic/Passion Plays.htm.

[78]Cardinal Kasper's remarks were given at the seventeenth meeting of the International Catholic-Jewish Liaison Committee (May 1-4, 2001) and can be found in full at http://www.bc.edu/bc org/research/cjl/articles/kasper dominus iesus.htm as well as summarized in the joint communiqué issued by the Committee, which can be found on the Vatican web site at http://www.vatican.va/roman curia/pontifical councils/chrstuni/relations-jews-doc/rc pc.

[79]For a quick introduction to some of the dimensions of the conversation from Catholic and Protestant perspectives, see "*Dominus Iesus*: A Panel Discussion," *Proceedings of the Catholic Theological Society of America* 56 (2001): 97-116, (for Mary Boys's remarks only see 111-16). For a deeper analysis inclusive of both Jewish and Muslim perspectives, see Stephen J. Pope and Charles Hefling, eds., *Sic et Non: Encountering Dominus Iesus* (Maryknoll, N.Y.: Orbis Books, 2002).

[80]Cunningham, *Education for Shalom*, 133.

[81]One student declared on an exam that "Jesus was a practicing Protestant Jew"!

[82]Eugene Fisher, "Catholics and Jews: Twenty Centuries and Counting," an unpublished paper forthcoming in a volume from Sacred Heart University Press; publication details not yet available.

[83]The document is available at http://www.vatican.va/roman curia/pontifical councils/chrstuni/relations-jews-docs/rc pc.

[84]See http://www.iccj.org.

[85]Visit CCJR at http://www.bc.edu/bc org/research/cjl/CCJR/Intro.htm.

[86]See the website at http://www.muhlenberg.edu/cultural/ijcu/.

[87]See a description of the program at http://www.xu.edu/dialogue/programs activities.cfm#7.

[88]See a description of the program at http://www.ajc.org/site/apps/nl/content3.asp?c=ijITI2PHKoG&b=846561&ct=1080787.

[89]See http://www.adl.org/bearing witness/default.asp and http://www.adl.org/PresRele/VaticanJewish 96/4765 01.htm.

[90]See note 4 above for information.

[91]See http://www.bc.edu/research/cjl/meta-elements/texts/cjrelations/resources/education/WALKING GODS PATHS/WGP entry page.htm for information.

[92]Ron Kronish, "Forty Years Since the Second Vatican Council—Central Challenges Facing Jewish-Christian Dialogue Today: A Jewish Point of View," *Ecumenical Trends* 34:6 (June 2005): 5/85.

[93]Michael A. Signer, "The Covenant in Recent Theological Statements," in Korn and Pawlikowski, eds., *Two Faiths, One Covenant: Jewish and Christian Identity in the Presence of the Other* (Lanham, Md.: Rowman and Littlefield Publishers, 2005), 111.

[94]See note 51 above.

[95]See John Pawlikowski, "A Faith without Shadows: Liberating Christian Faith from Anti-Semitism," *Theology Digest* 43:3 (Fall 1996): 212-13.

[96]Michael A. Signer, "The Covenant in Recent Theological Statements," 121.

[97]See Irving Greenberg, "Covenants of Redemption" in *For the Sake of Heaven and Earth*.

[98]See Peter C. Phan, "Jesus as the Universal Savior," in Boys, *Seeing Judaism Anew*, 132-36; and John T. Pawlikowski, "A Theology of Religious Pluralism," in Brooks, *Unanswered Questions*, 159-60.

[99]Mary Boys, *Has God Only One Blessing: Judaism as a Source of Christian Self-Understanding?* (Mahwah, N.J.: Paulist Press, 2000), 278.

Catholic Evangelicals and Ancient Christianity[1]

Phillip Luke Sinitiere

> *These [Catholics and Evangelicals] quite self-conscious heirs of the sixteenth-century Reformation and the Council of Trent need to face, understand, accept, and resolve their past if they are to be free to deal with the deep issues separating them and with the projects of common action for the common good. Each knows that there once was a man who tried to build a castle on sand (Mt. 7:24-27). What shall these parties build on? Is there a theological or even a religious foundation? What precisely are the limits to a structure erected on it?*[2]
>
> William M. Shea, *The Lion and the Lamb* (2004)

For some evangelicals, the passing of Pope John Paul II prompted interesting reflection on the terms "catholic" and "evangelical." Timothy George, Mark Noll, and other evangelicals recently offered thoughts and observations on the life and times of the late pontiff.

Historian and Beeson Divinity School founder Timothy George, in an interview in *Christianity Today*, said he believed that Pope John Paul II was *the* most important pope since the Reformation because of his extensive travel, ecumenical concern, support of the "culture of life," and his ability to "offer a visible, articulate, winsome, attractive, embracing face to world Christianity."[3]

In an April 2005 *Boston Globe* article titled "The Evangelical Pope?" historian Mark Noll offered several reasons for why he believes that the pontificate of John Paul II resulted in a "dramatic warming" of relations between evangelicals and Catholics.

According to Noll, "mutual suspicion" recently turned to "interchange, overlap, and cross-fertilization" exemplified by Evangelicals and Catholics Together, by a recent Dominican pamphlet titled "Catholic and Born Again," and by John Paul's attention to matters of Christian intellectual life. "To see these former antagonists talking to each other about prayer, the Bible, and the person of Jesus Christ," Noll concludes, "is of much greater importance for the whole history of Christianity."[4]

Agnieszka Tennant, a Pole and an editor at *Christianity Today*, offers a unique perspective in an article titled "How the Pope Turned Me into an Evangelical." Tennant believes that ecumenism is John Paul's most important legacy because this posture "gave me permission to explore the religion of Billy Graham." Several years ago Tennant enthusiastically embraced evangelicalism, yet after the pope's death "return[ed] to Mary as a sister whose obedience I wish I had" and offered a "prayer of gratitude" to the late pontiff.[5]

In "Protestants and the Papacy: In Need of a Pope?" Garrett-Evangelical Theological Seminary professor D. Stephen Long argues that John Paul's death underscored the fact that "the papacy is on the Protestant horizon in a way that would have been unthinkable even a generation ago." As such, Long proposes three reasons why Protestants "need" the papacy. First, Long observes, without the papacy Protestants would have nothing to "protest" and hence no real foundation to justify five hundred years of "protest and dissent against tradition." In addition, Protestants need the pope because within the fractured nature of Protestant Christianity there exists no conciliar or visible manifestation of Christ's incarnation. For Long, both scripture and tradition attest to the pope's embodiment of Christian unity. Finally, Long argues that Protestants often hesitate to embrace a subordination of power to truth. "John Paul II," Long concludes, "taught us to risk truth and not be content with the modern assumption that peace can only be had when we confess power as the most basic reality of our lives."[6]

These important observations about Pope John Paul II's impact on evangelicals and evangelicalism provide an entrée into larger questions surrounding evangelicals who wish to feast at ecumenical tables. Evidence indicates that growing numbers of evangelicals—whom I call "catholic evangelicals"[7]—adopt ecumenical and historical postures that draw significantly from the faith and practice of ancient Christianity (roughly the first five hundred years of Christianity). This article first demonstrates *that* a "catholic evangelical" trend is present within evangelicalism; second, it situates this trend within the wider stream of evangelical thought; and third, it constructively engages the future of evangelicalism in an ecumenical context.

It is helpful here to define evangelicalism. Historian David Bebbington offers what many scholars affirm to be evangelicalism's distinguishing marks: conversionism, a focus on the "born again" experience; activism, the necessity of evangelism; biblicism, a belief that the Bible is the sole authority in the life of a Christian; and crucicentrism, the centrality of Christ's substitutionary atonement for the sins of the world.[8] Catholic evangelicals embrace this four-fold definition yet remain committed to framing doctrinal conviction and spiritual experience with the faith and practices of the early church.

Many historians agree, more or less, that the germs of evangelical convictions emerged during the Protestant Reformation and were later popularized in British North America by individuals like Anglican preacher George Whitefield.[9] From this angle, then, one might argue that Protestant interest in ancient Christianity began with certain sixteenth-century Protestant Reformers,[10] remained an important topic in the eighteenth century with John Wesley's publication of various writings of the church fathers,[11] and garnered attention in the nineteenth century with the work of scholars like Phillip Schaff and "Anglo-Catholic" theologians such as J. B. Lightfoot.[12] The twentieth- and twenty-first-century conversations of and between catholic evangelicals sparked significant comment throughout the 1970s and 1980s, but witnessed massive growth starting in the mid-1990s.[13] This trend continues today.

Locating Catholic Evangelicals

To demonstrate that growing numbers of evangelicals are turning to ancient Christianity for reflection and renewal, we must first turn to three of the most prominent voices calling evangelicals to recall historical memories, renegotiate ecclesial boundaries, and (re)create religious identities: Thomas Oden, Robert Webber, and

D. H. Williams. While the work of Thomas Oden merits discussion here, his comments largely inform mainline Protestant traditions, with which this article is not concerned.[14] Similarly, Robert Webber's work focuses on incorporating ancient Christian elements into evangelical worship, again a topic with which this article does not engage.[15] The work of D. H. Williams, on the other hand, speaks directly to concerns this article addresses about the integration of ancient Christian faith and practice within a (catholic) evangelical context.

In *Retrieving the Tradition and Renewing Evangelicalism: A Primer for Suspicious Protestants* (1999), Baylor theologian D. H. Williams sketches the historic formulation of Christian tradition—what he defines as the patristic formulation of Christian doctrine and interpretation—and urges evangelicals to embrace, adopt, and appropriate these elements instead of embracing the false Protestant dichotomy that pits scripture against tradition. Furthermore, Williams argues, the Protestant penchant for pragmatic and utilitarian innovation has created a kind of historical amnesia in which thinking about the past is seen as detrimental and stifling. Rigorous and theological thinking about the past, Williams asserts, atrophies because many evangelicals envision a "fall" of the church wherein corrupt doctrine and practice followed the apostolic age only to find "orthodox" expression in the teaching of major Protestant reformers like Martin Luther and John Calvin. If evangelical churches continue to ignore the Christian past, Williams warns, such communions will devolve further into sectarianism. In fact, Williams points out, many of these churches uncritically adopt innovative (and often ahistorical) postures of ecclesiastical gurus. By "retrieving the tradition," Williams has in mind a "serious study" of the early church fathers that will integrate ancient wisdom into contemporary currents of evangelical thought while responsibly retaining the historical context of patristic theology. "If the aim of contemporary evangelicalism is to be doctrinally orthodox and exegetically faithful to Scripture," Williams observes, "it cannot be accomplished without recourse to and integration of the foundational tradition of the early church. . . . Tradition is not something evangelicals can take or leave."[16]

While Williams's *Retrieving the Tradition* presents a cogent case for evangelicals to consider ways ancient Christianity might inform doctrinal, spiritual, and ecclesial outlooks, *Evangelicals and Tradition: The Formative Influence of the Early Church* (2005) further articulates his vision for catholic evangelicalism and offers practical ways for evangelicals to integrate elements of ancient Christianity into faith and practice. Importantly, *Evangelicals and Tradition* is the first book in a new series, of which Williams is editor, titled Evangelical *Ressourcement*: Ancient Sources for the Church's Future.[17]

Evangelicals and Tradition first explains the formation, development, and application of Christian tradition. Williams points out that early Christians used "tradition" both to defend the faith and for catechesis. While the apologetic use of tradition had particular aims, the catechetical use of tradition, Williams argues, retains the memory of Christianity, embodied through ritual. Williams explains the historically rooted and contextually lived aspect of Christian tradition:

> If tradition is a preserver of the church's faith as the work of God in the body of Christ, then it is supposed to be a living and shared memory. In this characteristic of tradition, we are directed to the role of the church, which harbors the tradition and is also the agent for handing the tradition over to new believers and to the world. Tradition as memory is not the work of the individual believer, although the believer participates in it, but of the corporate body of Christ, the church. Only within the church can memory reside each time the Lord's Supper is observed or a new Christian is baptized, when the memory of the faith is called back and reexperienced. In effect, the tradition has to do with how it is transmitted through the acts of the church. As memory, tradition has to do with how the gospel is transmitted, how the divine presence is realized in the sacraments (or ordinances) among believers, and how lives are changed by Christian truth.[18]

Williams here contends that tradition is a living thing, simultaneously rooted in the past yet displayed publicly as believers participate in Christian ritual and encounter moral change directed by the Holy Spirit. Ritual traditions like the Lord's Supper, a Christian devotional life punctuated by the historic church calendar, or participation in weekly liturgy frame experience of tradition and adoption of a catholic Christian identity.

Williams sets the foundation of Christian tradition by noting that the early church fathers embraced an "apostolic canon of Scripture" and adopted a "theological canon of apostolicity." These trajectories, Williams insists, do not pit scripture against tradition or unnecessarily privilege tradition, but rather suggest that catholic evangelicals might "see the early church as canonical," a singularly formative period in the development of Christian doctrine. Drawing from the writings of church fathers like Irenaeus, Tertullian, and Hippolytus, and in general from the "functional canonicity of the patristic theological legacy," Williams likens his conception of the early church as canonical to a richly diverse coat of many colors, "a composite . . . garment of faith." For Williams such an image captures the model of orthodoxy present with the early church; not an essentialized period of history, but a generative moment in which the Holy Spirit sewed together the threads of faith. In this context Williams insists that the witness of the early church should not be worn "as an ecclesiastical charm bracelet" or used to "romantically reappropriate" patristic theology. Rather, the development of the patristic witness, indeed the canonicity of the early church, is a construction of particular times and particular places.[19]

Not only is Williams committed to carefully appropriating patristic elements into evangelical thought and life, but he regularly reminds readers that the Reformation touted by evangelicals as a "recovery" of sound doctrine was far more catholic and ecumenical than most evangelicals admit. Williams notes, for instance, that a "patristic" faith was latent in many of the Reformers' understanding of church history. Luther's insistence on the sufficiency and authority of scripture, for example, readily acknowledged the legitimacy and necessity of church tradition. Furthermore, patristic anthologies used during the Reformation had a decidedly medieval flavor, and were thus conscious of and indebted to the early church.[20]

If many of the major Reformers were more patristically minded than most evangelicals admit, then it follows that what many consider seminal Protestant doctrines like *sola scriptura*, *sola fide* and justification by faith have patristic roots. Williams carefully shows that fourth-century church fathers Marius Victorinus and Hilary of Poitiers wrote about justification by faith, and in general influenced early Western interest in Paul's writings. In addition, these doctrines found patristic expression during the Reformation. It is true as well that throughout Protestant history these doctrines have functioned as a kind of tradition themselves. Jan Hus, Williams shows, read scripture alongside many of the church fathers, and Luther found patristic precedent for his convictions regarding the doctrine of justification by faith. Others, like Andreas Musculus and Jakob Andreae, composed catechetical and liturgical texts that collated sayings of the church fathers. The value of these observations, Williams points out, serves to contextualize the catholic nature of some Protestant doctrines. "[I]t is not accurate to say that the Reformers were merely interested in repristinating patristic theology," Williams concludes. "Nor did they see themselves as limited to the authority of the early fathers. The development of theological principles (*sola fide*, and so on), however, was believed to be an extension of apostolic teaching vindicated by the text of the early fathers and therefore the basis of reforming catholicity."[21]

After making a case for the legitimacy of the church's tradition, Williams invites catholic evangelicals to draw from the ancient "deposits" of faith invested in the church.[22] These deposits include ancient creedal affirmations, sermons, biblical commentaries, theological treatises, and selected hymns. Careful appropriation of these deposits defines Williams's program for *ressourcement*.

> Evangelical *ressourcement* is . . . the necessary next step for contemporary evangelicals that it might grow with theological integrity and ecumenical prudence in a cultureless culture and Christless spirituality. If, indeed, the church must create its own culture to preserve a distinctive existence in the midst of the decay of Western culture, then such resources are critical fonts for believers to discover their roots and Christian identity.[23]

While the work of Thomas Oden and Robert Webber richly informs catholic evangelical interest, Williams's erudite examination of history and tradition contributes significantly to this discussion and urges forward the conversation about evangelical interest in ancient Christianity. And while Oden, Webber, and

Williams are three of the leading voices of this surge, there are countless others contributing to the larger conversation that encourages Protestant encounter with various facets of the early church.[24] It is to these voices we now turn.

Defining Catholic Evangelicalism

This literature that constitutes the catholic evangelical conversation falls roughly into five categories: 1) conversion narratives, 2) historical studies, 3) exegetical commentary, 4) ancient application, and 5) pastoral and popular perspectives.

Conversion narratives define the first category of catholic evangelical interest. Simply put, these stories of transformation explain why certain individuals left evangelicalism for either Eastern Orthodoxy or Roman Catholicism. While every story is unique, converts uniformly point to a discovery of church history, a fascination with and embrace of early Christian tradition that was not part of their Protestant religious experience. In his *Turning to Jesus: The Sociology of Conversion in the Gospels* (2002), North Park University theologian Scot McKnight analyzes the complexities that accompany conversion to the Christian faith. In a recent article, "From Wheaton to Rome: Why Evangelicals Become Roman Catholic," McKnight offers some well-known Protestant-turned-Catholic stories (John Michael Talbot, Scott Hahn) and the conversion accounts of some of his former students. Church history surfaces as one of the many factors that influence conversion. Many evangelical converts to Roman Catholicism, observes McKnight, describe a sense of "historical disenfranchisement" that stems from the "*temporality of modern evangelicalism.*" In the end, a sense of the past grounds and centers these evangelical converts to Roman Catholicism. Interestingly, McKnight notes that evangelical converts to Eastern Orthodoxy also cite church history as a reason for conversion.[25] These stories reinforce the fact that many consider what Stephen Holmes calls "historical locatedness" integral to sustaining the Christian faith.[26]

Historical analyses of early Christian traditions define the second focus of catholic evangelical literature. Like the conversion stories discussed above, these historical studies explore both Roman Catholicism and Eastern Orthodoxy and note the importance of patristic life and theology to Protestant identity.

Two major book-length studies examine ancient Christianity in the context of Eastern Orthodoxy: Daniel Clendenin's *Eastern Orthodox Christianity: A Western Perspective* (1994) and Donald Fairbairn's *Eastern Orthodoxy Through Western Eyes* (2002). Both Clendenin and Fairbairn ministered and studied in Russia and their work comes from personal and professional experience.

Clendenin argues that evangelicals must thoughtfully, critically, and humbly acknowledge the Christian East. Clendenin asserts that through careful study evangelicals will find Orthodoxy consistent with the "basic truths" of the Christian faith. Furthermore, the liturgical and theological mystery of Orthodoxy, observes Clendenin, can redirect evangelical "reductionism, barrenness, [and] minimalism." Clendenin also argues that the unity of Christ's body is at stake with the study of Orthodoxy; evangelicals, according to Clendenin, must "see beyond the narrow confines of their own particular experience of Christianity." Finally, employing what Clendenin terms a "hermeneutic of love," evangelicals can learn several things from Eastern Orthodoxy and develop a more balanced "historical consciousness" that will set essential Christian doctrine in its rightful context and lead to a healthy integration of doctrine and doxology.[27]

Donald Fairbairn's examination of Eastern Orthodoxy, published eight years after Clendenin's work, is a more extensive doctrinal analysis of Orthodox theology. Like Clendenin, Fairbairn addresses tradition and theosis; unlike Clendenin, Fairbairn more extensively examines Orthodoxy in the context of nationalism and the folk beliefs of Orthodoxy, what he calls "popular Orthodoxy." Pleading for patience and suggesting that evangelicals and the Orthodox should "see through each other's eyes," Fairbairn contends that evangelicals have much to learn from Eastern Orthodox Christians.[28] In addition to the illuminating work of Clendenin and Fairbairn, other evangelical and mainline theologians and scholars effectively (and historically) engage traditions of Eastern Orthodox Christianity.[29]

Another aspect of catholic evangelicalism's historical engagement with ancient Christianity is a growing interest in Mary. While a number of mainline theologians approach Mariology in a recent collection of essays edited by Beverly Roberts Gaventa and Cynthia L. Rigby, *Blessed One: Protestant Perspectives on Mary* (2002),[30] Baptist theologian Timothy George argues, "It is time for evangelicals to recover a fully biblical appreciation of the Blessed Virgin Mary and her role in the history of salvation, and to do so precisely as evangelicals." Situated under what George calls five "Marian [m]otifs," he urges evangelicals to envision Mary as a daughter of Zion, as a handmaiden of the Word, and as the mother of the church while simultaneously affirming the virgin birth and embracing Mary as Theotokos. George also carefully notes where Reformers like Luther and Zwingli extolled Mary and suggests that an evangelical Mary might ultimately infuse evangelicalism with a more focused incarnational theology and promote a healthier ecclesiology.[31]

As the previous works indicate, there are growing numbers of catholic evangelical scholars who rigorously and responsibly engage both Roman Catholicism and Eastern Orthodoxy in order to better understand the shared traditions of ancient Christianity. In a similar vein, this historical view has inspired important biblical commentary aimed particularly at evangelicals.

There is an important and growing number of biblical commentaries aimed at a recovery of patristic exegesis that are broadly ecumenical and quite accessible to evangelicals. The first commentary series, and the most well known, is the *Ancient Christian Commentary on Scripture* edited by Thomas Oden. It is important to point out that the goal of *ACCS* is to put patristic exegesis not only on scholars' bookshelves, but also into the hands of laypeople and ministers. According to Thomas Oden, the *ACCS*

> has as its goal the revitalization of Christian teaching based on classical Christian exegesis, the intensified study of Scripture by lay persons who wish to think with the early church about the canonical text, and the stimulation of Christian historical, biblical, theological and pastoral scholars toward further inquiry into scriptural interpretation by ancient Christian writers.[32]

Another series whose aim is to introduce evangelicals to the ancient Christian past is *The Church's Bible*, a new commentary series under the general editorship of Robert Wilken. Different from the *ACCS* in that this series includes medieval exegesis, only two volumes are available to date: *Song of Songs: Interpreted by Early Christian and Medieval Commentators* (2003), edited by

Union Seminary's Richard A. Norris, Jr., and *1 Corinthians: Interpreted by Early Christian Commentators* (2005), edited by Judith Kovacs.[33]

A third and equally important commentary series intent on recovering patristic exegesis is Brill Academic's *The Bible in Ancient Christianity*, edited by Dallas Seminary's Jeffrey Bingham. With only a handful of volumes published to date, this series promises to add crucial understanding to the earliest worlds of Christianity and how the faithful learned, understood, and applied the Bible. Volumes include Charles Kannengiesser's *Handbook of Patristic Exegesis: The Bible in Ancient Christianity* (2004); James Ernest's *The Bible in Athanasius of Alexandria* (2004); Angela Russell Christman's *"What Did Ezekiel See?": Christian Exegesis of Ezekiel's Vision of the Chariot from Irenaeus to Gregory the Great* (2005); Robert C. Hill's *Reading the Old Testament in Antioch* (2005); and Elizabeth Ann Dively Lauro's *The Soul and Spirit of Scripture within Origen's Exegesis* (2005).[34]

The *ACCS*, *The Church's Bible*, and *The Bible in Ancient Christianity* provide critical resources to address some of the exegetical and historical deficiencies within evangelicalism and thus equip both pastors and laypeople with the tools to enhance historical studies of the Bible. It is important to note that these commentaries on the Bible *specifically* seek to draw from the exegetical resources of the early church and offer catholic evangelicals a way to more faithfully engage the church's past.[35]

While catholic evangelicals offer important historical perspectives on various traditions within Christianity's history and provide resources for more historically informed biblical exegesis, other catholic evangelical work provides practical knowledge and applicatory guidance from the early church.

Eastern University theologian Christopher Hall offers the most accessible studies of the church fathers and effectively bridges the wisdom of the past to issues of the present. A student of Thomas Oden, Hall leads the way in making patristic life and thought popularly accessible to evangelical pastors and laypeople. Hall's *Reading Scripture with the Church Fathers* (1998) introduces the church fathers to the general reader and discusses major exegetes like Athanasius, John Chrysostom, Augustine, and Gregory the Great, among others. In *Learning Theology with the Church Fathers* (2002) Hall delves into the fathers' observations on and comments about key doctrines of the Christian faith such as Christ's divinity, the Trinity, sin, grace, providence, the Bible, and the church. Hall will round out his church fathers trilogy with a forthcoming work, *Praying with the Church Fathers*.[36]

In addition to Hall's accessible work, evangelical theologian Clint Arnold, among many others, offers another way to draw guidance from the early church. In a March 2004 article, "Early Church Catechesis and New Christians: Classes in Contemporary Evangelicalism," Arnold argues that evangelicals might learn from the way the early church fathers committed to training, teaching, and equipping those new to the Christian faith. Arnold suggests using the *Apostolic Tradition*, a guide to training catechumens associated with second-century Christian Hippolytus of Rome, and notes how patristic *scholars* engaged in the doctrinal and moral training of new church members. In the end, Arnold draws four broad applications from the early church catechumenate: he argues that this new approach necessitates an "immersion" in the Bible, that it can facilitate basic doctrinal instruction, train in spiritual discipline, and allow for what Arnold calls a "deliverance ministry," or "renunciation" of the Satan himself. While Arnold's article is both historical and doctrinal, he suggests that tapping the roots of the early church might better serve evangelical ecclesiology.[37]

The final major theme around which the growing body of evangelical literature on ancient Christianity clusters comes in both popular and pastoral expressions. By "popular" literature I mean books and articles aimed specifically at thoughtful laypeople. By "pastoral" I refer to either books or sermons authored by ministers. I will first address ancient Christianity in popular literature.

In circulation for nearly two decades now and published under the umbrella of *Christianity Today*, *Christian History & Biography* (formerly *Christian History*) devoted three of its recent issues to topics relating to ancient Christianity. For instance, the December 2003 issue, titled *The First Bible Teachers: Reading Over the Shoulders of the Church's Founding Fathers*, features articles on patristic interpretation, a look at monastic spirituality, and Augustine's historical understanding of scripture. Mary was the subject of the Summer 2004 issue of *Christian History & Biography* titled *All Generations Will Call Me Blessed: Mary in the Imagination of the Church*; this issue includes articles that address

Marian devotion, Marian art, and Martin Luther's praise of Mary. Most recently, the Winter 2005 issue of *Christian History & Biography* focused on the Nicene Creed and contained articles on the meeting at Nicaea, the theology of the Nicene Creed, fourth-century Arianism, and an interview with noted scholar Robert Louis Wilken.

Another example of popular reflection that borders on pastoral application comes from the observations of several leading members of a home-church collective known as the New Testament Restoration Foundation. The aim of this group is to create the "New Testament church" by hosting home meetings, partaking of the Lord's Supper weekly and as a communal meal, conducting church rule by elders, meeting for fellowship daily, and cultivating a "[c]hurch leadership that is male, plural, non-hierarchial, homegrown, [and upholds] servant leadership." Above all, the New Testament Restoration Foundation aims to adopt "apostolic" norms for ecclesiastical life.[38]

Some of the pastoral reflection on ancient Christianity surfaces in a growing body of literature some call the "emergent church," a post-Christian, postmodern, and simultaneously multi-denominational and nondenominational community of Christians that aims to be historically conscious, biblically sound, culturally creative, artistically expressive, doctrinally responsible, and faithfully missional. The emergent church focuses on cultivating a deeper sense of community within the diversity of the Christian church, and in various ways adopts perspectives and practices drawn from ancient Christianity.[39]

Pastor and leadership consultant Brian McLaren is one of the leading thinkers and practitioners of emergent Christianity. In a recent book, *A Generous Orthodoxy* (2004), McLaren notes that "generous orthodoxy . . . consistently, unequivocally, and unapologetically upholds and affirms the Apostles' and Nicene Creeds." Furthermore, writes McLaren, a generous orthodoxy "invites us as never before to study not only the history of the church, but also the history of writing the church's history." While in one sense the ancient creeds and history frame emergent discussions, McLaren details the practical aspects of a generous orthodoxy as well.[40]

In a chapter entitled "Why I am <u>c</u>atholic," McLaren comments on the Nicene Creed and its potential to shape conversations about Christian unity and describes what he has learned and applied from [Roman] Catholic Christianity. About the phrase, "We believe in one holy, catholic, and apostolic church," McLaren writes:

> "We believe in one . . . church," the creed says, and that's no easy-to-swallow statement because we're surrounded by denominations, divisions, arguments, grand polemics, and petty squabbles. That's where the "we believe" part comes in: you can only know the unity of the church by believing it, not by seeing it. When you believe it you see through the surface dirt and cracks to the beauty and unity shining beneath. Generous orthodoxy presumes that the divisions, though tragic, are superficial compared to Christianity's deep, though often unappreciated, unity. Perhaps the more we believe in and practice that unity, the easier it will be to grow beyond the disunity.[41]

Here, in a practical and pastoral phrase, McLaren urges contemporary Christians to embrace the ancient message of unity in diversity found in the Nicene Creed. In a similar vein, McLaren also describes what he finds most attractive about Roman Catholic Christianity and suggests that evangelical renewal might come from embracing some of the ancient elements of the Christian faith. McLaren embraces the sacramental aspects of Roman Catholicism that purport to see God's handiwork in its multiform manifestations of the sacred. He argues that liturgy can enhance the sometimes simplistic and thoughtless aspects of evangelical worship. He highlights the practicality of respecting tradition and urges evangelicals to adopt a healthy posture of veneration for Mary. He aso celebrates the incarnational focus of Catholic theology and life, and praises the spirit of forgiveness and healing in some Roman Catholic circles. Interestingly, McLaren situates his comments about tradition as a critique of the Protestant Reformation. "The Protestant Reformation separated two brothers," McLaren observes, "Scripture and tradition. The older brother tells the story that leads up to and through Christ, and the younger brother remembers what has happened since. These brothers aren't the same, but neither should they be enemies."[42] There is much for catholic evangelicals to digest in McLaren's chapter on catholicity and ecumenism, and his work demonstrates both a popular and pastoral emphasis on ancient Christianity.

Moving from the popular to the pastoral, I know of at least four ministers from Houston who seek to introduce aspects of ancient Christianity to their local setting. Leo Schuster, minister at Christ the King Presbyterian Church, preached a series of sermons on the Apostles' Creed in the fall of 2003. In early 2004, two ministers at one of Houston's megachurches, Second Baptist, preached on ancient topics. Ben Young, son of former Southern Baptist Convention President Ed Young, worked his way through a series titled "Ancient Spirituality: What You Can Learn from Monks and Mystics," and Jim DeLoach, a senior minister at Second Baptist, preached a series on the Apostles' Creed. Lance Waldie, a minister at Harvest Bible Church in northwest Houston, preached a series of sermons on the Nicene Creed in May 2004.[43] While this part of the argument is provincial and somewhat anecdotal, it is striking that evangelical ministers address themes and elements of ancient Christianity in various denominational settings.

Another pastoral application of ancient Christianity comes in what some call the "new monasticism." Comprised of many young evangelicals who protest things like materialism by living with and among the poor, the "new friars" focus on holistic ministry, prayer and contemplation, deep community, hospitality, and a host of other spiritual disciplines rooted in ancient Christian tradition. Several books and a recent *Christianity Today* article describe yet another way catholic evangelicals adopt perspectives rooted in ancient Christianity.[44]

This popular discussion about ancient Christianity reflects a larger academic and theological interest among evangelicals, brings more laypeople into conversations about ancient Christian history, and supplements some of the pastoral reflections on ancient Christianity. Moreover, the popular and pastoral literature does not necessarily possess the defined aspects of scholarly exploration of ancient Christianity, but it does indicate that the scholarly and academic reflection on the ancient Christian past has, at least to some degree, migrated to lay and popular conversations. Only time will tell how extensive the larger evangelical conversation about ancient Christianity actually is.

Conclusion

So how does one evaluate this growing evangelical interest in ancient Christianity? Is it just another fad in the storied history of evangelical innovation? Or, perhaps, is it something genuine, historic, and substantive, something holy, catholic, and apostolic? While space precludes a longer historical investigation of these trends, I will offer two observations. First, the evangelical surge of interest in ancient Christianity demonstrates the rumbles of what I call ecclesiological discontent, a kind of posture that opens up the possibility of genuine ecumenical encounter. Second, catholic evangelical interest in early Christianity offers a way to understand better the contours of what Mark Noll calls the "evangelical mind."

Evangelicals interested in thoughtful engagement and experiential encounter with ancient Christianity will invariably run into what I call ecclesiological discontent: a deep investigation of evangelical ecclesiology (or, more accurately, ecclesiologies) that interrogates the rather loose ecclesiological frameworks that often mar evangelical experiences. Catholic evangelical historian Timothy George, for example, reflects on these issues in a 2003 article, "The Sacramentality of the Church: An Evangelical Baptist Perspective." George situates the evangelical suspicion of using sacramental discourse about the church and suggests several ways in which evangelicals might describe the church in sacramental terms without sacrificing doctrinal clarity or conviction. He suggests that evangelicals might appropriate the incarnational aspects of the church (as understood by Roman Catholics) by living out the principles of Christ. Moreover, thoughtful evangelicals might begin a sacramental "journey" by appropriating the incarnational elements of their own traditions—what George terms a "churchly spirituality"—and the traditions of the church more generally and by recognizing when and where Roman Catholics uphold the authority of scripture. Finally, evangelicals might create more sacramentally oriented churches by realizing that the church on earth, the visible church, "always exists in a constant state of becoming, buffeted by struggles, under the sign of the cross." In a word, George suggests that by faithful living a sacramental evangelical church will ideally be "a sign that conveys that which it signifies."[45]

George is not the only evangelical to discuss publicly the crucial issues surrounding evangelical ecclesiology. Two recent collections of essays, *Evangelical Ecclesiology: Reality or Illlusion?* (2003) and *The Community of the Word: Toward an Evangelical Ecclesiology* (2005), explore further the complex issues that result from an honest look at evangelical ecclesiological structures.[46] Another commentator, catholic evangelical theologian J. I. Packer, concisely summarizes ecclesiological issues that divide evangelicals and Roman Catholics in a 2005 article, "Evangelicals and Catholics: The State of Play." Though Packer notes the areas of agreement between like-minded Catholics and evangelicals—a shared conviction for societal engagement, a deep respect for scripture, the work of Christ, the Trinity, the work of the Holy Spirit, and justification by faith, among others—he identifies the sacramental and ecclesiological divide that remains. "Catholics see the church as the extension of the incarnation . . . whose sacramental ministry of grace, mediated through priests in the apostolic succession of orders . . . will convey the blessings they signify," Packer writes, "[and] [e]vangelicals see the church as the extension of the resurrection, the community of the faithful linked in solidarity to each other in Christ because each is linked personally to the Holy Spirit in Christ." Despite these differences, Packer's tone is hopeful, and he believes that "mutual enrichment" might come from genuine "Catholic-evangelical exchanges."[47]

The current evangelical interest in ancient Christianity can also be seen as the next chapter—and certainly not the final chapter—in what Mark Noll terms *The Scandal of the Evangelical Mind*. "The scandal of the evangelical mind," Noll writes, "is that there is not much of an evangelical mind."[48] Published in 1994, Noll's important book sketched the historical contours of evangelical thought and argued that nineteenth-century revivalism and early-twentieth-century fundamentalism severed evangelicals from the rigorous and responsible intellectual engagement of historic evangelicalism. The scandal matters, Noll argues, because it is necessary to inform and educate future generations and because ideas have consequences. In short, Noll suggests, the evangelical mind is important because the worship of God is important.

While Noll's book painted a bleak picture of evangelical intellectual life, he noticed promising trends within evangelical political reflection, philosophy, and (much less so) science. In a 2001 article published in *First Things*, "Minding the Evangelical Mind," Noll praises a number of evangelical thinkers and suggested that some trends in scientific reflection (namely Intelligent Design) demonstrated a cultivated evangelical intellectual engagement. In a more recent update, "The Evangelical Mind Today," Noll praises evangelicals for consistent dialogue with Roman Catholics, for developments in philosophy, for increasing the academic rigor of Christian colleges and universities by a more conscious integration of faith and learning, for the increased presence of evangelicals in scientific circles, for a stronger scholarly contingent within "pluralistic" universities, and for contributing to forums like *Books & Culture*, *First Things*, and *Touchstone*.[49]

Yet what is perhaps most remarkable about Noll's *Scandal of the Evangelical Mind* comes in the fourth section of the book entitled "Hope?" Noll concludes with this observation: "Evangelicals who believe that God desires to be worshiped with thought as well as activity may well remain evangelicals, but they will find intellectual depth—a way of praising God through the mind—in ideas developed by confessional or mainline Protestants, Roman Catholics, or perhaps even the Eastern Orthodox."[50] Here Noll patently confesses that evangelicals keen on rigorous thought leading to "theological insight" might benefit from a more critical engagement with tradition and history. Evangelicals passionate for renewal, Noll insists, must open themselves up to ecumenical and historical conversations that might be uncomfortable, difficult, disconcerting, but ultimately profitable and transformative. In fact, in a 2002 autobiographical essay entitled "Teaching History as a Christian," Noll describes how his own faith is not only shaped by Calvinistic and Reformed traditions, but also rooted in the ancient creedal statements of the Christian church.[51]

While Noll is a respected historian of considerable faith and one who is gifted at telling stories about the past,[52] it would appear, given his comments above, that he is something of a prophet. Noll argued in 1994 that an evangelical intellectual life desiring more depth might pursue conversations with Roman Catholicism and Eastern Orthodoxy. It is quite striking that some of the more thoughtful and historical evangelical reflection does exactly what Noll suggested.

Given these comments in the context of catholic evangelicalism, what is equally notable is the publication of Noll's latest book (co-authored with Carolyn Nystrom): *Is the Reformation Over?: An Evangelical Assessment of Contemporary Roman Catholicism* (2005). Here Noll and Nystrom cover the history of evangelical-Catholic relations in both the United States and (to a lesser degree) Canada, account for the changing nature of this historically tense relationship, discuss the emergence of Evangelicals and Catholics Together (ECT), and sketch a number of keen comparisons between both bodies of faith. In a scenario that includes diverse expressions of the Christian faith in the context of ecumenical possibility, Noll and Nystrom imagine four strains of Christianity (Roman Catholic, Eastern Orthodox, Protestant, and Pentecostal) that each speak in a tongue of the global Christian language, what they call "Christian Tradition as Languages." This image explains the nature of dialogue between evangelicals and Catholics. Noll and Nystrom explain:

> What can we make of a world of multiple tongues? Continuing differences between Catholics and evangelicals should be regarded as both a problem and a gift. They constitute a problem because serious Christ-followers of one sort simply cannot understand why serious Christ-followers of another sort believe and act as they do. They represent a gift because, by the mercies of God, more and more Christ-followers of one sort are coming to recognize the sanctity, holiness, and telltale manifestations of the Holy Spirit among serious Christ-followers of other sorts. The gift in this realization is to see that God has always been bigger than our own group's grasp of God, that he has been manifesting himself at times, in places, and through venues where others have not expected him to be present at all.[53]

Here Noll and Nystrom courageously confront the differences that remain between evangelicals and Catholics, yet in the spirit of catholic evangelicalism they reflect not only an openness to dialogue, but also a willingness to learn from and understand deeply the diverse manifestations of the Holy Spirit, much of which takes place and is taking place outside of Protestantism and outside of North America.[54]

Serious evangelical thinking about history, tradition, memory, and identity, and by extension ecclesiology, acknowledges the importance *and* necessity of conversations with Roman Catholicism and Eastern Orthodoxy. This reflection, as hopefully demonstrated, is historically conscious, intellectually rigorous, and concerned with what Noll calls the ultimate scandal of the evangelical faith—the scandal of the Cross.[55]

While evangelical dialogue with Roman Catholicism and Eastern Orthodoxy is worthy of note, Roman Catholic engagement with Protestantism also garners significant interest. William M. Shea, for example, extensively chronicles this history in America in *The Lion and the Lamb* (2004), and William L. Portier, in a recent article titled "Here Come the Evangelical Catholics" (2004), traces the social dynamics of the "evangelical" impulse in Roman Catholicism.[56]

To return to where we started: How will evangelicalism's historical memory contribute to the future of evangelical identity and how will evangelicalism's future remember the church's past? Will catholic evangelicals and evangelical Catholics, to use the words of William Shea from the beginning of the article, "face, understand, accept, and resolve their past . . ."? Though these questions remain unanswered, it is clear that both "catholic evangelical" and "evangelical Catholic" conversations are underway. Whatever answers these questions receive, at this moment in time it appears, to use Robert Webber's words, that "the [catholic evangelical] road to the future is paved with the [church's] past."

Notes

[1]Earlier versions of this paper were presented at the Conference on Faith and History Student Research Meeting held in October 2004 at Hope College in Holland, Michigan, and at the College Theology Society Annual Meeting, held in June 2005 at Spring Hill College in Mobile, Alabama. An earlier version of this essay, absent the catholic evangelical focus, appeared as "Embracing the Early Church: Reflections on Evangelicals, Patristics, Ecclesiology, and Ecumenism," *Reformation & Revival Journal* 13/4 (Fall 2004): 13-43. I would like to thank D. H. Williams for permission to cite unpublished material, and Michael J. McClymond, Daniel Van Slyke, and two anonymous reviewers for comments on this version of the essay.

[2]William M. Shea, *The Lion and the Lamb: Evangelicals and Catholics in America* (New York: Oxford University Press, 2004), 5.

[3]Timothy George, "Pope Gave Evangelicals Moral Impetus We Didn't Have," *Christianity Today*, April 26, 2005 (accessed May 2005) <http://www.christianitytoday.com>.

[4]Mark Noll, "The Evangelical Pope?" *Boston Globe*, April 10, 2005 (accessed April 2005) <http://www.boston.com>.

[5]Agnieszka Tennant, "How the Pope Turned Me into an Evangelical," *Christianity Today*, April 4, 2005 (accessed May 2005) <http://www.christianitytoday.com>.

[6]D. Stephen Long, "Protestants and Power: In Need of a Pope," *Christian Century*, May 17, 2005, 10-11.

[7]Kenneth J. Collins, in *The Evangelical Moment: The Promise of an American Religion* (Grand Rapids: Baker, 2005), uses the term "catholic evangelicalism" (17) to describe evangelicals who express interest in Roman Catholicism and Eastern Orthodoxy. In this context Collins discusses Evangelicals and Catholics together as well as the work of Thomas Oden, among other things, and reflects theologically on these trends. Collins and I thus use similar terminology to discuss the same trend; Collins brings theological analysis to this movement (discussed specifically in chaps. 7-8) and writes from the Wesleyan perspective, while my aim is less theological and more historiographical.

[8]David Bebbington, *Evangelicalism in Modern Britain: A History from the 1730s to the 1980s* (Grand Rapids: Baker, 1989), 1-17.

[9]See, for example, Mark Noll, *The Rise of Evangelicalism: The Age of Edwards, Whitefield, and the Wesleys* (Downers Grove, Ill.: InterVarsity, 2003), 15-21; Bruce Hindmarsh, "Is Evangelical Ecclesiology an Oxymoron?: A Historical Perspective," in *Evangelical Ecclesiology*, ed. John G. Stackhouse (Grand Rapids: Baker, 2003), 15-38; D. G. Hart, *Deconstructing Evangelicalism: Conservative Protestantism in the Age of Billy Graham* (Grand Rapids: Baker, 2004), 1-61; and Douglas A. Sweeney, *The American Evangelical Story: A History of the Movement* (Grand Rapids: Baker, 2005), 17-26. Though a decade old, Alister McGrath offers another illuminatingly helpful description of evangelicalism in *Evangelicalism & the Future of Christianity* (Downers Grove, Ill.: InterVarsity, 1995), 53-87.

[10]See S. J. Barnett, "Where Was Your Church Before Luther?: Claims for the Antiquity of Protestantism Examined," *Church History* 68, no. 1 (March 1999): 14-41; Anthony N. S. Lane, *John Calvin: Student of the Church Fathers* (Grand Rapids: Baker, 1999); Phyllis Rodgerson Pleasants, "Sola Scriptura in Zurich," and D. H. Williams, "Scripture, Tradition, and the Church: Reformation and Post-Reformation," in *Free Church and Early Church*, ed. D. H. Williams (Grand Rapids: Eerdmans, 2002), 77-126; Irena Backus, *Historical Method and Confessional Identity in the Era of the Reformation, 1378-1615* (The Netherlands: Brill Academic, 2003); and D. H. Williams, "Justification by Faith: A Patristic Doctrine," *Journal of Ecclesiastical History* (2006).

[11]John C. English, "The Duration of the Primitive Church: An Issue for Seventeenth and Eighteenth Century Anglicans," *Anglican and Episcopal History* 73 (2004): 51.

[12]See William Tabbernee, "Alexander Campbell and the Apostolic Tradition," in Williams, *The Free Church and the Early Church*, 163-80; "Introduction," *Community Formation in the Early Church and in the Church Today*, ed. Richard N. Longenecker (Peabody, Mass.: Hendrickson, 2002), xi-xix.

[13]Bradley Nassif, "Eastern Orthodoxy and Evangelicalism: The Status of an Emerging Global Dialogue," 211-48, and Timothy P. Weber, "Looking for Home: Evangelical Orthodoxy and the Search for the Original Church," 249-72, in *Eastern Orthodox Theology: A Contemporary Reader*, 2d ed., ed. Daniel B. Clendenin (Grand Rapids: Baker, 2003); Thomas P. Rausch, ed., *Catholics and Evangelicals: Do They Share Any Common Future?* (Downers Grove, Ill.: InterVarsity, 2000); Robert Webber, *Evangelicals on the Canterbury Trail: Why Evangelicals Are Attracted to the Liturgical Church* (Waco, Tex.: Word, 1985).

[14]See Thomas C. Oden, *The Rebirth of Orthodoxy: Signs of Life in Christianity* (New York: Harper Collins, 2003), 86, 29-30, 58-59. See also "Introduction," in *Ancient and Postmodern Christianity, Paleo-Orthodoxy in the 21st Century: Essays in Honor of Thomas C. Oden*, ed. Kenneth Tanner and Christopher A. Hall (Downers Grove, Ill.: InterVarsity, 2002), 7-12; and "Can Anything Good Come Out of Liberalism?: One Pilgrim's Regress," in *Pilgrims on the Sawdust Trail: Evangelical Ecumenism and the Quest for Christian Identity*, ed. Timothy George (Grand Rapids: Baker, 2004), 157-74.

[15]See Robert E. Webber, *Ancient-Future Faith: Rethinking Evangelicalism for a Postmodern World* (Grand Rapids: Baker, 1999); *Ancient-Future Evangelism: Making Your Church a Faith-Forming Community* (Grand Rapids: Baker, 2003); and *Ancient-Future Time: Forming Spirituality Through the Christian Year* (Grand Rapids: Baker, 2004). On a related note, and for a look at the interest of younger generations (Protestant, Catholic, and Orthodox) in the spirituality of ancient Christianity, see Robert E. Webber, *The Younger Evangelicals: Facing the Challenges of the New World* (Grand Rapids: Baker, 2002) and Colleen Carroll, *The New Faithful: Why Young Adults Are Embracing Christian Orthodoxy* (Chicago: Loyola, 2002). Also, see Carroll's interview, "The Good News about Generations X & Y," *Christianity Today* 46, no. 9 (August 5, 2002): 40-45.

[16]D. H. Williams, *Retrieving the Tradition and Renewing Evangelicalism: A Primer for Suspicious Protestants* (Grand Rapids: Eerdmans, 1999), 4-5, 13, and *Evangelicals and Tradition: The Formative Influence of the Early Church* (Grand Rapids: Baker, 2005), 18.

[17]Williams discusses the aims of evangelical *ressourcement* in *Evangelicals and Tradition*, 9-10.

[18]Ibid., 36.

[19]Ibid., 56, 73, 62, 78. See also D. H. Williams, "The Patristic Tradition as Canon," *Perspectives in Religious Studies* (2006).

[20]Ibid., 73-78.

[21]Ibid, 115-44.

[22]Ibid., 147.

[23]Ibid., 179.

[24]In *Younger Evangelicals*, Webber praises the work of Oden and Williams along with other evangelicals like James Cutsinger, Rodney Clapp, Stanley Grenz, James McLendon, Jr., Gordon Lewis, and Gregory Boyd (75-79). See also Todd E. Johnson, ed., *The Conviction of Things Not Seen: Worship and Ministry in the 21st Century* (Grand Rapids: Brazos, 2002).

[25]For accounts of evangelical conversion to Roman Catholicism, see Thomas Howard, *Evangelical Is Not Enough* (Nashville: Thomas Nelson, 1984); "Recognizing the Church: A Personal Pilgrimage & the Discovery of Five Marks of the Church," in *Creed & Culture: A Touchstone Reader*, ed. James M. Kushiner (Wilmington, Del.: ISI, 2003), 115-28; and Scott and Kimberly Hahn, *Rome Sweet Home: Our Journey to Catholicism* (Ft. Collins, Col.: Ignatius Press, 1994). For accounts of evangelical conversion to Eastern Orthodoxy, see Peter Gillquist, *Becoming Orthodox: A Journey to the Ancient Christian Faith*, rev. ed. (Ben Lomond, Calif.: Conciliar, 2001); Peter Gillquist, ed., *Coming Home: Why Protestant Clergy Are Becoming Orthodox* (Ben Lomond, Calif.: Conciliar, 1995); Frank Shaeffer, *Dancing Alone: The Quest for Orthodox Faith in the Age of False Religion* (Boston: Regina Orthodox Press, [1994] 2002); Matthew Gallatin, *Thirsting for God in a Land of Shallow Wells* (Ben Lomond, Calif.: Conciliar, 2002); and Frederica Matthewes-Green, *Facing East: A Pilgrim's Journey into the Mysteries of Orthdoxy* (New York: HarperCollins, 1996). For unique reflections from an evangelical-turned-Orthodox on evangelical-Orthodox fellowship, see Sam Torode, "It's All About Jesus: A Convert to Orthodoxy Reconsiders Evangelicalism," *Christianity Today* 49, no. 8 (August 2005): 42-44. See also Scot McKnight, *Turning to Jesus: The Sociology of Conversion in the Gospels* (Louisville: Westminster/John Knox, 2002) and "From Wheaton to Rome: Why Evangelicals Become Roman Catholic," *Journal of the Evangelical Theological Society* 45 no. 3 (September 2002): 451-72, quotes from 464-65 (italics his). For accounts of evangelical interest in Orthodoxy in Canada, see Patricia Paddey, "Orthodox Through Evangelical Eyes: What Does an Ancient Form of Christianity Have to Offer Evangelicals?" *Faith Today* (November/December 2004); and Peter T. Chattaway, "Looking to the East," *ChristianWeek*, March 18, 2005 <http://www.christianweek.org> (accessed May 2005). Chattaway's article is also available at <http://www.christianity.ca>. For a look at evangelicals-turned-Orthodox from a British perspective, see Michael Harper, *A Faith Fulfilled: Why Are Chris-*

tians Across Britain Embracing Orthodoxy? (Ben Lomond, Calif.: Conciliar, 1999).

[26]Stephen R. Holmes, *Listening to the Past: The Place of Tradition in Theology* (Grand Rapids: Baker, 2002), 6.

[27]Daniel L. Clendenin, *Eastern Orthodox Christianity: A Western Perspective* (Grand Rapids: Baker, 1994), quotes from 18, 19, 22, 148, 27. See also Clendenin's *Eastern Orthodox Theology: A Contemporary Reader* (Grand Rapids: Baker, 1995). In 2003 Baker issued second editions of Clendenin's books; the only changes came with the addition of two articles in *A Contemporary Reader* (see n.13).

[28]Donald Fairbairn, *Eastern Orthodoxy Through Western Eyes* (Louisville: Westminster/John Knox, 2002), quotes from 131, 159, 133.

[29]See Robert V. Rakestraw, "Becoming Like God: An Evangelical Doctrine of Theosis," *Journal of the Evangelical Theological Society* 40, no. 2 (June 1997): 257-69; James S. Cutsinger, *Reclaiming the Great Tradition: Evangelicals, Catholics, and Orthodox in Dialogue* (Downers Grove, Ill.: InterVarsity, 1997); Mark Saucy, "Evanglicals, Catholics, and Orthodox Together: Is the Church the Extension of the Incarnation?" *Journal of the Evangelical Theological Society* 43, no. 2 (June 2000): 193-212; Bradley Nassif, Michael Horton, Vladimir Berzonsky, George Hancock-Stefan, and Edward Rommen, *Three Views on Eastern Orthodoxy and Evangelicalism* (Grand Rapids: Zondervan, 2004); Laurie Guy, *Introducing Early Christianity: A Topic Survey of Its Life, Beliefs & Practices* (Downers Grove, Ill.: InterVarsity, 2004); Paul Barnett, *The Birth of Christianity: The First Twenty Years* (Grand Rapids: Eerdmans, 2005); and David Willis, *Clues to the Nicene Creed: A Brief Outline of the Faith* (Grand Rapids: Eerdmans, 2005).

Other important studies on this score include the January 2004 issue of the mainline journal *Theology Today* and the July/August 2003 edition of *Touchstone*. The *Theology Today* issue, save Ellen Charry's editorial, features all Orthodox writers, including the Ecumenical Patriarch Bartholomew I and the British Orthodox Bishop Kallistos Ware, who address Orthodox artistic expression, monasticism, worship, and prayer. The *Touchstone* issue contains articles by Roman Catholic, Eastern Orthodox, and evangelical theologians like Richard John Neuhaus, Metropolitan Maximos, Timothy George, and Albert Mohler, among others, and deals with denominational, liturgical, sacramental, doctrinal, and historical issues.

[30]Beverly Roberts Gaventa and Cynthia L. Rigby, eds., *Blessed One: Protestant Perspectives on Mary* (Louisville: Westminster/John Knox, 2002). See also Dwight Longenecker and David Gustafson, *Mary: A Catholic-Evangelical Debate* (Grand Rapids: Brazos, 2001).

[31]Timothy George, "The Blessed Virgin Mary in Evangelical Perspective," in *Mary, Mother of God*, ed. Carl E. Braaten and Robert W. Jenson (Grand Rapids: Eerdmans, 2004), 100-22, quotes from 102, 104, 107, 110, 112, and

118. See also Timothy George, "The Blessed Evangelical Mary: Why We Shouldn't Ignore Her Any Longer," *Christianity Today* (December 2003): 34-39 and his interview "Recovering a Protestant View of Mary," *Christian History & Biography* 83 (Summer 2004): 13-15.

[32]Thomas C. Oden, "General Introduction," in *Ancient Christian Commentary on Scripture: Mark*, ed. Thomas C. Oden and Christopher A. Hall (Downers Grove, Ill.: InterVarsity, 1998), xi. For the latest information about the *ACCS*, visit <http://www.gospelcom.net/ivpress/accs/>.

[33]Richard A. Norris, Jr., ed., *Song of Songs: Interpreted by Early Christian and Medieval Commentators* (Grand Rapids: Eerdmans, 2003) and Judith L. Kovacs, ed., *1 Corinthians: Interpreted by Early Christian Commentators* (Grand Rapids: Eerdmans, 2005).

[34]For a full description of *The Bible in Ancient Christianity* series, visit the Brill Academic website <http://www.brill.nl>. In this vein readers may also wish to consult David Dunn-Wilson, *A Mirror for the Church: Preaching in the First Five Centuries* (Grand Rapids: Eerdmans, 2005); and Kathy Gaca and L. L. Welborn, *Early Patristic Readings of Romans* (London: T&T Clark, 2006).

[35]It is also important to point out that the writings of the early church fathers, first edited by Phillip Schaff in the late nineteenth century, are another resource for pastors and laypersons. Shaff's work is now available online at the Christian Classics Ethereal Library <http://www.ccel.org>.

[36]Christopher Hall, *Reading Scripture with the Church Fathers* (Downers Grove, Ill.: InterVarsity, 1998) and *Learning Theology with the Church Fathers* (Downers Grove, Ill.: InterVarsity, 2002). Hall's *Praying with the Church Fathers* will also be published by InterVarsity Press.

[37]Clinton E. Arnold, "Early Church Catechesis and New Christians' Classes in Contemporary Evangelicalism," *Journal of the Evangelical Theological Society* 47, no. 1 (March 2004): 39-54, quotes from 46, 51. Other studies that offer applicatory guidance from the early church include D. Jeffrey Bingham, "Evangelicals, Irenaeus, and the Bible," in *The Free Church and the Early Church*, 27-46; Roger E. Van Harn, *Exploring and Proclaiming the Apostles' Creed* (Grand Rapids: Eerdmans, 2004); and Richard Valantasis, *Centuries of Holiness: Ancient Spirituality for a Postmodern Age* (New York: Continuum, 2005). For books related to Christian ritual, see Leonard J. Vander Zee, *Christ, Baptism, and the Lord's Supper: Recovering the Sacraments for Evangelical Worship* (Downers Grove, Ill.: InterVarsity, 2004); Gordon T. Smith, *Holy Meal: The Lord's Supper in Light of the Church* (Grand Rapids: Baker, 2005); and Elizabeth Zelinsky and Lela Gilbert, *Windows to Heaven: Introducing Icons to Protestants and Catholics* (Grand Rapids: Brazos, 2004).

[38]For more information about the New Testament Restoration Foundation, visit <http://www.ntrf.org>. The quote is taken from the first chapter of Steve Atkerson, *Ekklesia: To the Roots of Biblical Church Life*, available on-

line with NTRF. While the NTRF helpfully saturates its literature with scripture quotations, there appears to be very little engagement with any of the relevant scholarship related to evangelical interest in ancient Christianity.

[39]The emergent church has received significant attention as of late. See Andy Crouch, "The Emergent Mystique," *Christianity Today* 48, no. 11 (November 2004): 36-41 and in the same issue a discussion between emergent pastor and leader Brian McLaren and Wheaton College President Duane Liftin titled "Emergent Evangelism" (41-42); Scott Bader-Saye, "A New Kind of Church?: The Emergent Matrix," *Christian Century* (November 30, 2004): 20-27; Geoff Thomas, "The Emerging Church," *Banner of Truth* (February 8, 2005), David Carmichael, "The 'Emerging Church' Further Considered," *Banner of Truth* (February 18, 2005), <http://www.bannerof truth.org> [Accessed May 2005]; Chuck Smith, Jr., "What Is Emerging?" *Worship Leader* 14, no. 2 (March/April 2005): 22-27; D. A. Carson, *Becoming Conversant with the Emerging Church: Understanding a Movement and Its Implications* (Grand Rapids: Zondervan, 2005); Albert R. Mohler, "What Should We Think of the Emerging Church? Part One," *Christian Post* (July 29, 2005), and "What Should We Think of the Emerging Church? Part 2," *Christian Post* (June 30, 2005), <http://www.christianpost.com> [Accessed July 2005]; D. A. Carson, "The Emerging Movement," *Modern Reformation* 14, no. 4 (July/August 2005): 11-18; Aaron Flores, "An Exploration of the Emerging Church in the United States: The Missiological Intent and Potential Implications for the Future" (M.A. thesis, Vanguard University, 2005); Gerardo Marti, *A Mosaic of Believers: Diversity and Innovation in a Multiethnic Church* (Bloomington: Indiana University Press, 2005); and Eddie Gibbs and Ryan Bolger, *Emerging Churches: Creating Community in Postmodern Cultures* (Grand Rapids: Baker, 2005). In addition to these works, The *White Horse Inn* radio program devoted its March 6, March 17, and July 17, 2005, shows to the emergent church and are archived at <http://www.whitehorseinn.org>. Also archived are the July 8 and July 15, 2005, episodes of *Religion & Ethics Newsweekly* devoted to the emerging church. Visit <http://www.pbs.org/wnet/religionandethics/>.

[40]Brian D. McLaren, *A Generous Orthodoxy* (Grand Rapids: Zondervan, 2004), 11, 28-29.

[41]Ibid., 222.

[42]Ibid., 225-30, quote from 227.

[43]For sermon notes visit the web sites of Second Baptist Church <http://www.second.org>, Harvest Bible Church <http://www.harvestbiblechurch.net>, and Christ the King Presbyterian Church <http://www.christtheking houston.org>.

[44]See Rutba House, ed., *School(s) for Conversion: 12 Marks of a New Monasticism* (Eugene, Ore: Wipf and Stock, 2005) and Rob Moll, "The New Monasticism," *Christianity Today* 49, no. 9 (September 2005): 38-46.

[45]Timothy George, "The Sacramentality of the Church: An Evangelical

Baptist Perspective," *Pro Ecclesia* 12, no. 3 (Summer 2003): 309-23, quote from 322. In another article, "An Evangelical Reflection on Scripture and Tradition" (*Pro Ecclesia* 9, no. 2 [Spring 2000]: 184-207), George sketches the evangelical distaste for tradition—what he calls "the heresy of contemporaneity"—and observes that "for [e]vangelicals . . . the Christian past is not so much something to be studied and appropriated as it is something to be overcome." George then demonstrates *how* many of the early reformers drew from the long stream of patristic theology and consciously read the scriptures, in part, through a patristic lens. George ends the article with a summary of post-WW II ecumenical conversations about tradition and, while cautious, sees significant potential in such discussions where there might be "a bridge upon which the estranged parties [evangelicals and Catholics] might at least meet even if they do not journey on to the other side."

[46]See John G. Stackhouse, ed., *Evangelical Ecclesiology: Reality or Illusion?* (Grand Rapids: Baker, 2003) and Mark Husbands and Daniel J. Treier, *The Community of the Word: Toward an Evangelical Ecclesiology* (Downers Grove, Ill.: InterVarsity, 2005). For a more popular examination of these issues, see Wes Roberts and Glenn Marshall, *Reclaiming God's Original Intent for the Church* (Colorado Springs: NavPress, 2004).

[47]J. I. Packer, "Catholics and Evangelicals: The State of Play," *Books&Culture* 11, no. 2 (March/April 2005): 10-11. Though I was aware of this article, I want to thank an anonymous reviewer for suggesting integration of Packer's essay into my article at this point.

[48]Mark A. Noll, *The Scandal of the Evangelical Mind* (Grand Rapids: Eerdmans, 1994), 3.

[49]Ibid., ix, and Mark A. Noll, "Minding the Evangelical Mind," *First Things* 109 (January 2001): 14-17. Within this conversation, Noll cites Alan Wolfe's "The Opening of the Evangelical Mind," *Atlantic Monthly* 286, no. 4 (October 2000), 55-76, an important article that recognizes several aspects of what Wolfe considers rigorous evangelical intellectual engagement. For Noll's most recent assessment of the evangelical mind, see "The Evangelical Mind Today," *First Things* 147 (October 2004): 34-39.

[50]Noll, *The Scandal of the Evangelical Mind*, 239.

[51]Ibid., 246. Mark A. Noll, "Teaching History as a Christian," in *Religion, Scholarship, and Higher Education: Perspectives, Models, and Future Prospects*, ed. Andrea Staerk (Notre Dame: University of Notre Dame Press, 2002), 161-71.

[52]See Shawn Mosher, "Mark Noll's Historiography" (Th.M. thesis, Dallas Theological Seminary, 2002).

[53]Mark A. Noll and Carolyn Nystrom, *Is the Reformation Over?: An Evangelical Assessment of Contemporary Roman Catholicism* (Grand Rapids: Baker, 2005), 229-51, quote from 246. See also Mark Noll and Carolyn Nystrom, "Is the Reformation Over?," *Books & Culture* 11, no. 4 (July/August 2005): 10-18.

[54]On the rise of Christianity in the global South and about the growing field of world Christianity, see Phillip Jenkins, *The Next Christendom: The Coming of Global Christianity* (New York: Oxford University Press, 2002), Justo Gonzalez, *The Changing Shape of Church History* (St. Louis: Chalice, 2002), and Lamin Sanneh, *Whose Religion Is Christianity? The Gospel Beyond the West* (Grand Rapids: Eerdmans, 2003).

[55]Noll, *Scandal of the Evangelical Mind*, 241-53.

[56]Shea, *The Lion and the Lamb*, and William L. Portier, "Here Come the Evangelical Catholics," *Communio* 31 (Spring 2004): 35-66. Also important here are the essays found in Robert Barron, *Bridging the Great Divide: Musings of a Post-Liberal, Post-Conservative, Evangelical Catholic* (Lanham, Md.: Rowman & Littlefield, 2004) and Richard John Neuhaus, "Why Catholics and Evangelicals Belong Together," in *Pilgrims on the Sawdust Trail: Evangelical Ecumenism and the Quest for Christian Identity*, ed. Timothy George (Grand Rapids: Baker, 2004), 103-11. For an evangelical assessment of these kinds of discussions (and of Shea's work in particular), see Packer, "Evangelicals and Catholics: The State of Play."

Contributors

Victor Lee Austin, Ph.D., is theologian-in-residence at Saint Thomas Church, Fifth Avenue, New York City. Previously he was assistant professor of religious studies, philosophy, and theology at Mount Aloysius College, Cresson, Pennsylvania. He has taught on the adjunct faculty of Marist College in Poughkeepsie, New York, and the General Theological Seminary in New York City. A moral theologian with training in systematics, his ongoing research interests are in political theology and political ethics.

Christopher D. Denny is assistant professor in the Department of Theology and Religious Studies at St. John's University in Queens, New York. He completed his Ph.D. at The Catholic University of America with a dissertation on literary criticism in Hans Urs von Balthasar's theological anthropology. His current research projects include the anthropological continuities between tragedy and modern Christianity, and damnation and tragedy as interpretive frameworks for alienation in medieval and modern theologies.

Philip A. Franco is originally from Brooklyn, New York. He recently completed his doctorate at Fordham University and is currently an adjunct professor at St. John's University, Staten Island Campus. His primary research interests include the conversation between theology and popular culture, particularly as this influences the catechesis of youth and young adults. He has also authored "Educating toward Communion: The Educative Potential of Popular Religious Traditions," which will be appearing in the journal *Religious Education*.

William French teaches in the theology department of Loyola University of Chicago. He received his Ph.D. from the University of Chicago Divinity School. He has written on a number of topics in environmental ethics and creation-oriented theology. Among some of his recent publications are "Ecological Security and the Policies of Restraint" in *Christianity and Ecology*; a survey of Christian and Hindu responses to ecological concerns in *The Blackwell Companion to Religious Ethics* (2005); and an article on "Roman Catholicism" in *The Encyclopedia of Religion and Nature* (2005).

Christine Firer Hinze is associate professor of Christian ethics at Marquette University, where she has taught since 1990. She received her Ph.D. in Christian social ethics at the University of Chicago Divinity School in 1989. Her research, teaching, and writing center on foundational and applied questions in Christian social ethics, with emphasis on contemporary Catholic social thought. Among the numerous articles and book chapters she has authored are "What Is Enough? Catholic Social Perspectives on Consumption and Sufficiency," in C. Matthewes & W. Schweiker, eds. *Having: Religious Perspectives on Property and Possessions* (Eerdmans, 2004) and a commentary on *Quadragesimo Anno* in Kenneth Himes, ed., *Modern Catholic Social Teaching: Commentaries and Interpretations* (Georgetown University Press, 2005). She is currently working on her second book, *Making a Living Together: Transforming the Family Living Wage Agenda for a New Century.*

Francis Holland is associate professor of theology at St. John's University in New York. He received his Ph.D. from the Department of Near Eastern Languages in University College in Dublin, Ireland. His research interests include Hebrew Wisdom literature, biblical theology, and hermeneutics.

Jason King received his Ph.D. in Catholic moral theology from The Catholic University of America in Washington, D.C. He currently teaches at St. Vincent College in Latrobe, Pennsylvania. His publications include "Sex, Time, and Meaning: A Theology of Dating" in *Horizons* (2003) and the book *Save the Date: A Spirituality of Dating, Love, Dinner and the Divine*

(Crossroads, 2003). He is currently working on *After the Death of God: The Theological Vision in Philip Pullman's* His Dark Materials (Jossey-Bass, forthcoming).

Paul F. Knitter, emeritus professor of theology at Xavier University, Cincinnati, received a licentiate in theology from the Pontifical Gregorian University in Rome and a doctorate from the University of Marburg, Germany. Most of his research and publications have dealt with religious pluralism and interreligious dialogue. Since his ground-breaking 1985 book, *No Other Name?* he has been exploring how the religious communities of the world can cooperate in promoting human and ecological well-being. This is the topic of: *One Earth Many Religions: Multifaith Dialogue and Global Responsibility* (Orbis, 1995) and *Jesus and the Other Names: Christian Mission and Global Responsibility* (Orbis, 1996). He has recently published a critical survey of Christian approaches to other religions: *Introducing Theologies of Religions* (Orbis, 2002). Knitter is general editor of Orbis Books' series "Faith Meets Faith" and serves on the Board of Trustees for the International, Interreligious Peace Council, formed after the 1993 World Parliament of Religions, to promote interreligious peace-making projects.

Reid B. Locklin, assistant professor, teaches in the Christianity and Culture Program at Saint Michael's College and the University of Toronto. He is the author of *Spiritual But Not Religious? An Oar Stroke Closer to the Farther Shore* (Liturgical Press, 2005).

Alice Laffey has a doctorate in sacred scripture from the Pontifical Biblical Institute in Rome and is associate professor in the Department of Religious Studies at the College of the Holy Cross. In addition to many articles and book reviews, she is the author of *Introduction to the Old Testament: A Feminist Perspective*; *The Pentateuch: A Liberation Critical Perspective*; *1 and 2 Kings*; *1 and 2 Chronicles*; and *Appreciating Creation Through Scripture*.

Harriet A. Luckman is associate professor of religious studies and director of the Spirituality Institute at the College of Mount

Saint Joseph, Cincinnati, Ohio. She holds a Ph.D. in historical theology from Marquette University, with a concentration in spirituality and early Christianity.

Elaine Catherine MacMillan, assistant professor of theology at the University of San Diego, holds a Ph.D. from the University of St. Michael's College (Toronto) and an S.T.L. from Saint Paul University (Ottawa). She is appointed by the USCCB as a Roman Catholic Commissioner to the Faith and Order Commission of the National Council of Churches (U.S.A.) and serves on the Authority of the Church in the World Section of the Commission.

William Madges, professor and recent chair of the Department of Theology at Xavier University (Cincinnati), received his Ph.D. from the University of Chicago. His research interests include the history of Christian thought and theology in the modern period. Among recent books that he has edited are: *Vatican II: Forty Personal Stories* (Bayard/Twenty-Third Publications, 2003) and *God and the World* (Orbis, 1998). A new book on the marks of the church will be published in 2006.

Peter C. Phan has earned three doctoral degrees: in theology from the Salesian Pontifical University, Rome; in philosophy and in divinity from the University of London. He taught theology at the University of Dallas in Irving, Texas, for thirteen years before going to The Catholic University of America in 1988, where he taught in and chaired the Department of Theology. Later he joined the Department of Religion and Religious Education, where he held the Warren-Blanding Chair of Religion and Culture. In 2003 he moved to Georgetown University as the inaugural holder of the Ignacio Ellacuría Chair in Catholic Social Thought. Phan has published and edited over thirty books and two hundred and fifty essays. His scholarly interests include the theology of the icon, the theology of Rahner, missiology, and interreligious dialogue. His latest work is a trilogy: *Christianity with an Asian Face*, *In Our Own Tongues*, and *Being Religious Interrreligiously* (Orbis).

Elena Procario-Foley holds the positions of Driscoll Professor of Jewish-Catholic Studies and associate professor of religious studies at Iona College (New Rochelle, N.Y.), where she has served on the faculty since 1998. She received the Ph.D. from The Divinity School of the University of Chicago in 1995 and her dissertation was "Orthodoxy or Orthopraxy? An Analysis of the Relationship between Experience and Thought in the Christological Trilogy of Edward Schillebeeckx." Her recent engagement with Jewish-Catholic studies has provided a transformative lens through which to conduct systematic studies. She has been regularly active in the CTS and has served as convener of the Contemporary Theologies section and as a member of the Awards Committee.

Phillip Luke Sinitiere is a Ph.D. student in history at the University of Houston, studying American evangelicalism, world history, and African history. He also teaches history in the Upper School at Second Baptist School in Houston, Texas.

John Sniegocki is an assistant professor in the Department of Theology at Xavier University (Cincinnati). His main areas of interest include Catholic social teaching, globalization, the ethics of war and nonviolence, environmental ethics, and interreligious dialogue. His doctoral dissertation on "Catholic Social Teaching and the Third World" explored the contributions that Catholic social teaching can make to the quest for more just and ecologically sustainable alternatives to conventional forms of economic development.